summoner

式神X少女

GIRL

4-11
11 00

Summoner Girl Volume 1
Created by Hiroshi Kubota

Translation - Su Mon Han
English Adaptation - Paul Morrissey
Copy Editor - Joseph Heller
Retouch and Lettering - Star Print Brokers
Production Artist - Rui Kyo
Graphic Designer - Kenneth Chan

Editor - Lillian Diaz-Przybyl
Print Production Manager - Lucas Rivera
Managing Editor - Vy Nguyen
Senior Designer - Louis Csontos
Art Director - Al-Insan Lashley
Director of Sales and Manufacturing - Allyson De Simone
Associate Publisher - Marco F. Pavia
President and C.O.O. - John Parker
C.E.O. and Chief Creative Officer - Stu Levy

A  Manga

TOKYOPOP Inc.
5900 Wilshire Blvd. Suite 2000
Los Angeles, CA 90036

E-mail: info@TOKYOPOP.com
Come visit us online at www.TOKYOPOP.com

ISBN: 978-1-4278-1568-2

First TOKYOPOP printing: November 2010
10 9 8 7 6 5 4 3 2 1
Printed in the USA

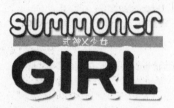

summoner GIRL

式神×少女

Volume 1
by Hiroshi Kubota

TOKYOPOP®

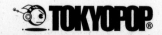

HAMBURG // LONDON // LOS ANGELES // TOKYO

Table of contents

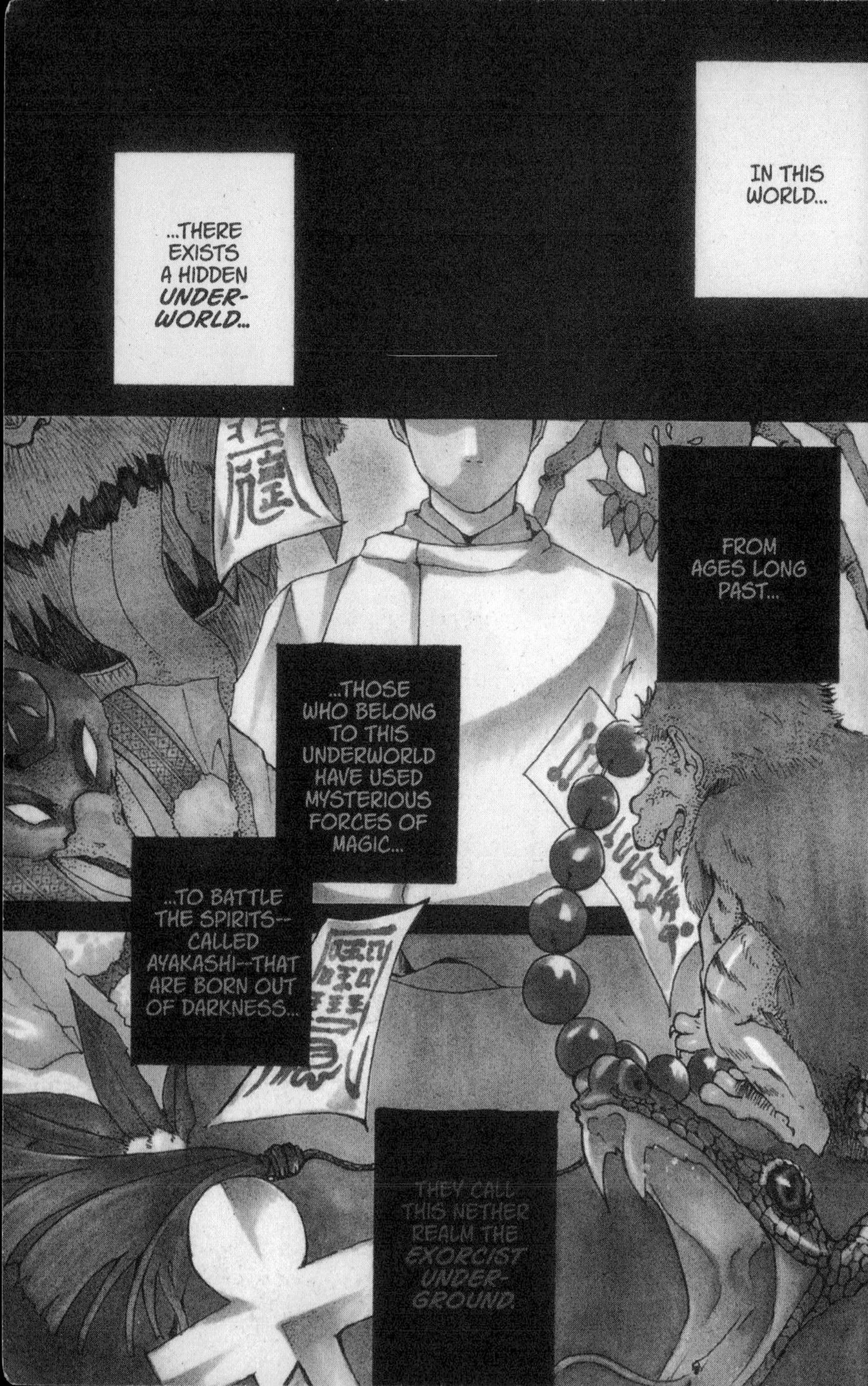
IN THIS WORLD...
...THERE EXISTS A HIDDEN UNDER-WORLD...
FROM AGES LONG PAST...
...THOSE WHO BELONG TO THIS UNDERWORLD HAVE USED MYSTERIOUS FORCES OF MAGIC...
...TO BATTLE THE SPIRITS--CALLED AYAKASHI--THAT ARE BORN OUT OF DARKNESS...
THEY CALL THIS NETHER REALM THE EXORCIST UNDER-GROUND.

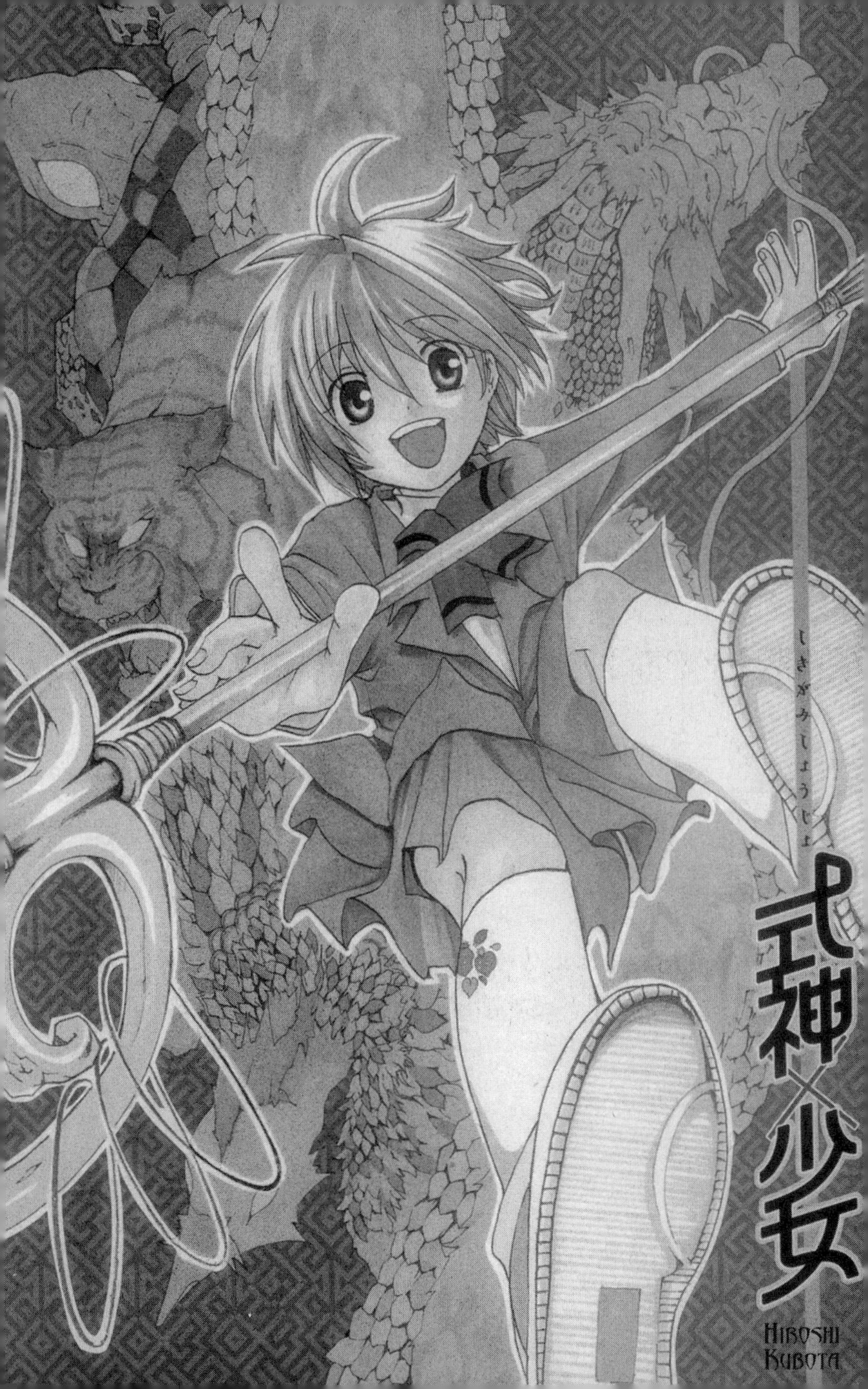
しきがみしょうじょ
式神×少女
HIROSHI KUBOTA

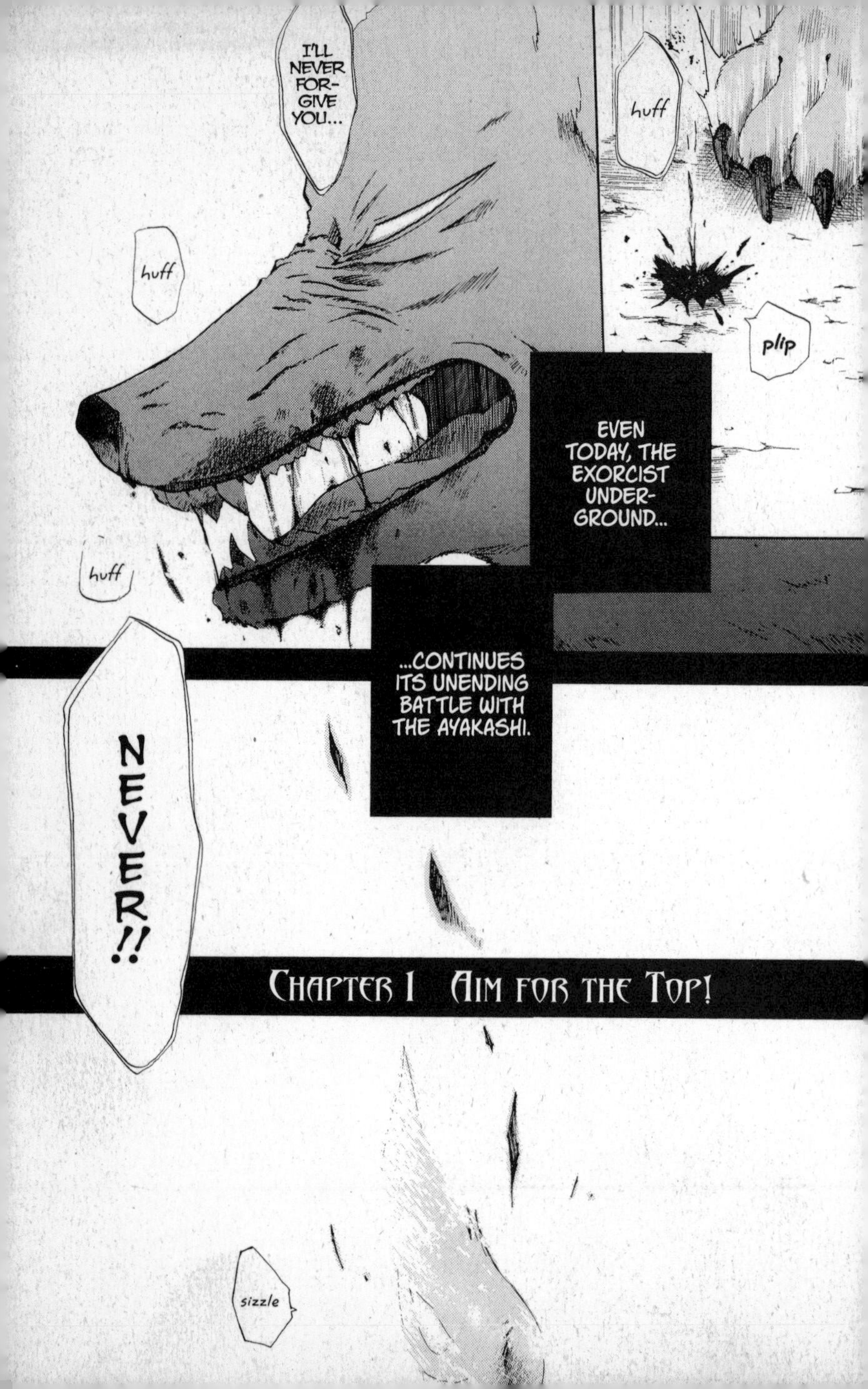
huff
plip
I'LL NEVER FORGIVE YOU...
huff
huff
EVEN TODAY, THE EXORCIST UNDERGROUND...
...CONTINUES ITS UNENDING BATTLE WITH THE AYAKASHI.
NEVER!!
CHAPTER 1 AIM FOR THE TOP!
sizzle

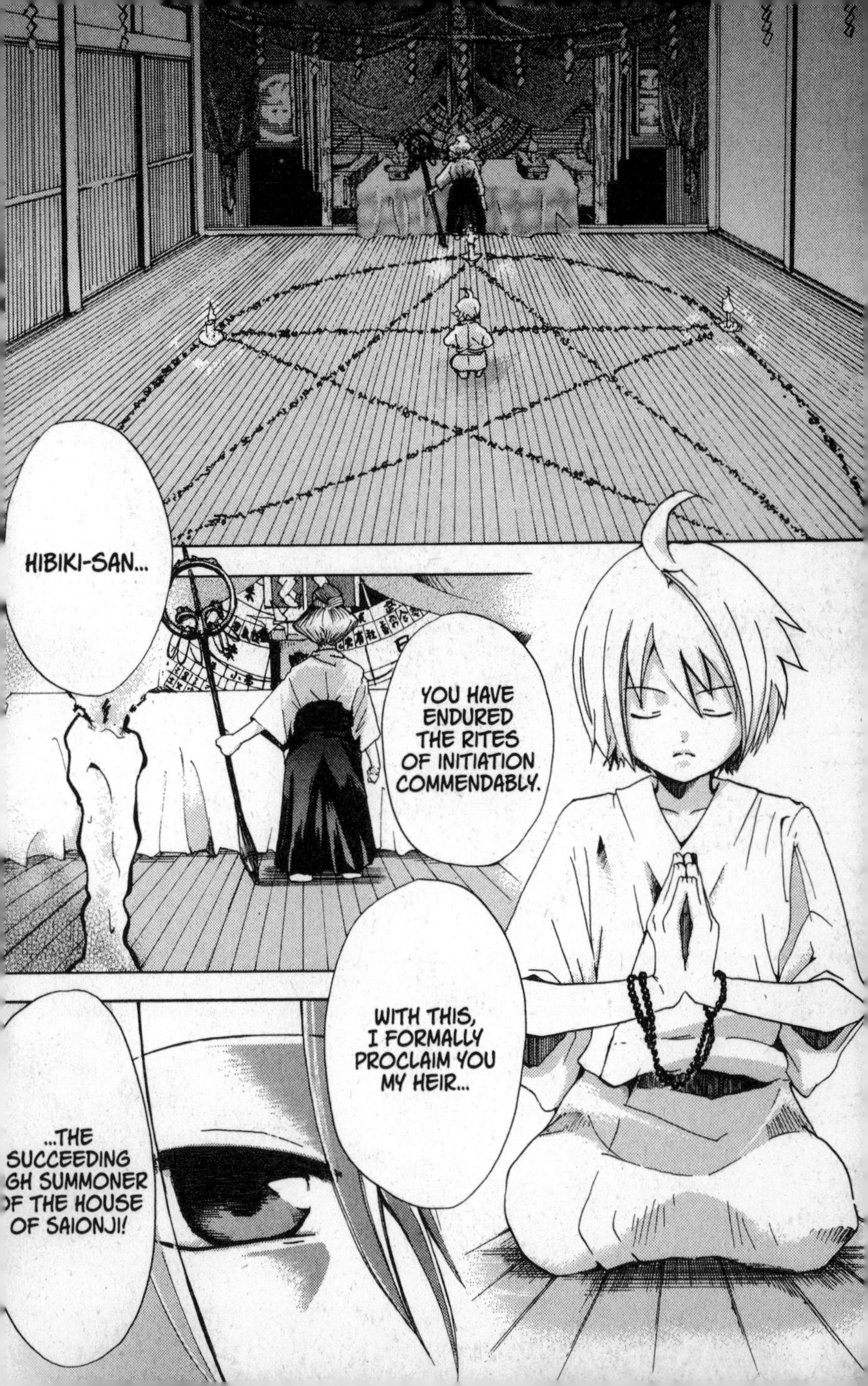
HIBIKI-SAN...
YOU HAVE ENDURED THE RITES OF INITIATION COMMENDABLY.
WITH THIS, I FORMALLY PROCLAIM YOU MY HEIR...
...THE SUCCEEDING GH SUMMONER F THE HOUSE OF SAIONJI!

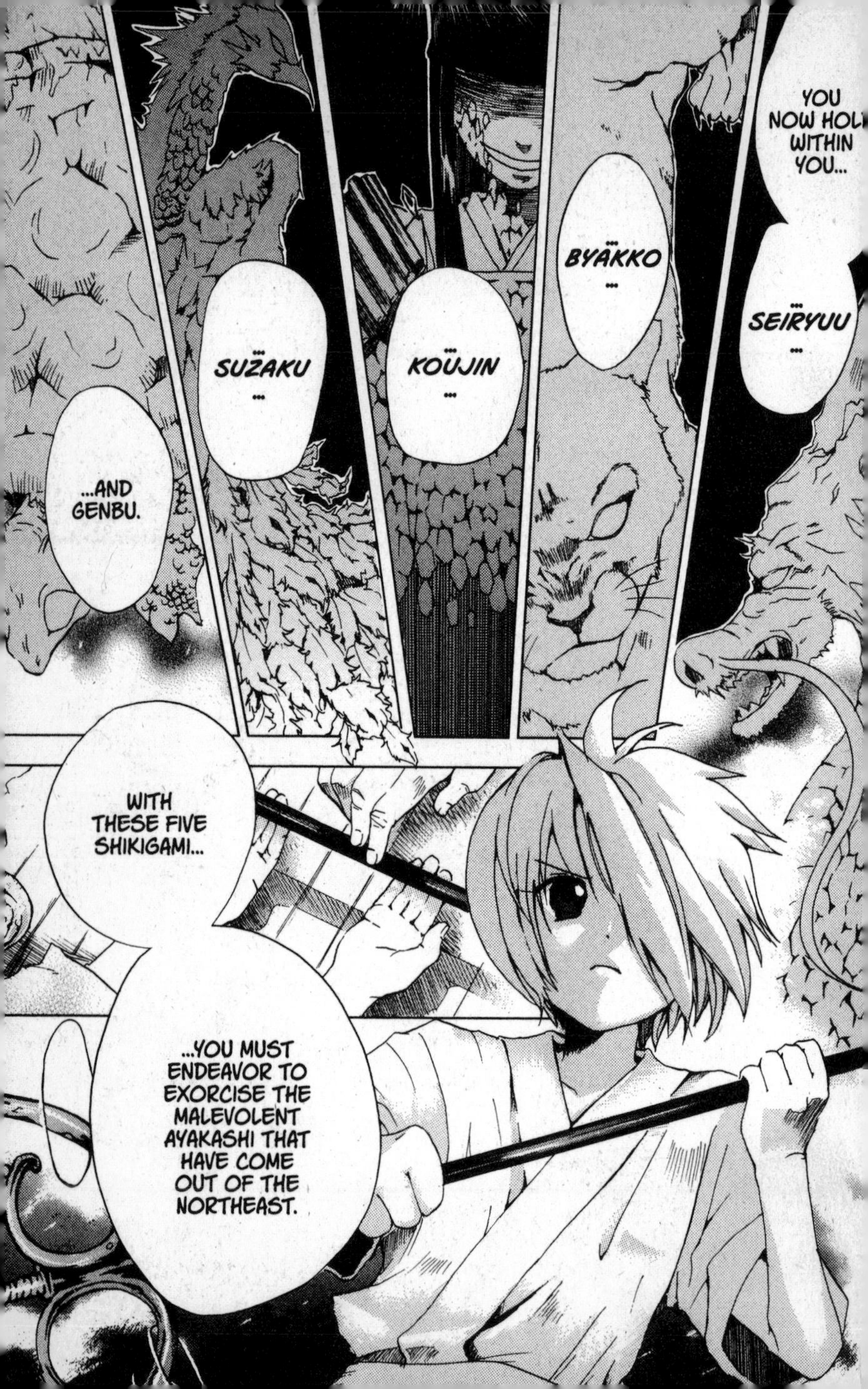

YOU NOW HOL WITHIN YOU...
...SEIRYUU...
...BYAKKO...
...KOUJIN...
...SUZAKU...
...AND GENBU.
WITH THESE FIVE SHIKIGAMI...
...YOU MUST ENDEAVOR TO EXORCISE THE MALEVOLENT AYAKASHI THAT HAVE COME OUT OF THE NORTHEAST.

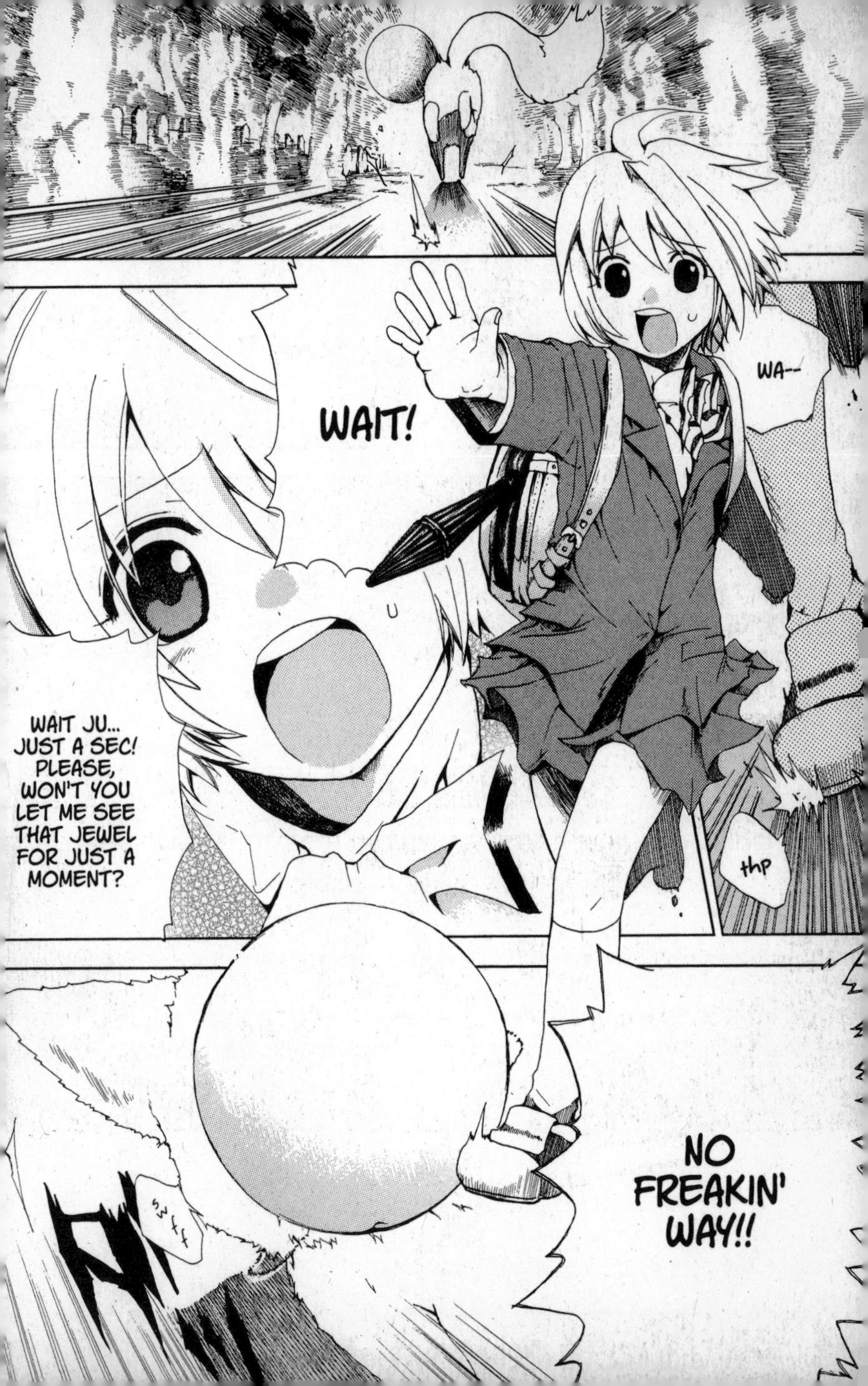
WA--
thp
WAIT!
WAIT JU... JUST A SEC! PLEASE, WON'T YOU LET ME SEE THAT JEWEL FOR JUST A MOMENT?
NO FREAKIN' WAY!!
swff

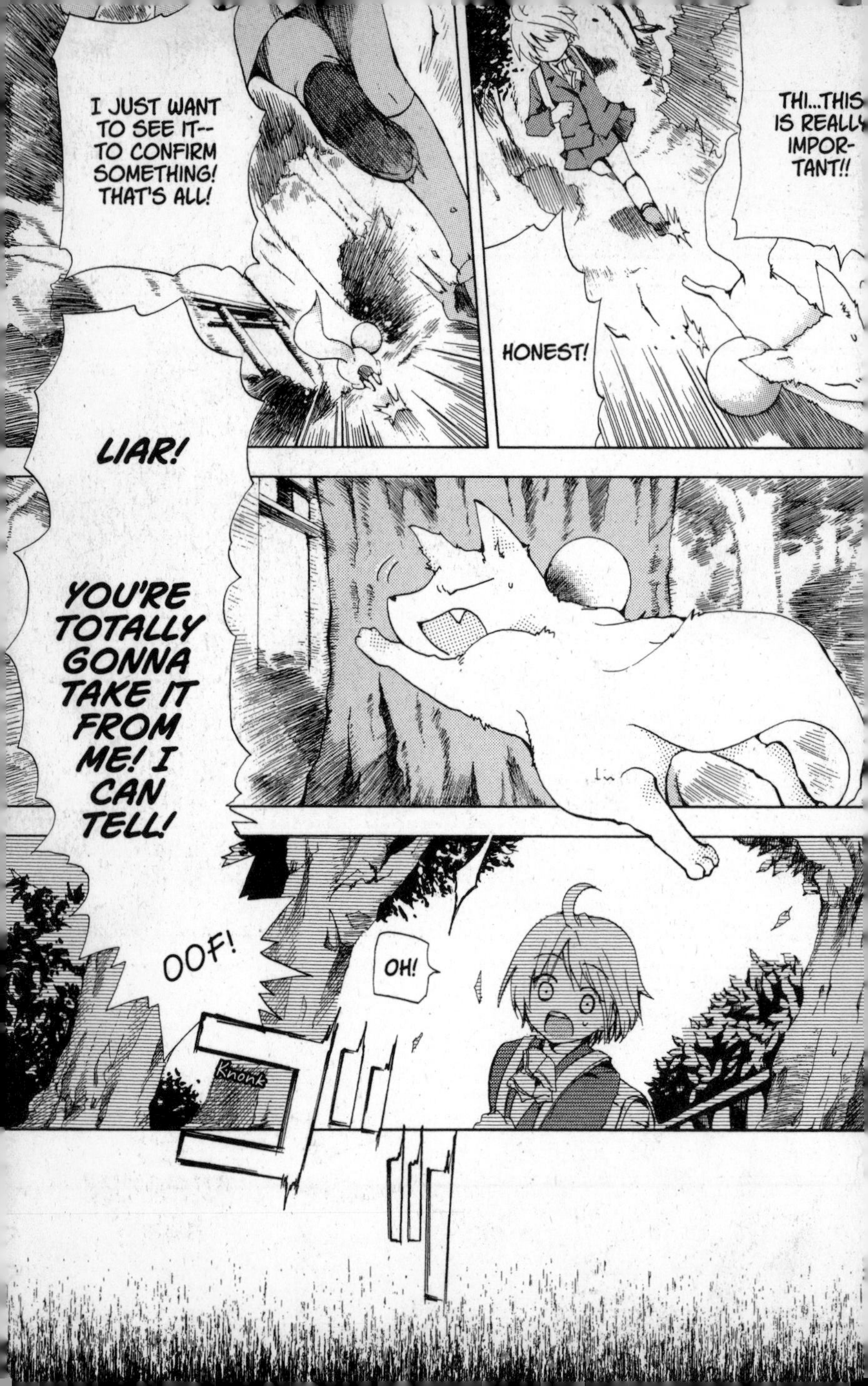
THI...THIS IS REALLY IMPORTANT!!
HONEST!
I JUST WANT TO SEE IT-- TO CONFIRM SOMETHING! THAT'S ALL!
LIAR!
YOU'RE TOTALLY GONNA TAKE IT FROM ME! I CAN TELL!
OH!
OOF!
Knonk

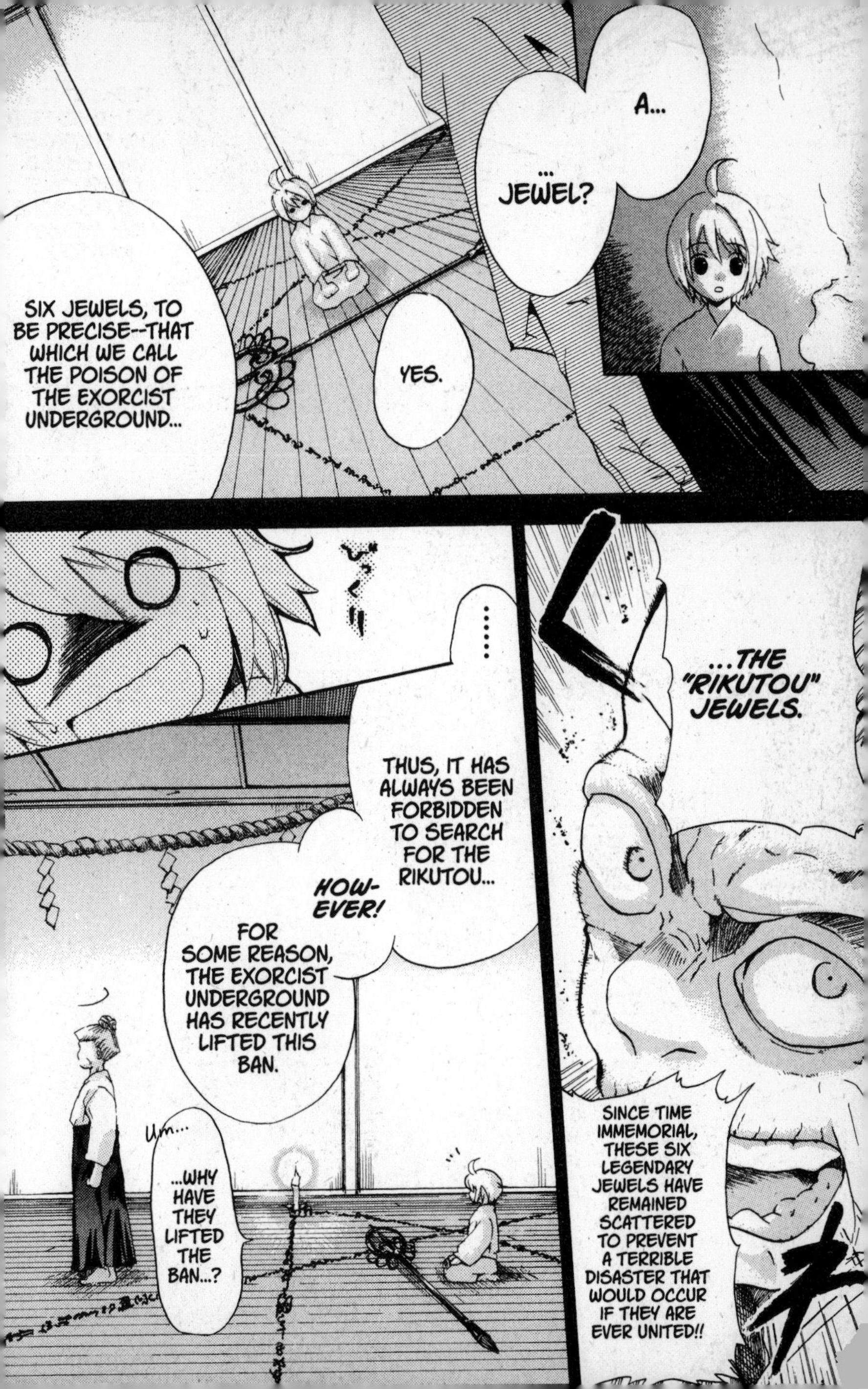
A...
...JEWEL?
YES.
SIX JEWELS, TO BE PRECISE--THAT WHICH WE CALL THE POISON OF THE EXORCIST UNDERGROUND...
...THE "RIKUTOU" JEWELS.
SINCE TIME IMMEMORIAL, THESE SIX LEGENDARY JEWELS HAVE REMAINED SCATTERED TO PREVENT A TERRIBLE DISASTER THAT WOULD OCCUR IF THEY ARE EVER UNITED!!
......
THUS, IT HAS ALWAYS BEEN FORBIDDEN TO SEARCH FOR THE RIKUTOU...
HOW-EVER!
FOR SOME REASON, THE EXORCIST UNDERGROUND HAS RECENTLY LIFTED THIS BAN.
Um...
...WHY HAVE THEY LIFTED THE BAN...?

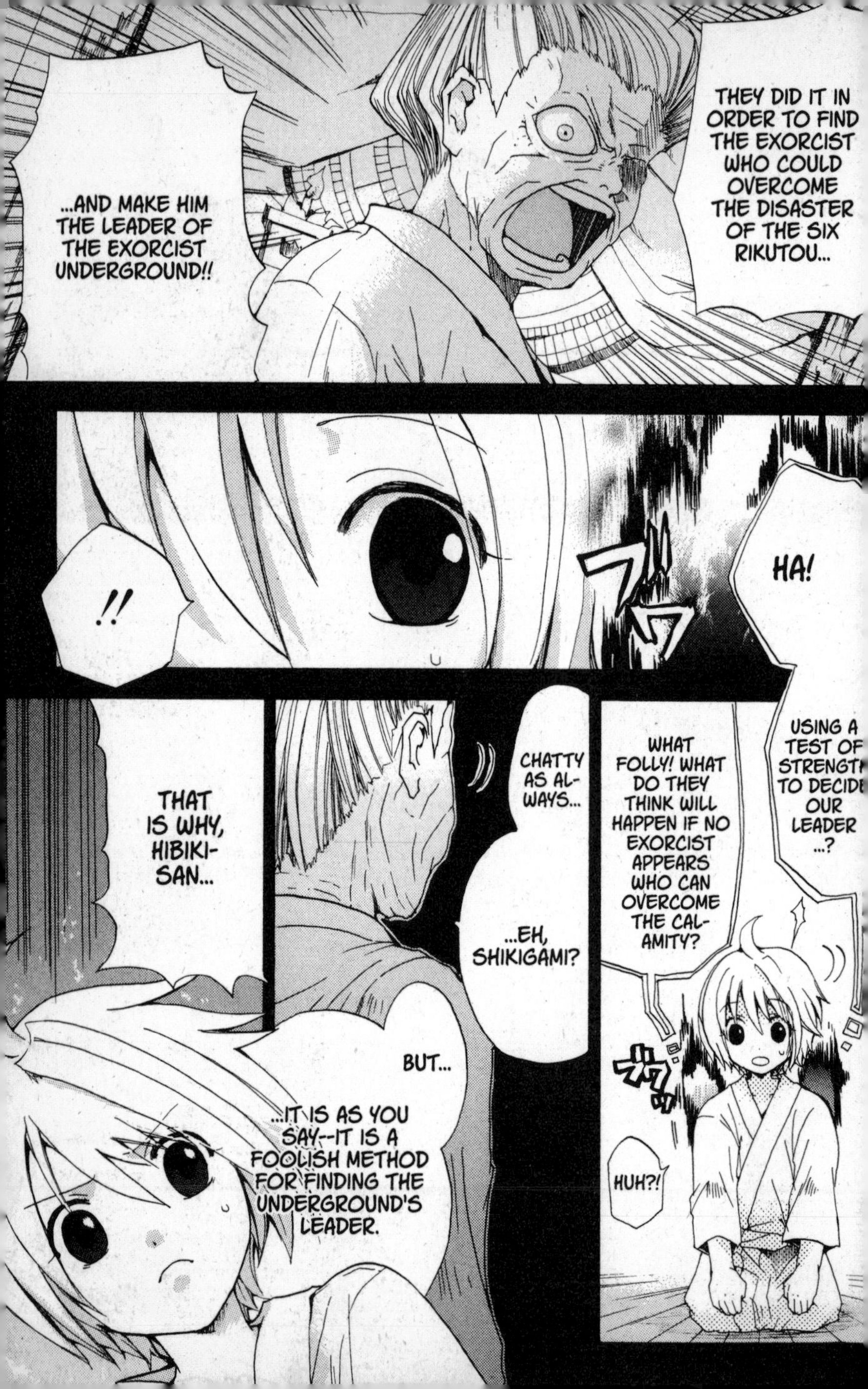
THEY DID IT IN ORDER TO FIND THE EXORCIST WHO COULD OVERCOME THE DISASTER OF THE SIX RIKUTOU...
...AND MAKE HIM THE LEADER OF THE EXORCIST UNDERGROUND!!
HA!
!!
USING A TEST OF STRENGT TO DECIDE OUR LEADER ...?
WHAT FOLLY! WHAT DO THEY THINK WILL HAPPEN IF NO EXORCIST APPEARS WHO CAN OVERCOME THE CAL-AMITY?
HUH?!
CHATTY AS AL-WAYS...
...EH, SHIKIGAMI?
THAT IS WHY, HIBIKI-SAN...
BUT...
...IT IS AS YOU SAY--IT IS A FOOLISH METHOD FOR FINDING THE UNDERGROUND'S LEADER.

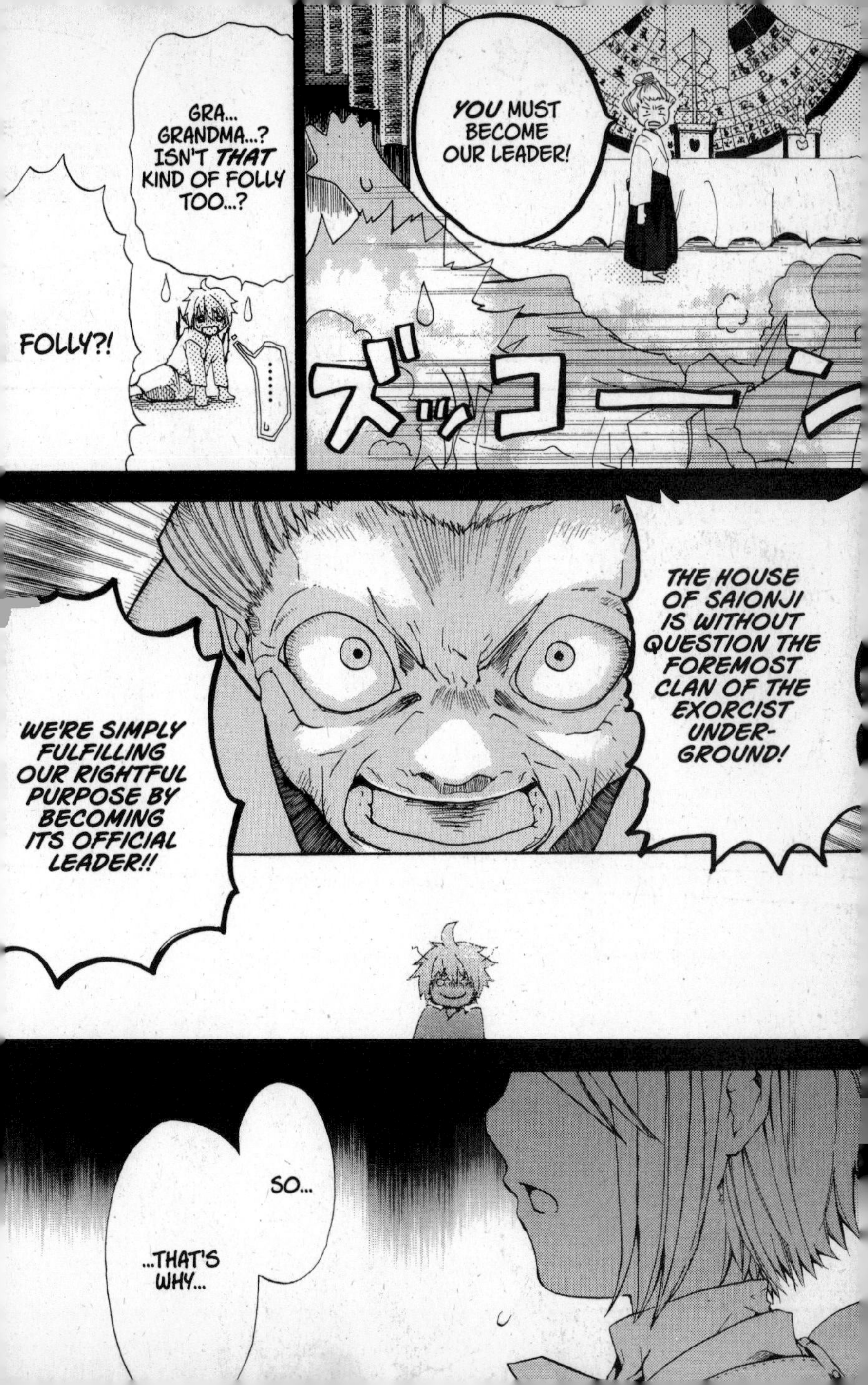
YOU MUST BECOME OUR LEADER!
ズッコーン
GRA... GRANDMA...? ISN'T THAT KIND OF FOLLY TOO...?
......
FOLLY?!
THE HOUSE OF SAIONJI IS WITHOUT QUESTION THE FOREMOST CLAN OF THE EXORCIST UNDER-GROUND!
WE'RE SIMPLY FULFILLING OUR RIGHTFUL PURPOSE BY BECOMING ITS OFFICIAL LEADER!!
SO...
...THAT'S WHY...

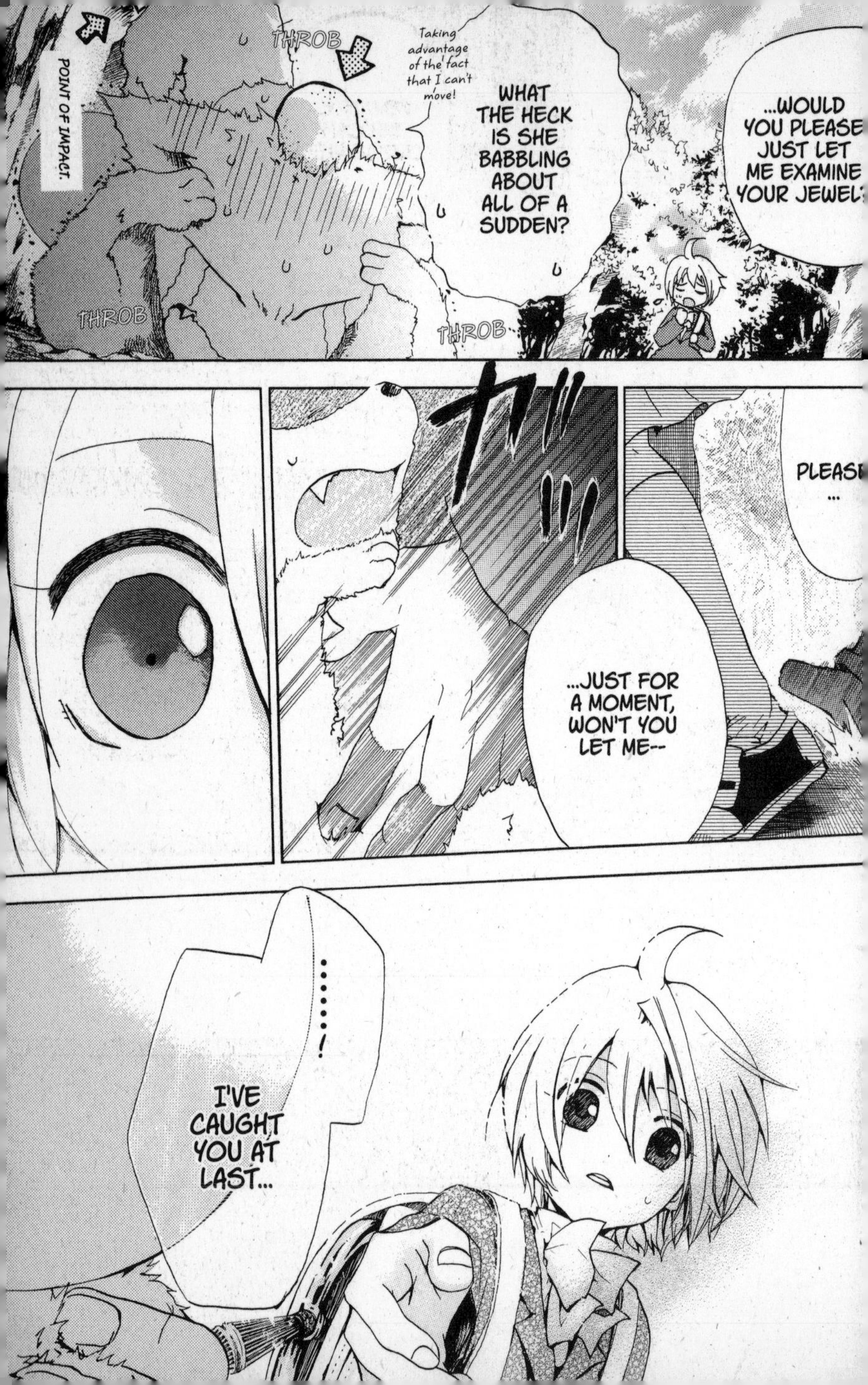
...WOULD YOU PLEASE JUST LET ME EXAMINE YOUR JEWEL
WHAT THE HECK IS SHE BABBLING ABOUT ALL OF A SUDDEN?
Taking advantage of the fact that I can't move!
THROB
THROB
THROB
POINT OF IMPACT.
PLEASE ...
...JUST FOR A MOMENT, WON'T YOU LET ME--
......!
I'VE CAUGHT YOU AT LAST...

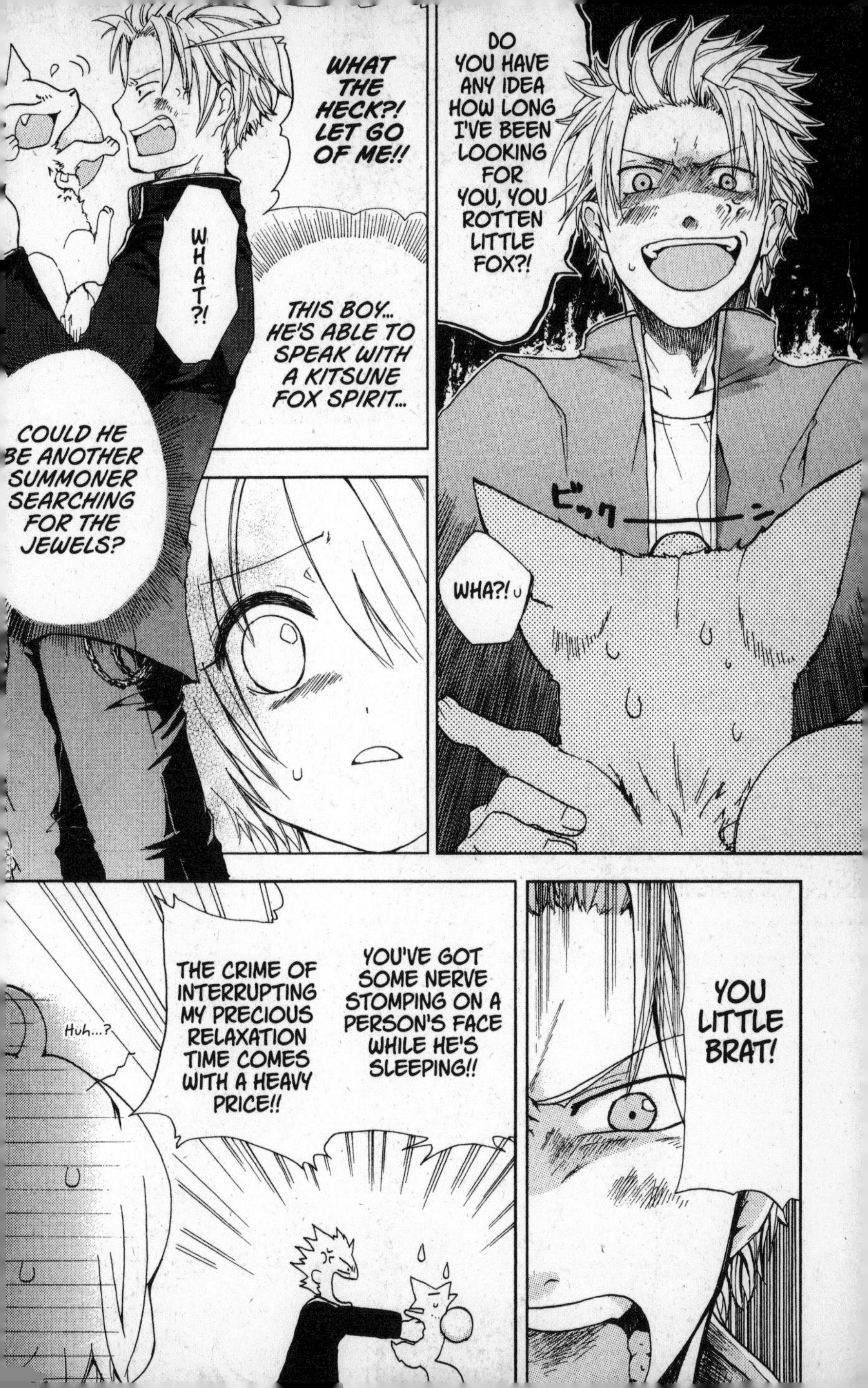
DO YOU HAVE ANY IDEA HOW LONG I'VE BEEN LOOKING FOR YOU, YOU ROTTEN LITTLE FOX?!
ビックーーーッ
WHA?!
WHAT THE HECK?! LET GO OF ME!!
WHAT?!
THIS BOY... HE'S ABLE TO SPEAK WITH A KITSUNE FOX SPIRIT...
COULD HE BE ANOTHER SUMMONER SEARCHING FOR THE JEWELS?
YOU LITTLE BRAT!
YOU'VE GOT SOME NERVE STOMPING ON A PERSON'S FACE WHILE HE'S SLEEPING!!
THE CRIME OF INTERRUPTING MY PRECIOUS RELAXATION TIME COMES WITH A HEAVY PRICE!!
Huh...?

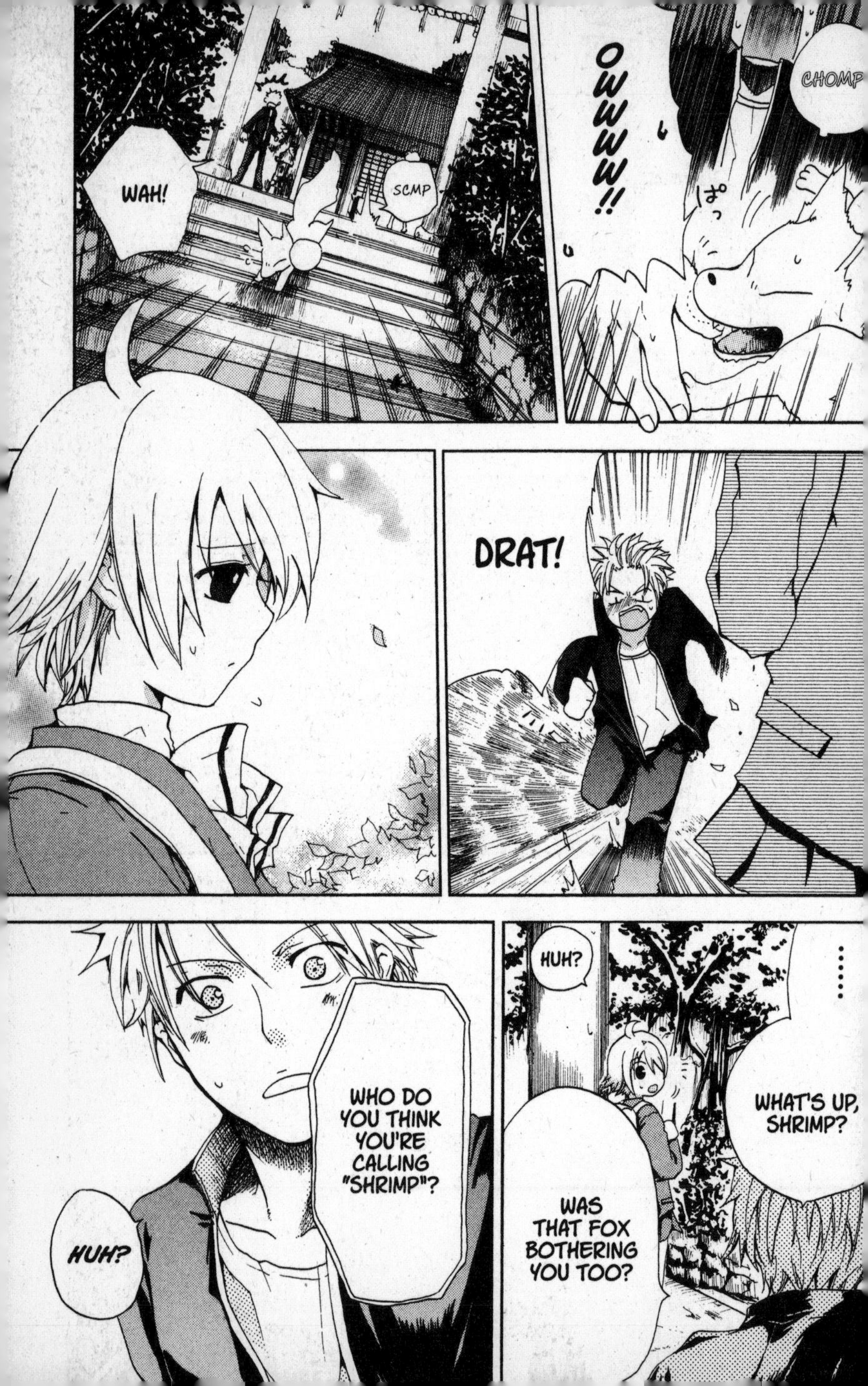
CHOMP
OWWWWW!!
ぱっ
SCMP
WAH!
DRAT!
......
HUH?
WHAT'S UP, SHRIMP?
WAS THAT FOX BOTHERING YOU TOO?
WHO DO YOU THINK YOU'RE CALLING "SHRIMP"?
HUH?

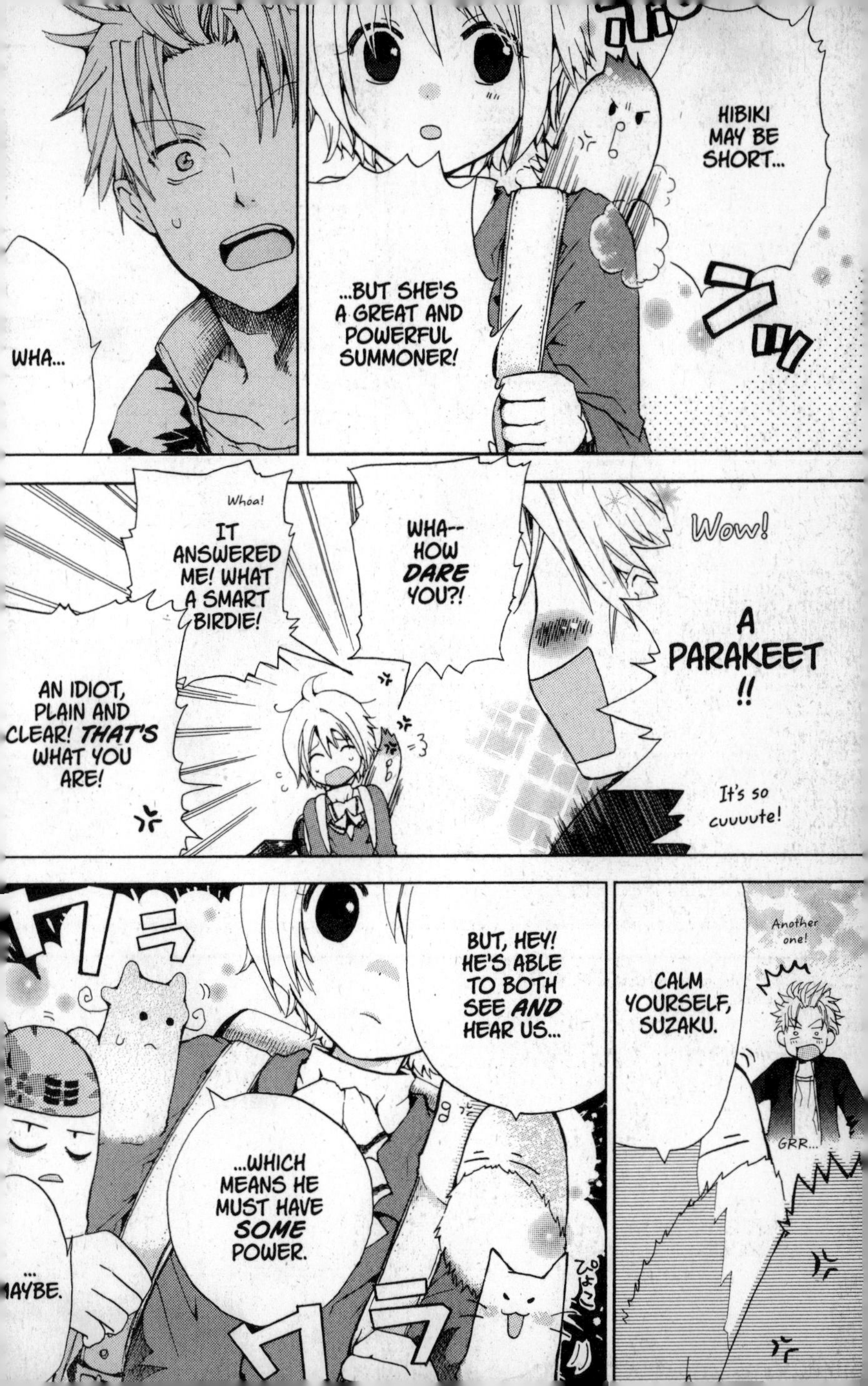
HIBIKI MAY BE SHORT...
...BUT SHE'S A GREAT AND POWERFUL SUMMONER!
WHA...
Wow!
A PARAKEET!!
It's so cuuuute!
WHA-- HOW *DARE* YOU?!
Whoa!
IT ANSWERED ME! WHAT A SMART BIRDIE!
AN IDIOT, PLAIN AND CLEAR! *THAT'S* WHAT YOU ARE!
Another one!
CALM YOURSELF, SUZAKU.
GRR...
BUT, HEY! HE'S ABLE TO BOTH SEE *AND* HEAR US...
...WHICH MEANS HE MUST HAVE *SOME* POWER.
ぴょこ
...MAYBE.

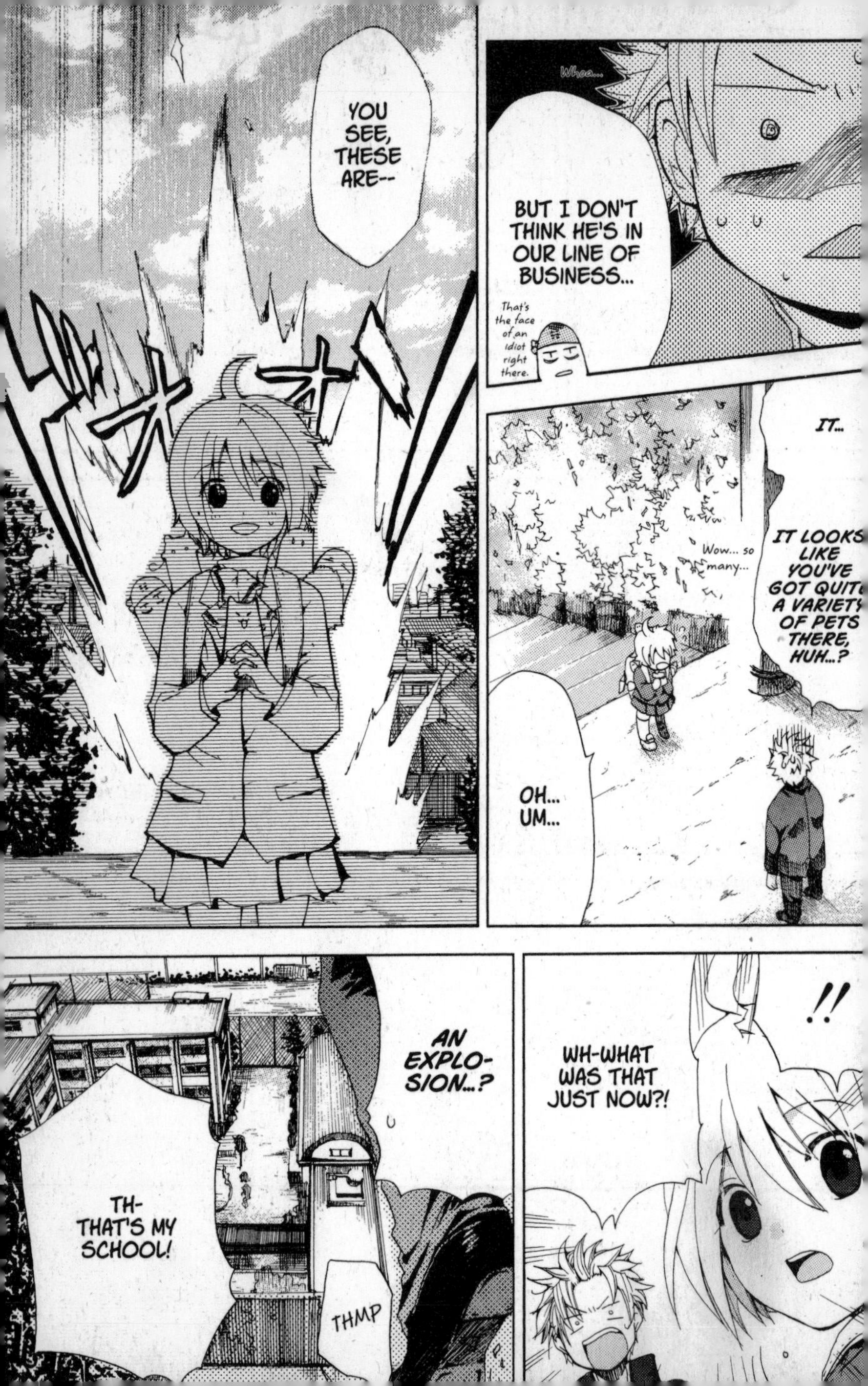
Whoa...
BUT I DON'T THINK HE'S IN OUR LINE OF BUSINESS...
That's the face of an idiot right there.
IT...
IT LOOKS LIKE YOU'VE GOT QUIT A VARIET OF PETS THERE, HUH...?
Wow... so many...
OH... UM...
YOU SEE, THESE ARE--
!!
WH-WHAT WAS THAT JUST NOW?!
AN EXPLOSION...?
TH-THAT'S MY SCHOOL!
THMP

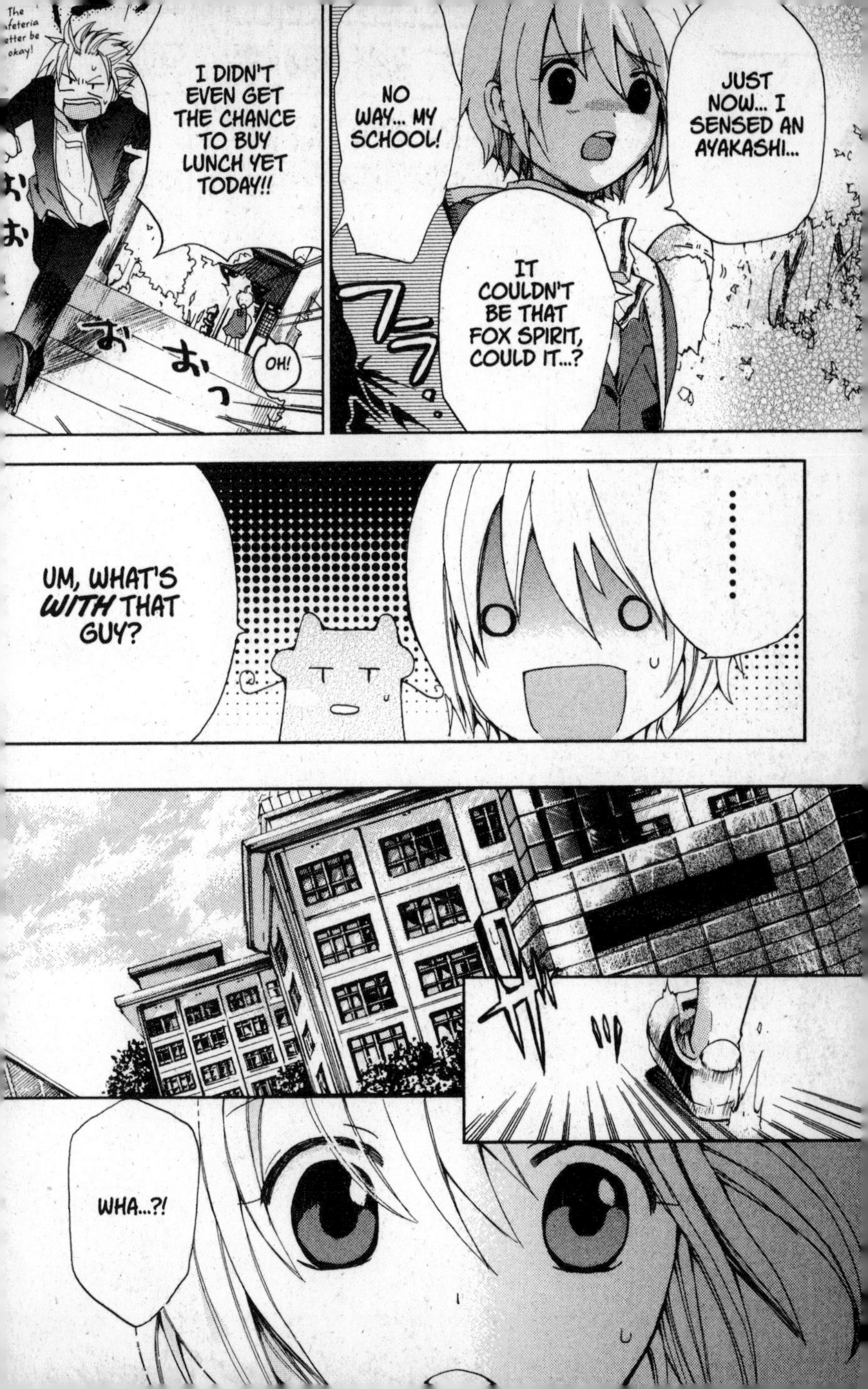
JUST NOW... I SENSED AN AYAKASHI...
NO WAY... MY SCHOOL!
IT COULDN'T BE THAT FOX SPIRIT, COULD IT...?
I DIDN'T EVEN GET THE CHANCE TO BUY LUNCH YET TODAY!!
The afeteria etter be okay!
OH!
......
UM, WHAT'S *WITH* THAT GUY?
WHA...?!

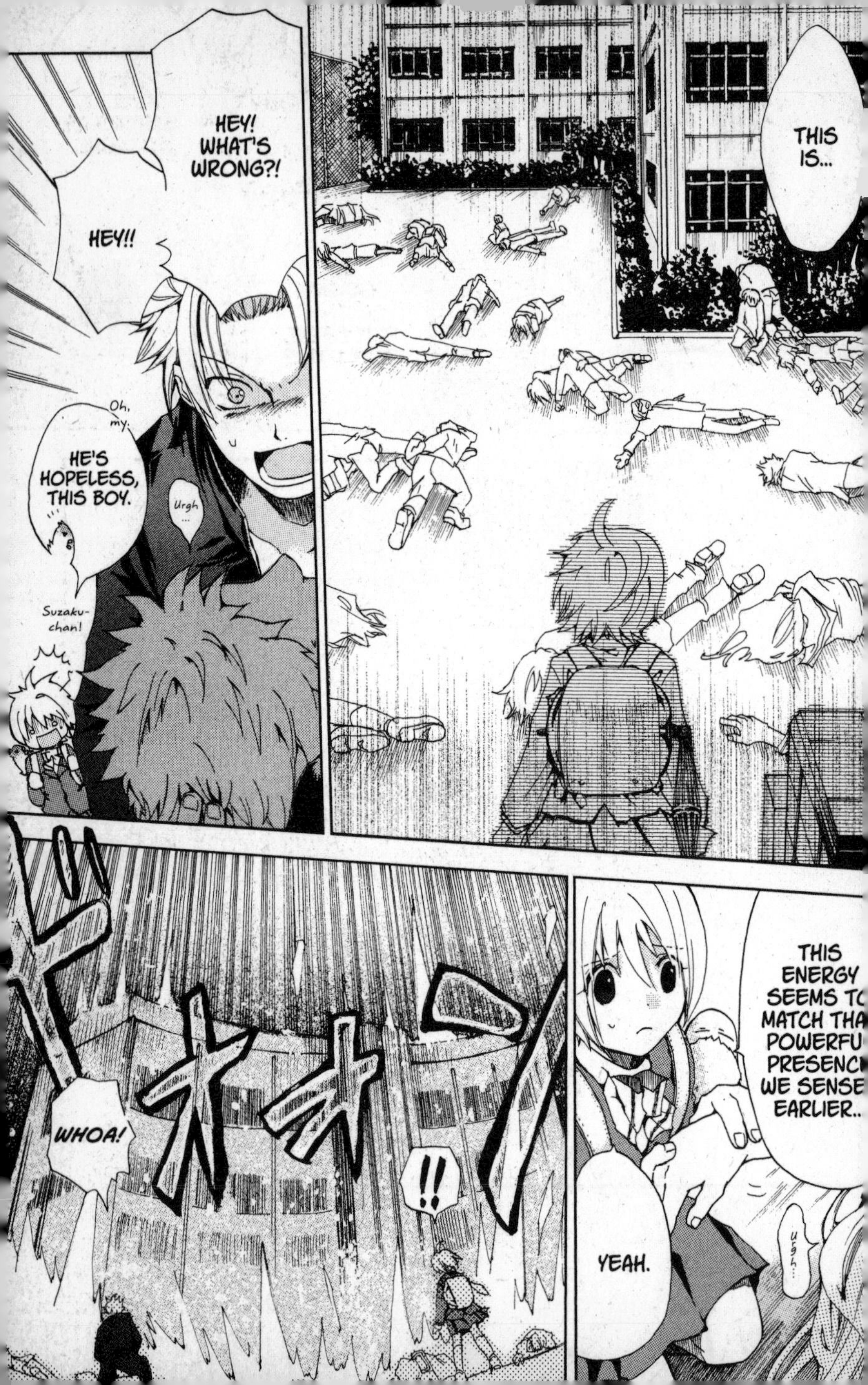

THIS IS...
HEY! WHAT'S WRONG?!
HEY!!
Urgh...
Oh, my.
HE'S HOPELESS, THIS BOY.
Suzaku-chan!
THIS ENERGY SEEMS TC MATCH THA POWERFU PRESENC WE SENSE EARLIER..
YEAH.
Urgh...
WHOA!
!!

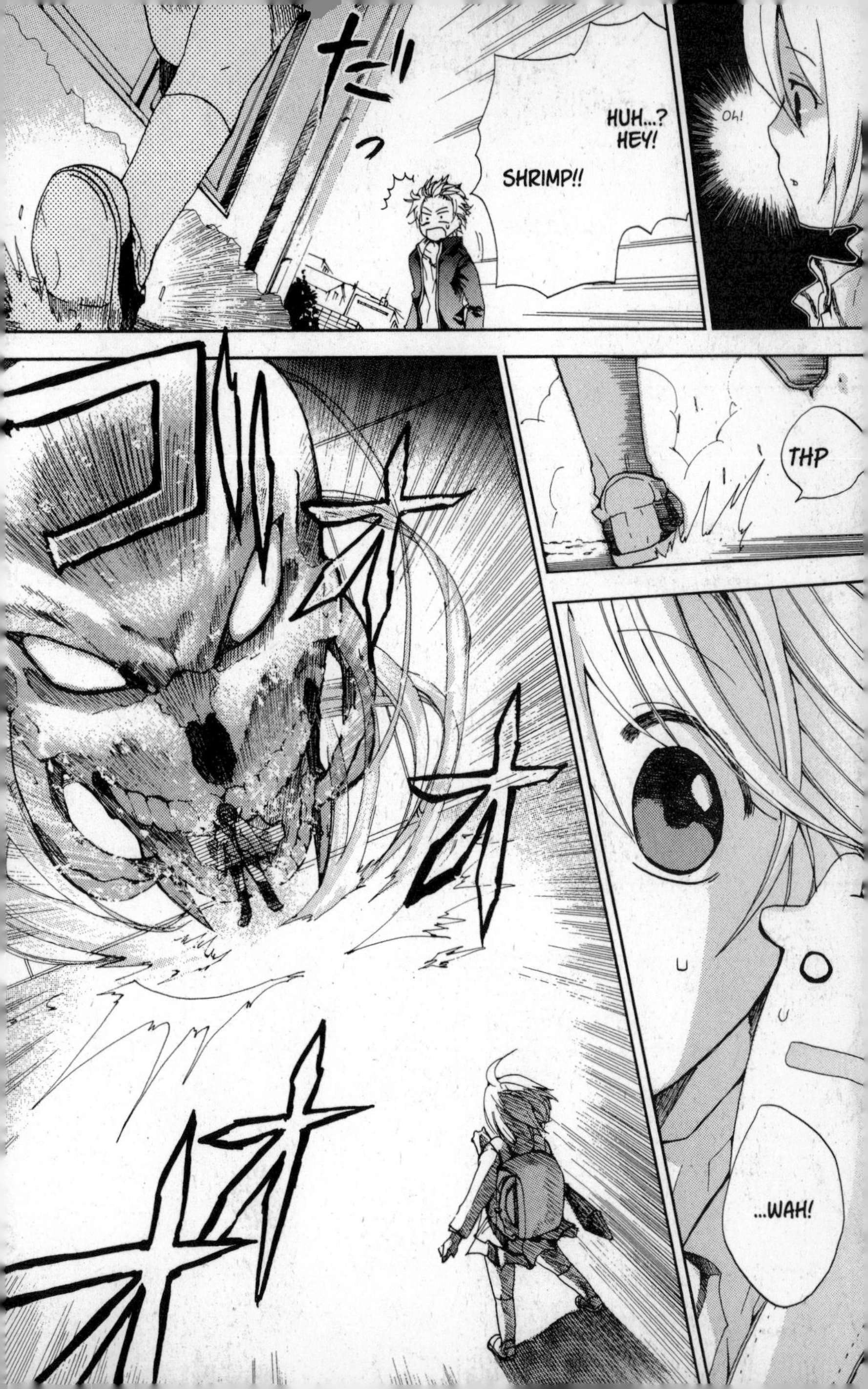
Oh!
HUH...? HEY!
SHRIMP!!
だっ
THP
...WAH!

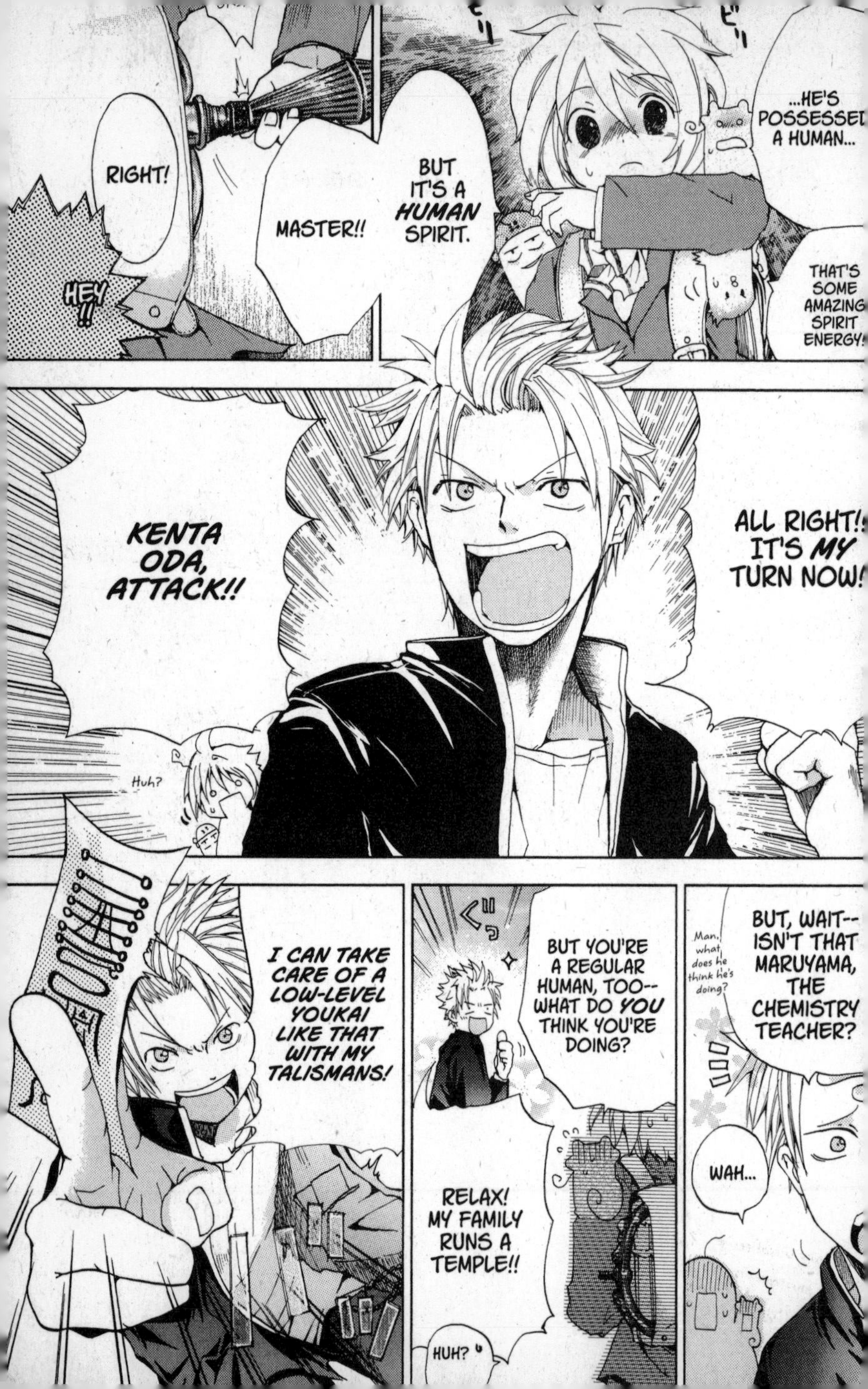
...HE'S POSSESSED A HUMAN...
THAT'S SOME AMAZING SPIRIT ENERGY!
BUT IT'S A *HUMAN* SPIRIT.
MASTER!!
RIGHT!
HEY!!
ALL RIGHT!! IT'S *MY* TURN NOW!
KENTA ODA, ATTACK!!
Huh?
BUT, WAIT-- ISN'T THAT MARUYAMA, THE CHEMISTRY TEACHER?
Man, what does he think he's doing?
WAH...
BUT YOU'RE A REGULAR HUMAN, TOO-- WHAT DO *YOU* THINK YOU'RE DOING?
RELAX! MY FAMILY RUNS A TEMPLE!!
HUH?
I CAN TAKE CARE OF A LOW-LEVEL YOUKAI LIKE THAT WITH MY TALISMANS!

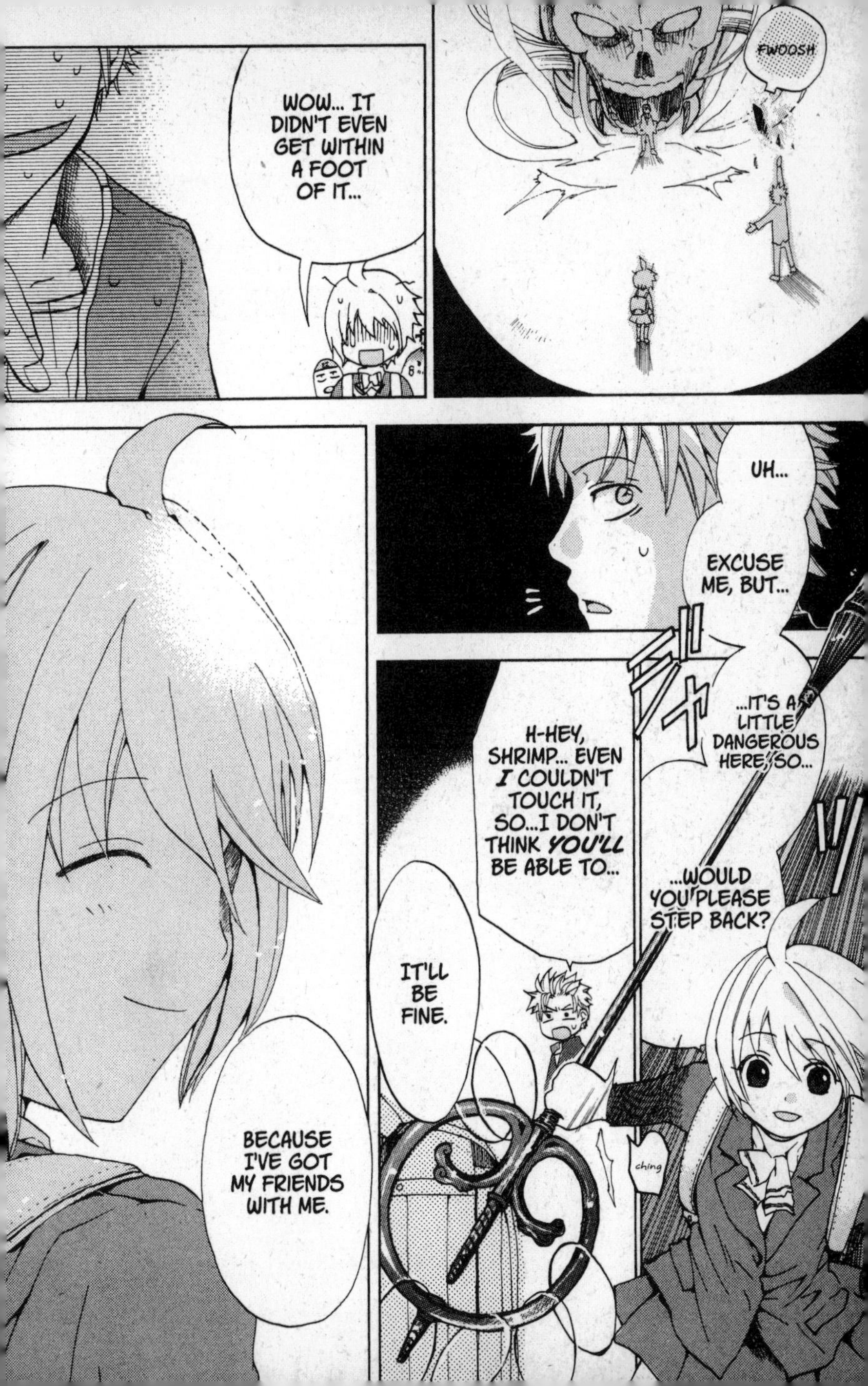
FWOOSH
WOW... IT DIDN'T EVEN GET WITHIN A FOOT OF IT...
UH...
EXCUSE ME, BUT...
...IT'S A LITTLE DANGEROUS HERE, SO...
...WOULD YOU PLEASE STEP BACK?
H-HEY, SHRIMP... EVEN *I* COULDN'T TOUCH IT, SO...I DON'T THINK *YOU'LL* BE ABLE TO...
IT'LL BE FINE.
ching
BECAUSE I'VE GOT MY FRIENDS WITH ME.

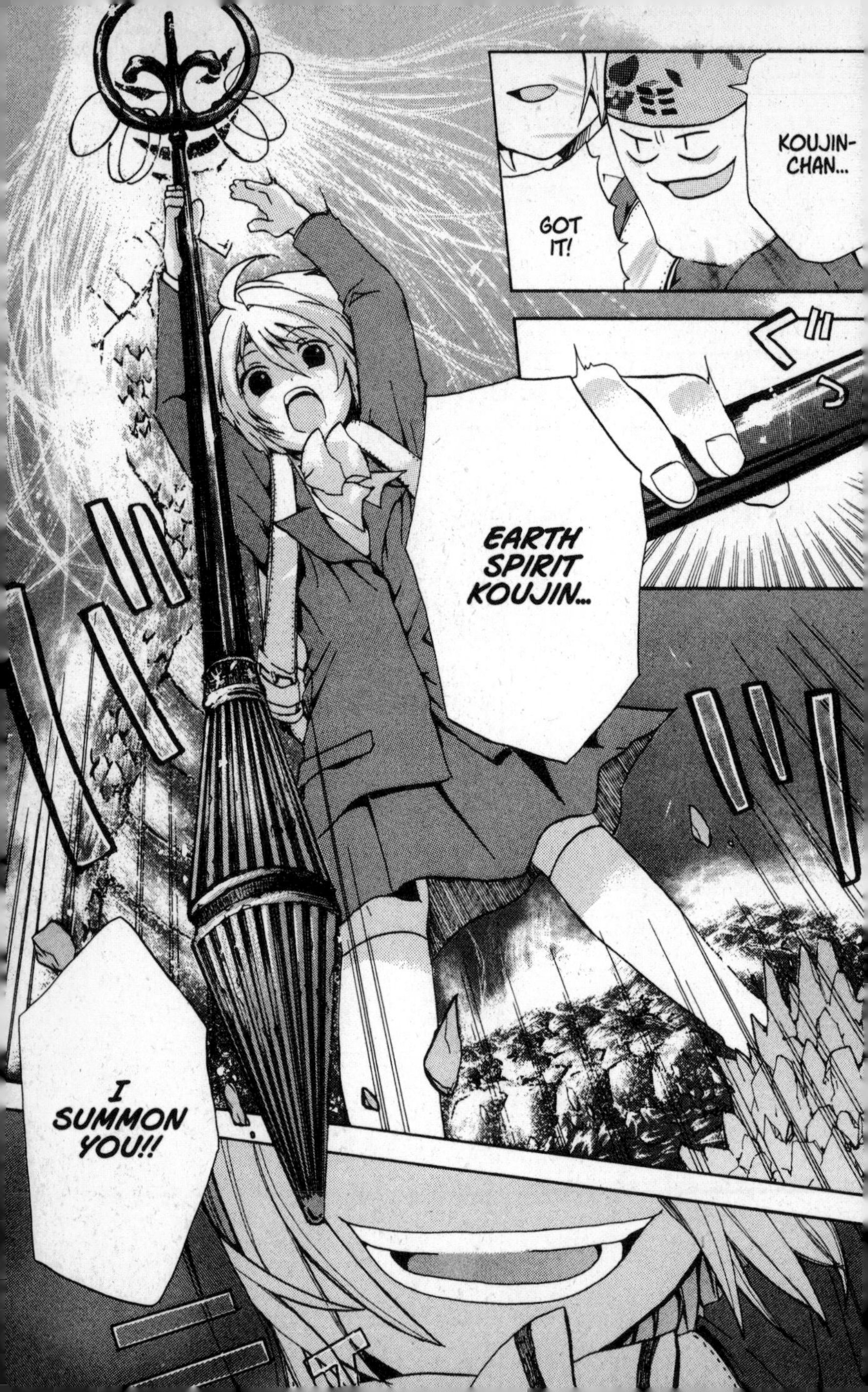
KOUJIN-CHAN...
GOT IT!
EARTH SPIRIT KOUJIN...
I SUMMON YOU!!

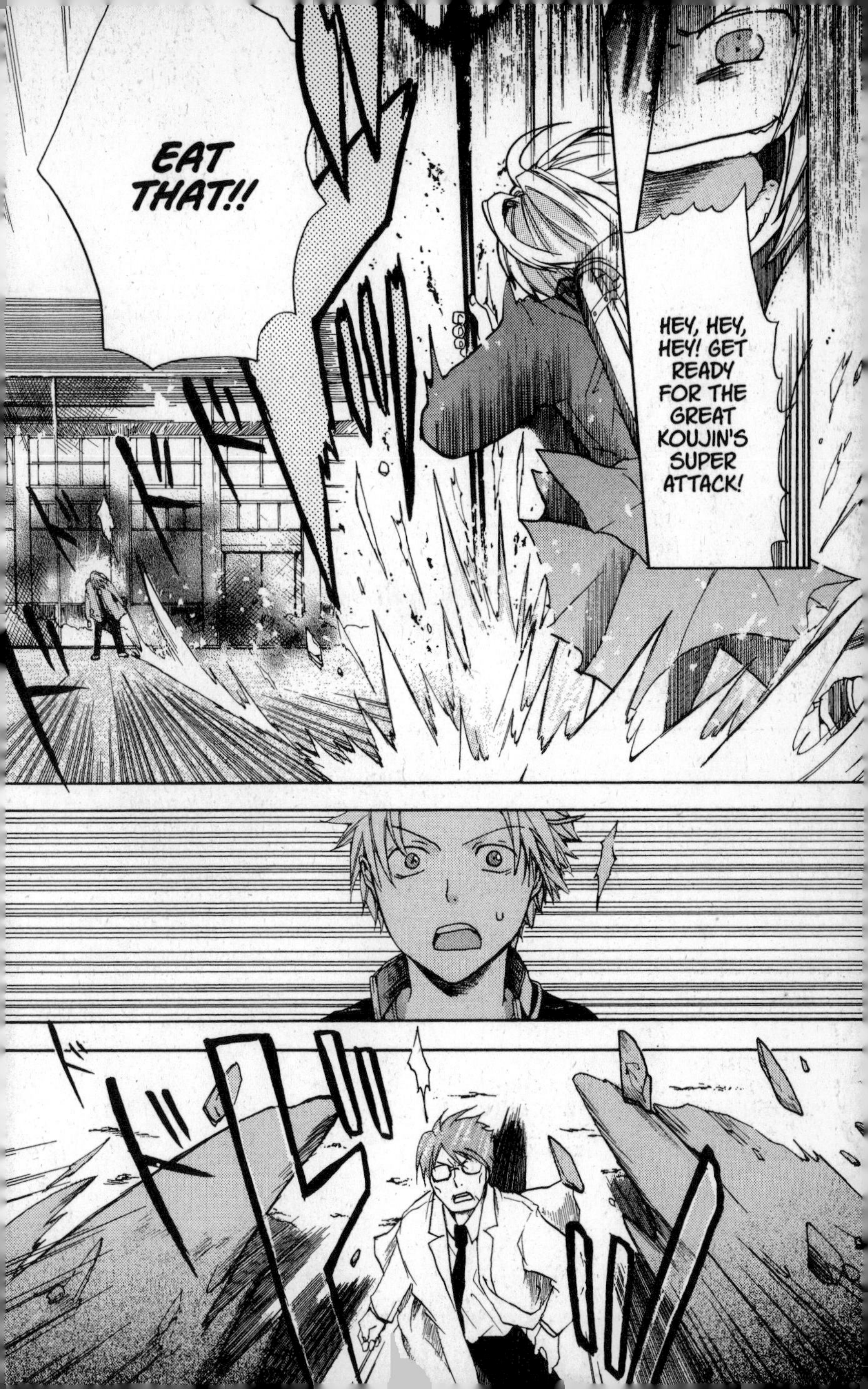
HEY, HEY, HEY! GET READY FOR THE GREAT KOUJIN'S SUPER ATTACK!
EAT THAT!!

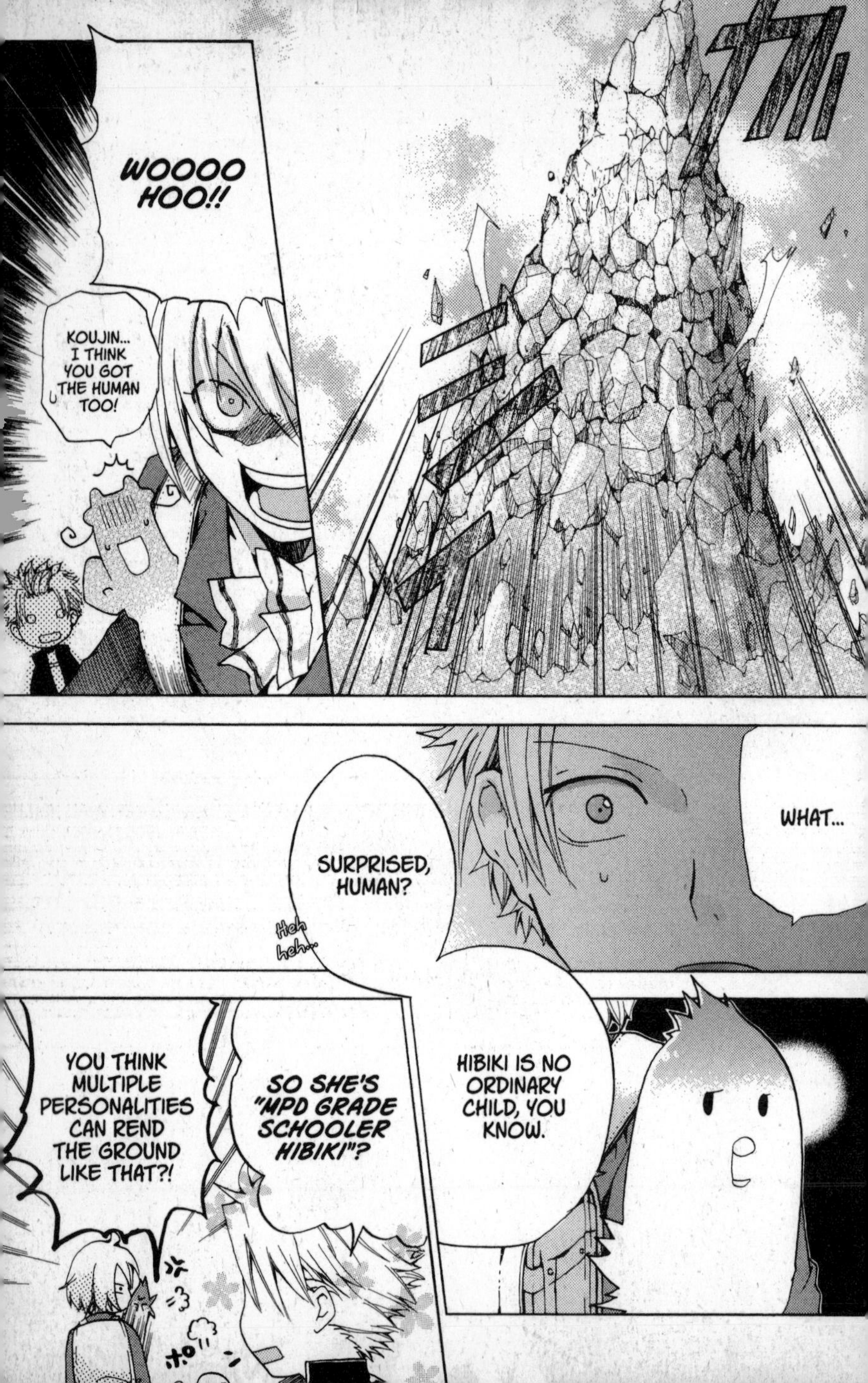
WOOOO HOO!!
KOUJIN... I THINK YOU GOT THE HUMAN TOO!
WHAT...
SURPRISED, HUMAN?
Heh heh...
HIBIKI IS NO ORDINARY CHILD, YOU KNOW.
SO SHE'S "MPD GRADE SCHOOLER HIBIKI"?
YOU THINK MULTIPLE PERSONALITIES CAN REND THE GROUND LIKE THAT?!

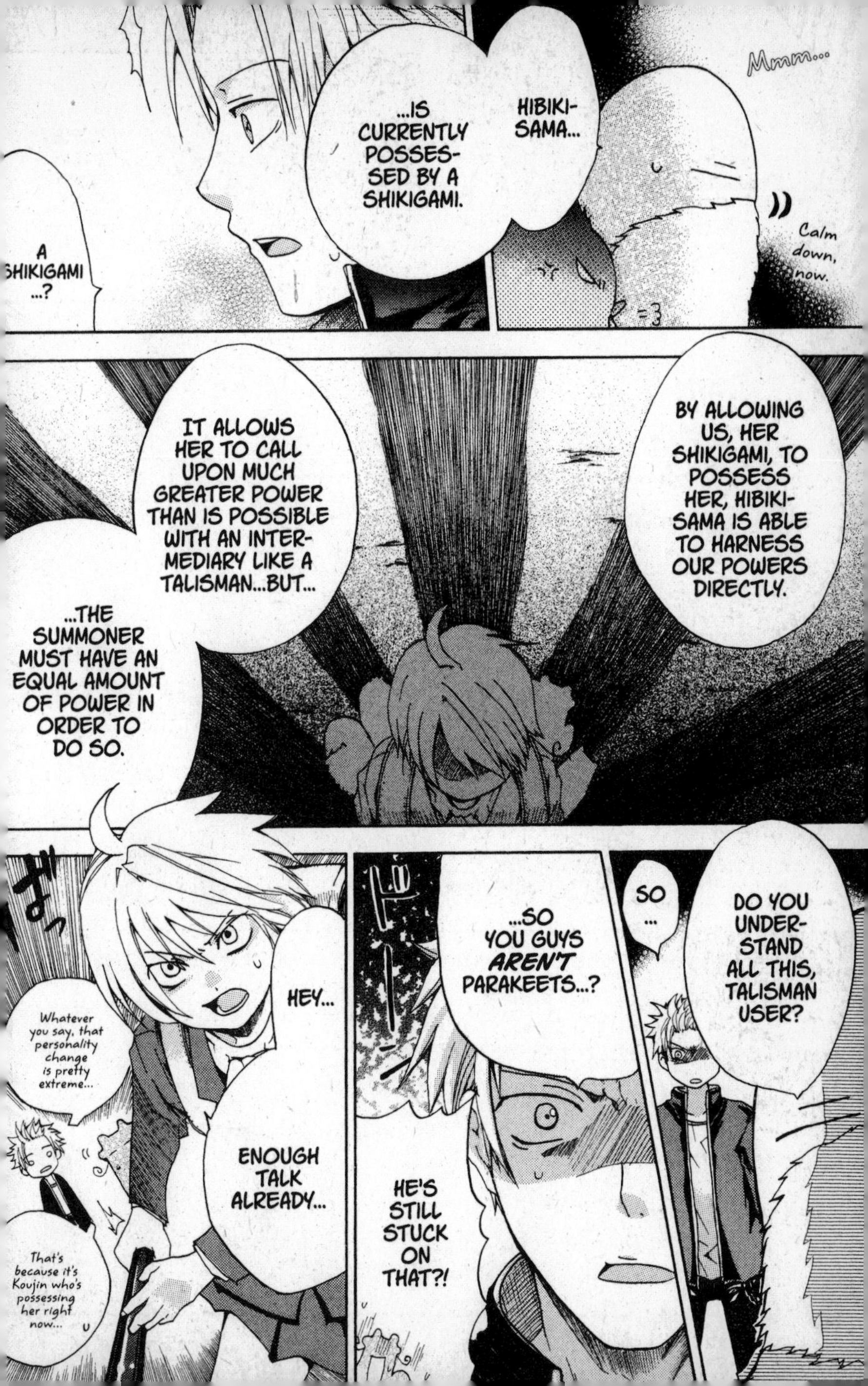
Mmmm...
HIBIKI-SAMA...
Calm down, now.
...IS CURRENTLY POSSES-SED BY A SHIKIGAMI.
A SHIKIGAMI ...?
BY ALLOWING US, HER SHIKIGAMI, TO POSSESS HER, HIBIKI-SAMA IS ABLE TO HARNESS OUR POWERS DIRECTLY.
IT ALLOWS HER TO CALL UPON MUCH GREATER POWER THAN IS POSSIBLE WITH AN INTER-MEDIARY LIKE A TALISMAN...BUT...
...THE SUMMONER MUST HAVE AN EQUAL AMOUNT OF POWER IN ORDER TO DO SO.
DO YOU UNDER-STAND ALL THIS, TALISMAN USER?
SO ...
...SO YOU GUYS *AREN'T* PARAKEETS...?
HE'S STILL STUCK ON THAT?!
HEY...
Whatever you say, that personality change is pretty extreme...
ENOUGH TALK ALREADY...
That's because it's Koujin who's possessing her right now...

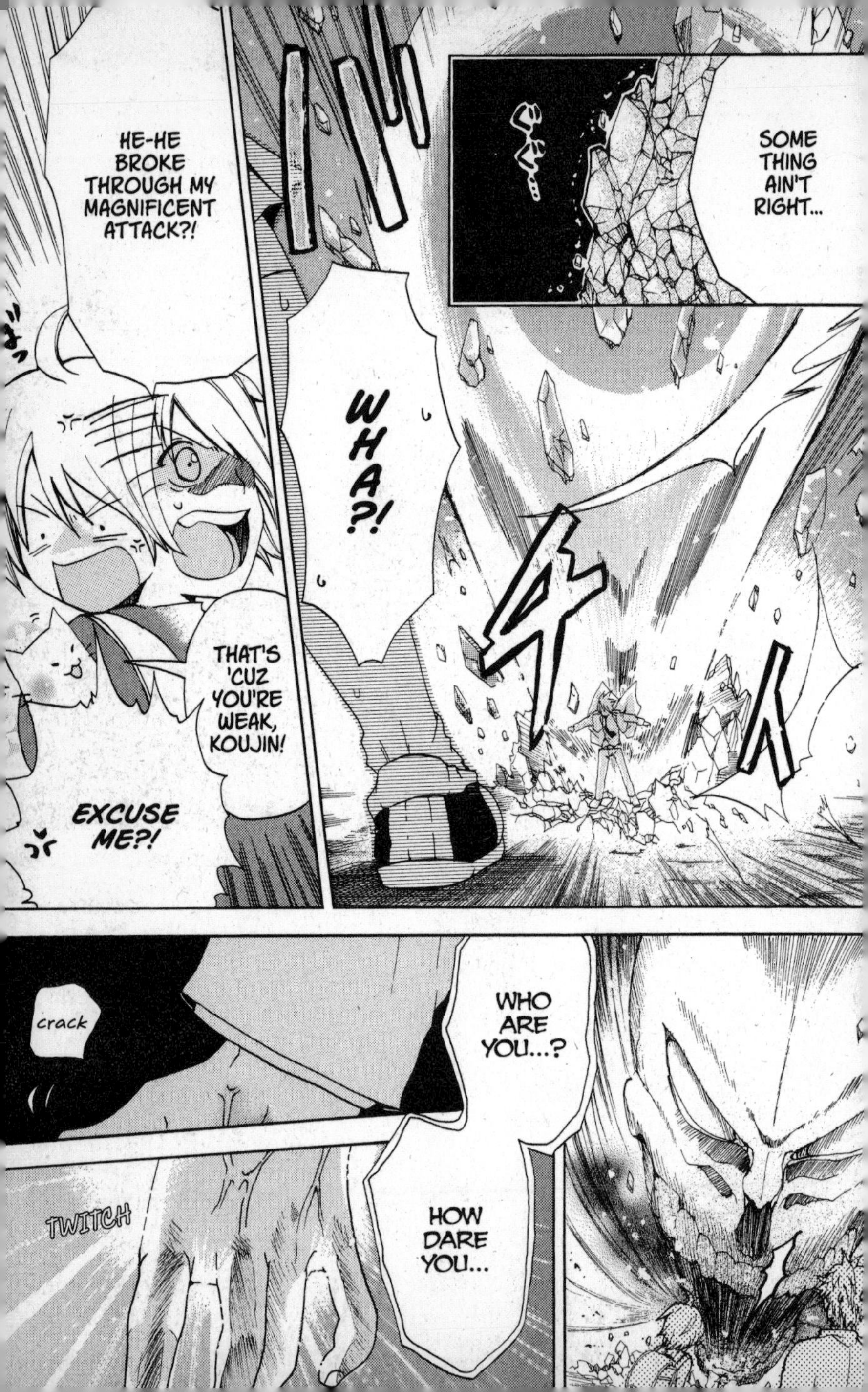
SOME THING AIN'T RIGHT...
WHA?!
HE-HE BROKE THROUGH MY MAGNIFICENT ATTACK?!
THAT'S 'CUZ YOU'RE WEAK, KOUJIN!
EXCUSE ME?!
WHO ARE YOU...?
HOW DARE YOU...
crack
TWITCH

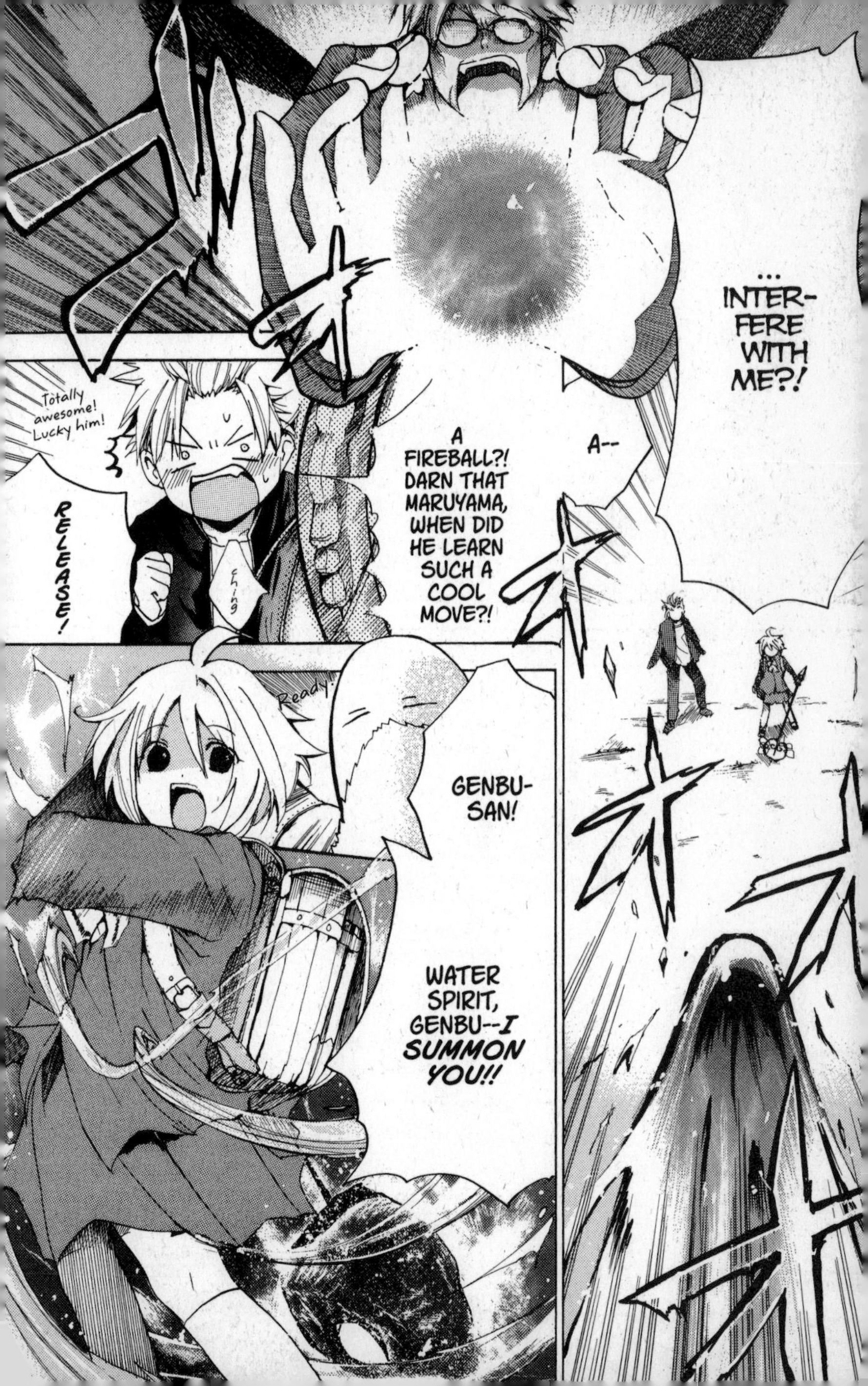

... INTER- FERE WITH ME?!
A--
A FIREBALL?! DARN THAT MARUYAMA, WHEN DID HE LEARN SUCH A COOL MOVE?!
Totally awesome! Lucky him!
RELEASE!
ching
GENBU-SAN!
Ready
WATER SPIRIT, GENBU--I SUMMON YOU!!

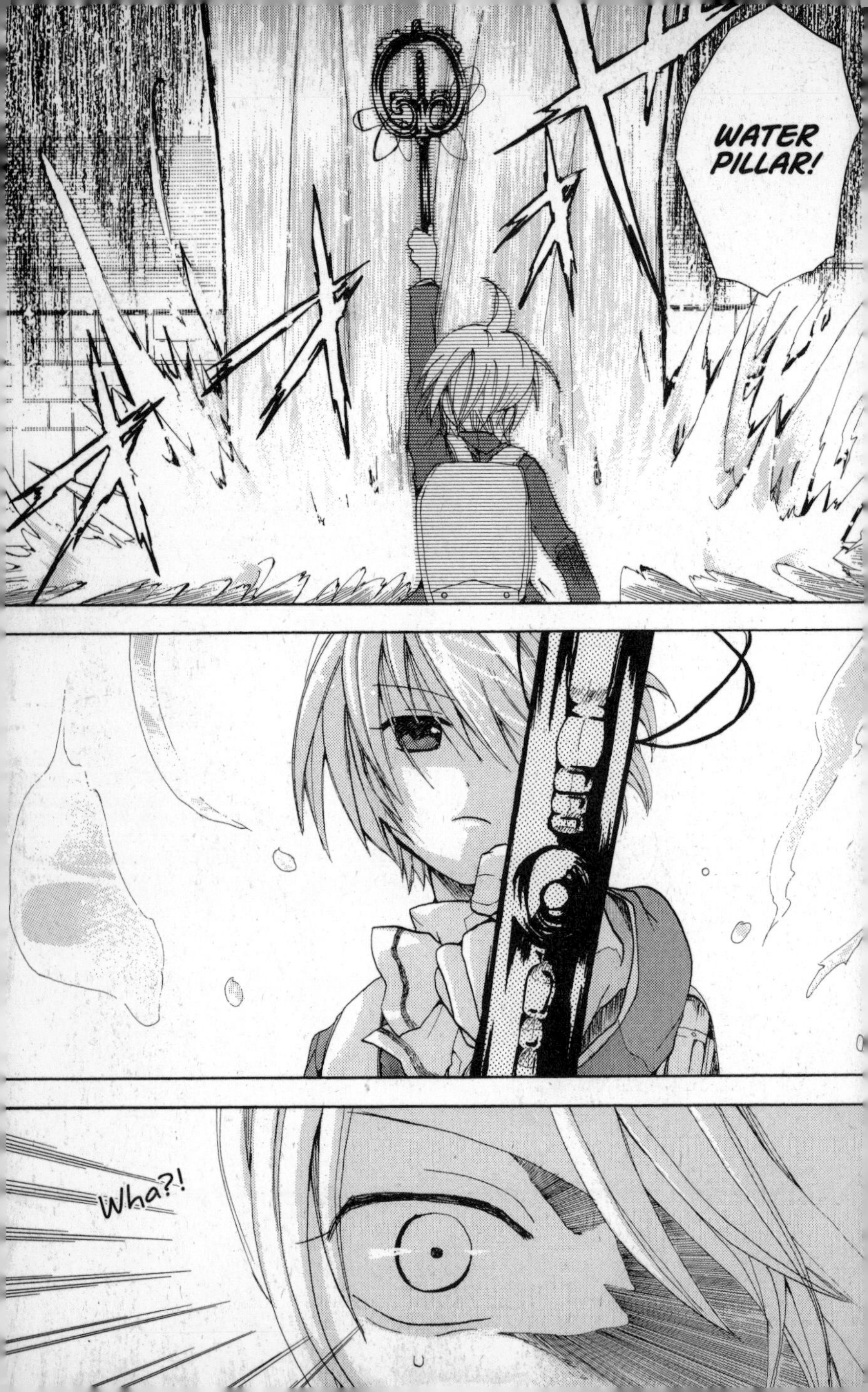
WATER PILLAR!
Wha?!

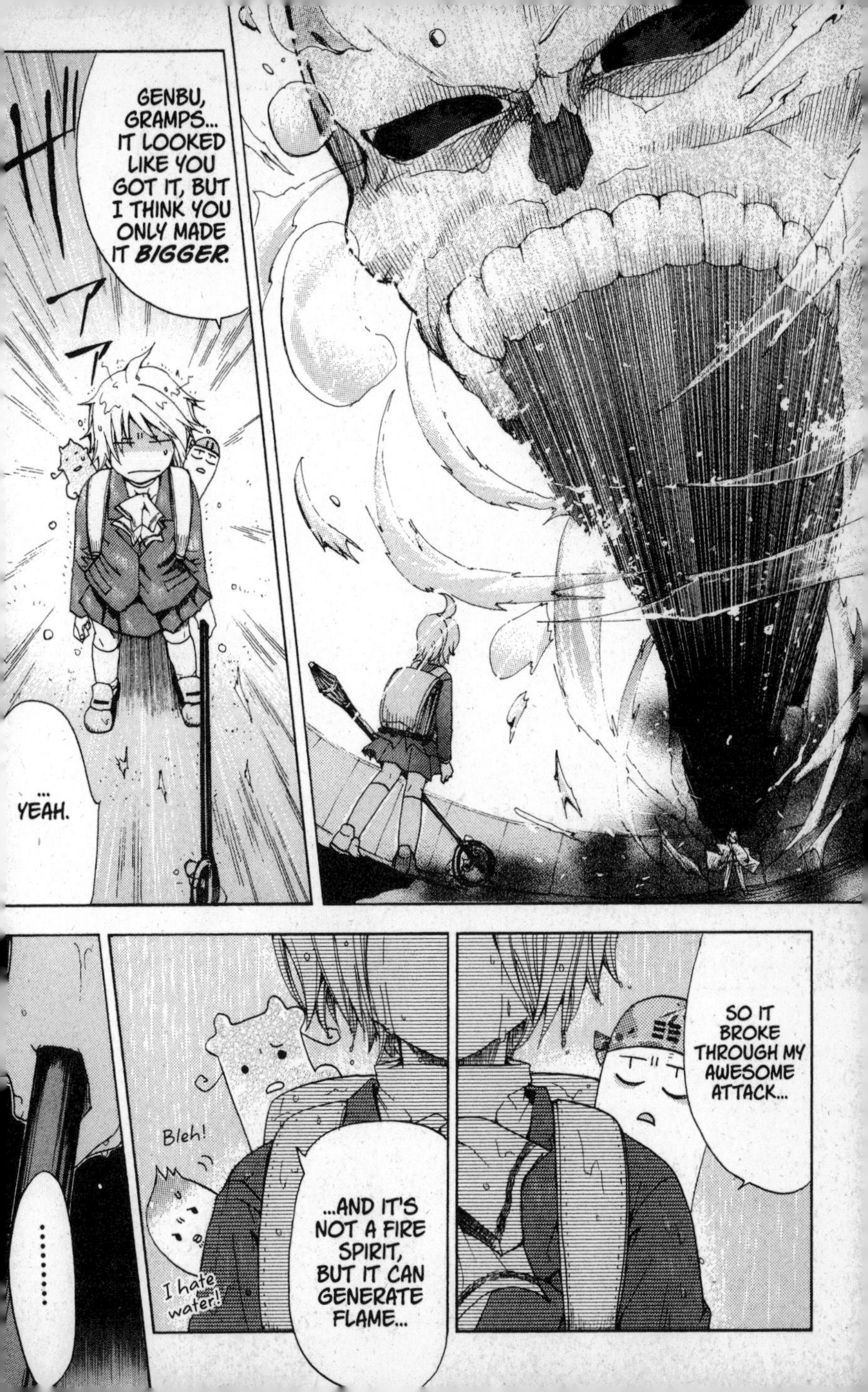
GENBU, GRAMPS... IT LOOKED LIKE YOU GOT IT, BUT I THINK YOU ONLY MADE IT ***BIGGER.***
...
YEAH.
SO IT BROKE THROUGH MY AWESOME ATTACK...
...AND IT'S NOT A FIRE SPIRIT, BUT IT CAN GENERATE FLAME...
Bleh!
I hate water!
......

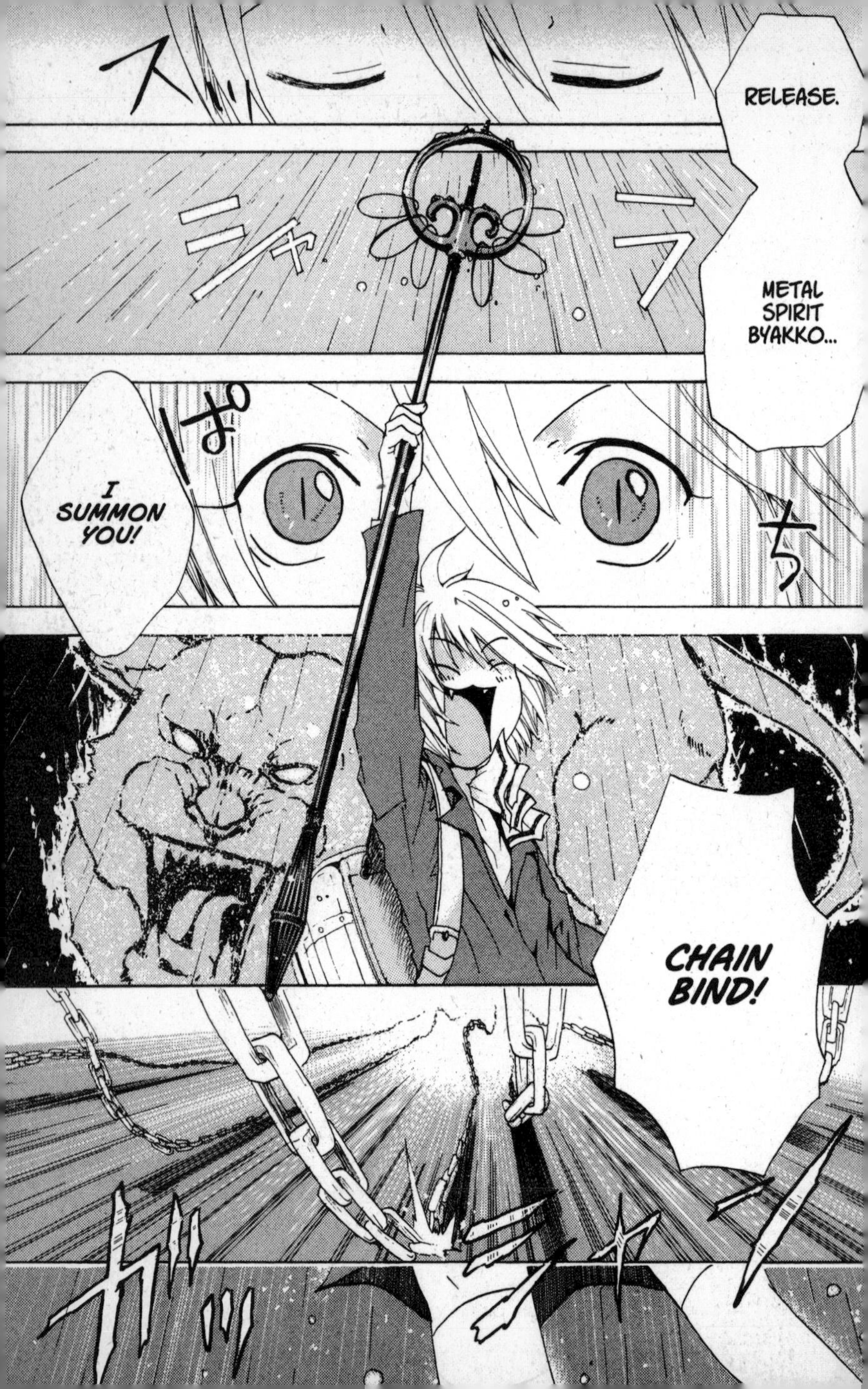
RELEASE.
METAL SPIRIT BYAKKO...
I SUMMON YOU!
CHAIN BIND!

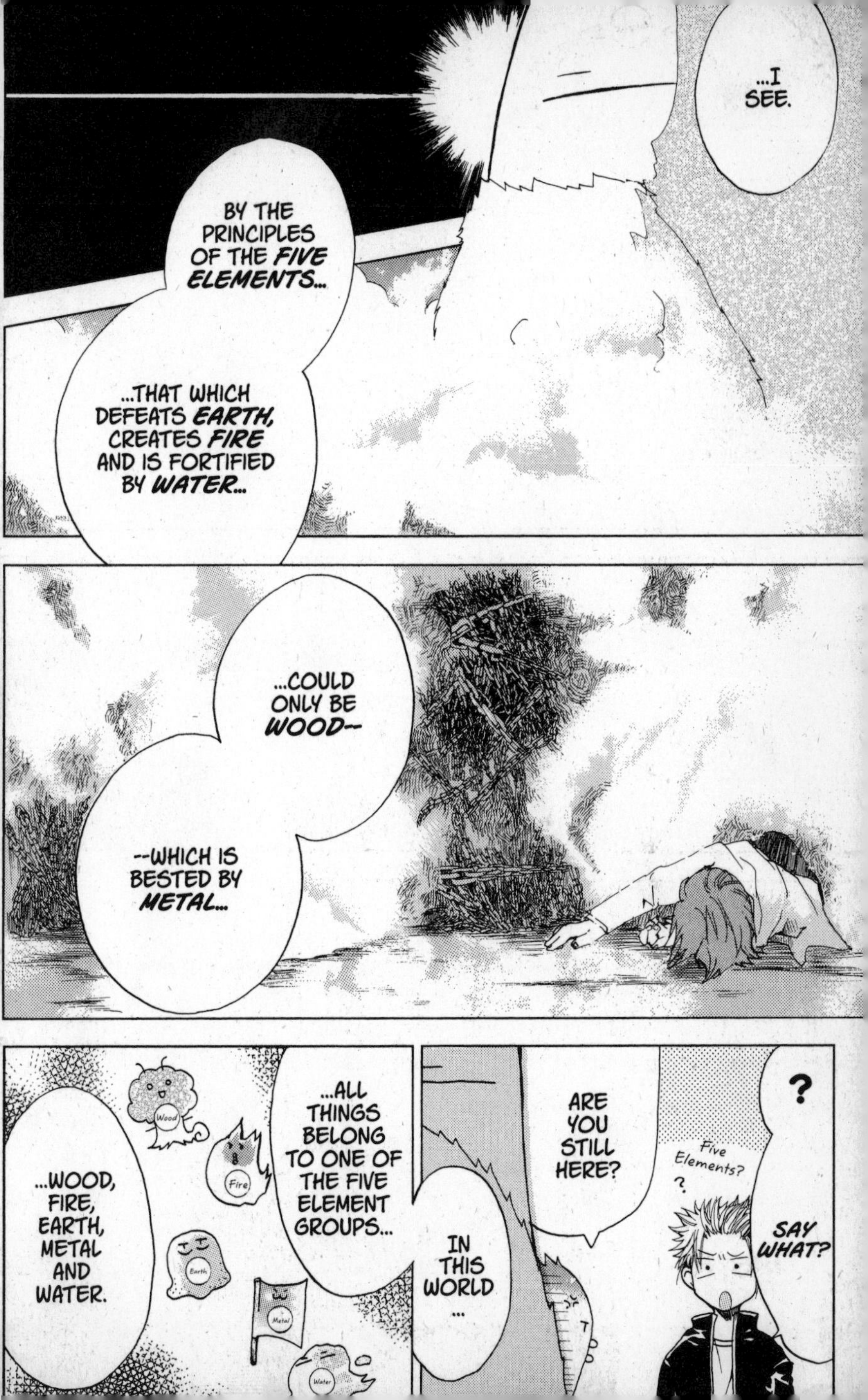
...I SEE.
BY THE PRINCIPLES OF THE *FIVE ELEMENTS*...
...THAT WHICH DEFEATS *EARTH*, CREATES *FIRE* AND IS FORTIFIED BY *WATER*...
...COULD ONLY BE *WOOD*--
--WHICH IS BESTED BY *METAL*...
?
Five Elements?
?
SAY WHAT?
ARE YOU STILL HERE?
IN THIS WORLD ...
...ALL THINGS BELONG TO ONE OF THE FIVE ELEMENT GROUPS...
...WOOD, FIRE, EARTH, METAL AND WATER.
Wood
Fire
Earth
Metal
Water

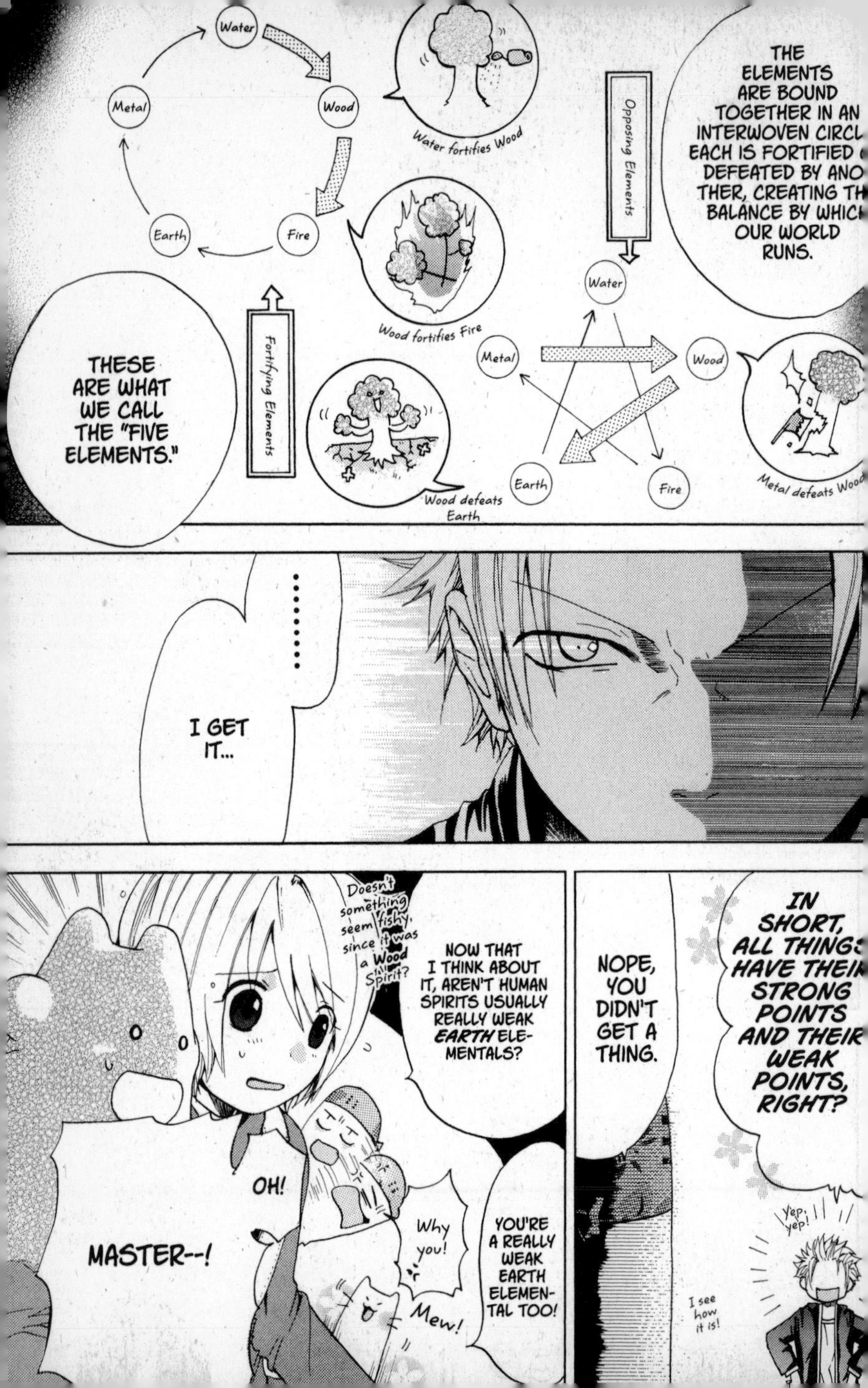
THE ELEMENTS ARE BOUND TOGETHER IN AN INTERWOVEN CIRCL EACH IS FORTIFIED DEFEATED BY ANO THER, CREATING TH BALANCE BY WHIC OUR WORLD RUNS.
Opposing Elements
Water
Wood
Fire
Earth
Metal
Metal defeats Woo
Water
Wood
Fire
Earth
Metal
Water fortifies Wood
Wood fortifies Fire
Fortifying Elements
Wood defeats Earth
THESE ARE WHAT WE CALL THE "FIVE ELEMENTS."
......
I GET IT...
IN SHORT, ALL THING HAVE THEI STRONG POINTS AND THEI WEAK POINTS, RIGHT?
Yep, yep!
NOPE, YOU DIDN'T GET A THING.
I see how it is!
Doesn't something seem fishy, since it was a Wood Spirit?
NOW THAT I THINK ABOUT IT, AREN'T HUMAN SPIRITS USUALLY REALLY WEAK EARTH ELEMENTALS?
YOU'RE A REALLY WEAK EARTH ELEMENTAL TOO!
Why you!
OH!
MASTER--!
Mew!

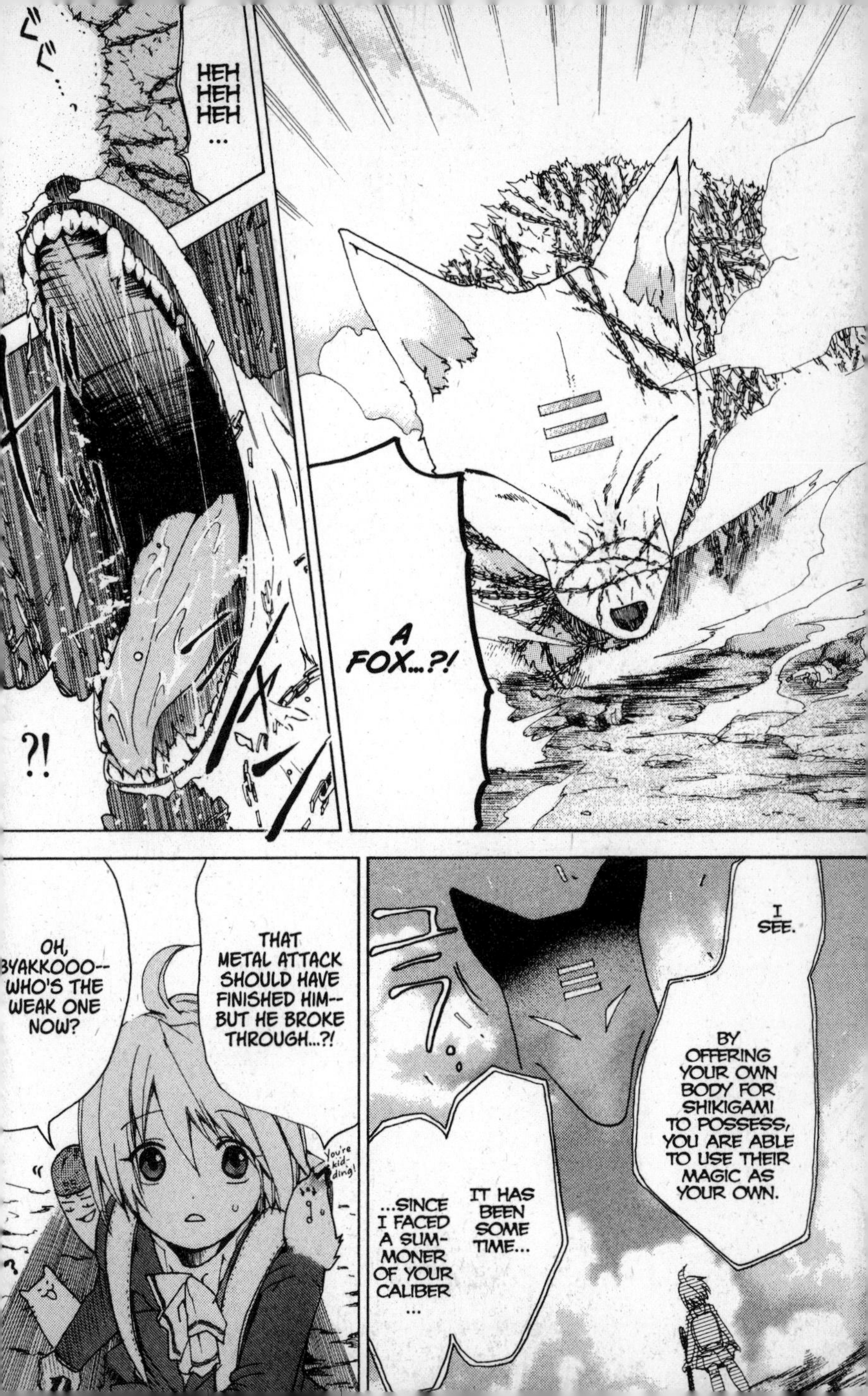
A FOX...?!
HEH HEH HEH ...
?!
I SEE.
BY OFFERING YOUR OWN BODY FOR SHIKIGAMI TO POSSESS, YOU ARE ABLE TO USE THEIR MAGIC AS YOUR OWN.
IT HAS BEEN SOME TIME...
...SINCE I FACED A SUM-MONER OF YOUR CALIBER ...
THAT METAL ATTACK SHOULD HAVE FINISHED HIM-- BUT HE BROKE THROUGH...?!
OH, BYAKKOOO-- WHO'S THE WEAK ONE NOW?
You're kid-ding!

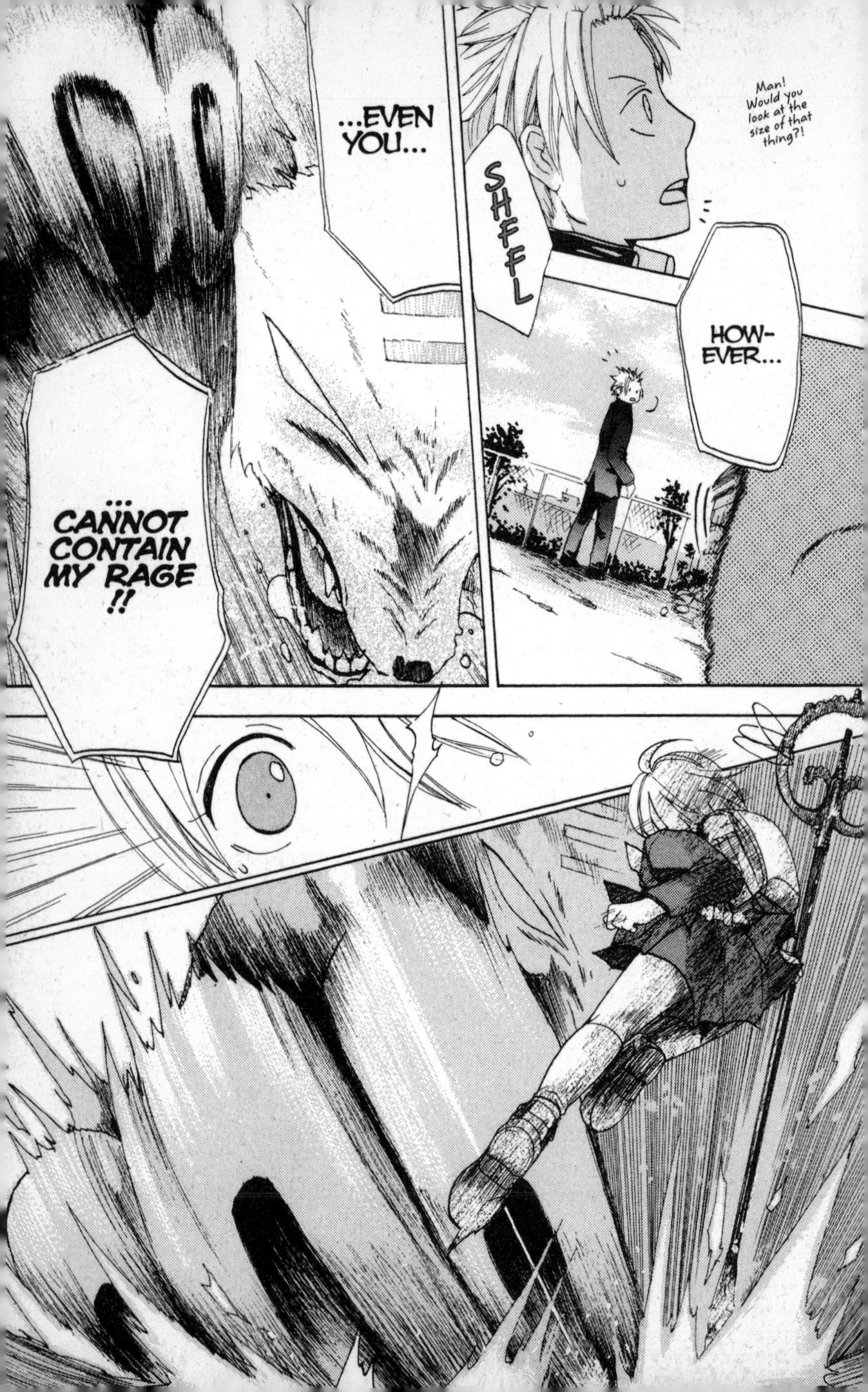
Man! Would you look at the size of that thing?!
SHFFL
HOW-EVER...
...EVEN YOU...
...CANNOT CONTAIN MY RAGE!!

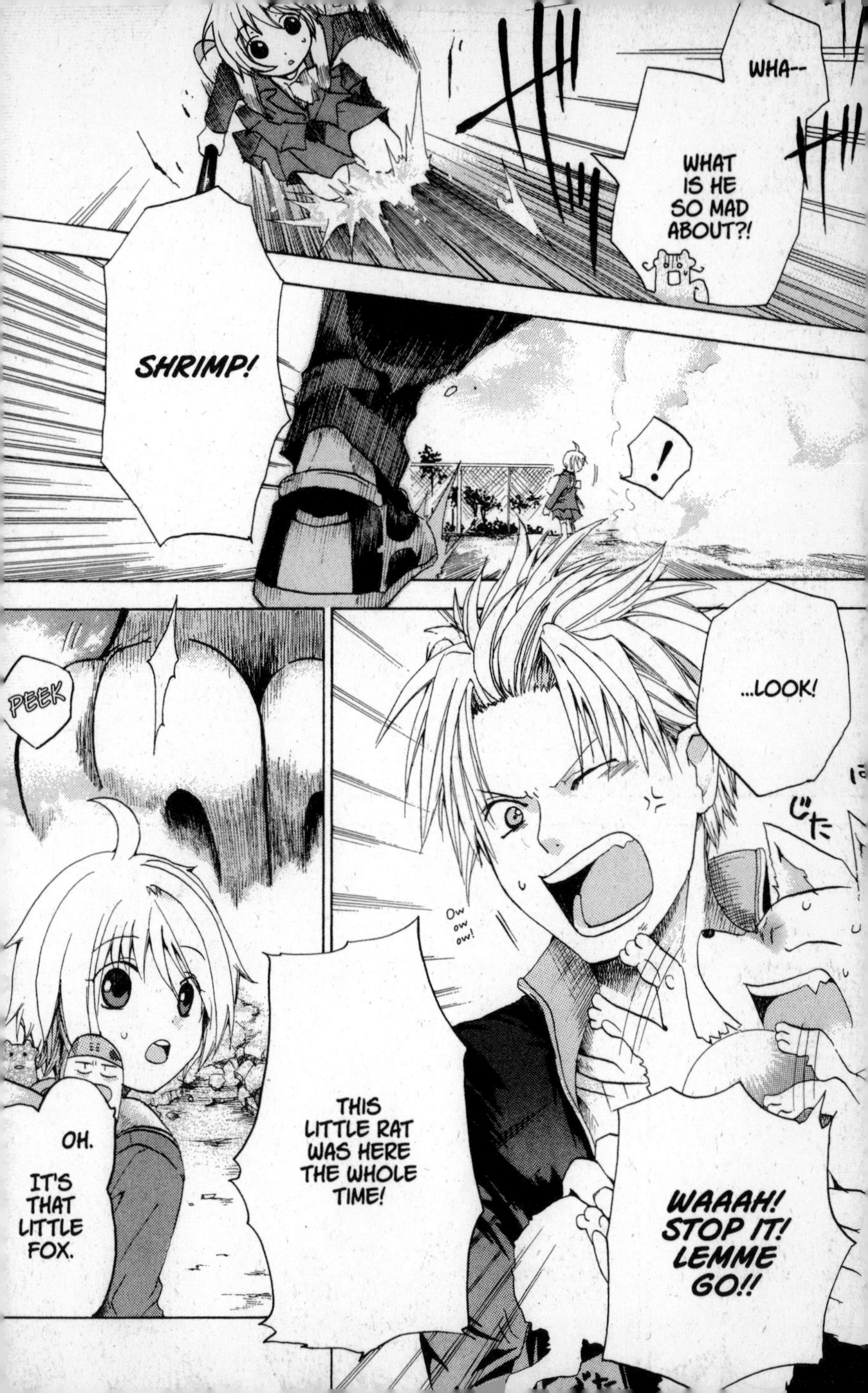
WHA--
WHAT IS HE SO MAD ABOUT?!
SHRIMP!
!
...LOOK!
Ow ow ow!
THIS LITTLE RAT WAS HERE THE WHOLE TIME!
WAAAH! STOP IT! LEMME GO!!
PEEK
OH.
IT'S THAT LITTLE FOX.

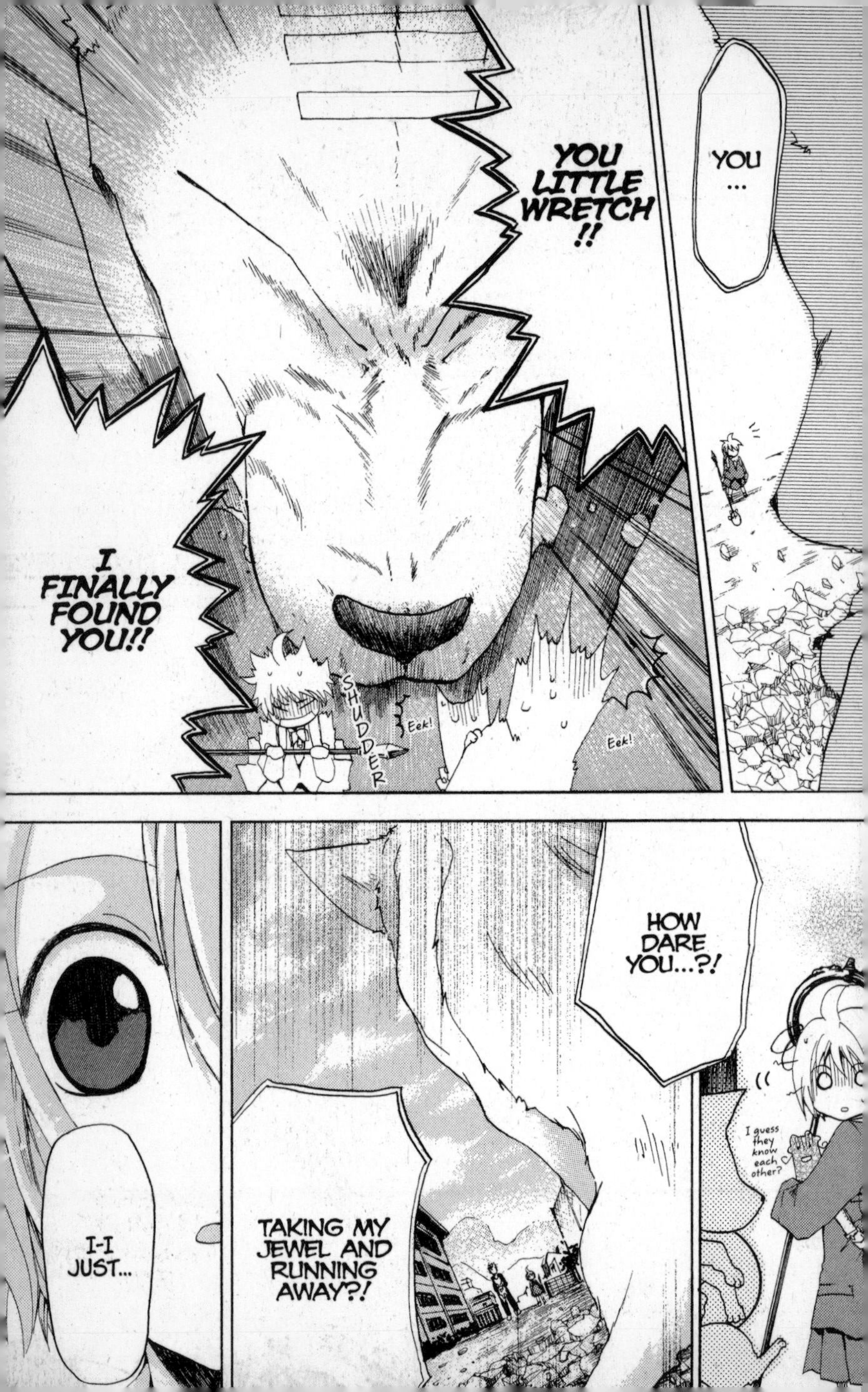
YOU ...
YOU LITTLE WRETCH!!
I FINALLY FOUND YOU!!
SHUDDER
Eek!
Eek!
I guess they know each other?
HOW DARE YOU...?!
TAKING MY JEWEL AND RUNNING AWAY?!
I-I JUST...

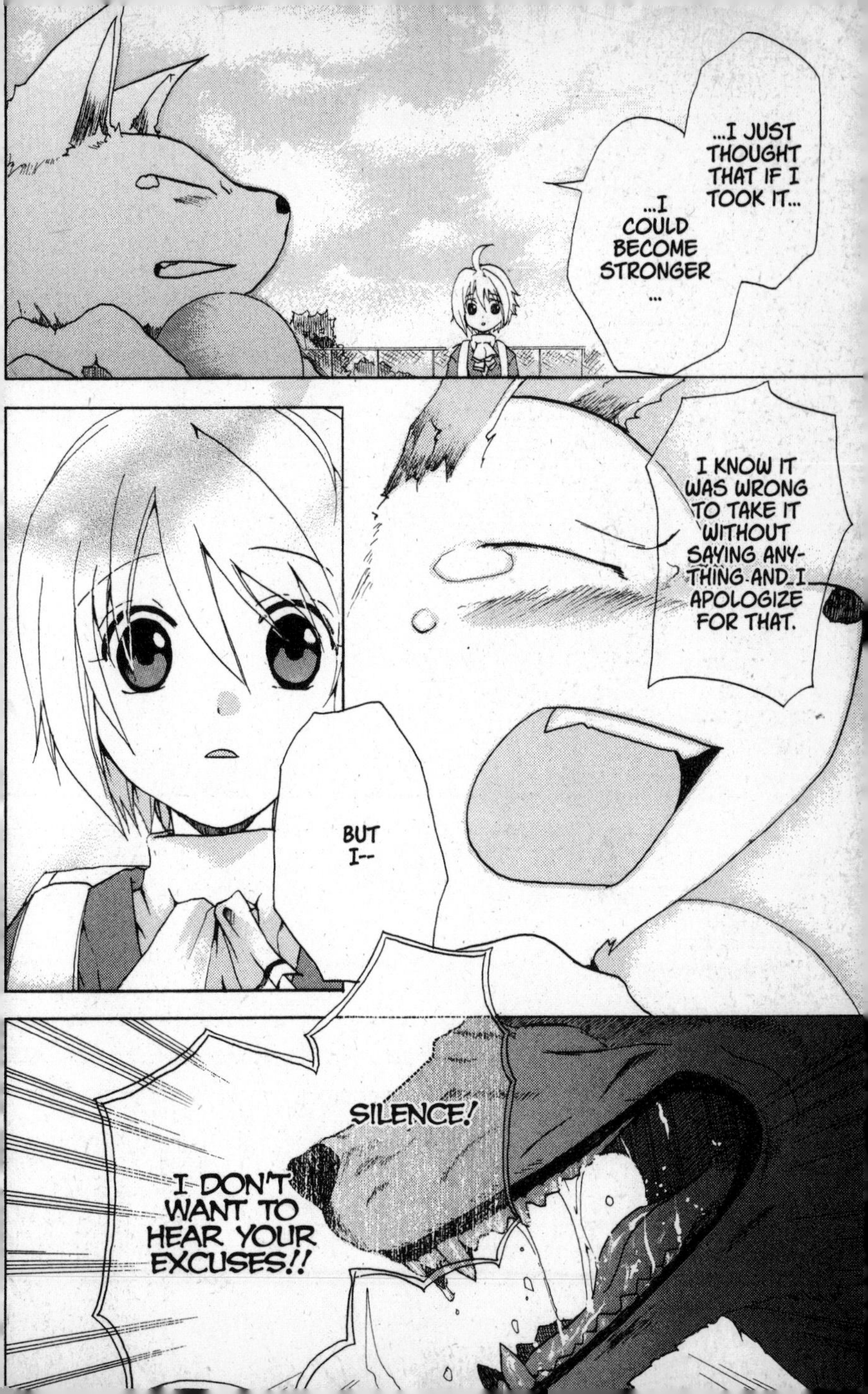
...I JUST THOUGHT THAT IF I TOOK IT...
...I COULD BECOME STRONGER ...
I KNOW IT WAS WRONG TO TAKE IT WITHOUT SAYING ANY-THING AND I APOLOGIZE FOR THAT.
BUT I--
SILENCE!
I DON'T WANT TO HEAR YOUR EXCUSES!!

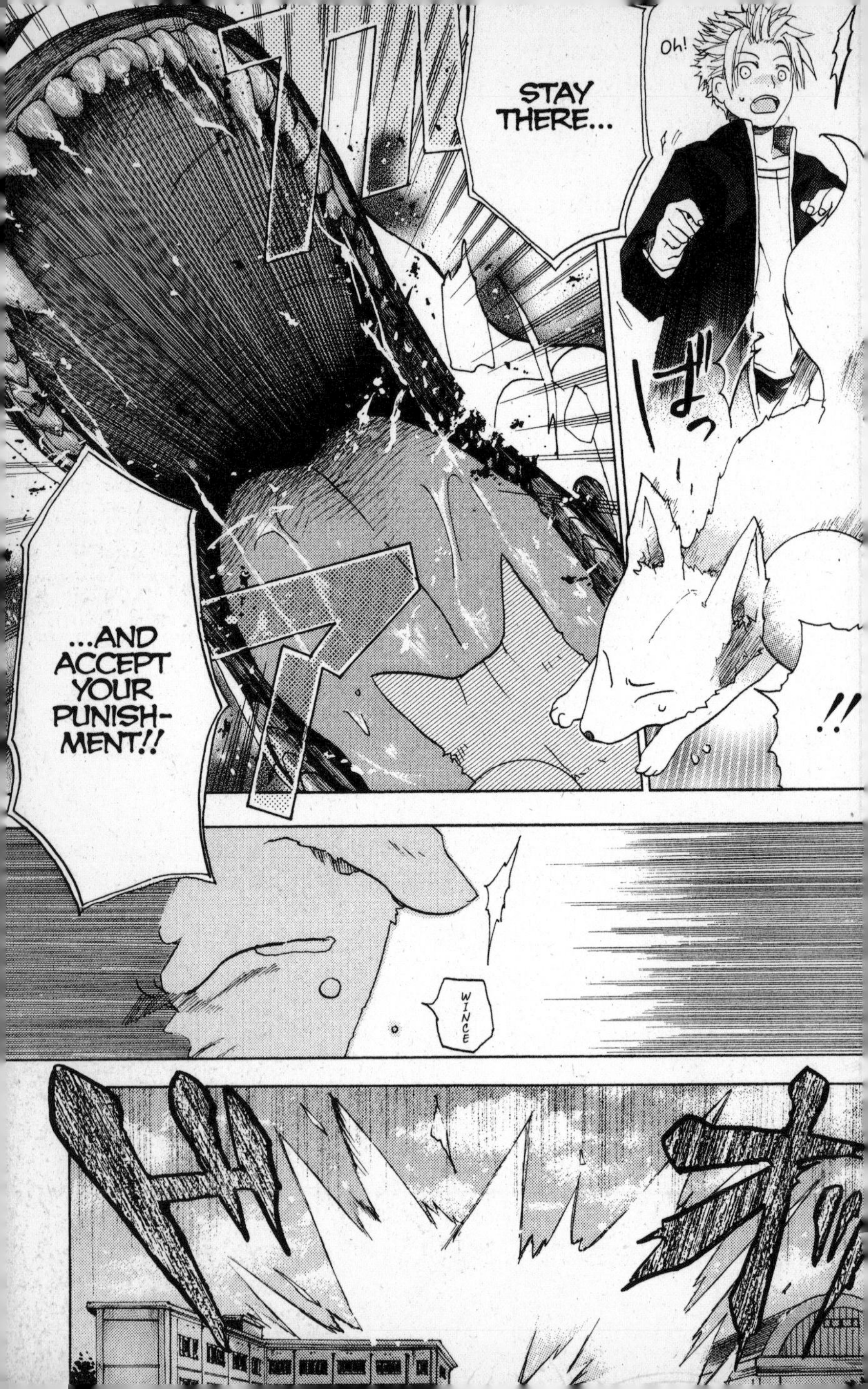
Oh!
STAY THERE...
ばっ
!!
...AND ACCEPT YOUR PUNISH-MENT!!
WINCE

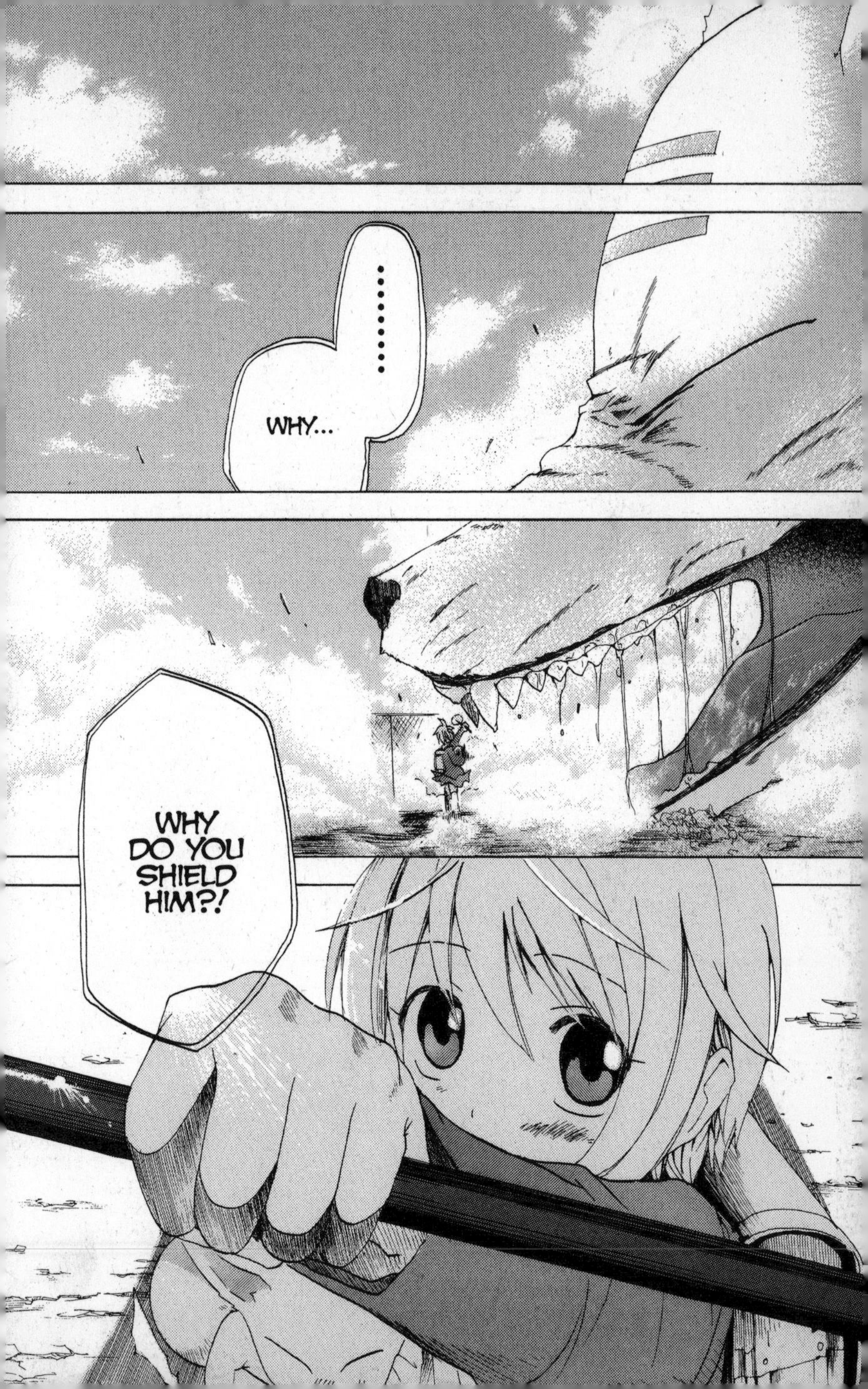
......
WHY...
WHY DO YOU SHIELD HIM?!

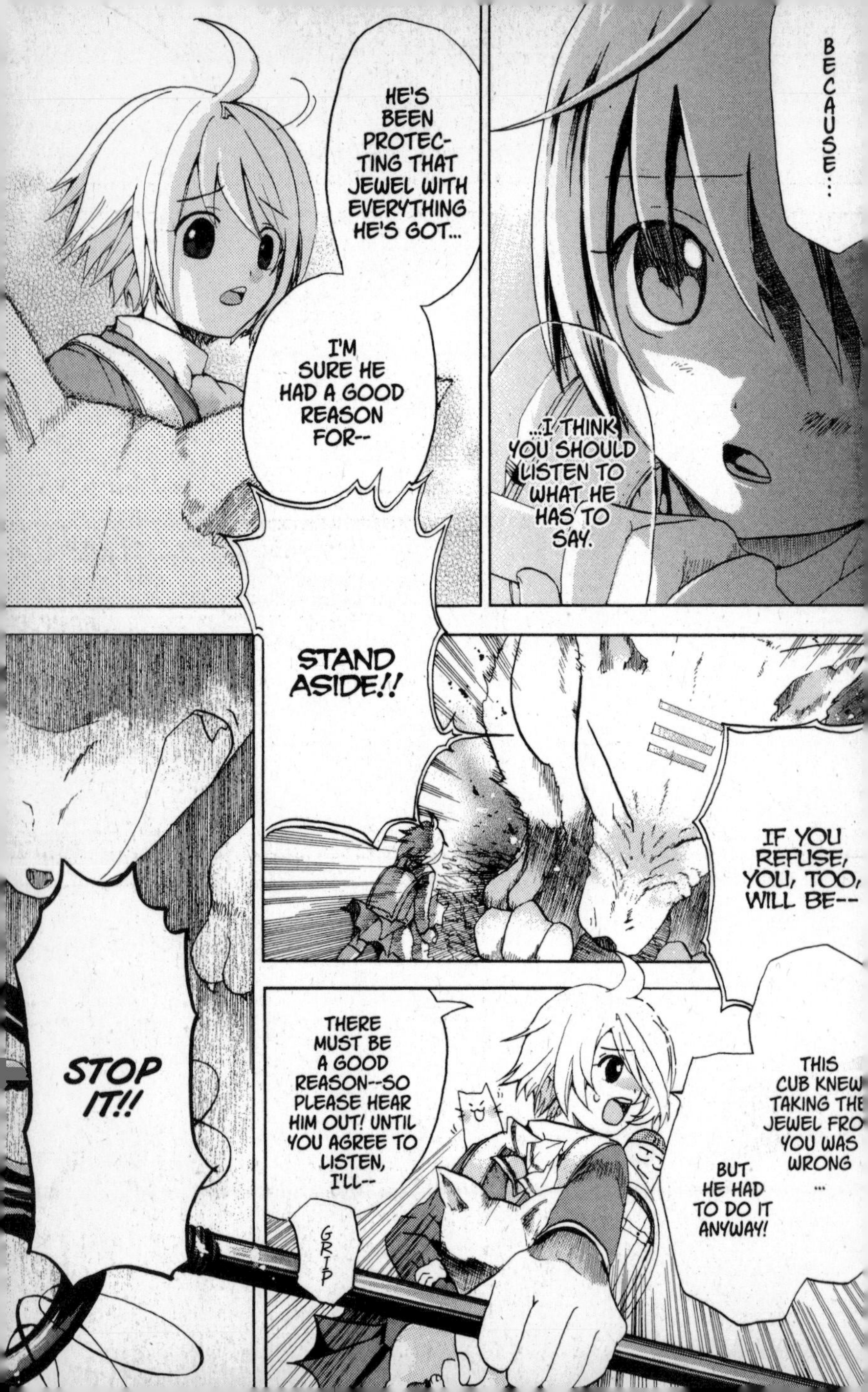
BECAUSE...
...I THINK YOU SHOULD LISTEN TO WHAT HE HAS TO SAY.
HE'S BEEN PROTECTING THAT JEWEL WITH EVERYTHING HE'S GOT...
I'M SURE HE HAD A GOOD REASON FOR--
STAND ASIDE!!
IF YOU REFUSE, YOU, TOO, WILL BE--
THIS CUB KNEW TAKING THE JEWEL FRO YOU WAS WRONG...
BUT HE HAD TO DO IT ANYWAY!
THERE MUST BE A GOOD REASON--SO PLEASE HEAR HIM OUT! UNTIL YOU AGREE TO LISTEN, I'LL--
GRIP
STOP IT!!

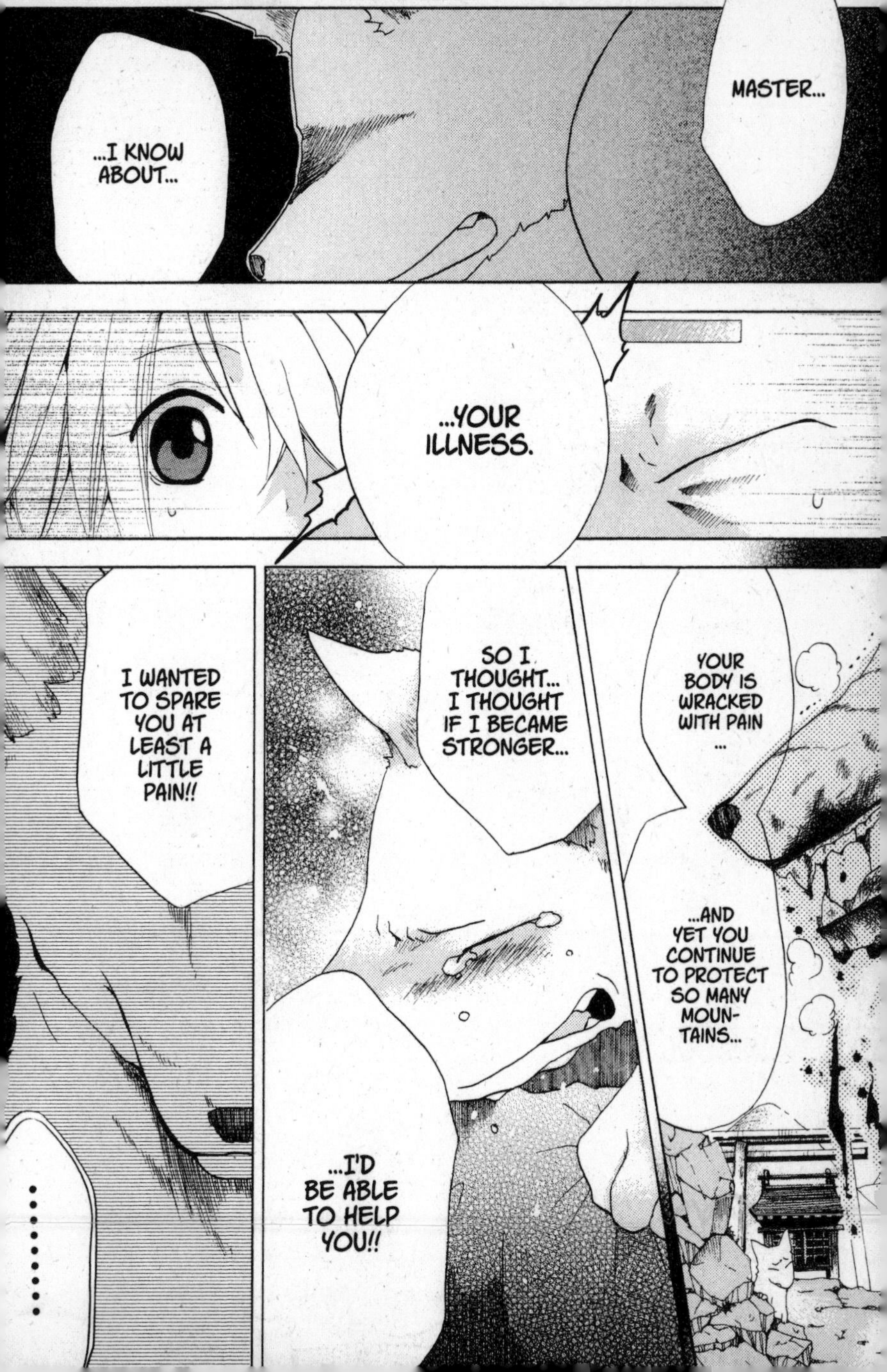
MASTER...
...I KNOW ABOUT...
...YOUR ILLNESS.
YOUR BODY IS WRACKED WITH PAIN ...
...AND YET YOU CONTINUE TO PROTECT SO MANY MOUN-TAINS...
SO I THOUGHT... I THOUGHT IF I BECAME STRONGER...
...I'D BE ABLE TO HELP YOU!!
I WANTED TO SPARE YOU AT LEAST A LITTLE PAIN!!
....

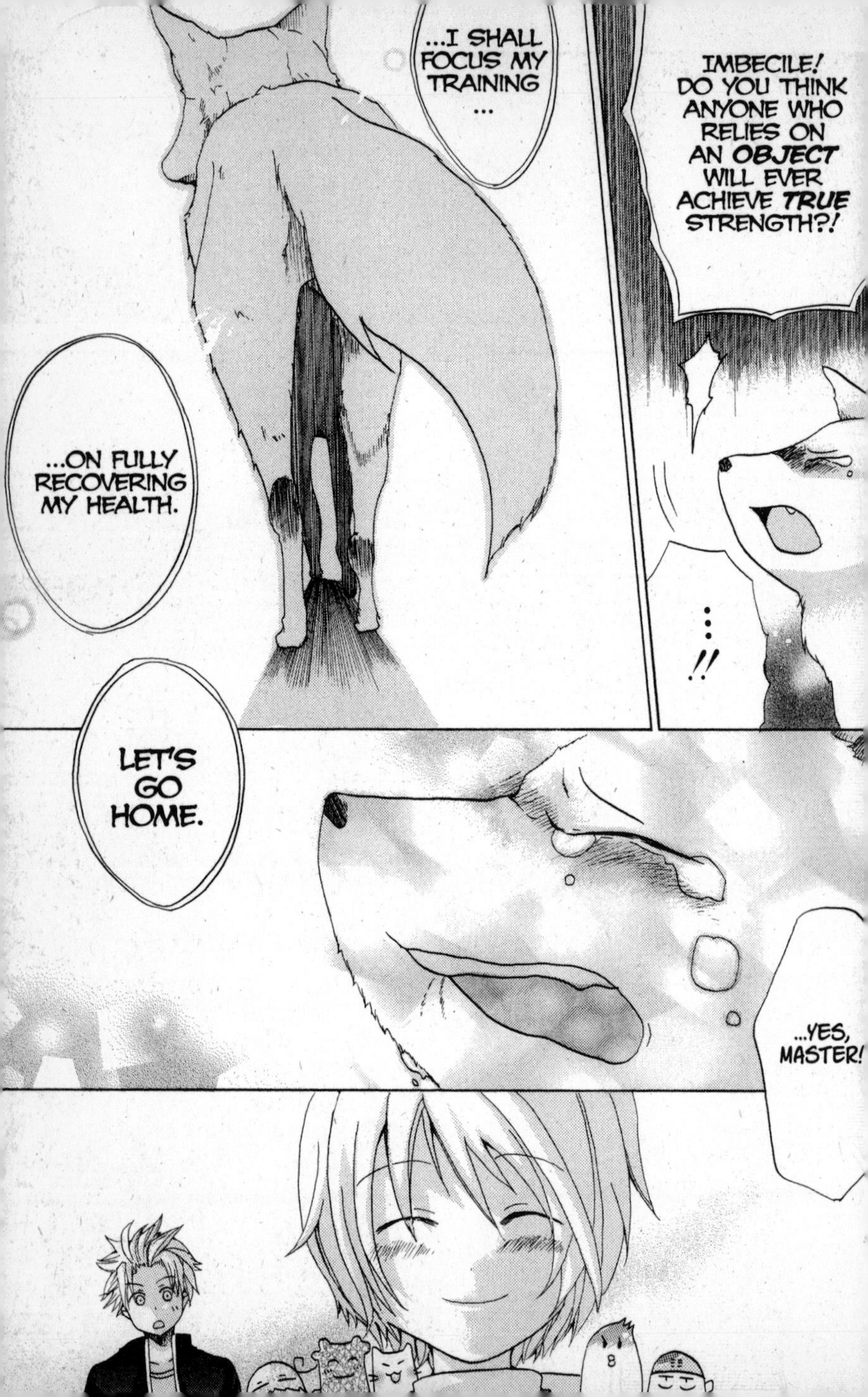
IMBECILE! DO YOU THINK ANYONE WHO RELIES ON AN *OBJECT* WILL EVER ACHIEVE *TRUE* STRENGTH?!
...!!
...I SHALL FOCUS MY TRAINING ...
...ON FULLY RECOVERING MY HEALTH.
LET'S GO HOME.
...YES, MASTER!

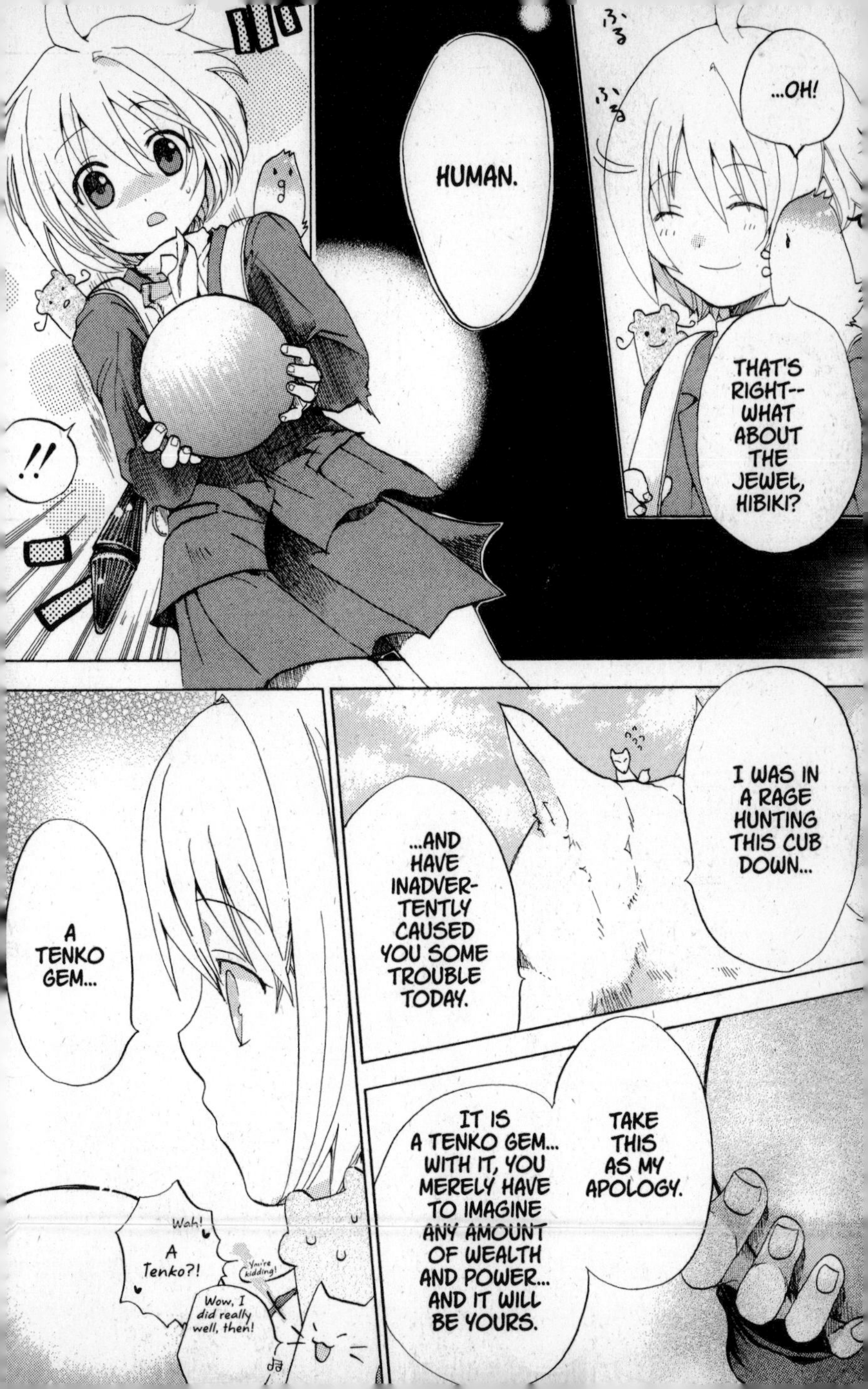
ふる
ふる
...OH!
THAT'S RIGHT-- WHAT ABOUT THE JEWEL, HIBIKI?
HUMAN.
!!
I WAS IN A RAGE HUNTING THIS CUB DOWN...
...AND HAVE INADVERTENTLY CAUSED YOU SOME TROUBLE TODAY.
TAKE THIS AS MY APOLOGY.
IT IS A TENKO GEM... WITH IT, YOU MERELY HAVE TO IMAGINE ANY AMOUNT OF WEALTH AND POWER... AND IT WILL BE YOURS.
A TENKO GEM...
Wah! A Tenko?!
You're kidding!
Wow, I did really well, then!

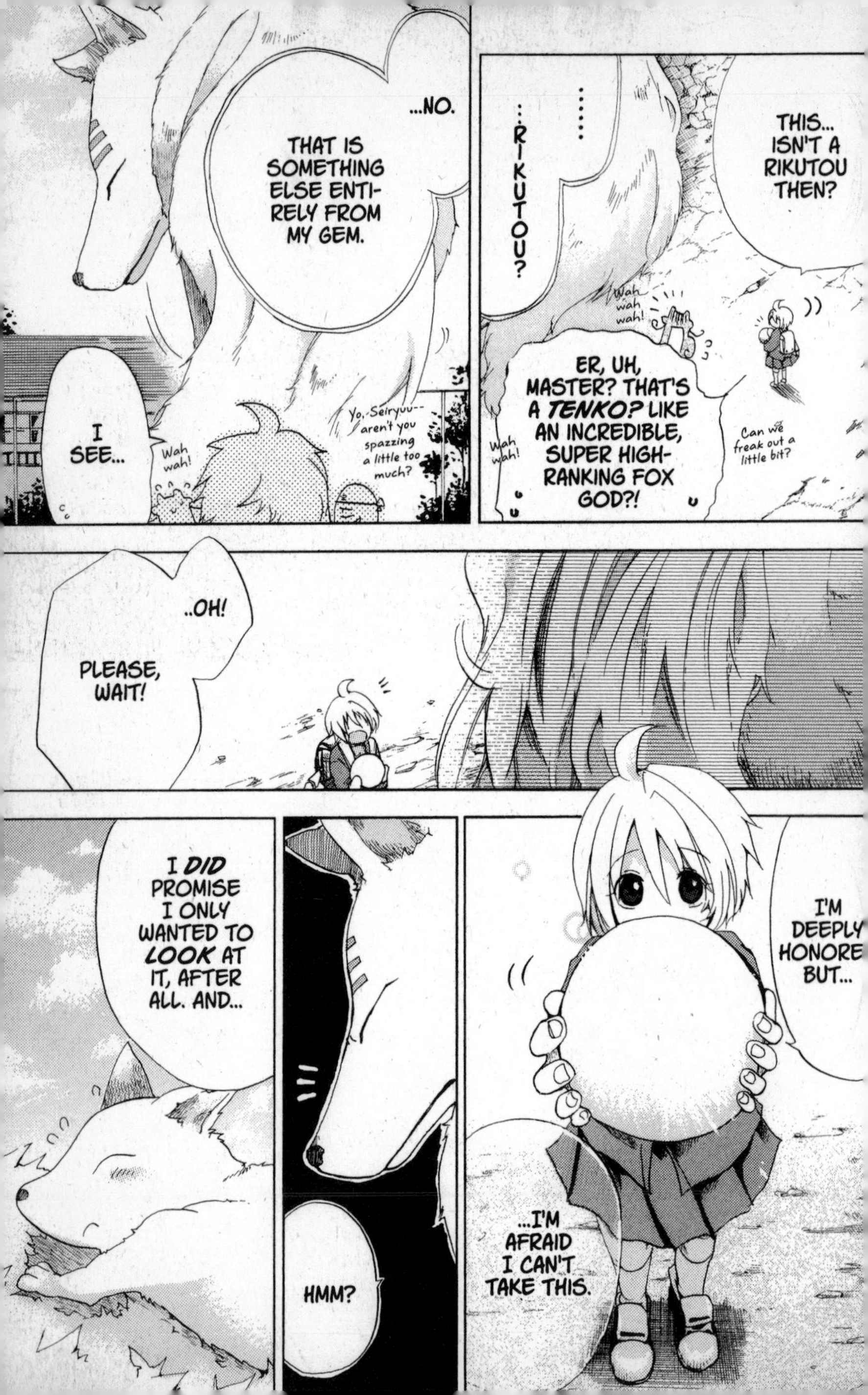
THIS... ISN'T A RIKUTOU THEN?
......
...RIKUTOU?
Wah wah wah!
ER, UH, MASTER? THAT'S A *TENKO?* LIKE AN INCREDIBLE, SUPER HIGH-RANKING FOX GOD?!
Wah wah!
Can we freak out a little bit?
...NO.
THAT IS SOMETHING ELSE ENTIRELY FROM MY GEM.
Yo, Seiryuu-- aren't you spazzing a little too much?
Wah wah!
I SEE...
..OH!
PLEASE, WAIT!
I'M DEEPLY HONORE BUT...
...I'M AFRAID I CAN'T TAKE THIS.
HMM?
I *DID* PROMISE I ONLY WANTED TO *LOOK* AT IT, AFTER ALL. AND...

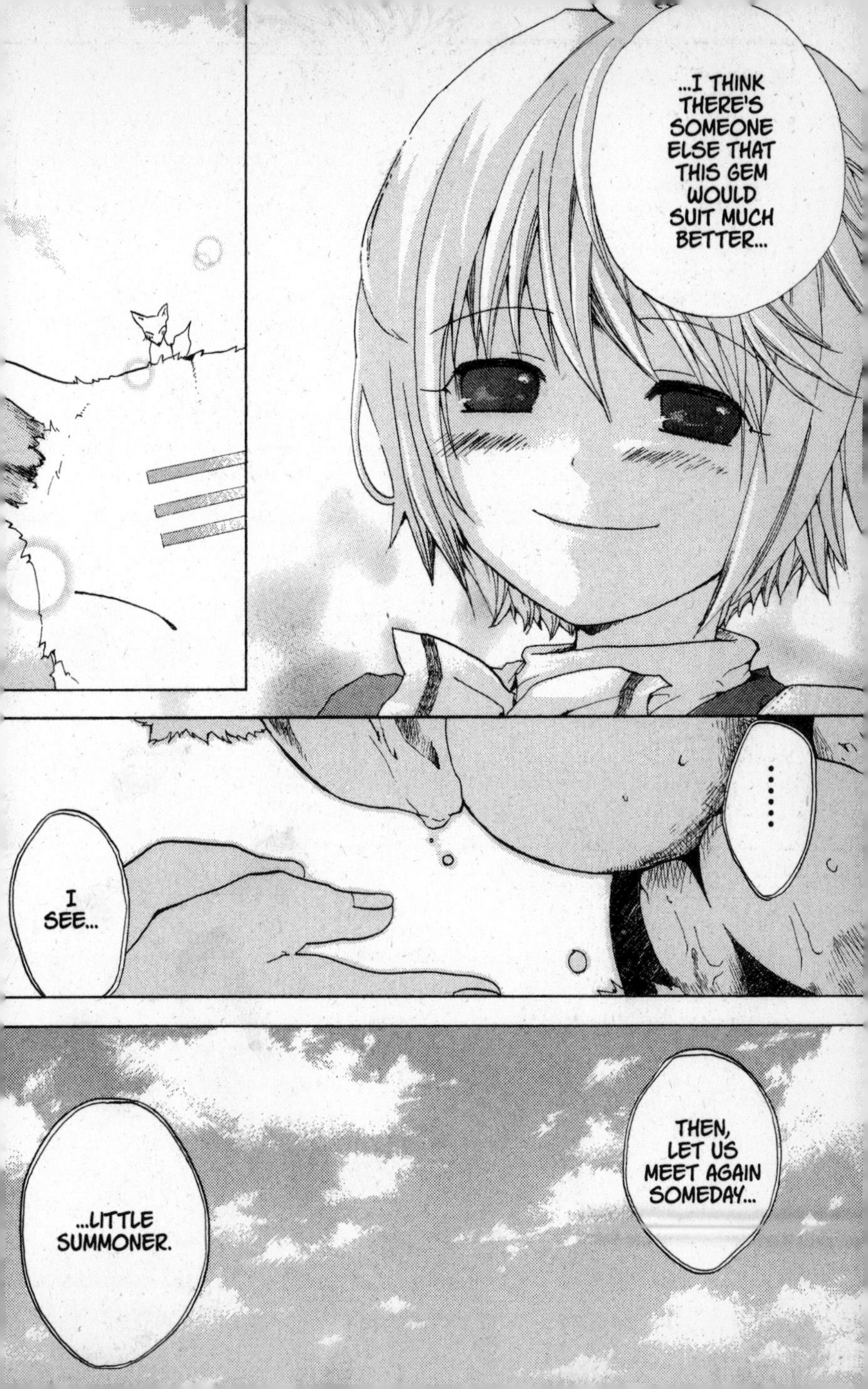
...I THINK THERE'S SOMEONE ELSE THAT THIS GEM WOULD SUIT MUCH BETTER...
......
I SEE...
THEN, LET US MEET AGAIN SOMEDAY...
...LITTLE SUMMONER.

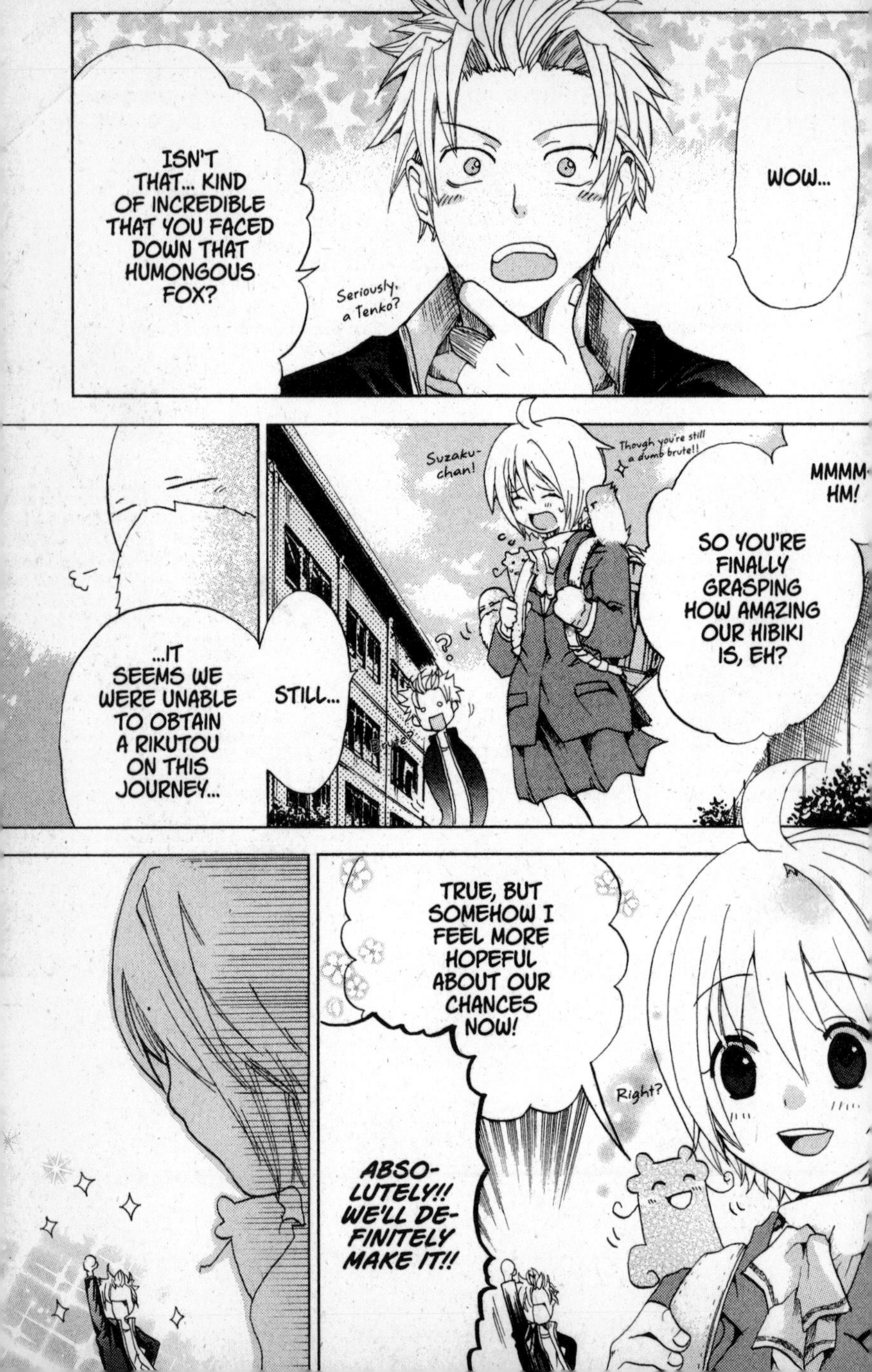
WOW...
ISN'T THAT... KIND OF INCREDIBLE THAT YOU FACED DOWN THAT HUMONGOUS FOX?
Seriously, a Tenko?
MMMM-HM!
SO YOU'RE FINALLY GRASPING HOW AMAZING OUR HIBIKI IS, EH?
Though you're still a dumb brute!!
Suzaku-chan!
Brute
STILL...
...IT SEEMS WE WERE UNABLE TO OBTAIN A RIKUTOU ON THIS JOURNEY...
TRUE, BUT SOMEHOW I FEEL MORE HOPEFUL ABOUT OUR CHANCES NOW!
Right?
ABSO-LUTELY!! WE'LL DE-FINITELY MAKE IT!!

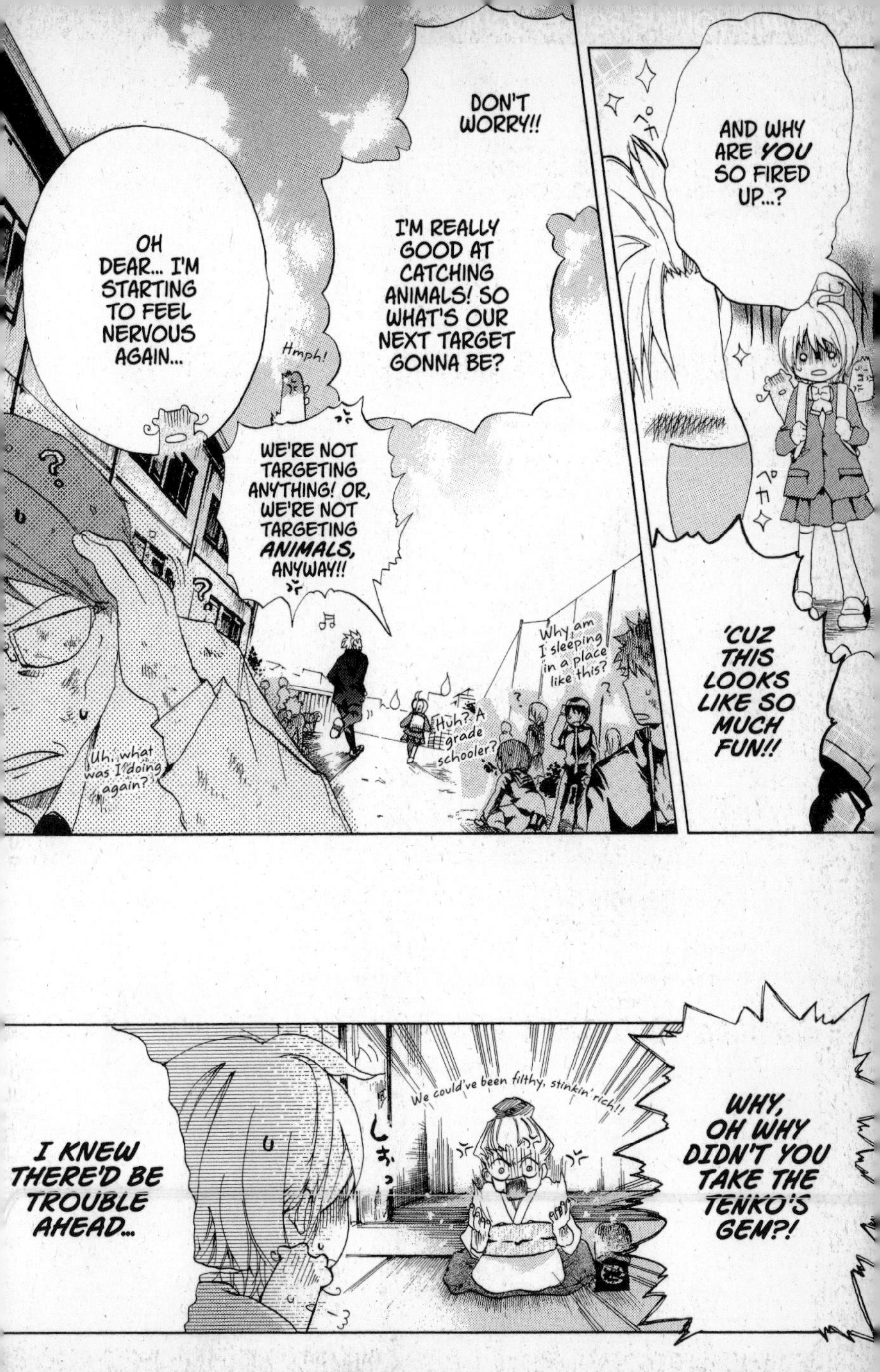
AND WHY ARE YOU SO FIRED UP...?
'CUZ THIS LOOKS LIKE SO MUCH FUN!!
DON'T WORRY!!
I'M REALLY GOOD AT CATCHING ANIMALS! SO WHAT'S OUR NEXT TARGET GONNA BE?
Hmph!
WE'RE NOT TARGETING ANYTHING! OR, WE'RE NOT TARGETING ANIMALS, ANYWAY!!
OH DEAR... I'M STARTING TO FEEL NERVOUS AGAIN...
Why am I sleeping in a place like this?
Huh? A grade schooler?
Uh, what was I doing again?
WHY, OH WHY DIDN'T YOU TAKE THE TENKO'S GEM?!
We could've been filthy, stinkin' rich!!
I KNEW THERE'D BE TROUBLE AHEAD...

A DAY IN THE LIFE OF A SHIKIGAMI (PART 1).

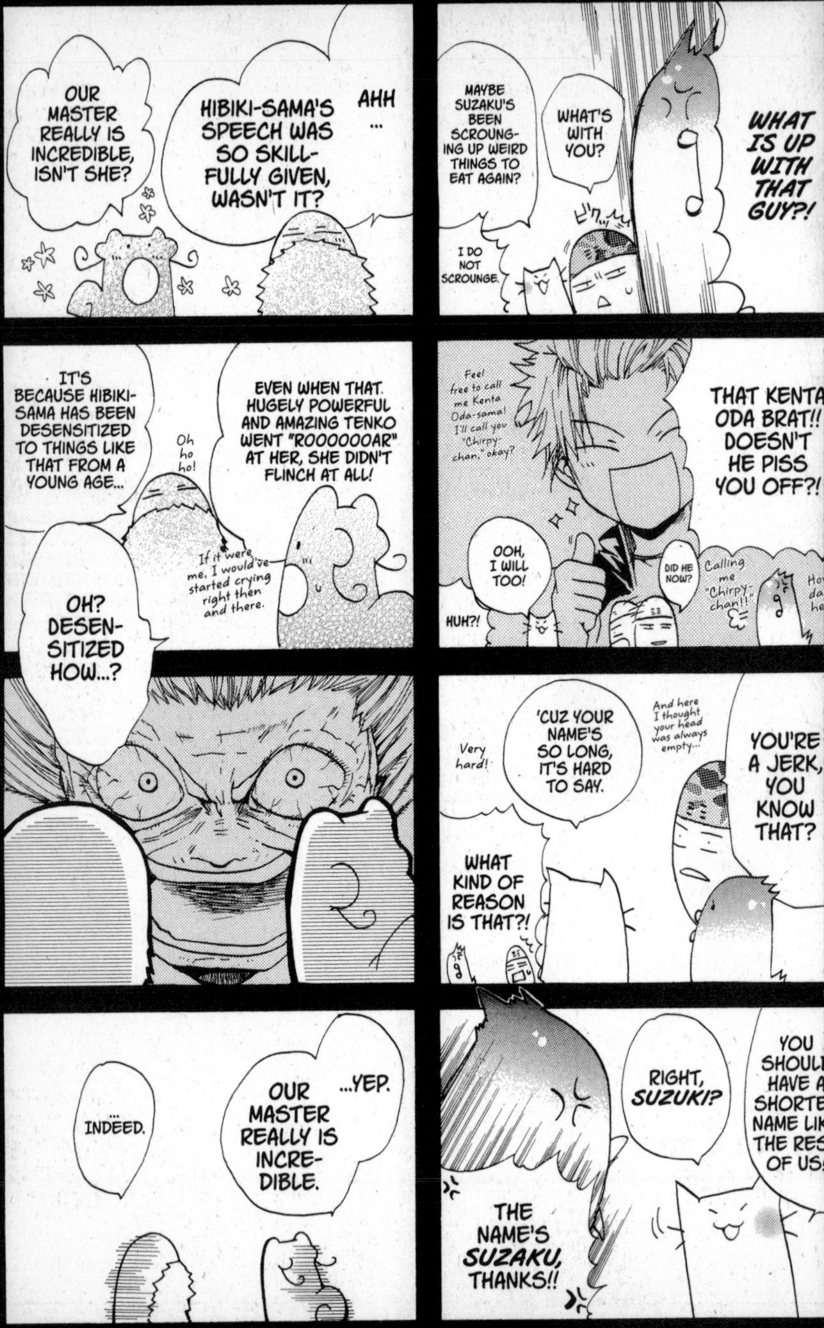
WHAT IS UP WITH THAT GUY?!
WHAT'S WITH YOU?
MAYBE SUZAKU'S BEEN SCROUNGING UP WEIRD THINGS TO EAT AGAIN?
I DO NOT SCROUNGE.
THAT KENTA ODA BRAT!! DOESN'T HE PISS YOU OFF?!
Calling me "Chirpy-chan!!"
DID HE NOW?
Feel free to call me Kenta Oda-sama! I'll call you "Chirpy-chan," okay?
OOH, I WILL TOO!
HUH?!
YOU'RE A JERK, YOU KNOW THAT?
And here I thought your head was always empty...
'CUZ YOUR NAME'S SO LONG, IT'S HARD TO SAY.
Very hard!
WHAT KIND OF REASON IS THAT?!
YOU SHOUL HAVE A SHORTE NAME LIK THE RES OF US
RIGHT, SUZUKI?
THE NAME'S SUZAKU, THANKS!!
AHH ...
HIBIKI-SAMA'S SPEECH WAS SO SKILLFULLY GIVEN, WASN'T IT?
OUR MASTER REALLY IS INCREDIBLE, ISN'T SHE?
EVEN WHEN THAT HUGELY POWERFUL AND AMAZING TENKO WENT "ROOOOOOAR" AT HER, SHE DIDN'T FLINCH AT ALL!
Oh ho ho!
IT'S BECAUSE HIBIKI-SAMA HAS BEEN DESENSITIZED TO THINGS LIKE THAT FROM A YOUNG AGE...
If it were me, I would've started crying right then and there.
OH? DESENSITIZED HOW...?
...YEP.
OUR MASTER REALLY IS INCREDIBLE.
... INDEED.

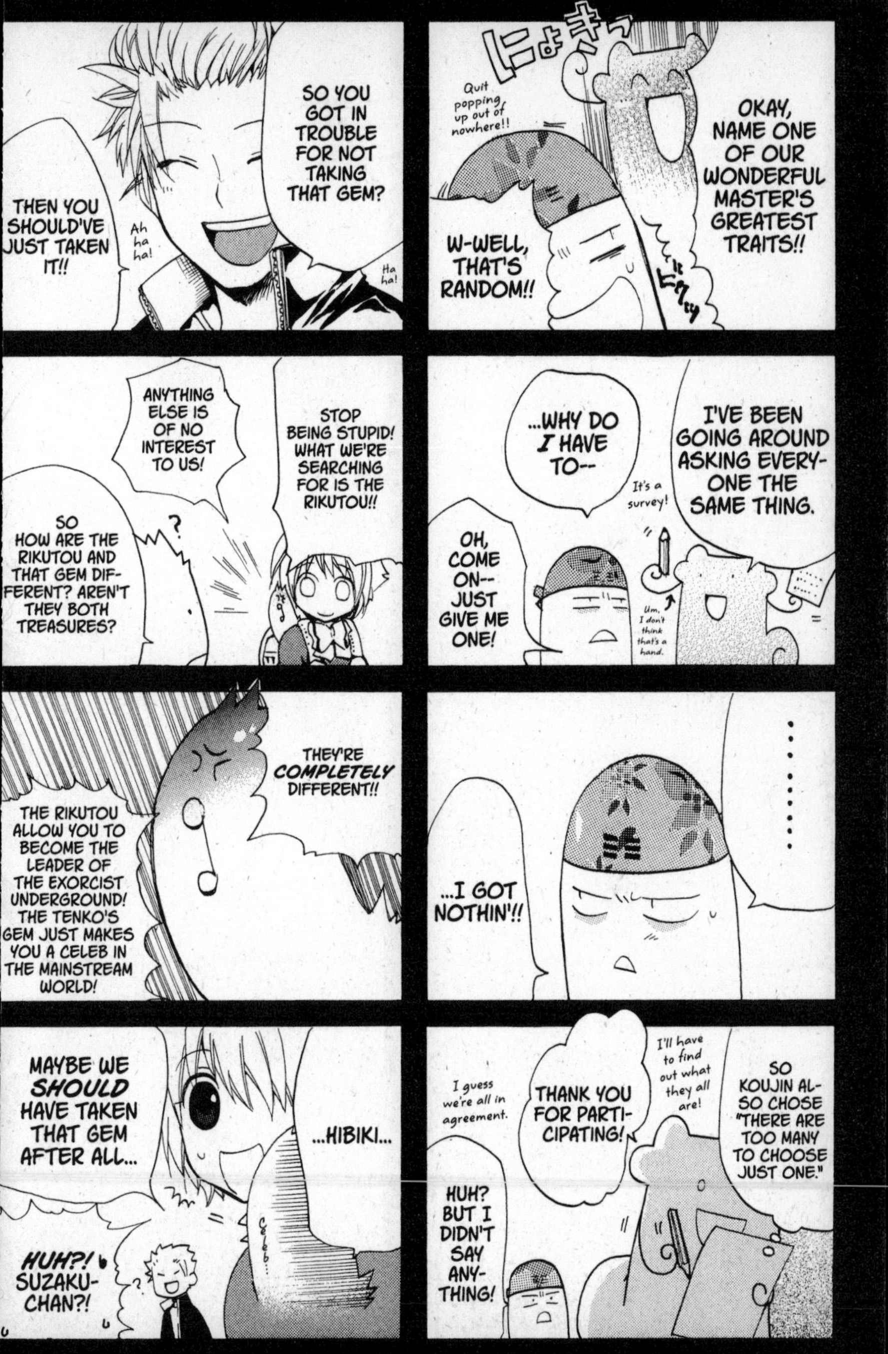
にょきっ
OKAY, NAME ONE OF OUR WONDERFUL MASTER'S GREATEST TRAITS!!
Quit popping up out of nowhere!!
W-WELL, THAT'S RANDOM!!
I'VE BEEN GOING AROUND ASKING EVERY-ONE THE SAME THING.
It's a survey!
...WHY DO I HAVE TO--
OH, COME ON-- JUST GIVE ME ONE!
Um, I don't think that's a hand.
....
...I GOT NOTHIN'!!
SO KOUJIN AL-SO CHOSE "THERE ARE TOO MANY TO CHOOSE JUST ONE."
I'll have to find out what they all are!
THANK YOU FOR PARTI-CIPATING!
I guess we're all in agreement.
HUH? BUT I DIDN'T SAY ANY-THING!
SO YOU GOT IN TROUBLE FOR NOT TAKING THAT GEM?
Ah ha ha!
Ha ha!
THEN YOU SHOULD'VE JUST TAKEN IT!!
STOP BEING STUPID! WHAT WE'RE SEARCHING FOR IS THE RIKUTOU!!
ANYTHING ELSE IS OF NO INTEREST TO US!
SO HOW ARE THE RIKUTOU AND THAT GEM DIF-FERENT? AREN'T THEY BOTH TREASURES?
THEY'RE COMPLETELY DIFFERENT!!
THE RIKUTOU ALLOW YOU TO BECOME THE LEADER OF THE EXORCIST UNDERGROUND! THE TENKO'S GEM JUST MAKES YOU A CELEB IN THE MAINSTREAM WORLD!
...HIBIKI...
MAYBE WE SHOULD HAVE TAKEN THAT GEM AFTER ALL...
Celeb...
HUH?! SUZAKU-CHAN?!

TO BE CONTINUED...

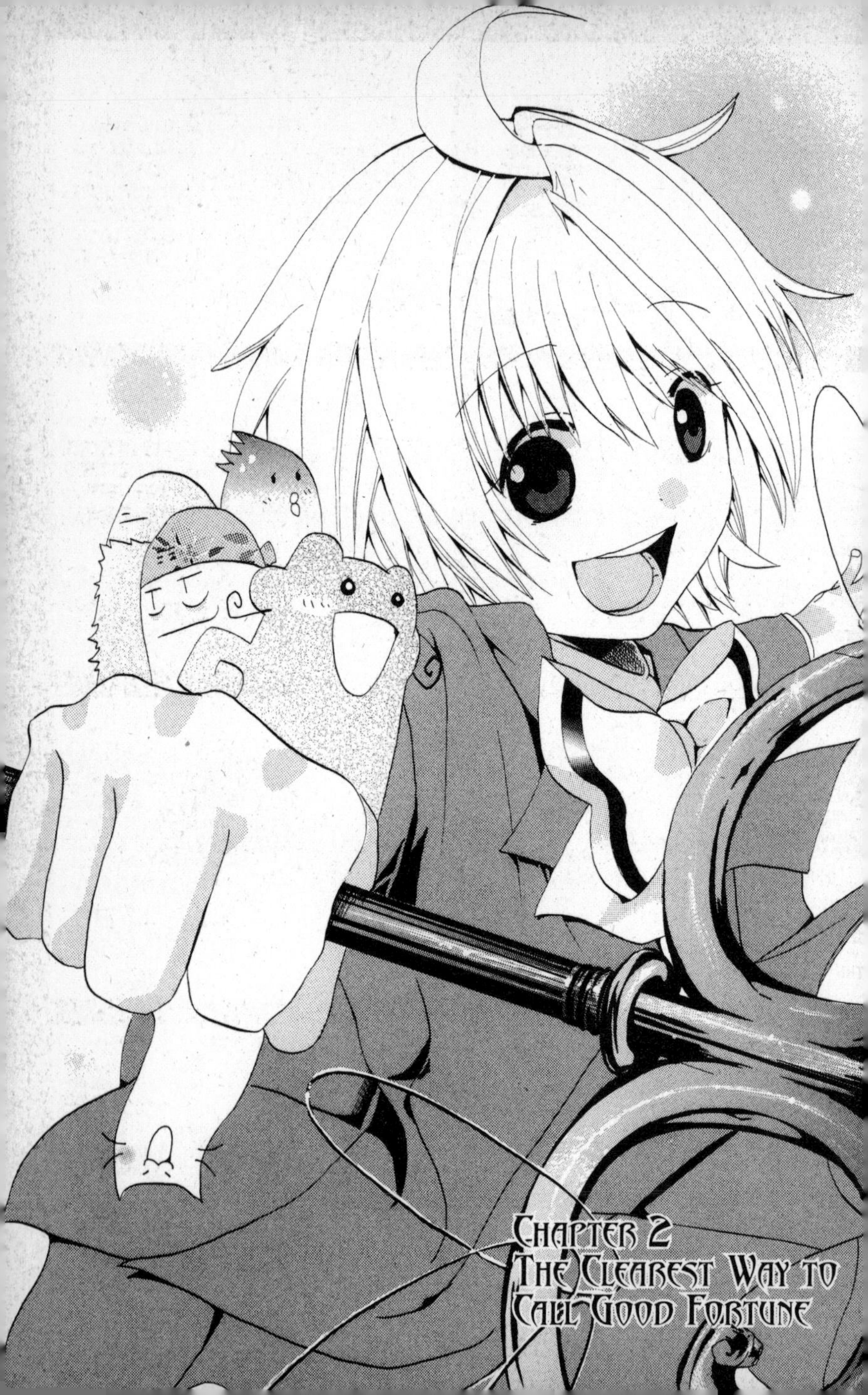
Chapter 2
The Clearest Way to Call Good Fortune

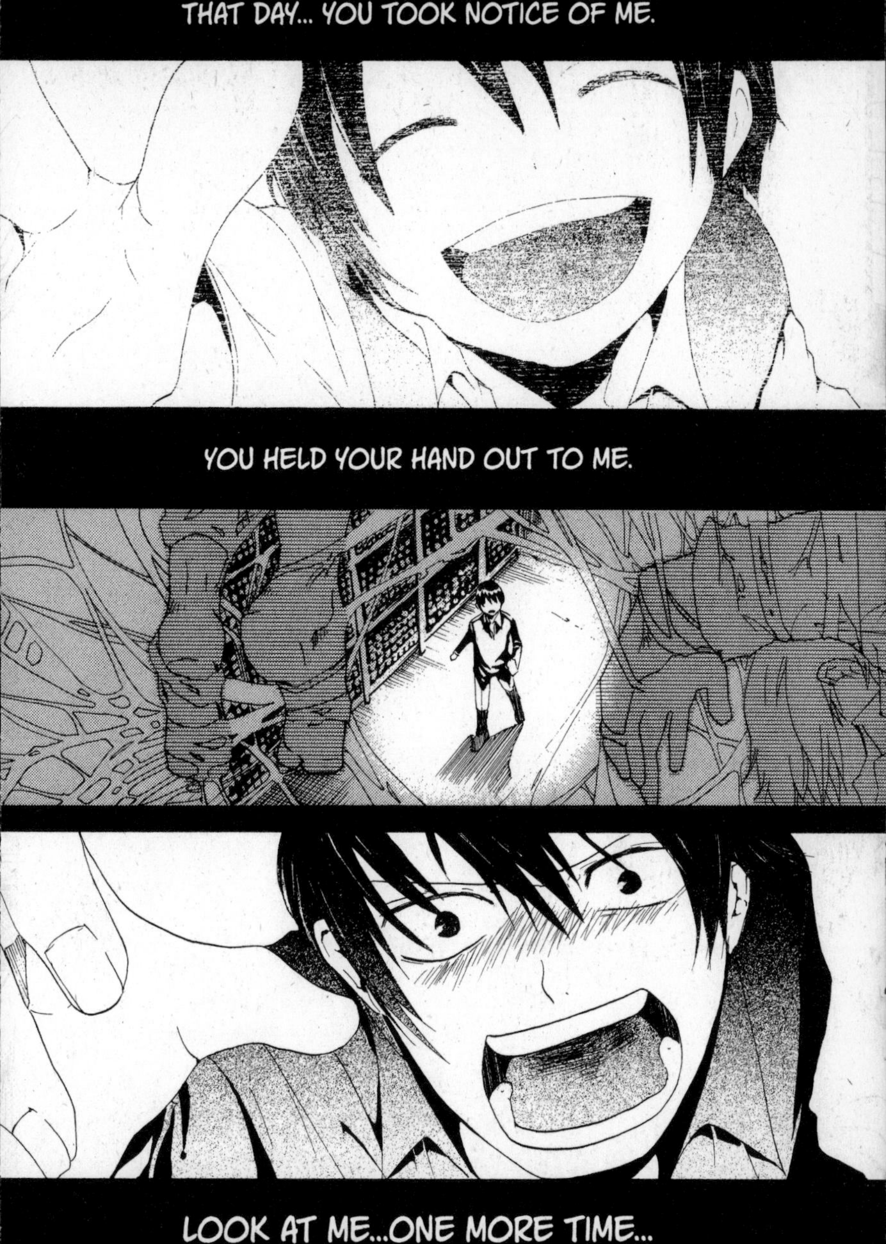
THAT DAY... YOU TOOK NOTICE OF ME.
YOU HELD YOUR HAND OUT TO ME.
LOOK AT ME...ONE MORE TIME...

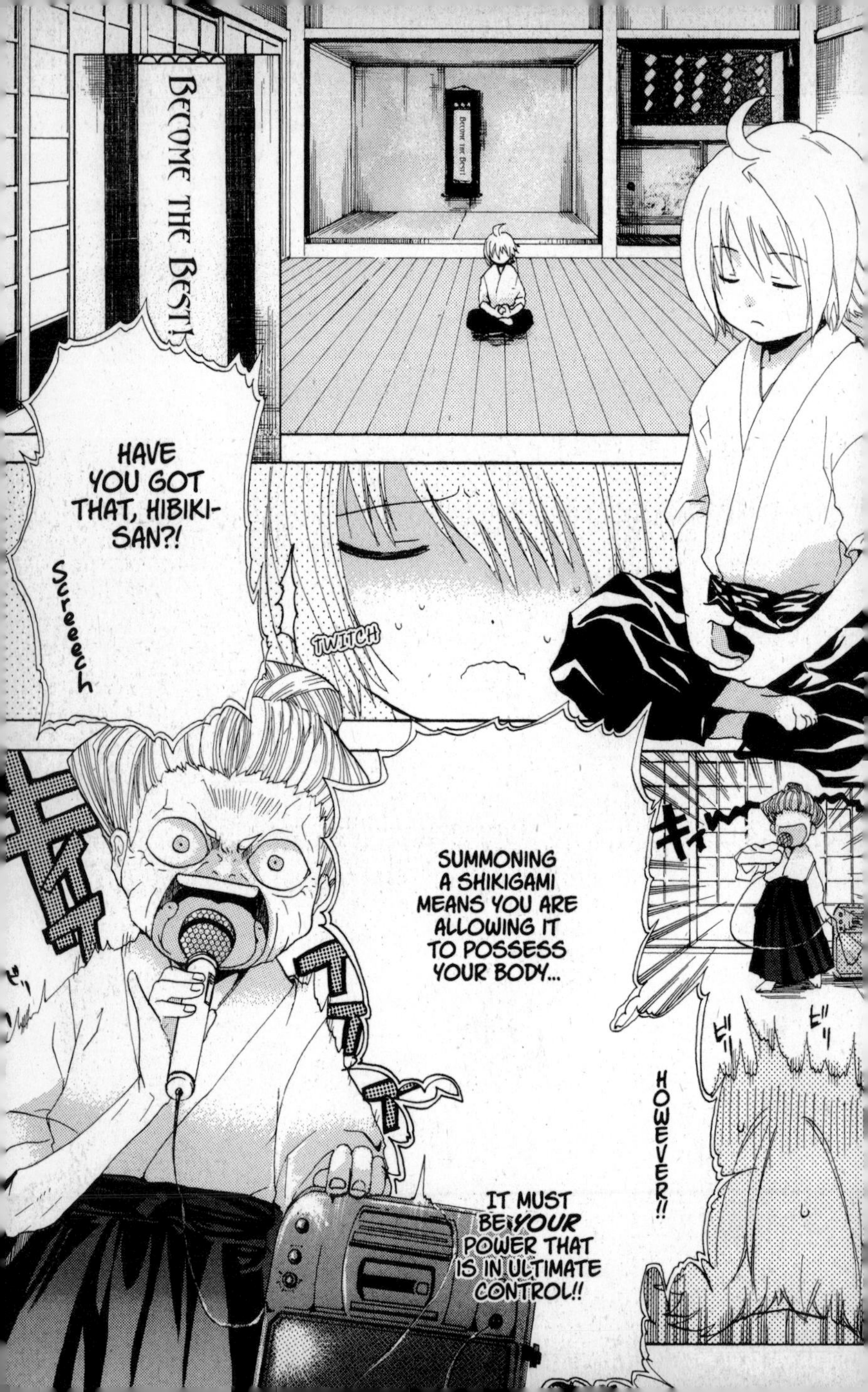

BECOME THE BEST!
BECOME THE BEST!
HAVE YOU GOT THAT, HIBIKI-SAN?!
Screeeech
TWITCH
SUMMONING A SHIKIGAMI MEANS YOU ARE ALLOWING IT TO POSSESS YOUR BODY...
HOWEVER!!
IT MUST BE *YOUR* POWER THAT IS IN ULTIMATE CONTROL!!

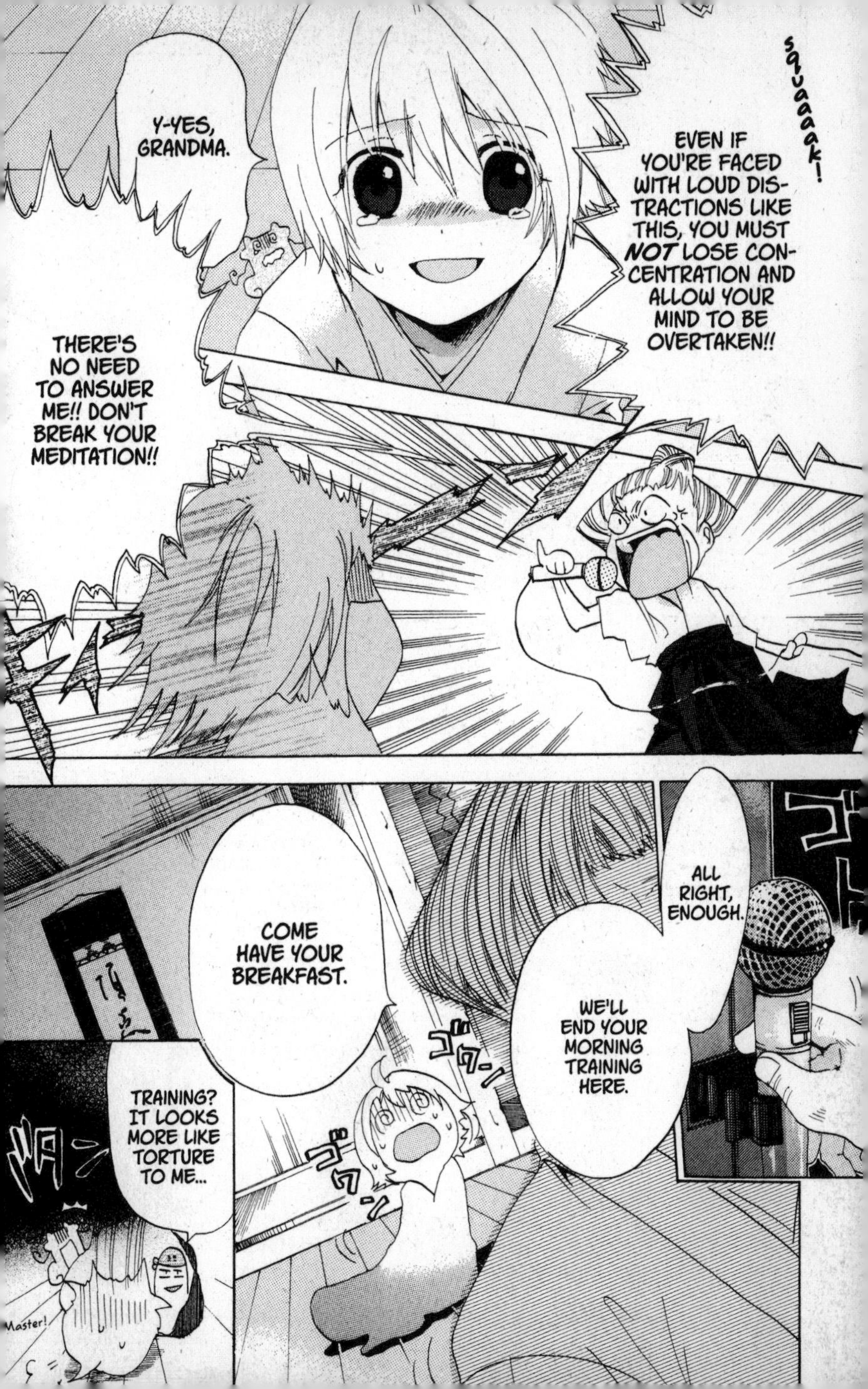
squaaaak!
EVEN IF YOU'RE FACED WITH LOUD DISTRACTIONS LIKE THIS, YOU MUST ***NOT*** LOSE CONCENTRATION AND ALLOW YOUR MIND TO BE OVERTAKEN!!
Y-YES, GRANDMA.
THERE'S NO NEED TO ANSWER ME!! DON'T BREAK YOUR MEDITATION!!
ALL RIGHT, ENOUGH.
WE'LL END YOUR MORNING TRAINING HERE.
COME HAVE YOUR BREAKFAST.
TRAINING? IT LOOKS MORE LIKE TORTURE TO ME...
Master!

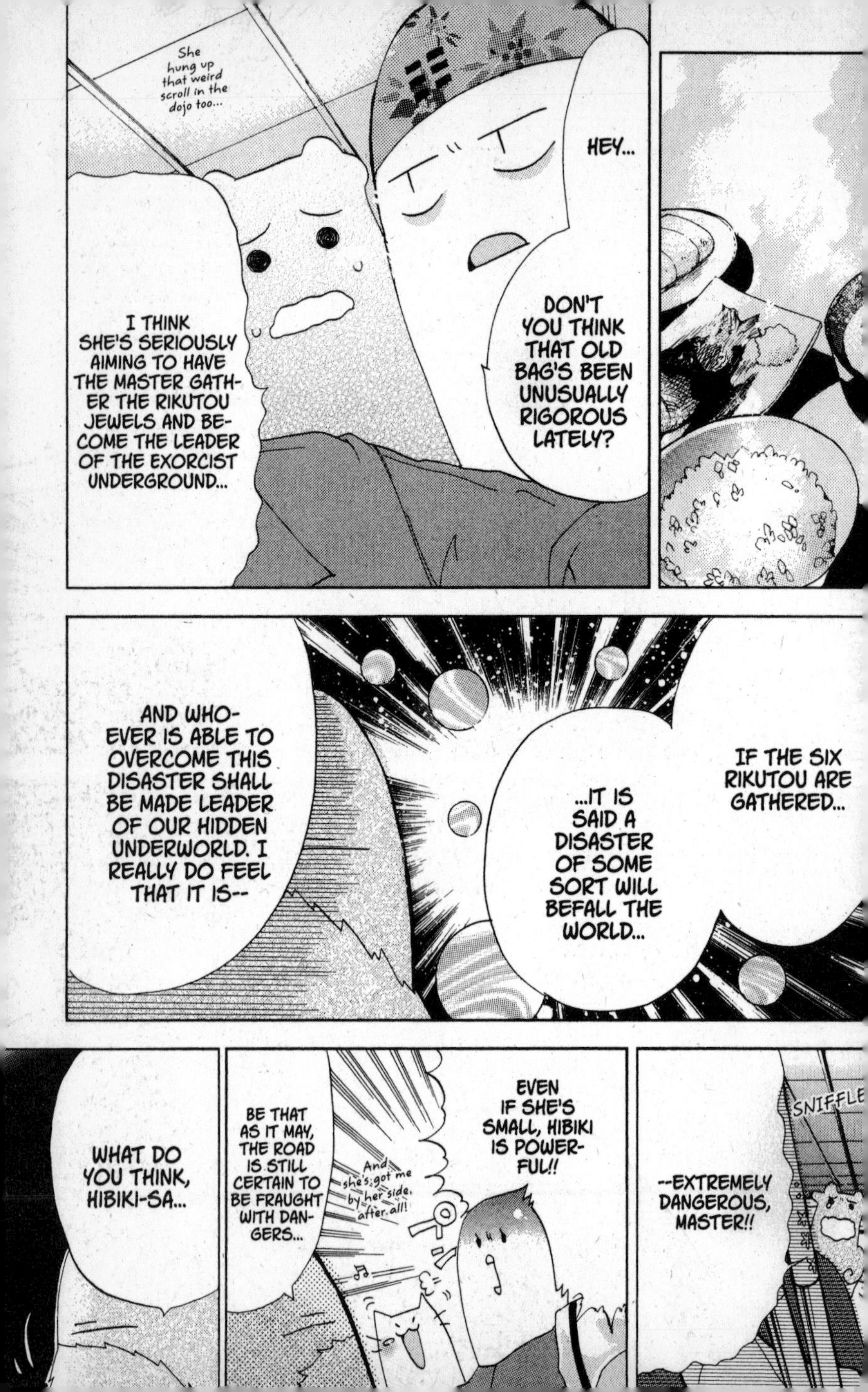
HEY...
DON'T YOU THINK THAT OLD BAG'S BEEN UNUSUALLY RIGOROUS LATELY?
She hung up that weird scroll in the dojo too...
I THINK SHE'S SERIOUSLY AIMING TO HAVE THE MASTER GATHER THE RIKUTOU JEWELS AND BECOME THE LEADER OF THE EXORCIST UNDERGROUND...
IF THE SIX RIKUTOU ARE GATHERED...
...IT IS SAID A DISASTER OF SOME SORT WILL BEFALL THE WORLD...
AND WHOEVER IS ABLE TO OVERCOME THIS DISASTER SHALL BE MADE LEADER OF OUR HIDDEN UNDERWORLD. I REALLY DO FEEL THAT IT IS--
SNIFFLE
--EXTREMELY DANGEROUS, MASTER!!
EVEN IF SHE'S SMALL, HIBIKI IS POWERFUL!!
And she's got me by her side, after all!
BE THAT AS IT MAY, THE ROAD IS STILL CERTAIN TO BE FRAUGHT WITH DANGERS...
WHAT DO YOU THINK, HIBIKI-SA...

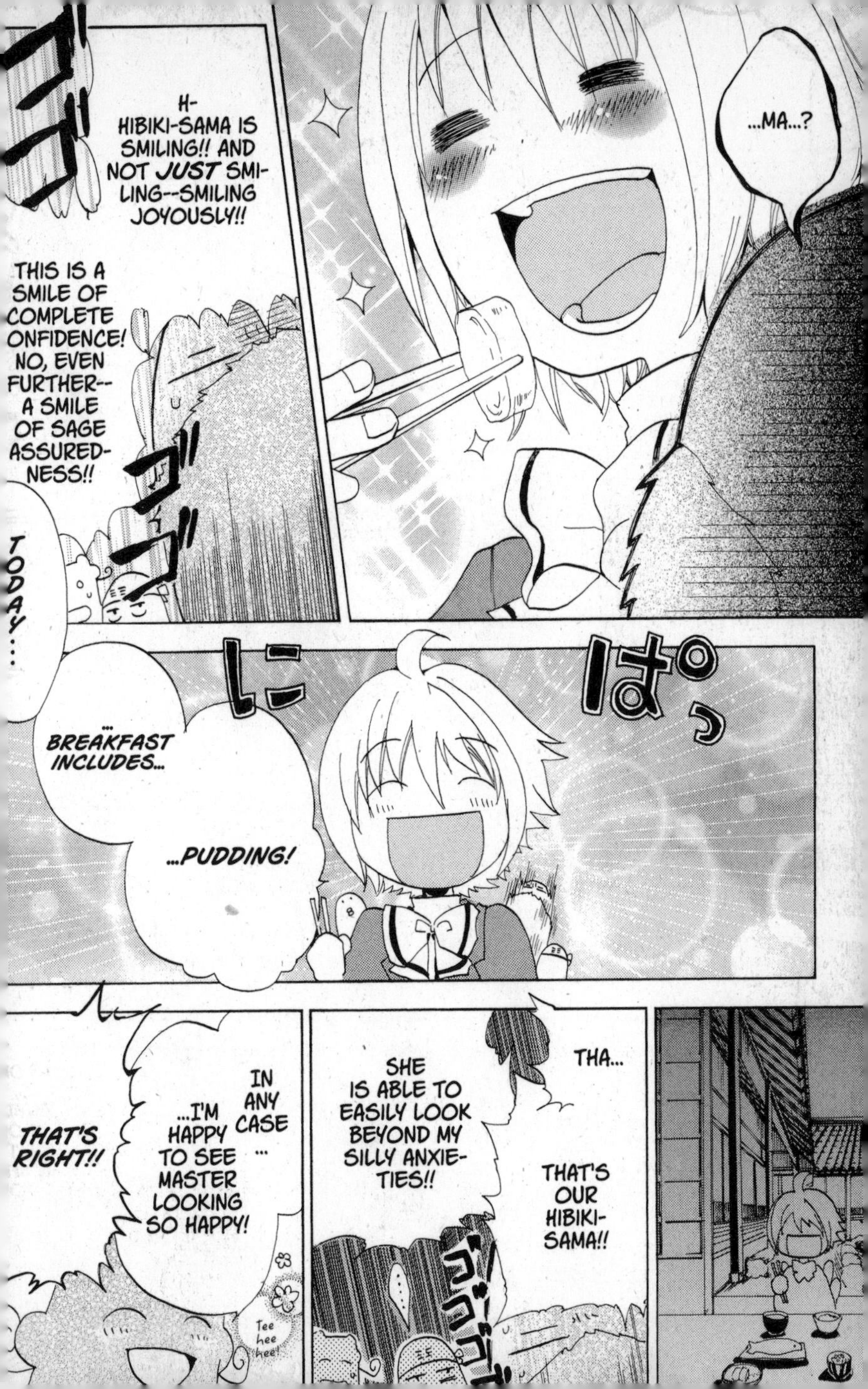
...MA...?
ゴゴ
H-HIBIKI-SAMA IS SMILING!! AND NOT *JUST* SMILING--SMILING JOYOUSLY!!
THIS IS A SMILE OF COMPLETE ONFIDENCE! NO, EVEN FURTHER-- A SMILE OF SAGE ASSUREDNESS!!
ゴゴ
ゴゴ
TODAY...
にぱっ
...BREAKFAST INCLUDES...
...PUDDING!
THA...
THAT'S OUR HIBIKI-SAMA!!
SHE IS ABLE TO EASILY LOOK BEYOND MY SILLY ANXIETIES!!
IN ANY CASE...
...I'M HAPPY TO SEE MASTER LOOKING SO HAPPY!
THAT'S RIGHT!!
Tee hee hee!

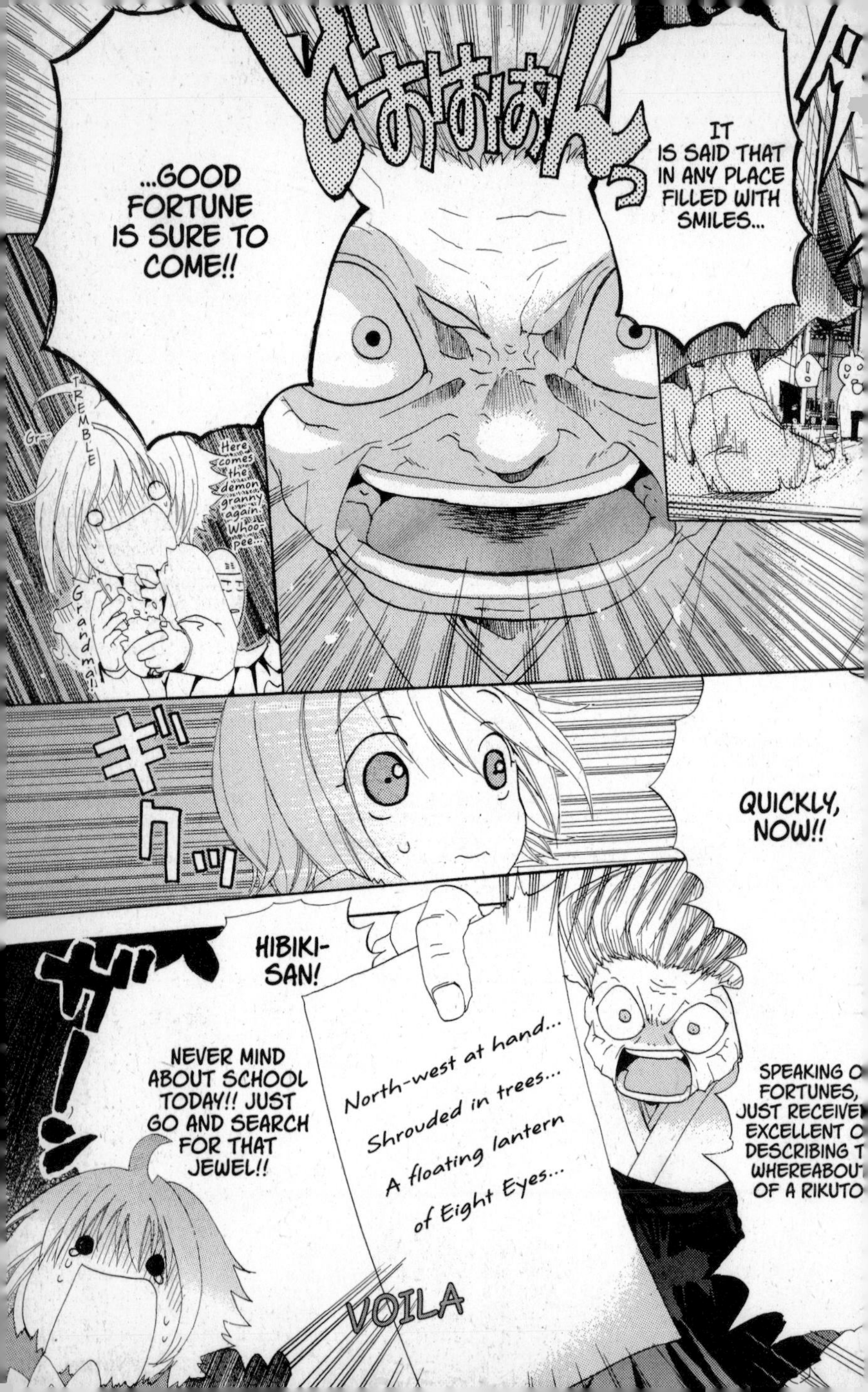

IT IS SAID THAT IN ANY PLACE FILLED WITH SMILES...
...GOOD FORTUNE IS SURE TO COME!!
TREMBLE
Gr--
Here comes the demon granny again. Whoo-pee...
Grandma!!
QUICKLY, NOW!!
ギクッ
SPEAKING O
FORTUNES,
JUST RECEIVE
EXCELLENT O
DESCRIBING T
WHEREABOU
OF A RIKUTO
HIBIKI-SAN!
North-west at hand...
Shrouded in trees...
A floating lantern
of Eight Eyes...
NEVER MIND ABOUT SCHOOL TODAY!! JUST GO AND SEARCH FOR THAT JEWEL!!
VOILA

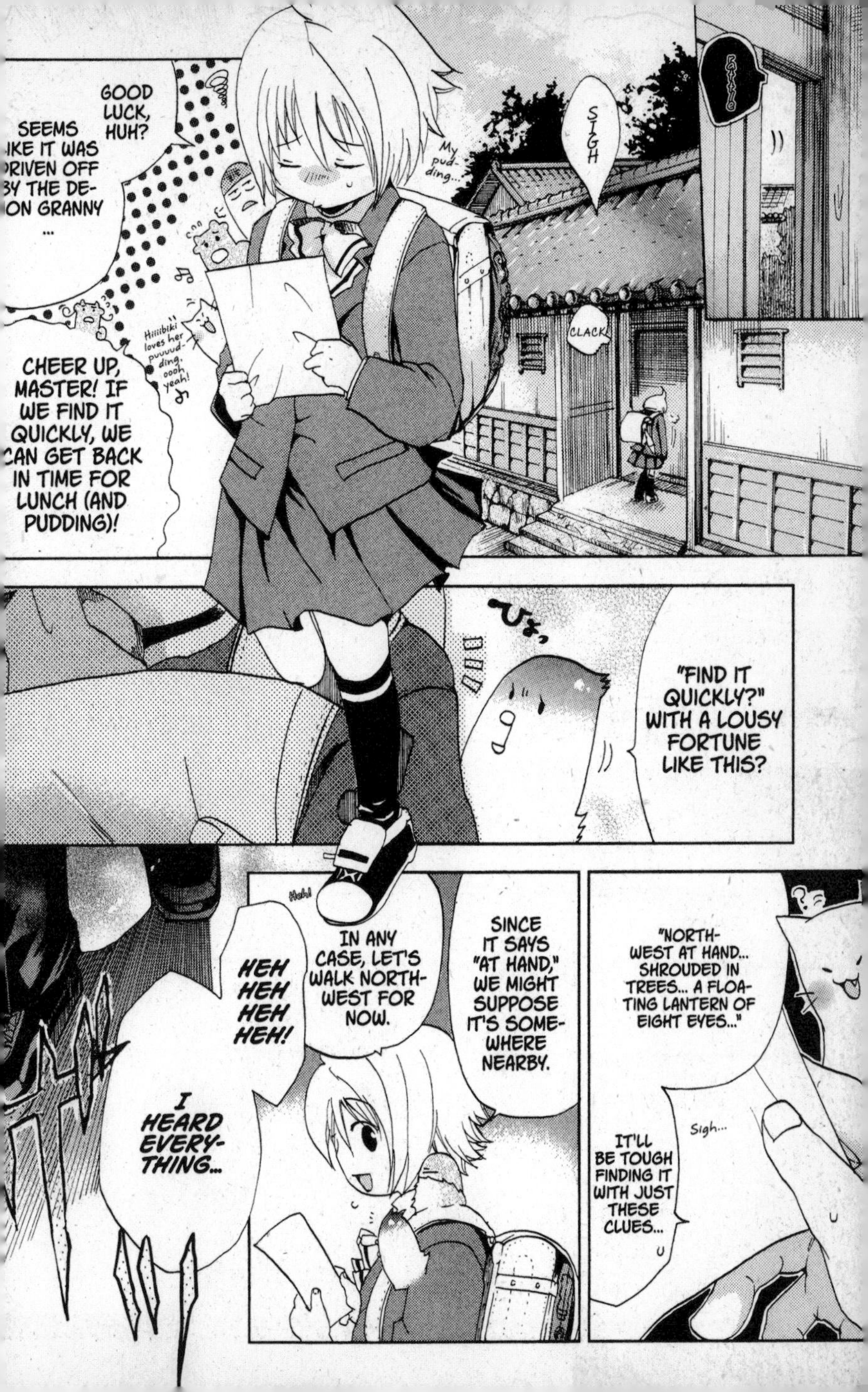
rattle
SIGH
CLACK
My pudding...
GOOD LUCK, HUH?
SEEMS LIKE IT WAS DRIVEN OFF BY THE DEMON GRANNY ...
Hiiiibiki loves her puuuudding. oooh yeah!
CHEER UP, MASTER! IF WE FIND IT QUICKLY, WE CAN GET BACK IN TIME FOR LUNCH (AND PUDDING)!
"FIND IT QUICKLY?" WITH A LOUSY FORTUNE LIKE THIS?
"NORTH-WEST AT HAND... SHROUDED IN TREES... A FLOATING LANTERN OF EIGHT EYES..."
Sigh...
IT'LL BE TOUGH FINDING IT WITH JUST THESE CLUES...
SINCE IT SAYS "AT HAND," WE MIGHT SUPPOSE IT'S SOMEWHERE NEARBY.
Heh!
IN ANY CASE, LET'S WALK NORTHWEST FOR NOW.
HEH HEH HEH HEH!
I HEARD EVERYTHING...

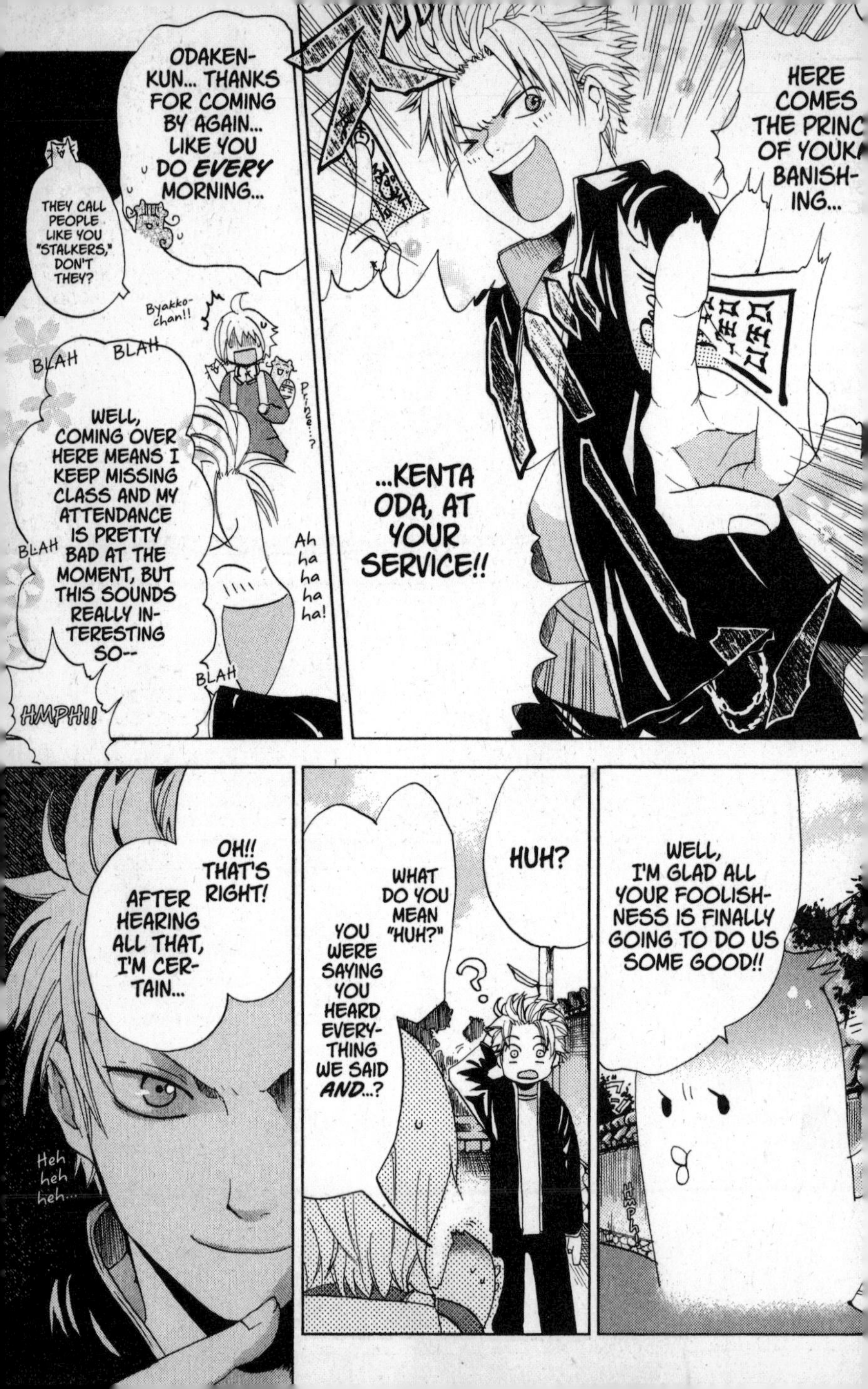
HERE COMES THE PRINC OF YOUKA BANISH-ING...
...KENTA ODA, AT YOUR SERVICE!!
ODAKEN-KUN... THANKS FOR COMING BY AGAIN... LIKE YOU DO *EVERY* MORNING...
THEY CALL PEOPLE LIKE YOU "STALKERS," DON'T THEY?
Byakko-chan!!
Prince...?
BLAH BLAH
WELL, COMING OVER HERE MEANS I KEEP MISSING CLASS AND MY ATTENDANCE IS PRETTY BAD AT THE MOMENT, BUT THIS SOUNDS REALLY IN-TERESTING SO--
BLAH
BLAH
Ah ha ha ha ha!
HMPH!!
WELL, I'M GLAD ALL YOUR FOOLISH-NESS IS FINALLY GOING TO DO US SOME GOOD!!
Hmph
HUH?
WHAT DO YOU MEAN "HUH?"
YOU WERE SAYING YOU HEARD EVERY-THING WE SAID *AND*...?
OH!! THAT'S RIGHT!
AFTER HEARING ALL THAT, I'M CER-TAIN...
Heh heh heh...

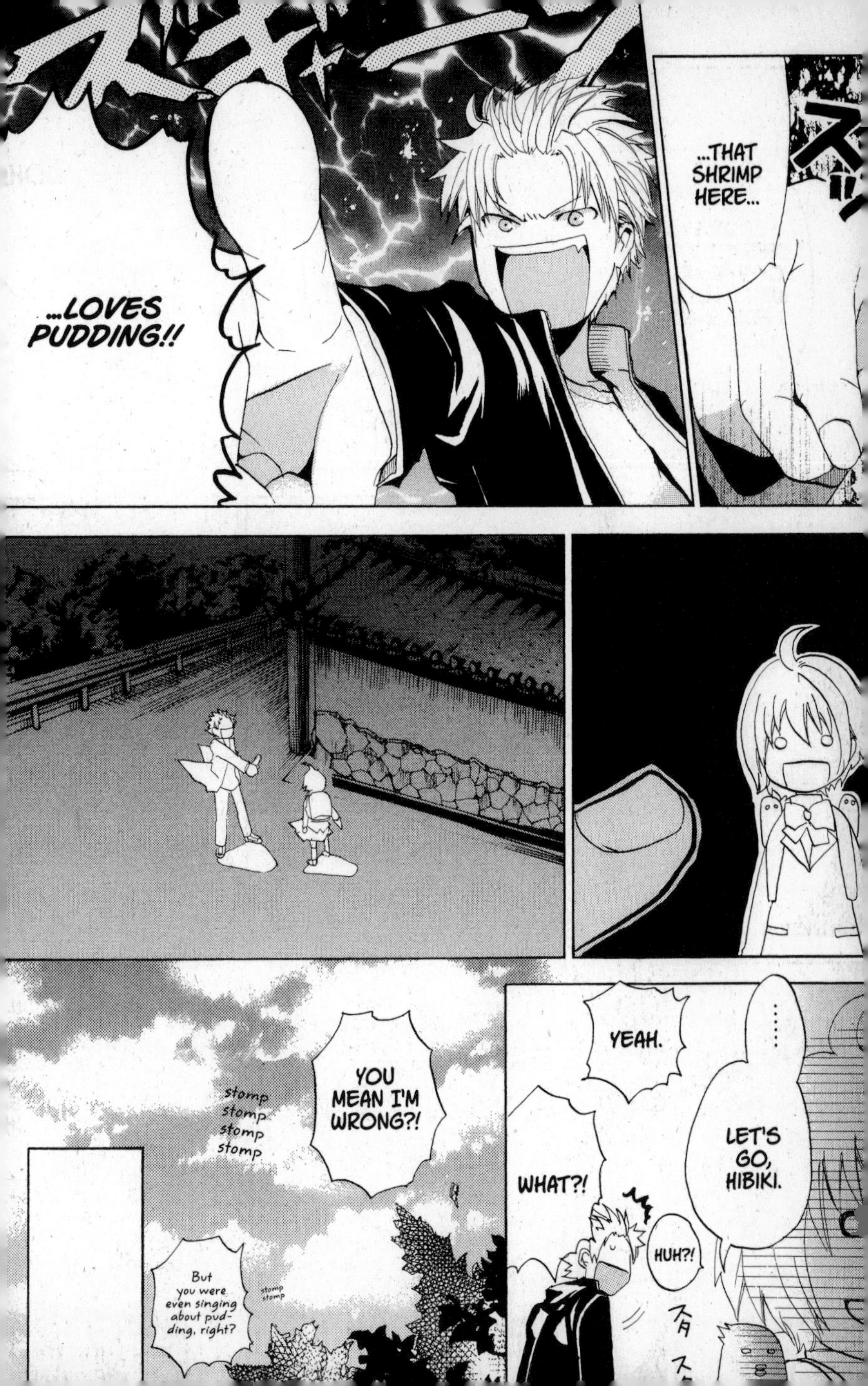
...THAT SHRIMP HERE...
...LOVES PUDDING!!
......
LET'S GO, HIBIKI.
YEAH.
HUH?!
WHAT?!
YOU MEAN I'M WRONG?!
stomp stomp stomp stomp
But you were even singing about pud-ding, right?
stomp stomp

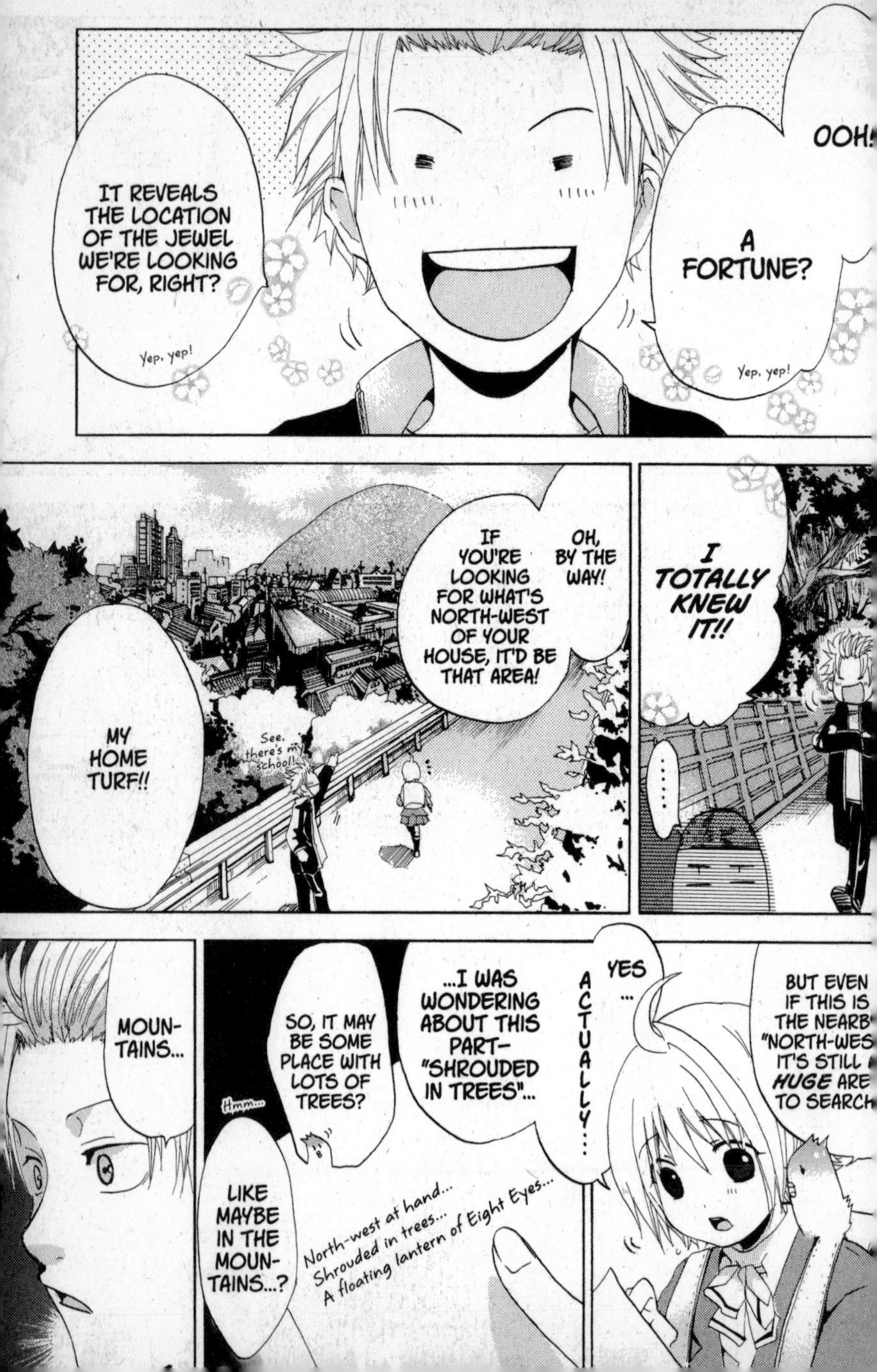
OOH!
A FORTUNE?
Yep, yep!
IT REVEALS THE LOCATION OF THE JEWEL WE'RE LOOKING FOR, RIGHT?
Yep, yep!
I TOTALLY KNEW IT!!
......
OH, BY THE WAY!
IF YOU'RE LOOKING FOR WHAT'S NORTH-WEST OF YOUR HOUSE, IT'D BE THAT AREA!
See, there's my school!
MY HOME TURF!!
BUT EVEN IF THIS IS THE NEARB "NORTH-WES IT'S STILL HUGE ARE TO SEARCH
YES ...
ACTUALLY...
...I WAS WONDERING ABOUT THIS PART— "SHROUDED IN TREES"...
North-west at hand... Shrouded in trees... A floating lantern of Eight Eyes...
SO, IT MAY BE SOME PLACE WITH LOTS OF TREES?
Hmm...
LIKE MAYBE IN THE MOUNTAINS...?
MOUNTAINS...

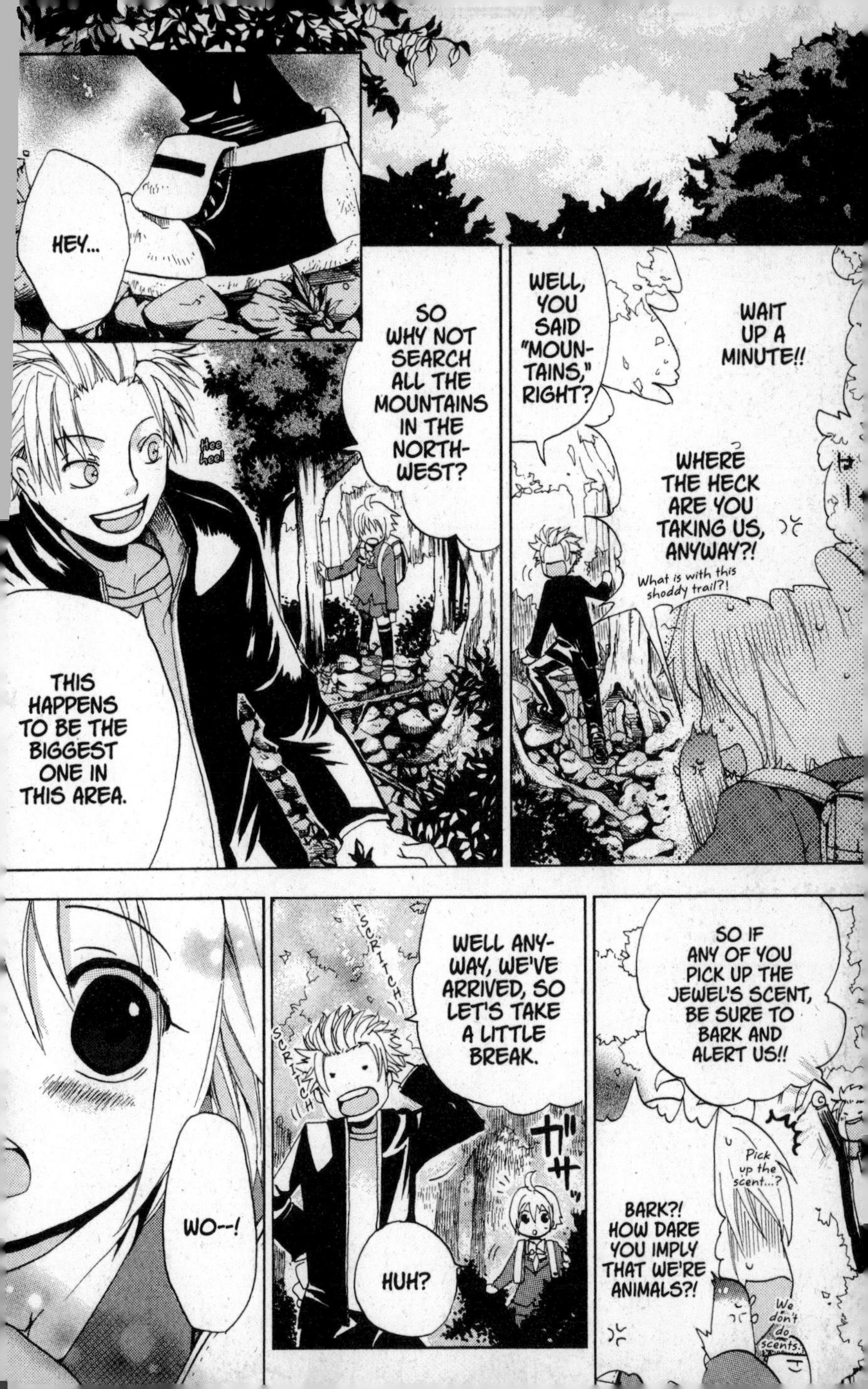
HEY...
WAIT UP A MINUTE!!
WHERE THE HECK ARE YOU TAKING US, ANYWAY?!
What is with this shoddy trail?!
WELL, YOU SAID "MOUN-TAINS," RIGHT?
SO WHY NOT SEARCH ALL THE MOUNTAINS IN THE NORTH-WEST?
Hee hee!
THIS HAPPENS TO BE THE BIGGEST ONE IN THIS AREA.
SO IF ANY OF YOU PICK UP THE JEWEL'S SCENT, BE SURE TO BARK AND ALERT US!!
Pick up the scent...?
BARK?! HOW DARE YOU IMPLY THAT WE'RE ANIMALS?!
We don't do scents.
SCRITCH
SCRITCH
WELL ANY-WAY, WE'VE ARRIVED, SO LET'S TAKE A LITTLE BREAK.
ガサ
HUH?
WO--!

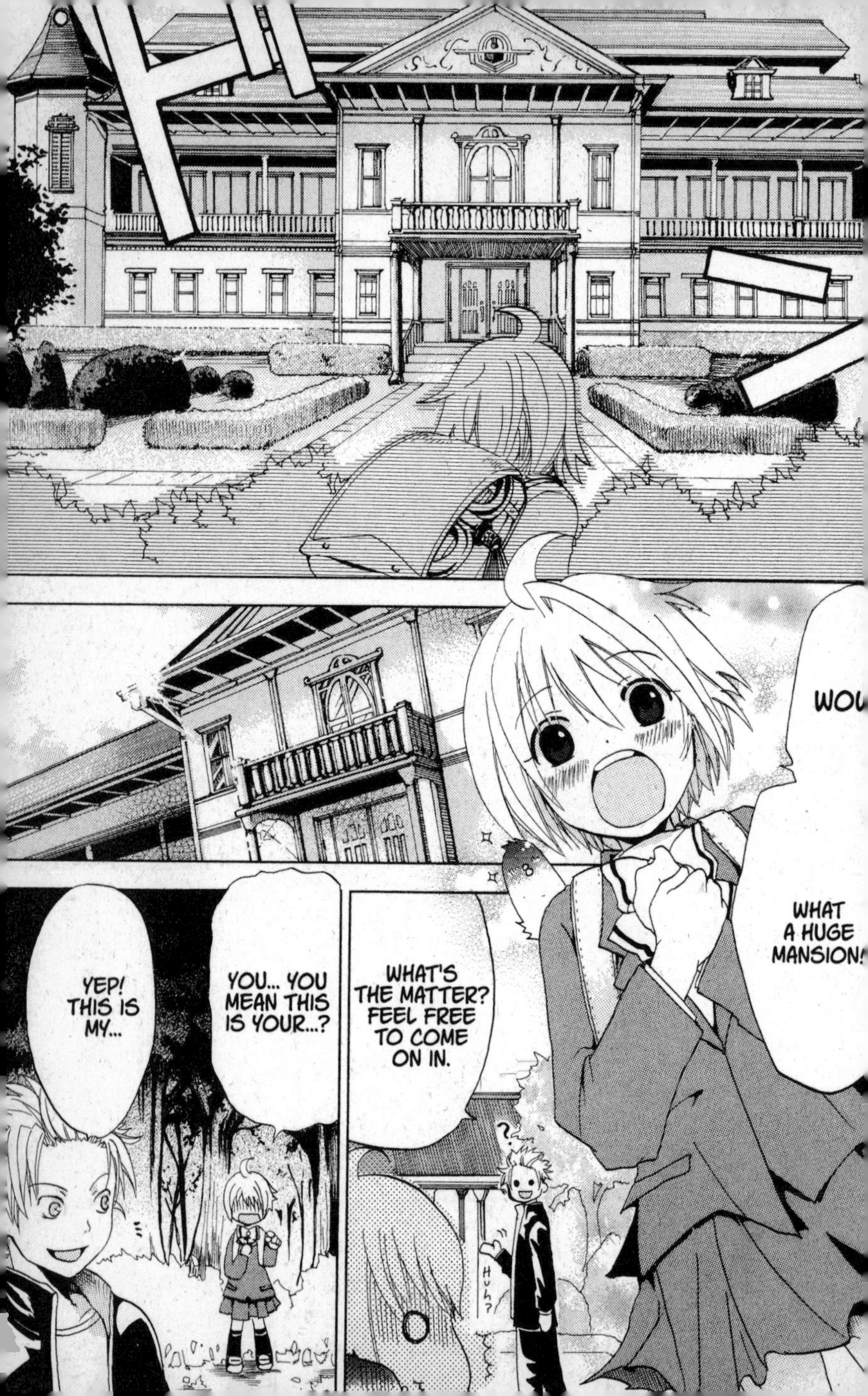
WOU
WHAT A HUGE MANSION!
WHAT'S THE MATTER? FEEL FREE TO COME ON IN.
HUH?
YOU... YOU MEAN THIS IS YOUR...?
YEP! THIS IS MY...

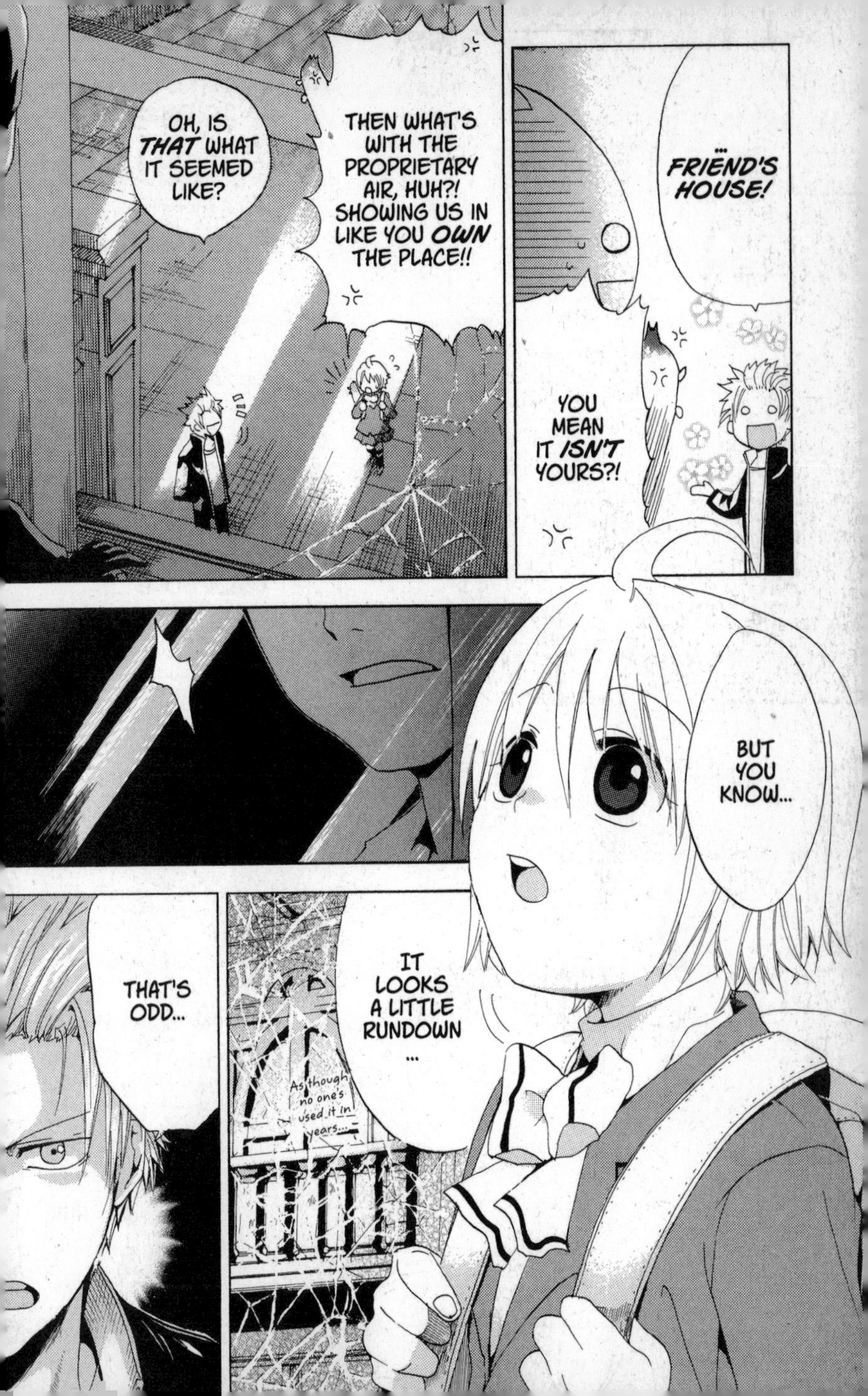
...FRIEND'S HOUSE!
YOU MEAN IT ISN'T YOURS?!
OH, IS THAT WHAT IT SEEMED LIKE?
THEN WHAT'S WITH THE PROPRIETARY AIR, HUH?! SHOWING US IN LIKE YOU OWN THE PLACE!!
BUT YOU KNOW...
IT LOOKS A LITTLE RUNDOWN...
As though no one's used it in years...
THAT'S ODD...

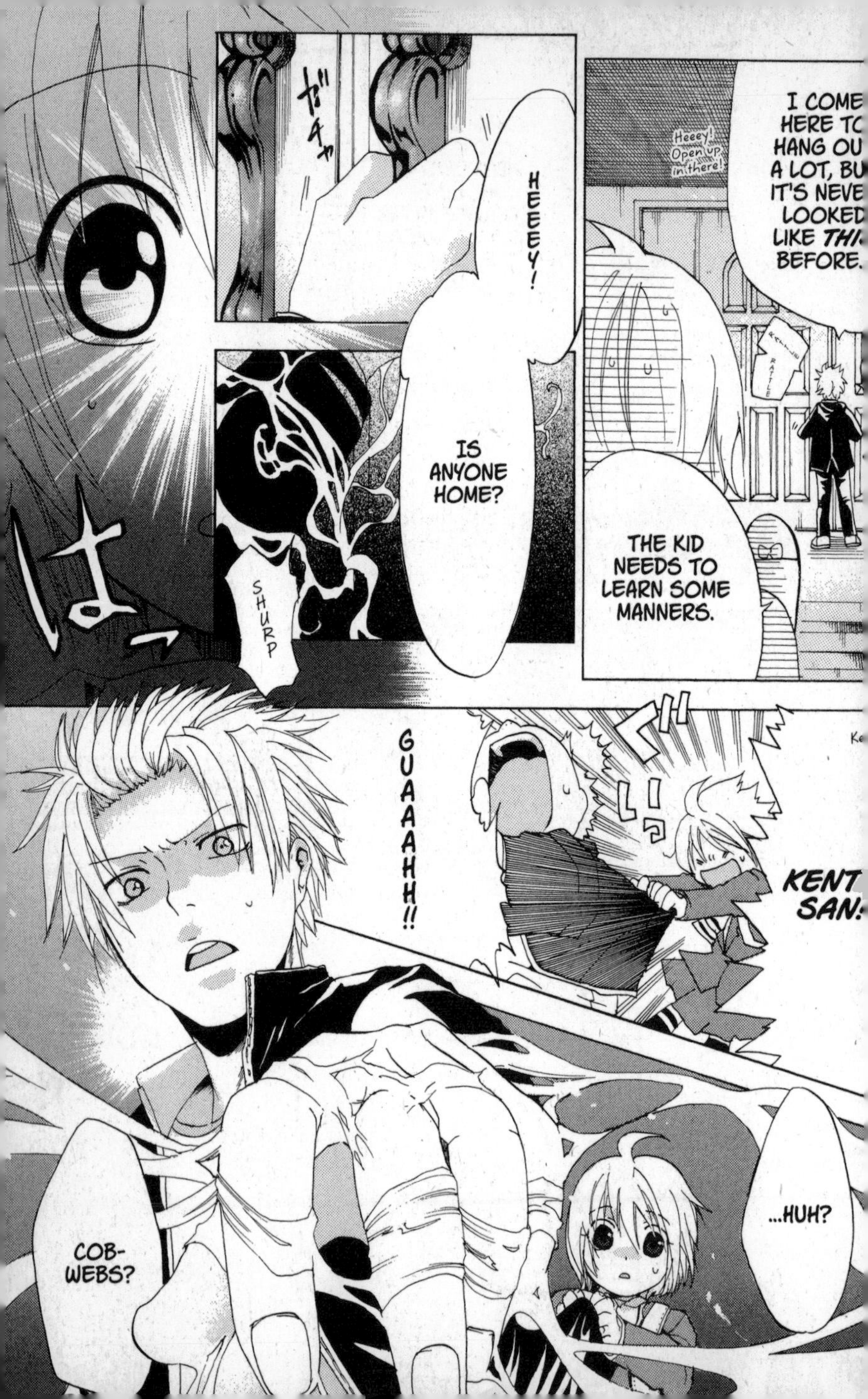
I COME HERE TO HANG OU A LOT, BU IT'S NEVE LOOKED LIKE THI BEFORE.
Heeey! Open up in there!
RATTLE
THE KID NEEDS TO LEARN SOME MANNERS.
ガチャ
HEEEEY!
IS ANYONE HOME?
SHURP
はっ
KENT SAN!
GUAAAAHH!!
ぐいっ
...HUH?
COB-WEBS?

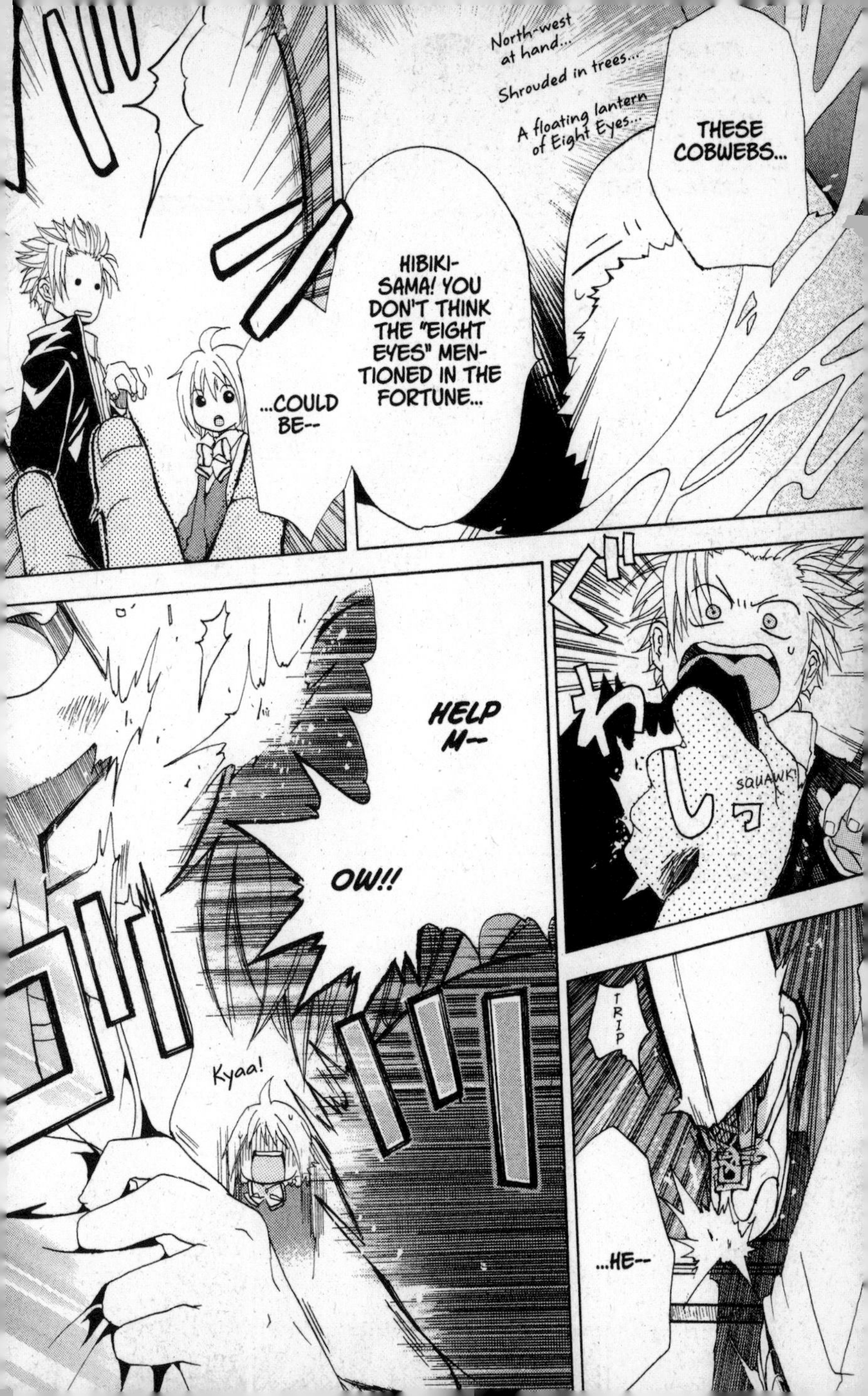
North-west at hand...
Shrouded in trees...
A floating lantern of Eight Eyes...
THESE COBWEBS...
HIBIKI-SAMA! YOU DON'T THINK THE "EIGHT EYES" MENTIONED IN THE FORTUNE...
...COULD BE--
ぐわしっ
SQUAWK!
TRIP
...HE--
HELP M--
OW!!
Kyaa!

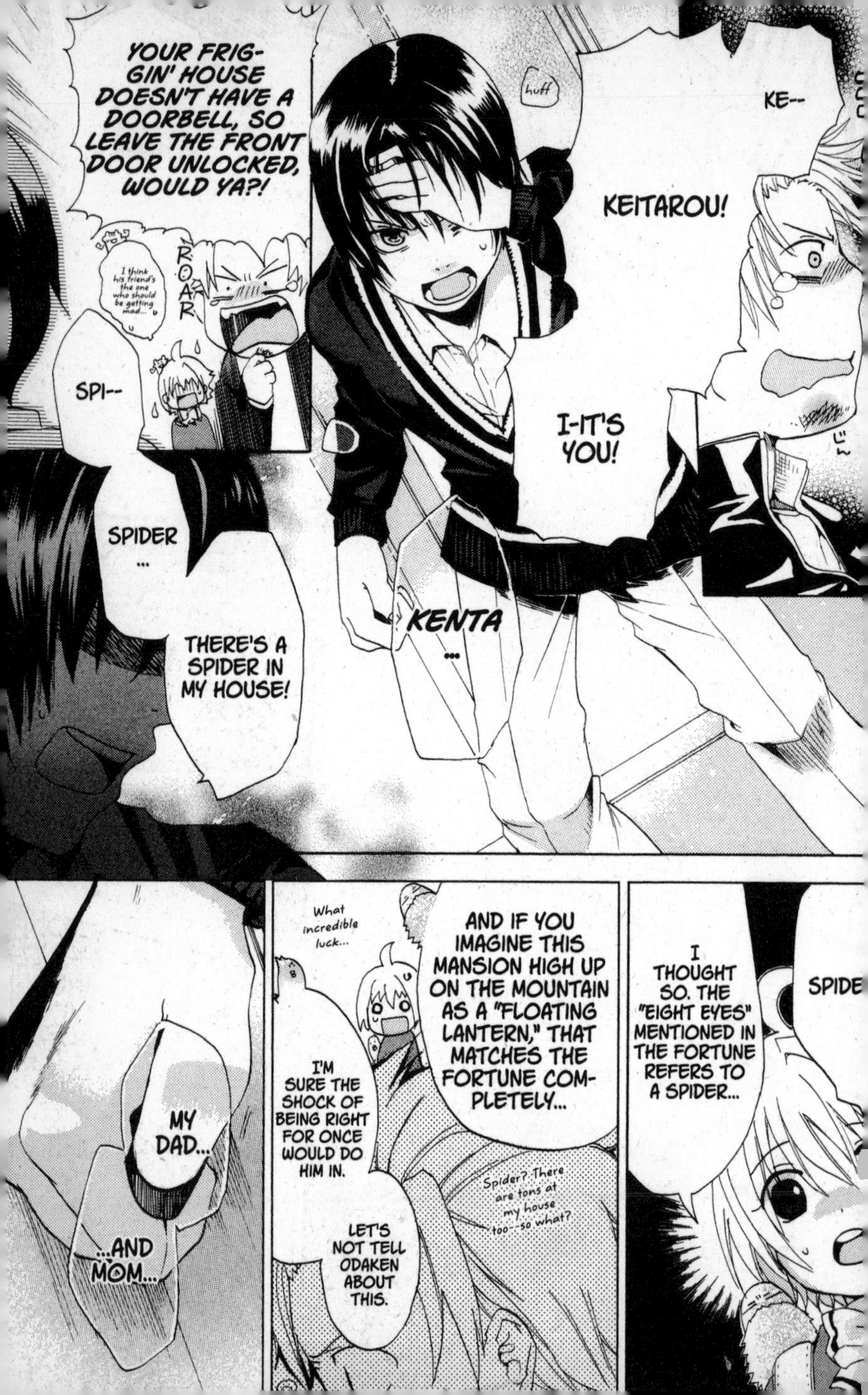
KE--
KEITAROU!
I-IT'S YOU!
huff
KENTA ...
YOUR FRIG-GIN' HOUSE DOESN'T HAVE A DOORBELL, SO LEAVE THE FRONT DOOR UNLOCKED, WOULD YA?!
ROAR
I think his friend's the one who should be getting mad...
SPI--
SPIDER ...
THERE'S A SPIDER IN MY HOUSE!
SPIDE
I THOUGHT SO. THE "EIGHT EYES" MENTIONED IN THE FORTUNE REFERS TO A SPIDER...
AND IF YOU IMAGINE THIS MANSION HIGH UP ON THE MOUNTAIN AS A "FLOATING LANTERN," THAT MATCHES THE FORTUNE COM-PLETELY...
What incredible luck...
Spider? There are tons at my house too--so what?
I'M SURE THE SHOCK OF BEING RIGHT FOR ONCE WOULD DO HIM IN.
LET'S NOT TELL ODAKEN ABOUT THIS.
MY DAD...
...AND MOM...

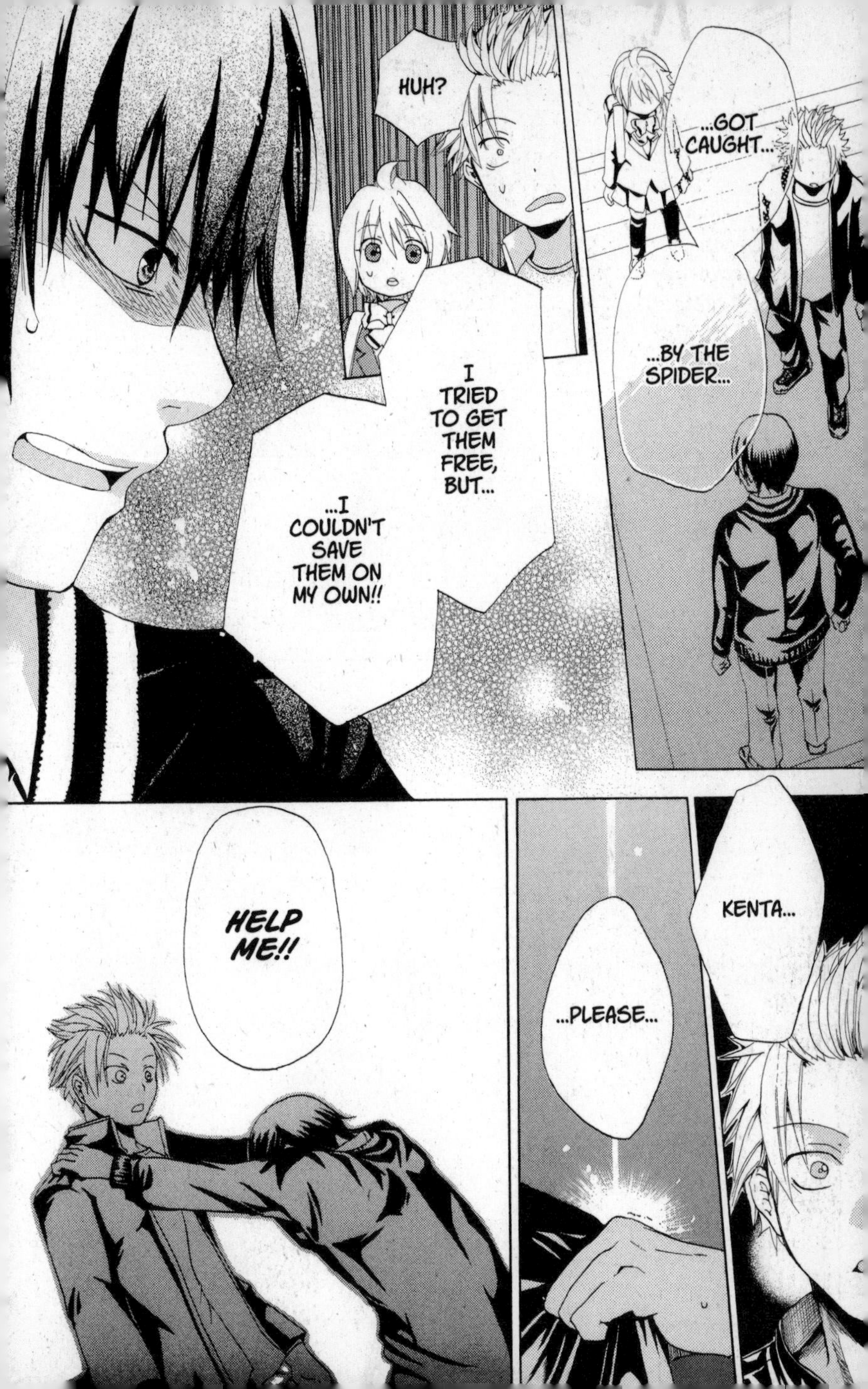
...GOT CAUGHT...
...BY THE SPIDER...
HUH?
I TRIED TO GET THEM FREE, BUT...
...I COULDN'T SAVE THEM ON MY OWN!!
KENTA...
...PLEASE...
HELP ME!!

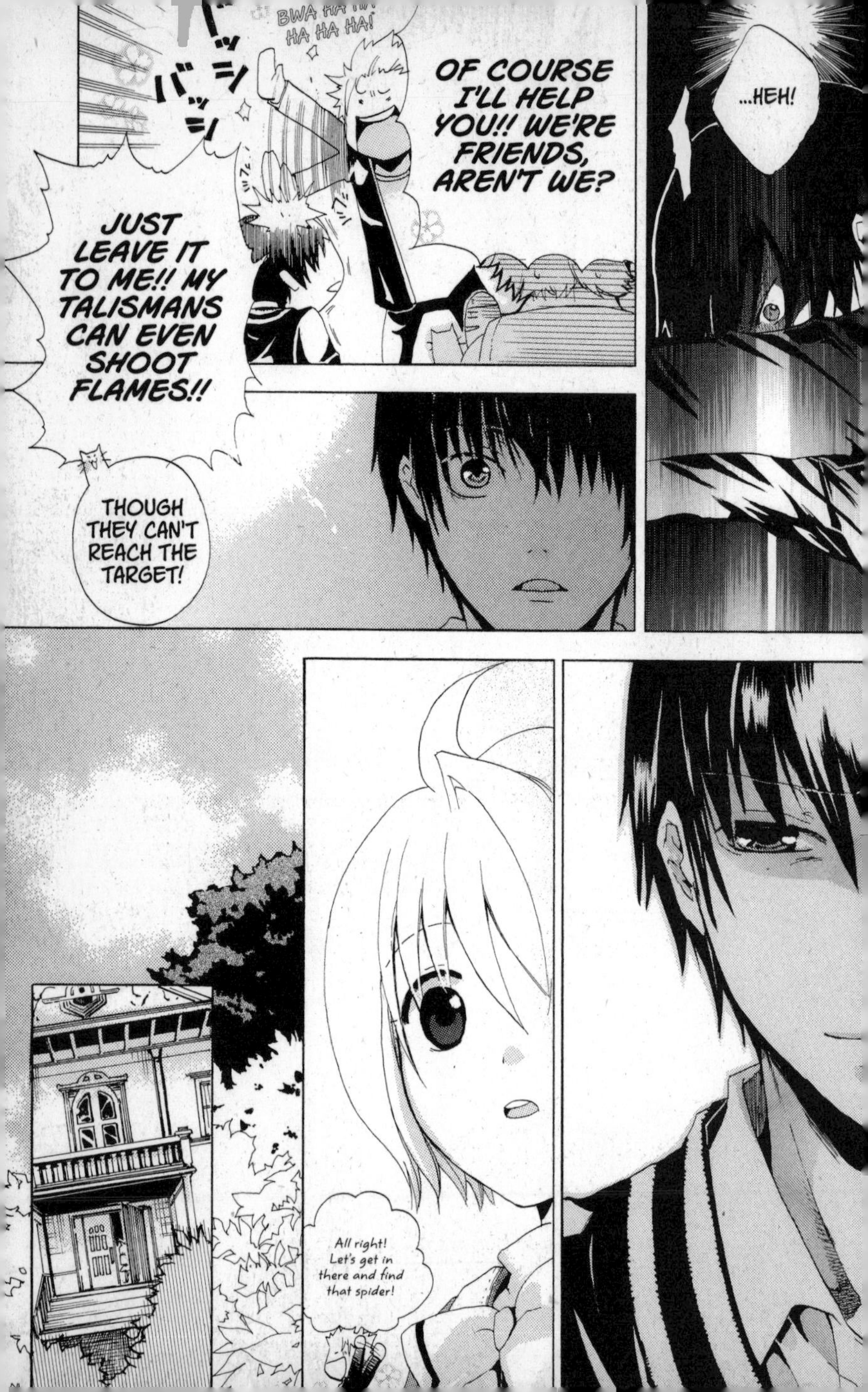
...HEH!
OF COURSE I'LL HELP YOU!! WE'RE FRIENDS, AREN'T WE?
BWA HA HA! HA HA HA!
JUST LEAVE IT TO ME!! MY TALISMANS CAN EVEN SHOOT FLAMES!!
THOUGH THEY CAN'T REACH THE TARGET!
All right! Let's get in there and find that spider!

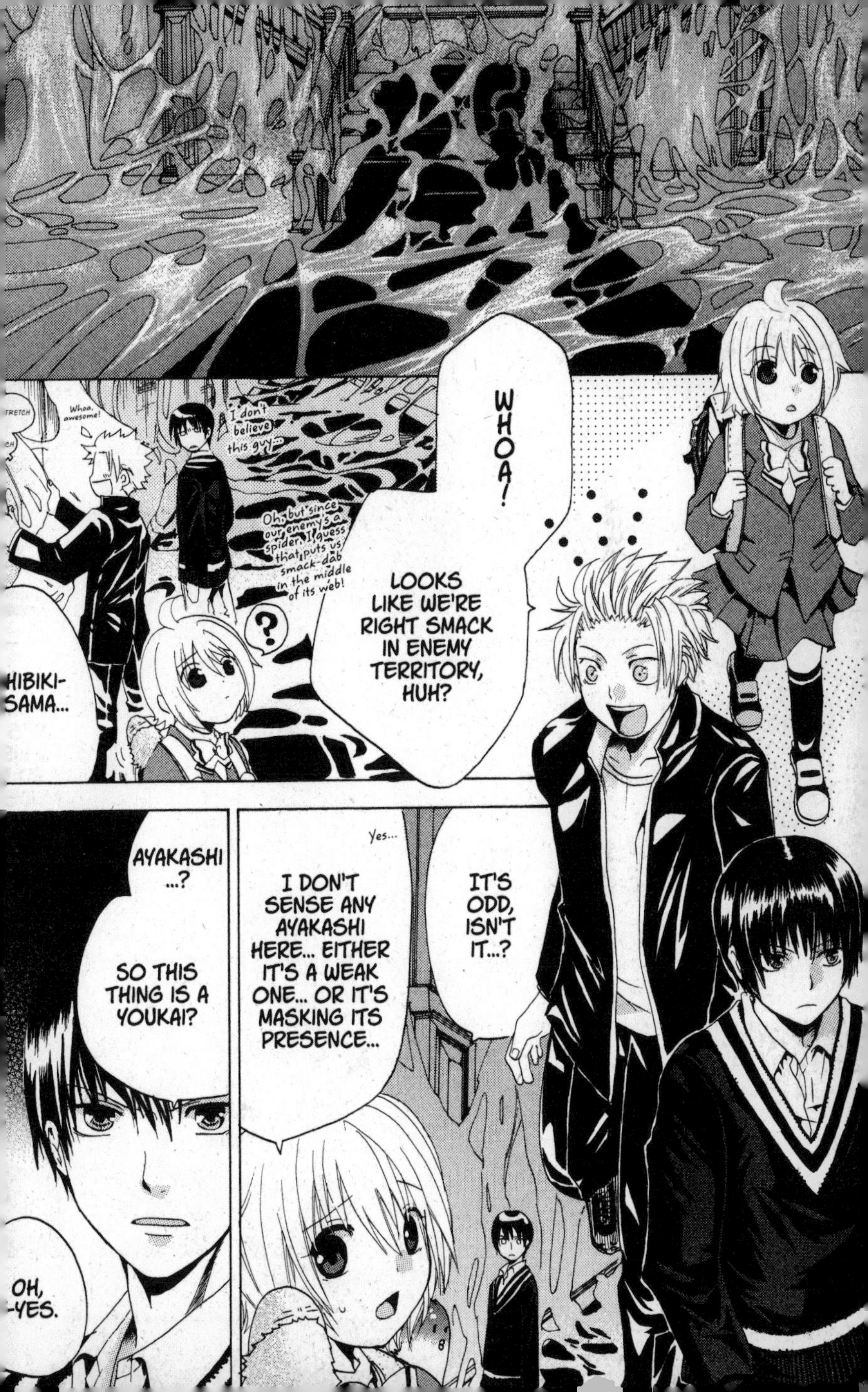
WHOA!
LOOKS LIKE WE'RE RIGHT SMACK IN ENEMY TERRITORY, HUH?
Whoa, awesome!
I don't believe this guy...
Oh, but since our enemy's a spider, I guess that puts us smack-dab in the middle of its web!
?
HIBIKI-SAMA...
IT'S ODD, ISN'T IT...?
Yes...
I DON'T SENSE ANY AYAKASHI HERE... EITHER IT'S A WEAK ONE... OR IT'S MASKING ITS PRESENCE...
AYAKASHI ...?
SO THIS THING IS A YOUKAI?
OH, -YES.

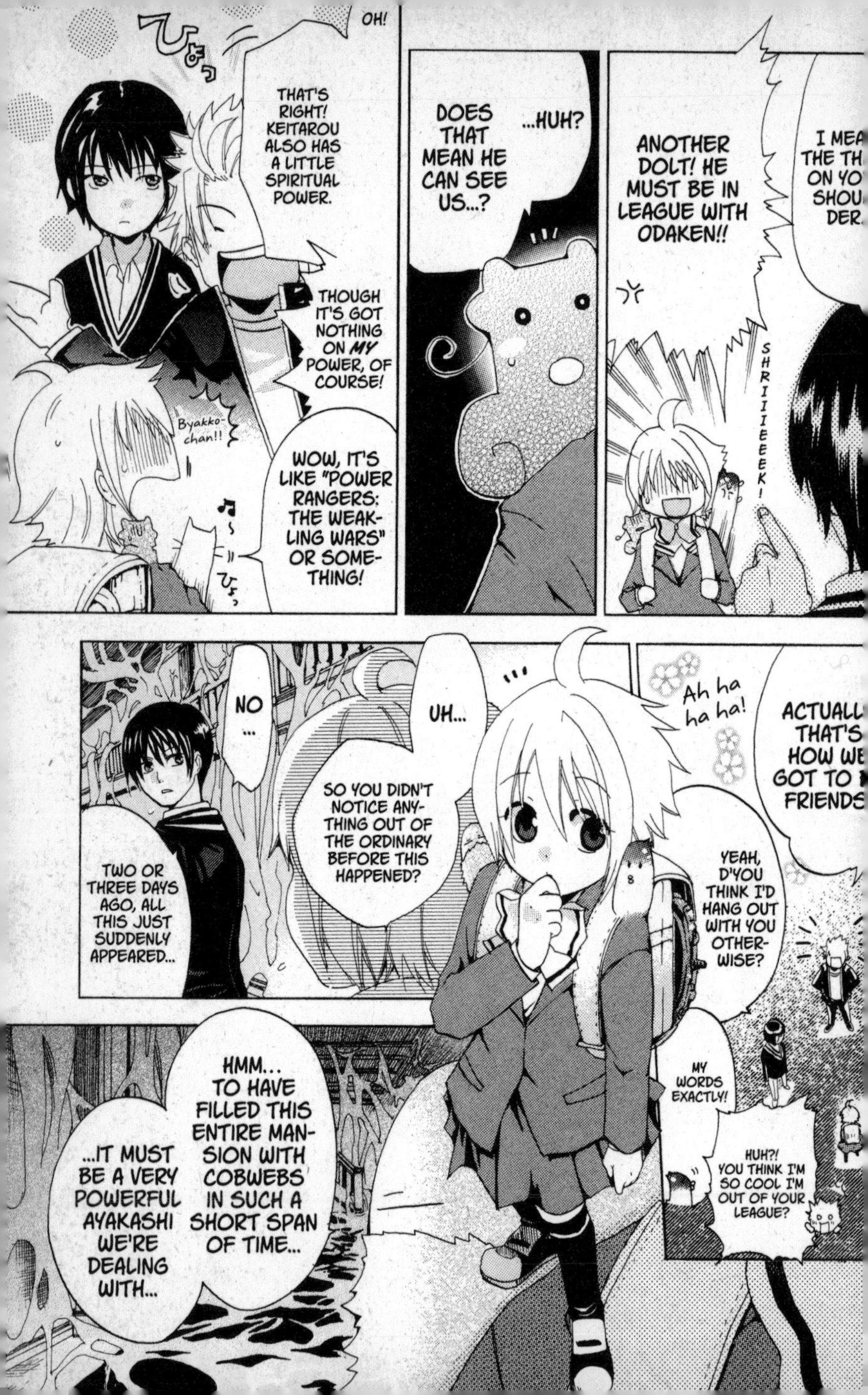
I MEA THE TH ON YO SHOU DER.
ANOTHER DOLT! HE MUST BE IN LEAGUE WITH ODAKEN!!
SHRIIIEEEEK!
...HUH?
DOES THAT MEAN HE CAN SEE US...?
OH!
THAT'S RIGHT! KEITAROU ALSO HAS A LITTLE SPIRITUAL POWER.
THOUGH IT'S GOT NOTHING ON *MY* POWER, OF COURSE!
Byakko-chan!!
WOW, IT'S LIKE "POWER RANGERS: THE WEAKLING WARS" OR SOMETHING!
ACTUALL THAT'S HOW WE GOT TO FRIENDS
Ah ha ha ha!
YEAH, D'YOU THINK I'D HANG OUT WITH YOU OTHERWISE?
MY WORDS EXACTLY!
HUH?! YOU THINK I'M SO COOL I'M OUT OF YOUR LEAGUE?
UH...
SO YOU DIDN'T NOTICE ANYTHING OUT OF THE ORDINARY BEFORE THIS HAPPENED?
NO ...
TWO OR THREE DAYS AGO, ALL THIS JUST SUDDENLY APPEARED...
HMM... TO HAVE FILLED THIS ENTIRE MANSION WITH COBWEBS IN SUCH A SHORT SPAN OF TIME...
...IT MUST BE A VERY POWERFUL AYAKASHI WE'RE DEALING WITH...

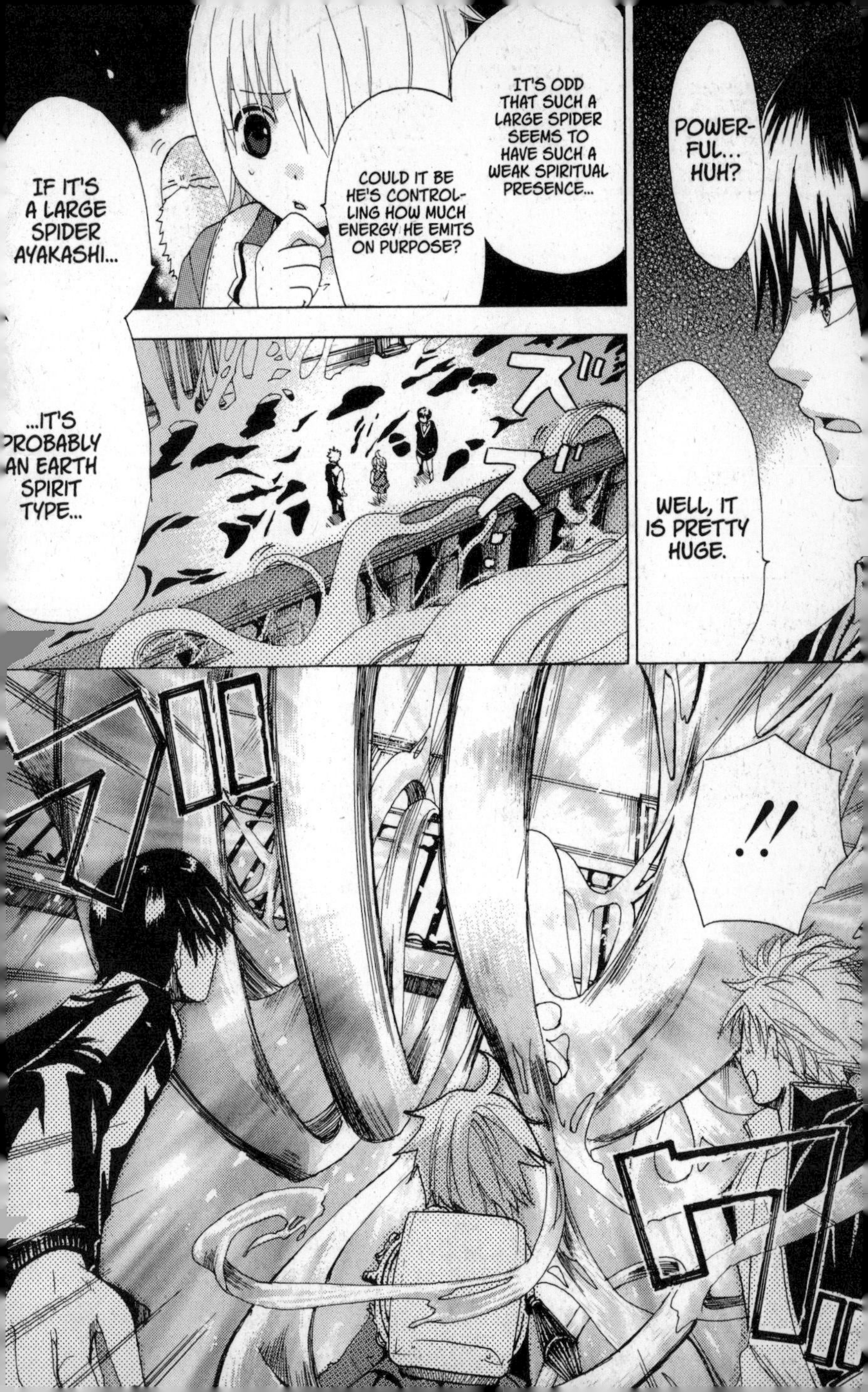
POWER-FUL... HUH?
WELL, IT IS PRETTY HUGE.
IT'S ODD THAT SUCH A LARGE SPIDER SEEMS TO HAVE SUCH A WEAK SPIRITUAL PRESENCE...
COULD IT BE HE'S CONTROL-LING HOW MUCH ENERGY HE EMITS ON PURPOSE?
IF IT'S A LARGE SPIDER AYAKASHI...
...IT'S PROBABLY AN EARTH SPIRIT TYPE...
!!

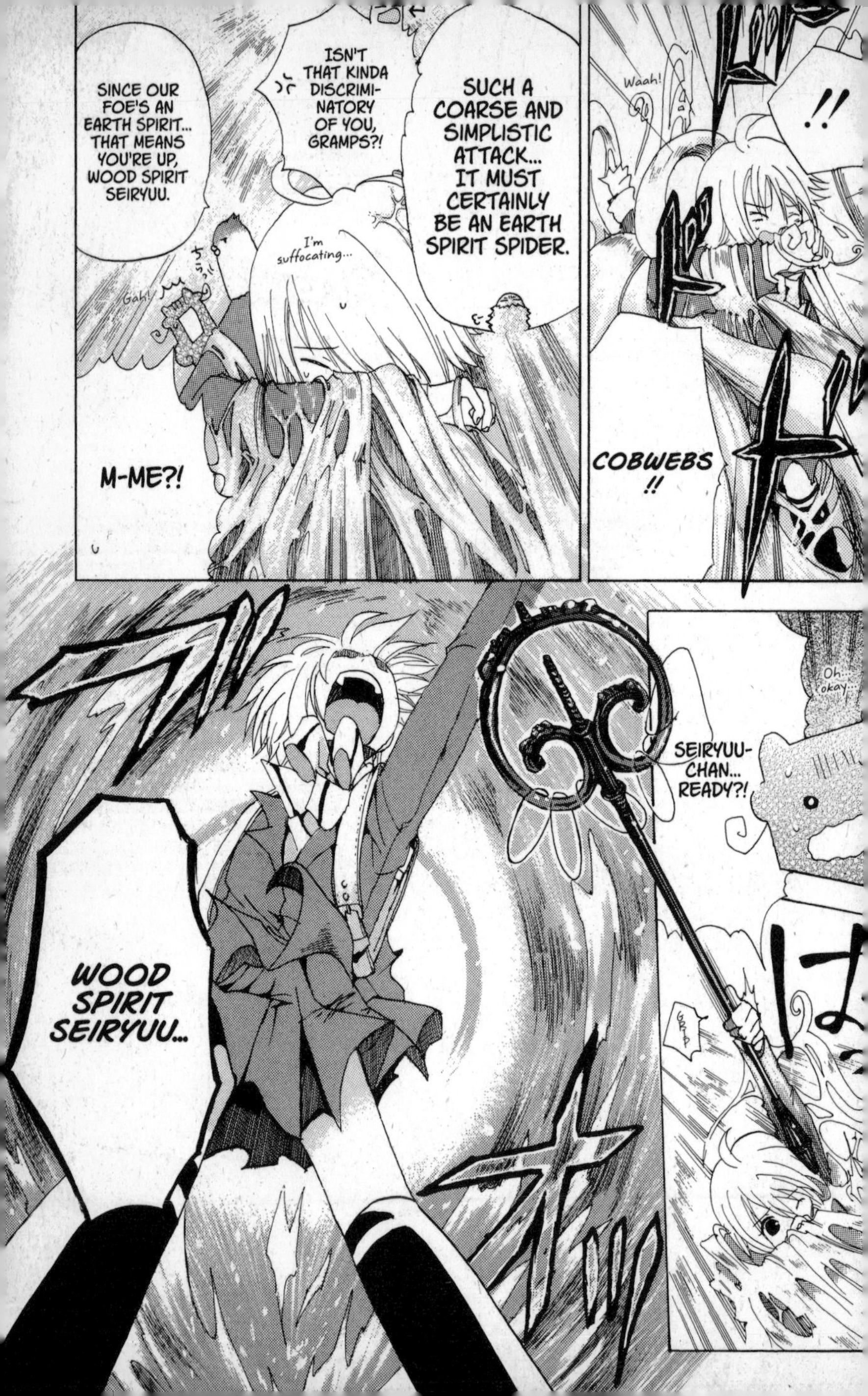
Waah!
!!
COBWEBS !!
SUCH A COARSE AND SIMPLISTIC ATTACK... IT MUST CERTAINLY BE AN EARTH SPIRIT SPIDER.
ISN'T THAT KINDA DISCRIMINATORY OF YOU, GRAMPS?!
SINCE OUR FOE'S AN EARTH SPIRIT... THAT MEANS YOU'RE UP, WOOD SPIRIT SEIRYUU.
I'm suffocating...
Gah!
M-ME?!
Oh... okay...
SEIRYUU-CHAN... READY?!
GRIP
WOOD SPIRIT SEIRYUU...

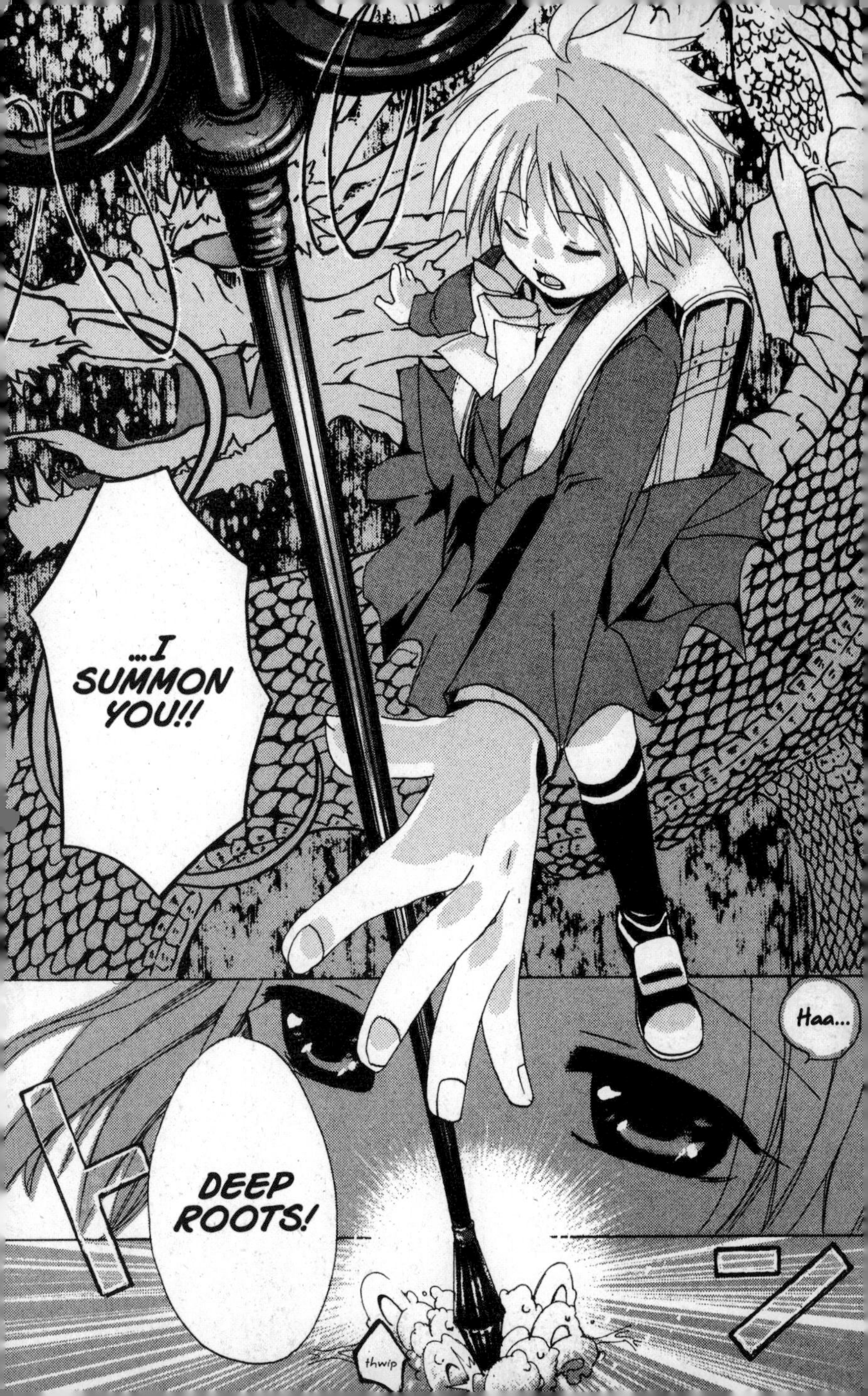
...I SUMMON YOU!!
Haa...
DEEP ROOTS!
thwip

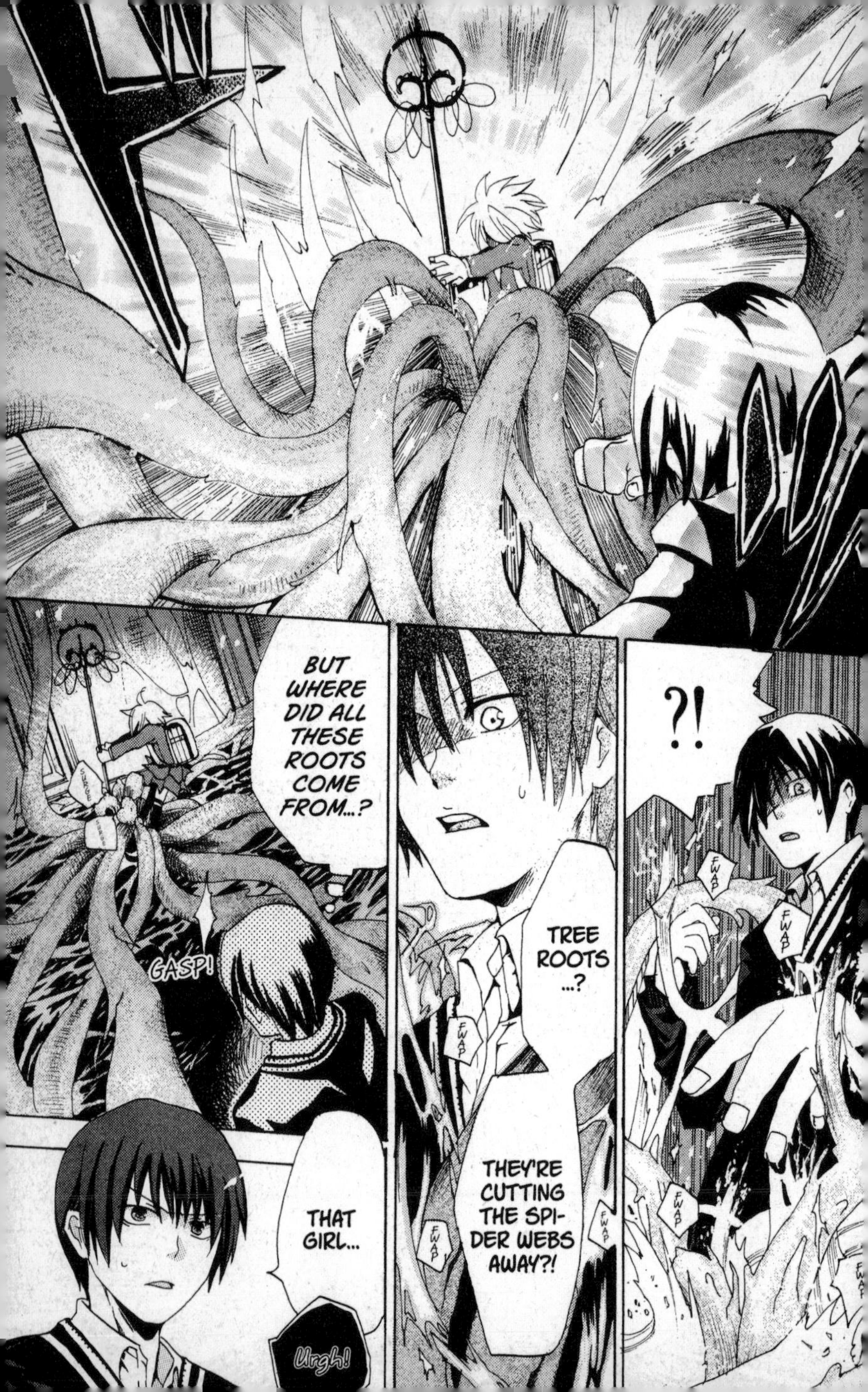
?!
FWAP
FWAP
FWAP
TREE ROOTS ...?
FWAP
THEY'RE CUTTING THE SPI-DER WEBS AWAY?!
FWAP
FWAP
BUT WHERE DID ALL THESE ROOTS COME FROM...?
SURGE
SURGE
GASP!
THAT GIRL...
Urgh!

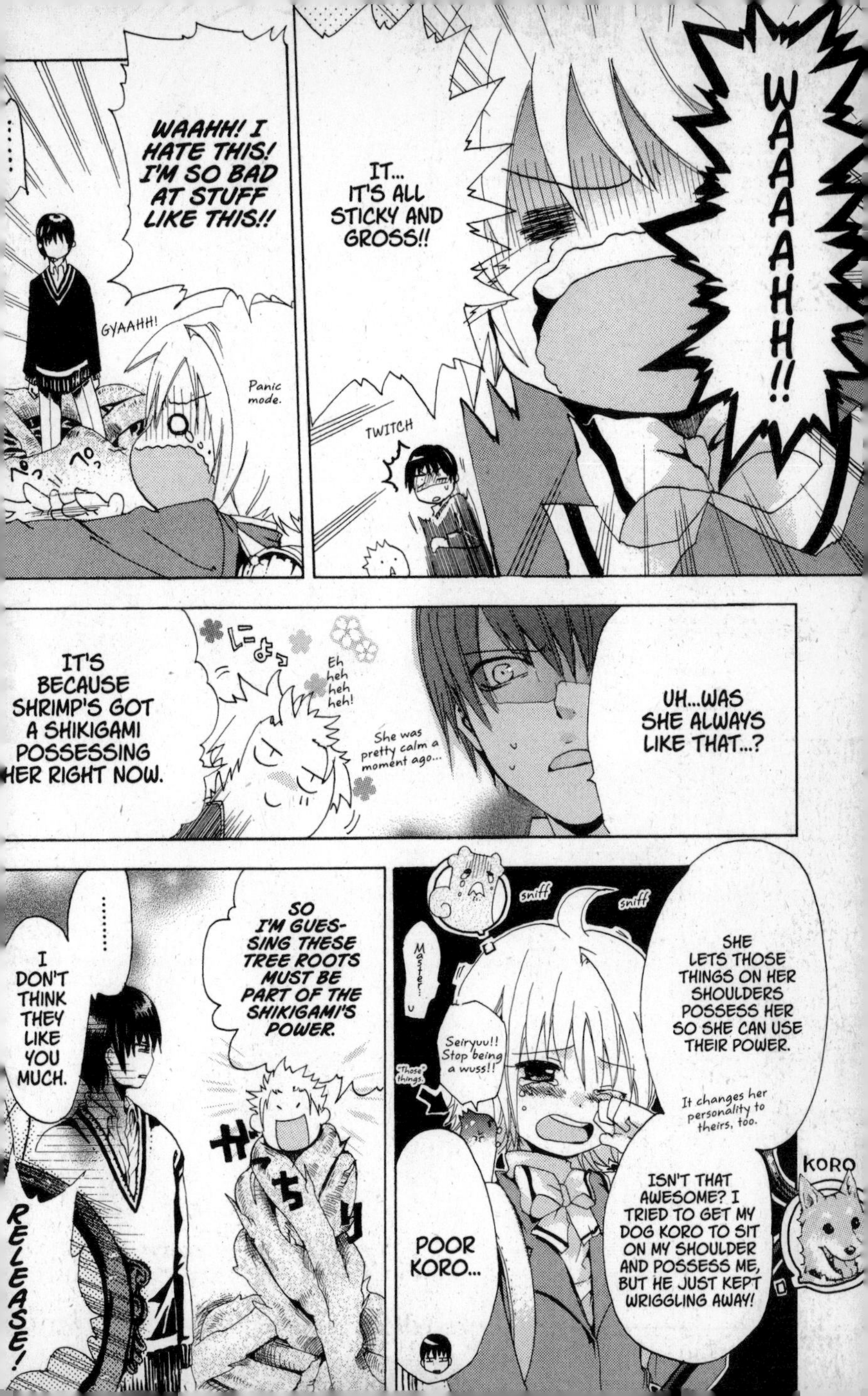
WAAAAAHH!!
IT... IT'S ALL STICKY AND GROSS!!
TWITCH
WAAHH! I HATE THIS! I'M SO BAD AT STUFF LIKE THIS!!
......
GYAAHH!
Panic mode.
UH...WAS SHE ALWAYS LIKE THAT...?
Eh heh heh heh!
She was pretty calm a moment ago...
IT'S BECAUSE SHRIMP'S GOT A SHIKIGAMI POSSESSING HER RIGHT NOW.
SHE LETS THOSE THINGS ON HER SHOULDERS POSSESS HER SO SHE CAN USE THEIR POWER.
It changes her personality to theirs, too.
sniff
sniff
Master...
Seiryuu!! Stop being a wuss!!
"Those" things.
KORO
ISN'T THAT AWESOME? I TRIED TO GET MY DOG KORO TO SIT ON MY SHOULDER AND POSSESS ME, BUT HE JUST KEPT WRIGGLING AWAY!
POOR KORO...
SO I'M GUESSING THESE TREE ROOTS MUST BE PART OF THE SHIKIGAMI'S POWER.
......
I DON'T THINK THEY LIKE YOU MUCH.
RELEASE!

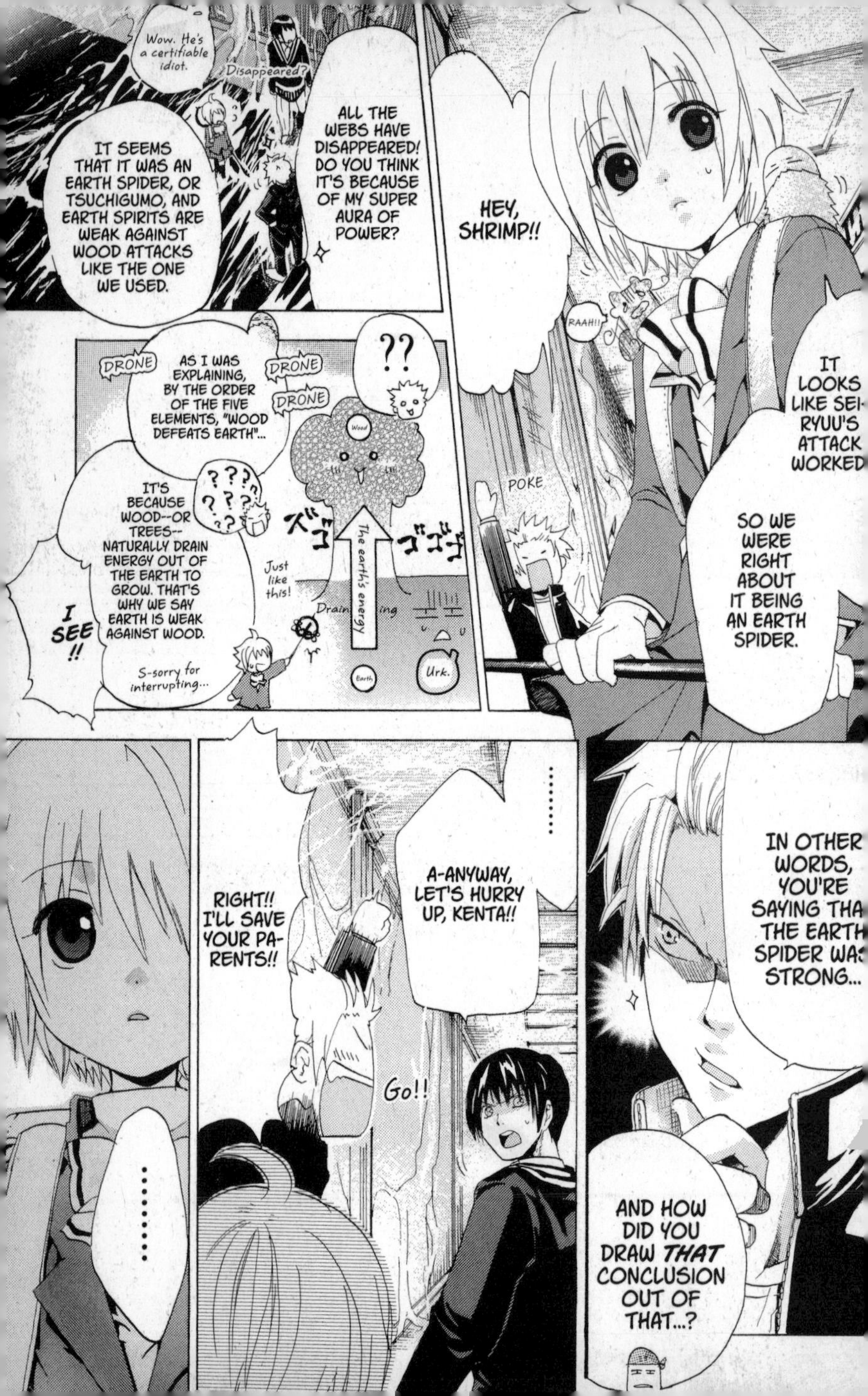
HEY, SHRIMP!!
RAAH!!
IT LOOKS LIKE SEI-RYUU'S ATTACK WORKED
POKE
SO WE WERE RIGHT ABOUT IT BEING AN EARTH SPIDER.
ALL THE WEBS HAVE DISAPPEARED! DO YOU THINK IT'S BECAUSE OF MY SUPER AURA OF POWER?
Disappeared?
Wow. He's a certifiable idiot.
IT SEEMS THAT IT WAS AN EARTH SPIDER, OR TSUCHIGUMO, AND EARTH SPIRITS ARE WEAK AGAINST WOOD ATTACKS LIKE THE ONE WE USED.
??
DRONE
DRONE
DRONE
AS I WAS EXPLAINING, BY THE ORDER OF THE FIVE ELEMENTS, "WOOD DEFEATS EARTH"...
Wood
IT'S BECAUSE WOOD--OR TREES--NATURALLY DRAIN ENERGY OUT OF THE EARTH TO GROW. THAT'S WHY WE SAY EARTH IS WEAK AGAINST WOOD.
The earth's energy
Just like this!
Drain ing
Earth
Urk.
I SEE!!
S-sorry for interrupting...
IN OTHER WORDS, YOU'RE SAYING THA THE EARTH SPIDER WA STRONG...
AND HOW DID YOU DRAW THAT CONCLUSION OUT OF THAT...?
......
A-ANYWAY, LET'S HURRY UP, KENTA!!
RIGHT!! I'LL SAVE YOUR PA-RENTS!!
Go!!
......

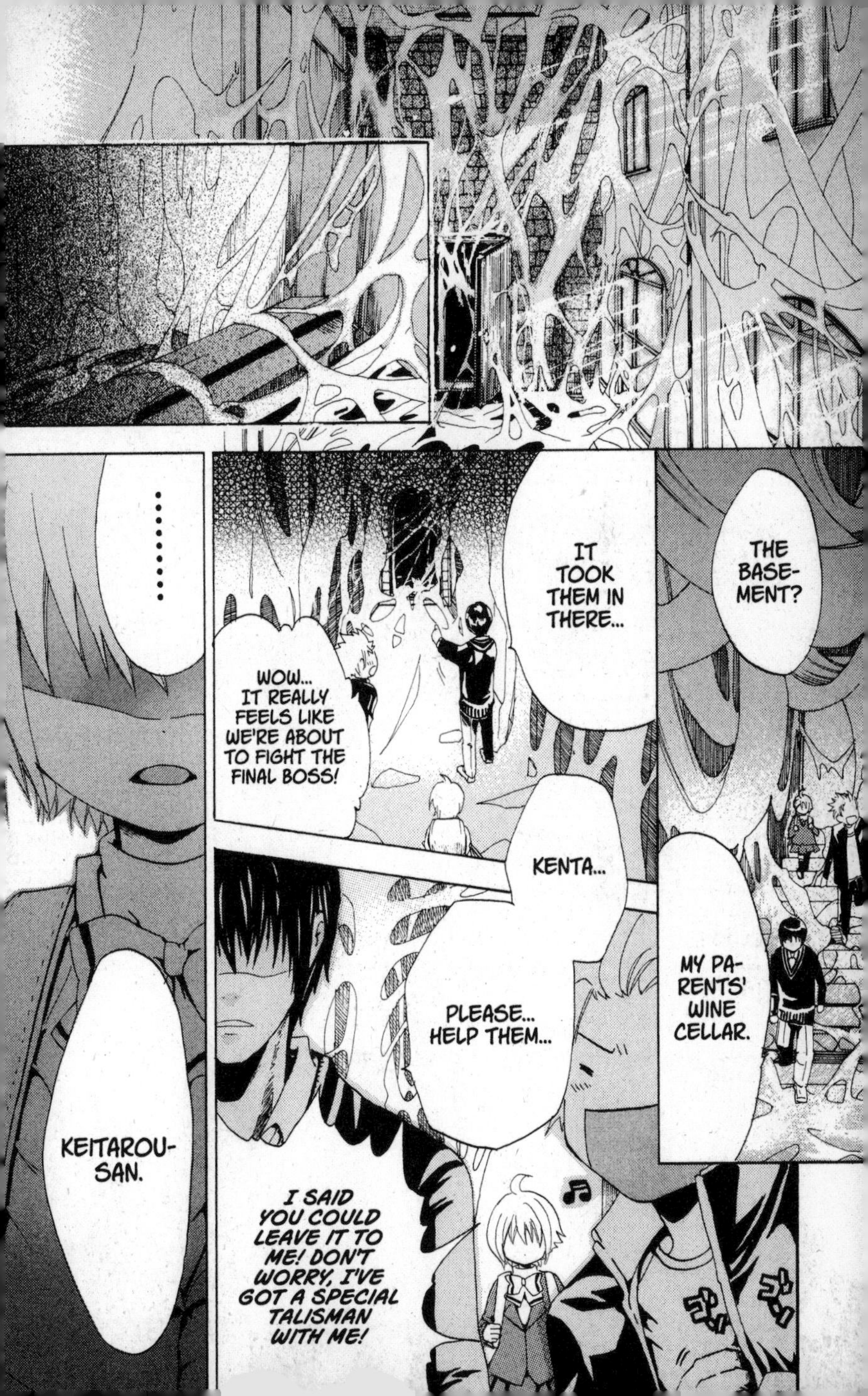
THE BASE-MENT?
MY PA-RENTS' WINE CELLAR.
IT TOOK THEM IN THERE...
WOW... IT REALLY FEELS LIKE WE'RE ABOUT TO FIGHT THE FINAL BOSS!
KENTA...
PLEASE... HELP THEM...
I SAID YOU COULD LEAVE IT TO ME! DON'T WORRY, I'VE GOT A SPECIAL TALISMAN WITH ME!
......
KEITAROU-SAN.

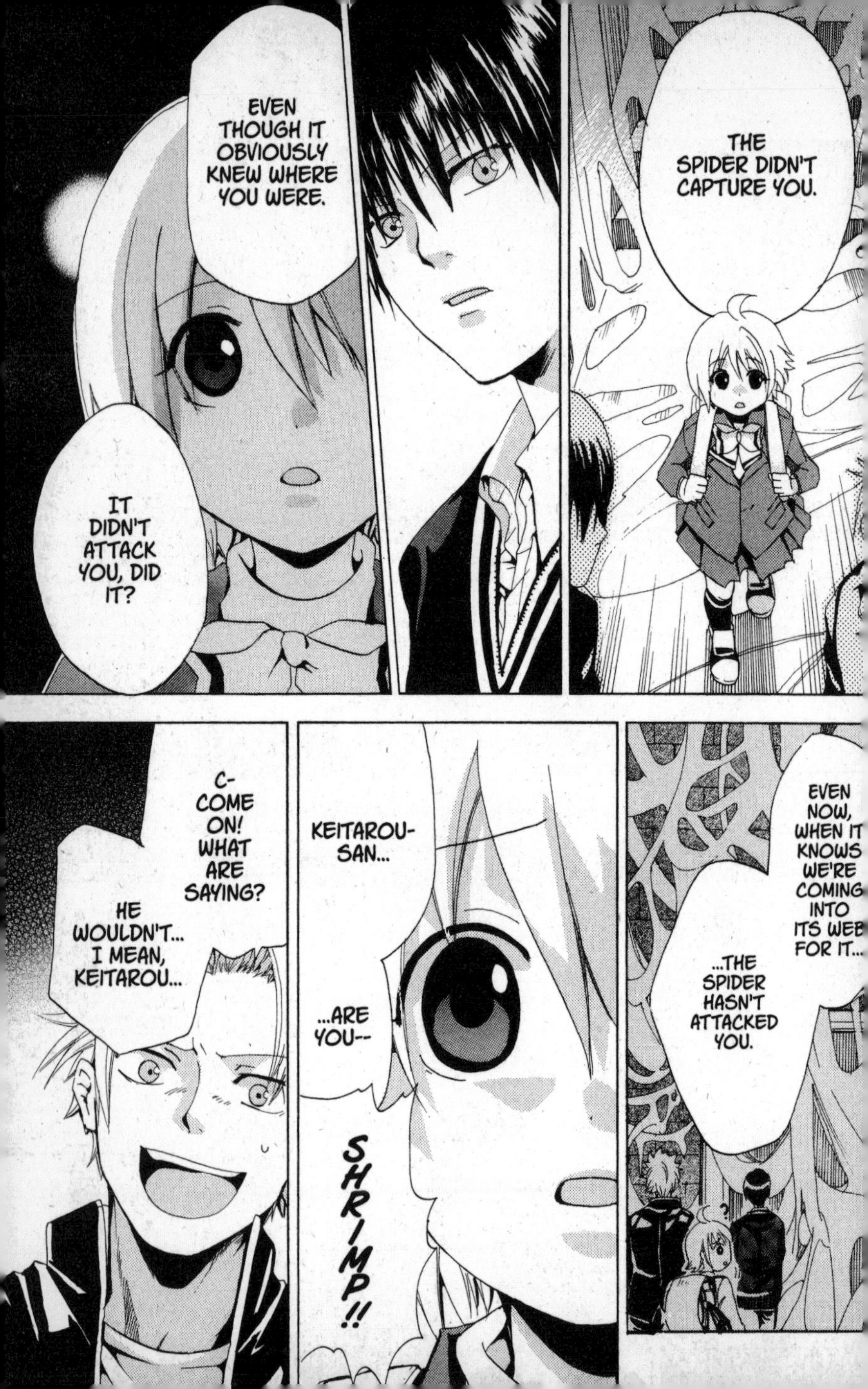
THE SPIDER DIDN'T CAPTURE YOU.
EVEN THOUGH IT OBVIOUSLY KNEW WHERE YOU WERE.
IT DIDN'T ATTACK YOU, DID IT?
EVEN NOW, WHEN IT KNOWS WE'RE COMING INTO ITS WEB FOR IT...
...THE SPIDER HASN'T ATTACKED YOU.
KEITAROU-SAN...
...ARE YOU--
SHRIMP!!
C-COME ON! WHAT ARE SAYING?
HE WOULDN'T... I MEAN, KEITAROU...

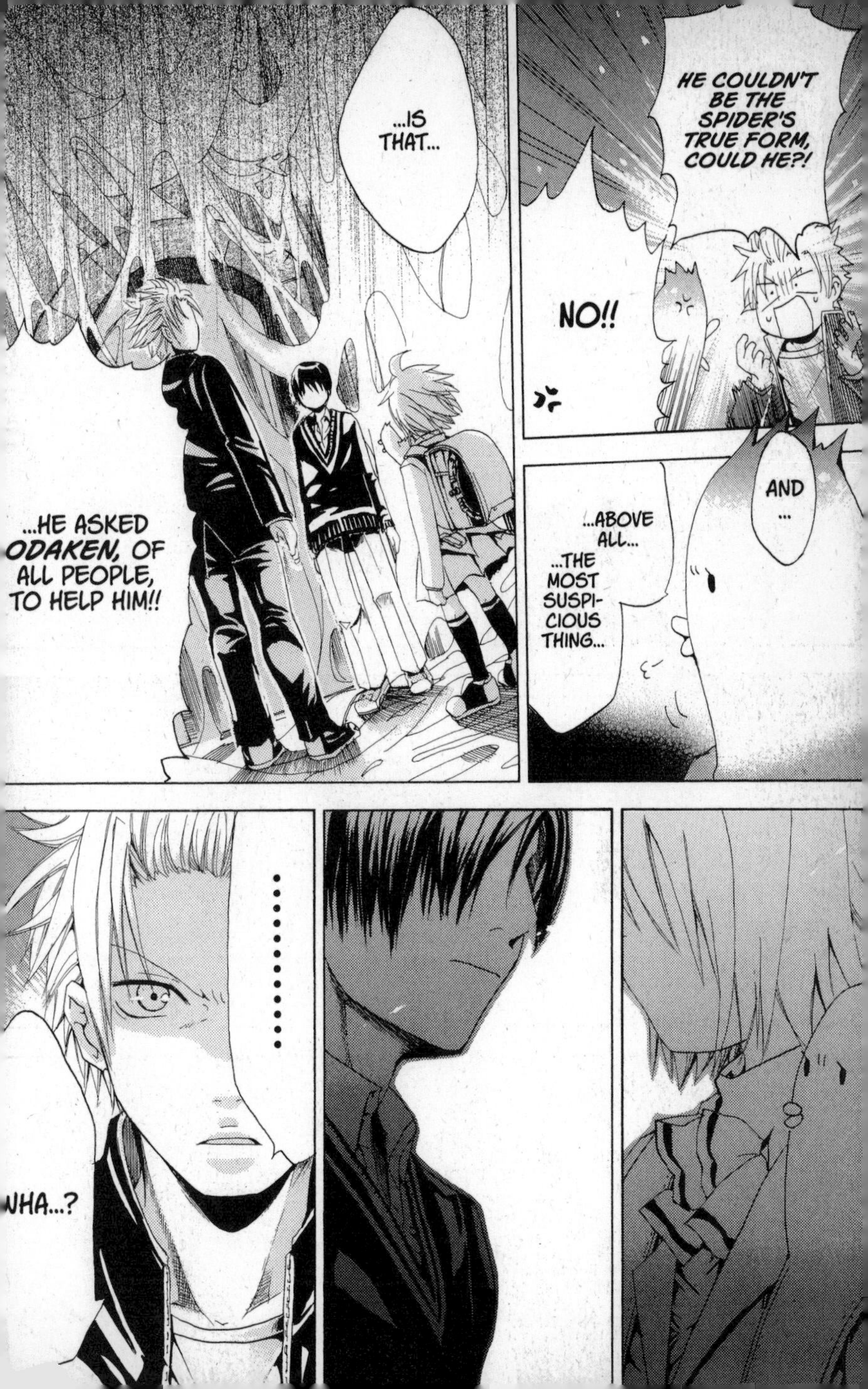

HE COULDN'T BE THE SPIDER'S TRUE FORM, COULD HE?!
NO!!
AND...
...ABOVE ALL... ...THE MOST SUSPICIOUS THING...
...IS THAT...
...HE ASKED ODAKEN, OF ALL PEOPLE, TO HELP HIM!!
....
WHA...?

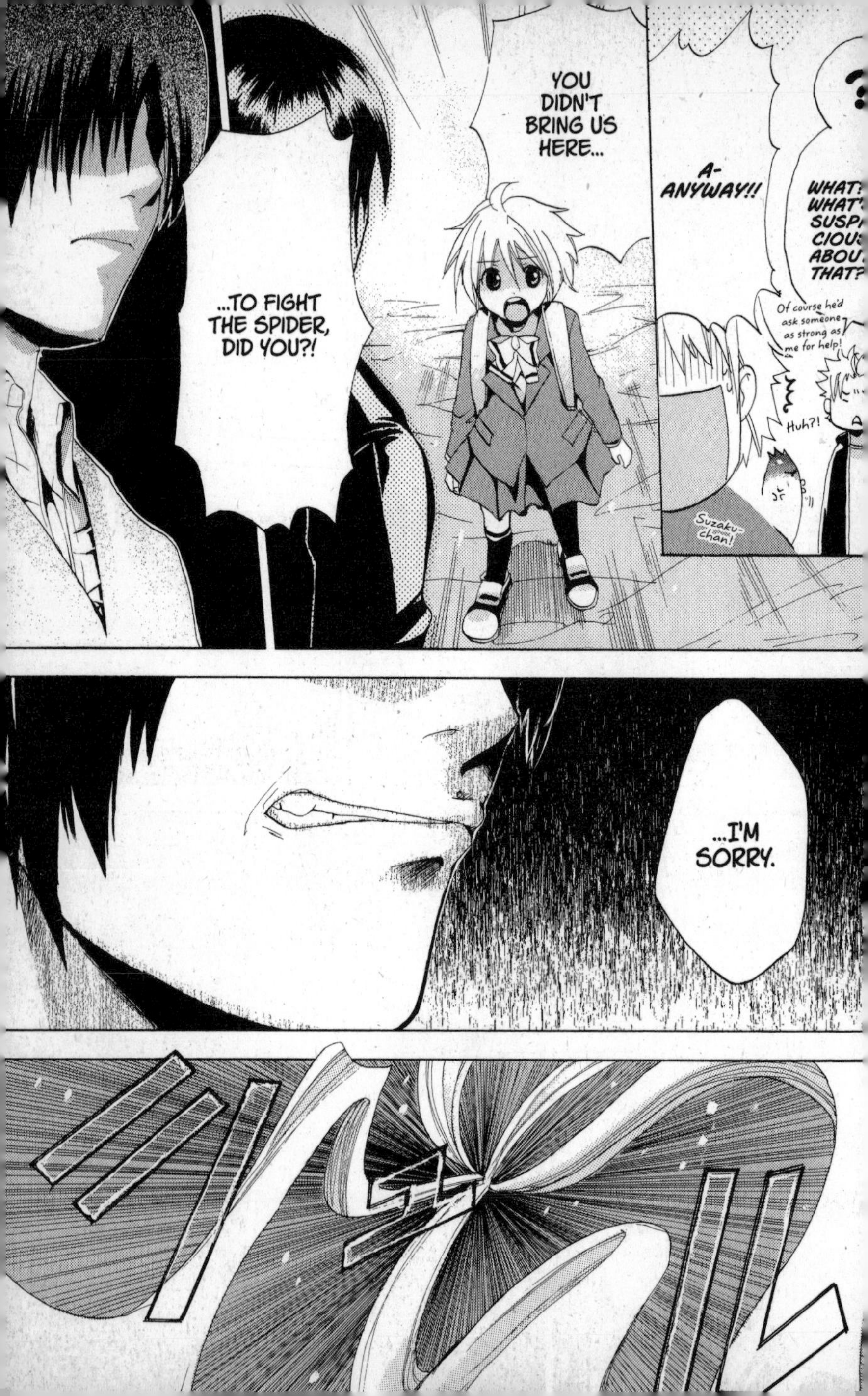
?
WHAT WHAT'S SUSP CIOUS ABOU THAT?
Of course he'd ask someone as strong as me for help!
Huh?!
Suzaku-chan!
A- ANYWAY!!
YOU DIDN'T BRING US HERE...
...TO FIGHT THE SPIDER, DID YOU?!
...I'M SORRY.

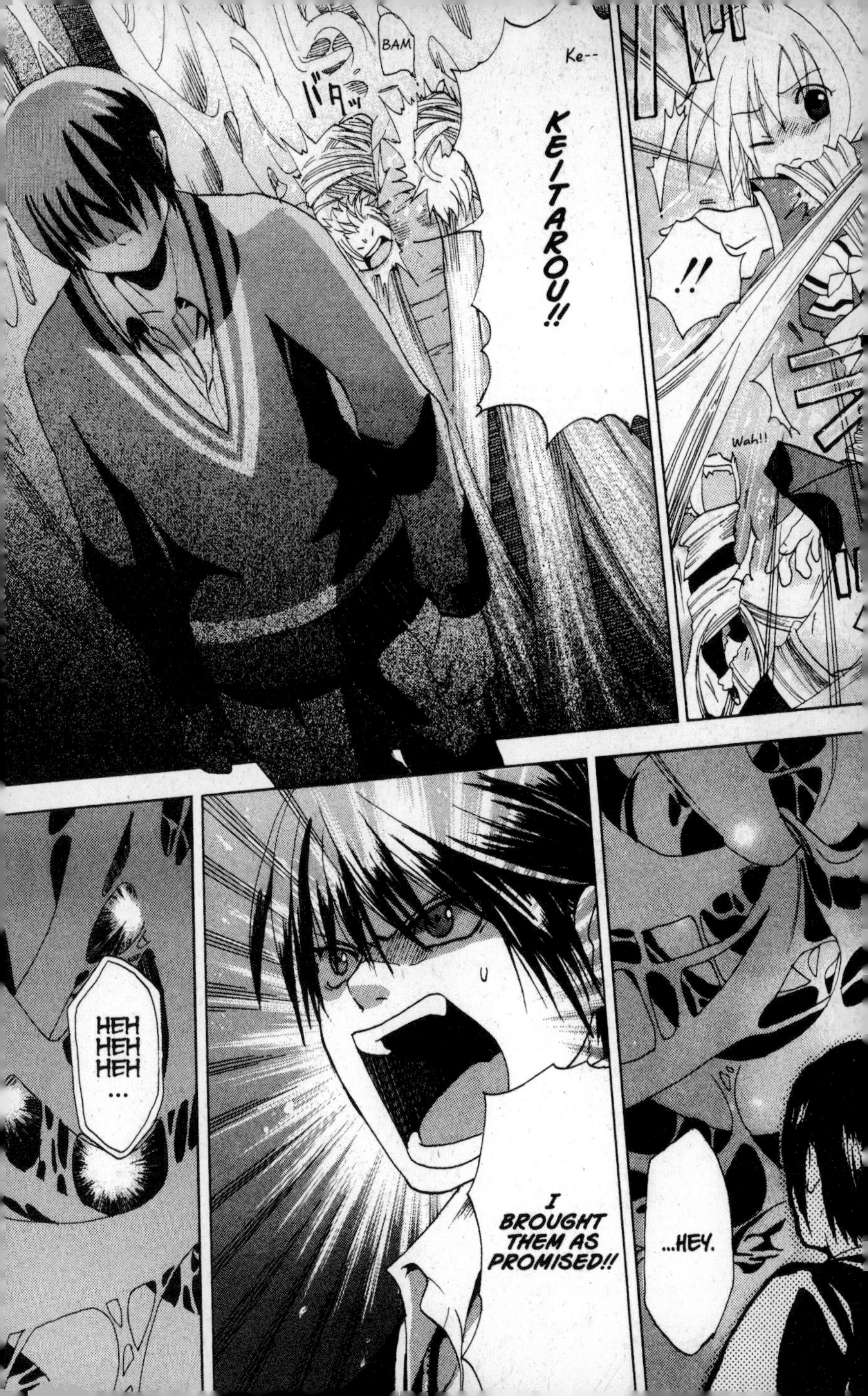
!!
Wah!!
Ke--
KEITAROU!!
BAM
バタッ
...HEY.
I BROUGHT THEM AS PROMISED!!
HEH HEH HEH ...

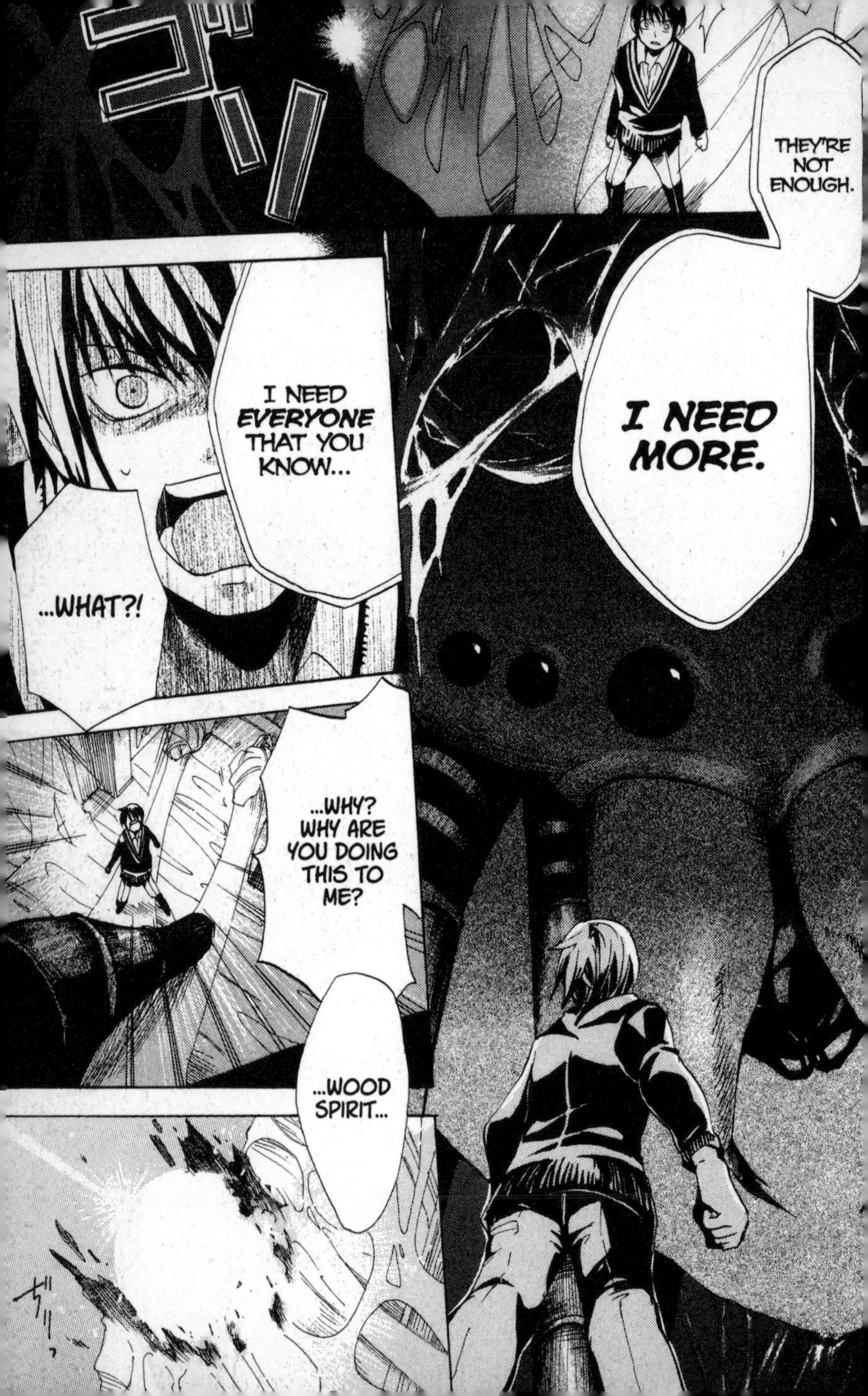
THEY'RE NOT ENOUGH.
I NEED MORE.
I NEED *EVERYONE* THAT YOU KNOW...
...WHAT?!
...WHY? WHY ARE YOU DOING THIS TO ME?
...WOOD SPIRIT...

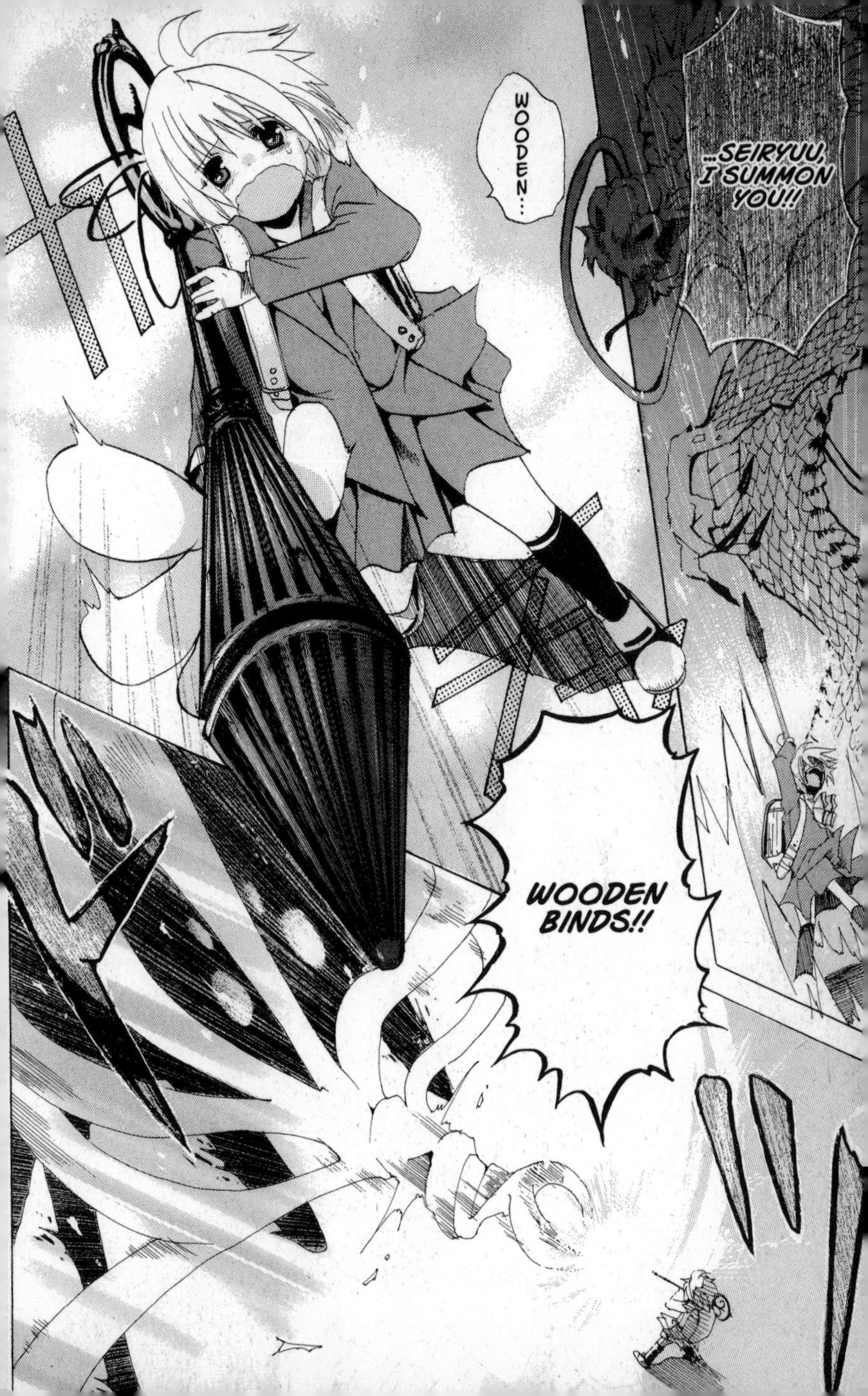
...SEIRYUU, I SUMMON YOU!!
WOODEN...
WOODEN BINDS!!

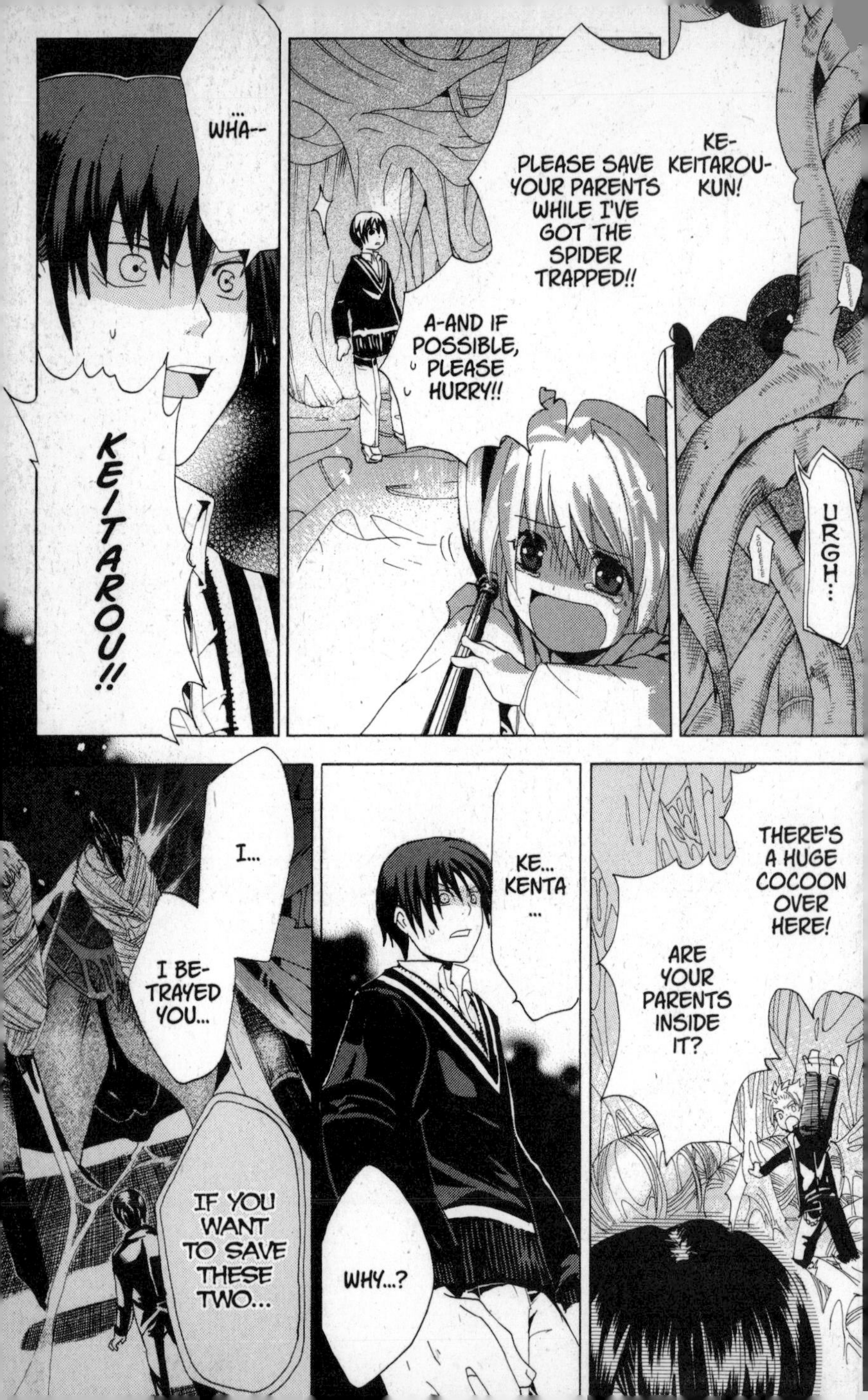
SQUEEZE
URGH...
SQUEEZE
KE-KEITAROU-KUN!
PLEASE SAVE YOUR PARENTS WHILE I'VE GOT THE SPIDER TRAPPED!!
A-AND IF POSSIBLE, PLEASE HURRY!!
...WHA--
KEITAROU!!
THERE'S A HUGE COCOON OVER HERE!
ARE YOUR PARENTS INSIDE IT?
KE... KENTA...
WHY...?
I...
I BE-TRAYED YOU...
IF YOU WANT TO SAVE THESE TWO...

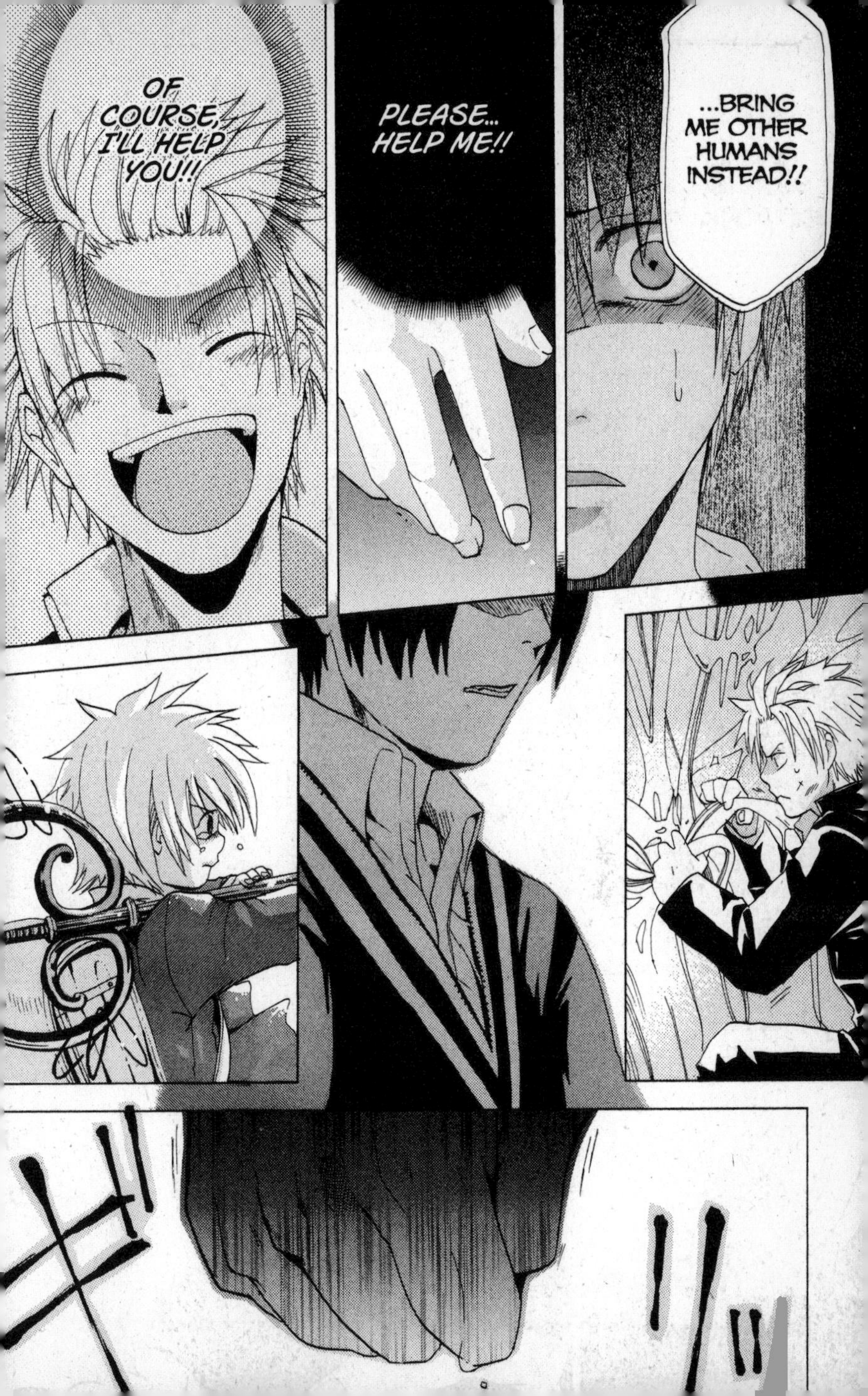
...BRING ME OTHER HUMANS INSTEAD!!
PLEASE... HELP ME!!
OF COURSE, I'LL HELP YOU!!

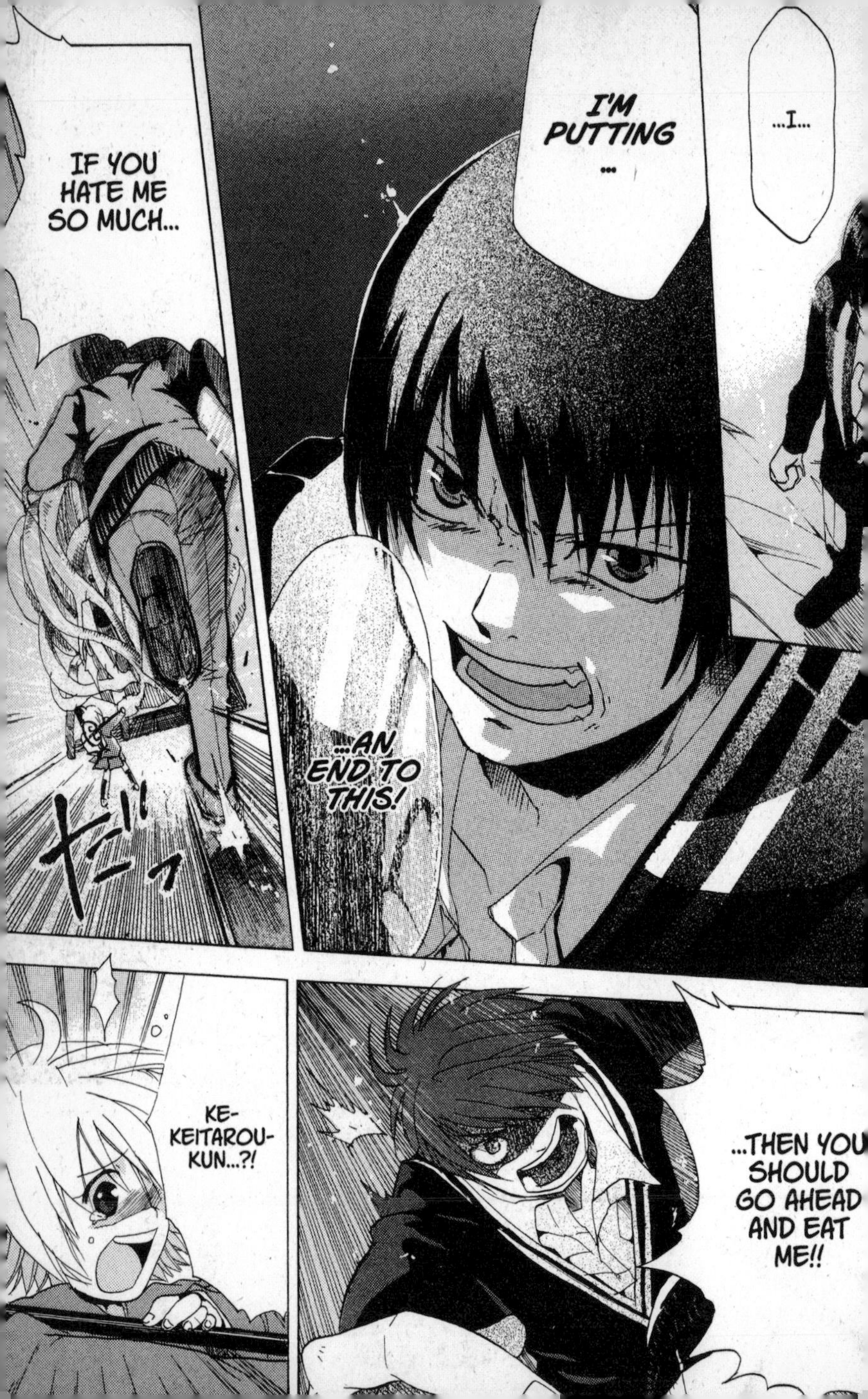
...I...
I'M PUTTING ...
...AN END TO THIS!
IF YOU HATE ME SO MUCH...
...THEN YOU SHOULD GO AHEAD AND EAT ME!!
KE-KEITAROU-KUN...?!

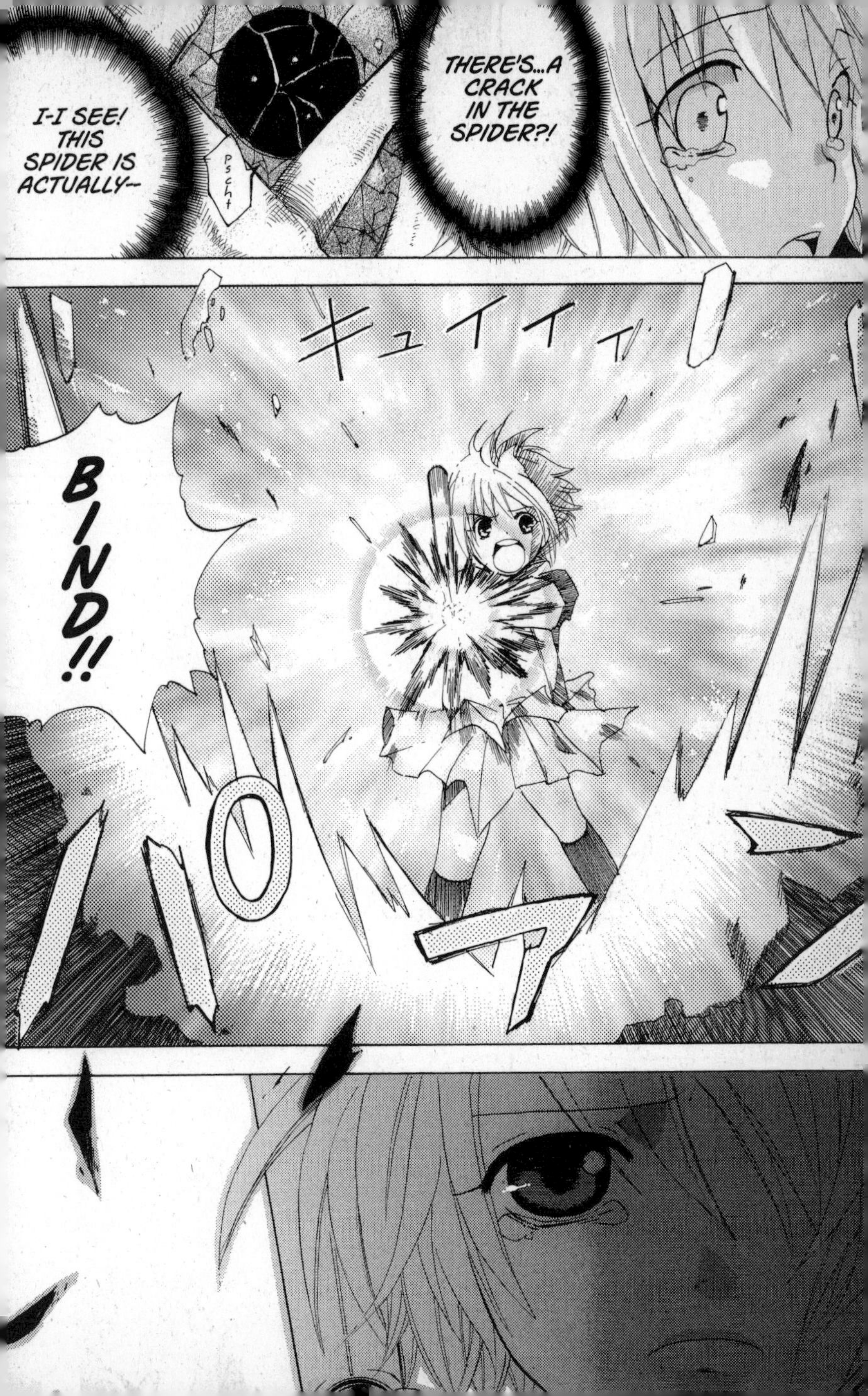
THERE'S...A CRACK IN THE SPIDER?!
Pscht
I-I SEE! THIS SPIDER IS ACTUALLY--
キュイイィ
BIND!!

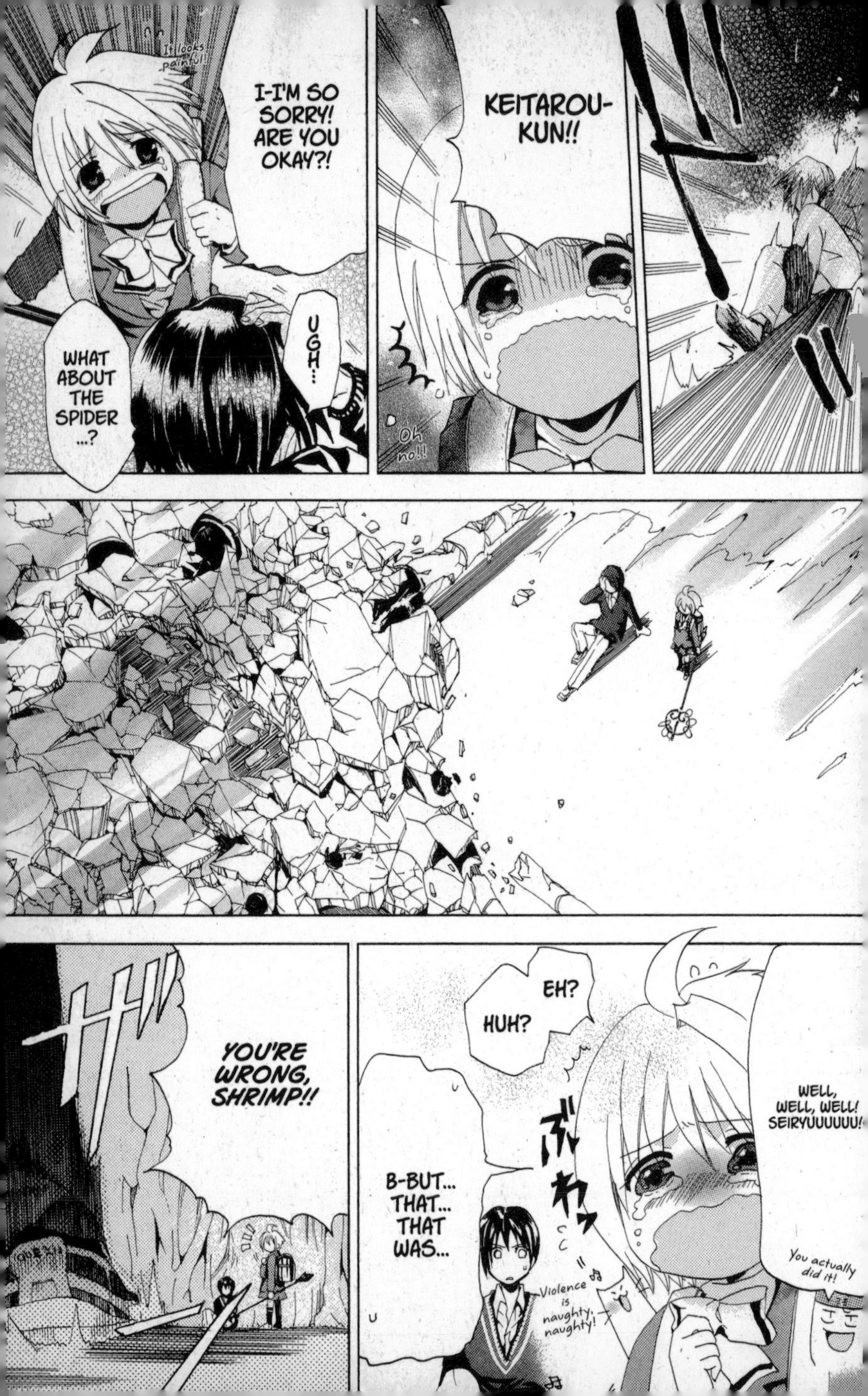
KEITAROU-KUN!!
Oh no!!
It looks painful!
I-I'M SO SORRY! ARE YOU OKAY?!
UGH...
WHAT ABOUT THE SPIDER ...?
EH?
HUH?
WELL, WELL, WELL! SEIRYUUUUUU!
You actually did it!
ぶわっ
B-BUT... THAT... THAT WAS...
Violence is naughty, naughty!
YOU'RE WRONG, SHRIMP!!

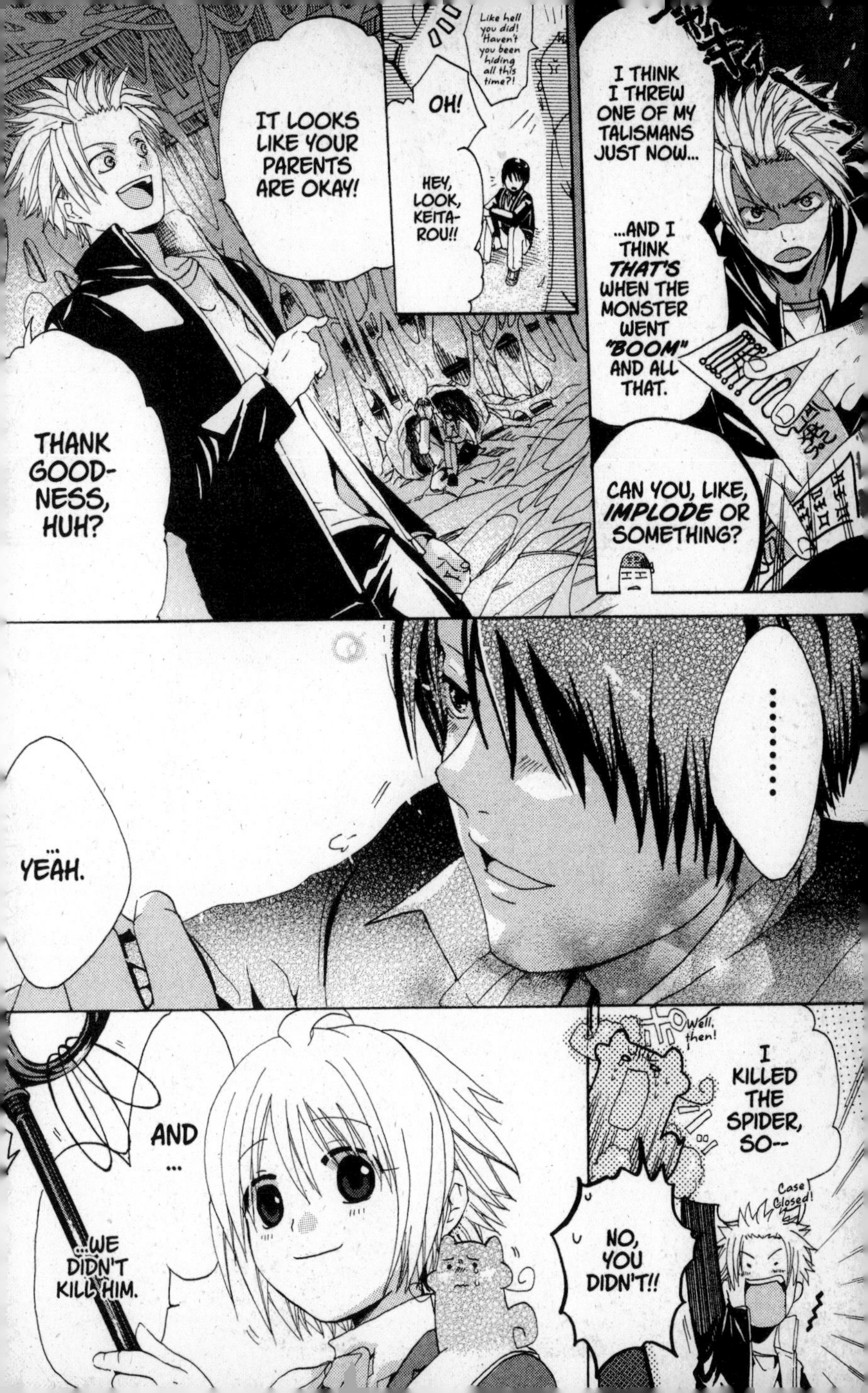
I THINK I THREW ONE OF MY TALISMANS JUST NOW...
...AND I THINK *THAT'S* WHEN THE MONSTER WENT *"BOOM"* AND ALL THAT.
CAN YOU, LIKE, *IMPLODE* OR SOMETHING?
Like hell you did! Haven't you been hiding all this time?!
OH!
HEY, LOOK, KEITA-ROU!!
IT LOOKS LIKE YOUR PARENTS ARE OKAY!
THANK GOOD-NESS, HUH?
......
...YEAH.
Well, then!
I KILLED THE SPIDER, SO--
Case Closed!
NO, YOU DIDN'T!!
AND ...
...WE DIDN'T KILL HIM.

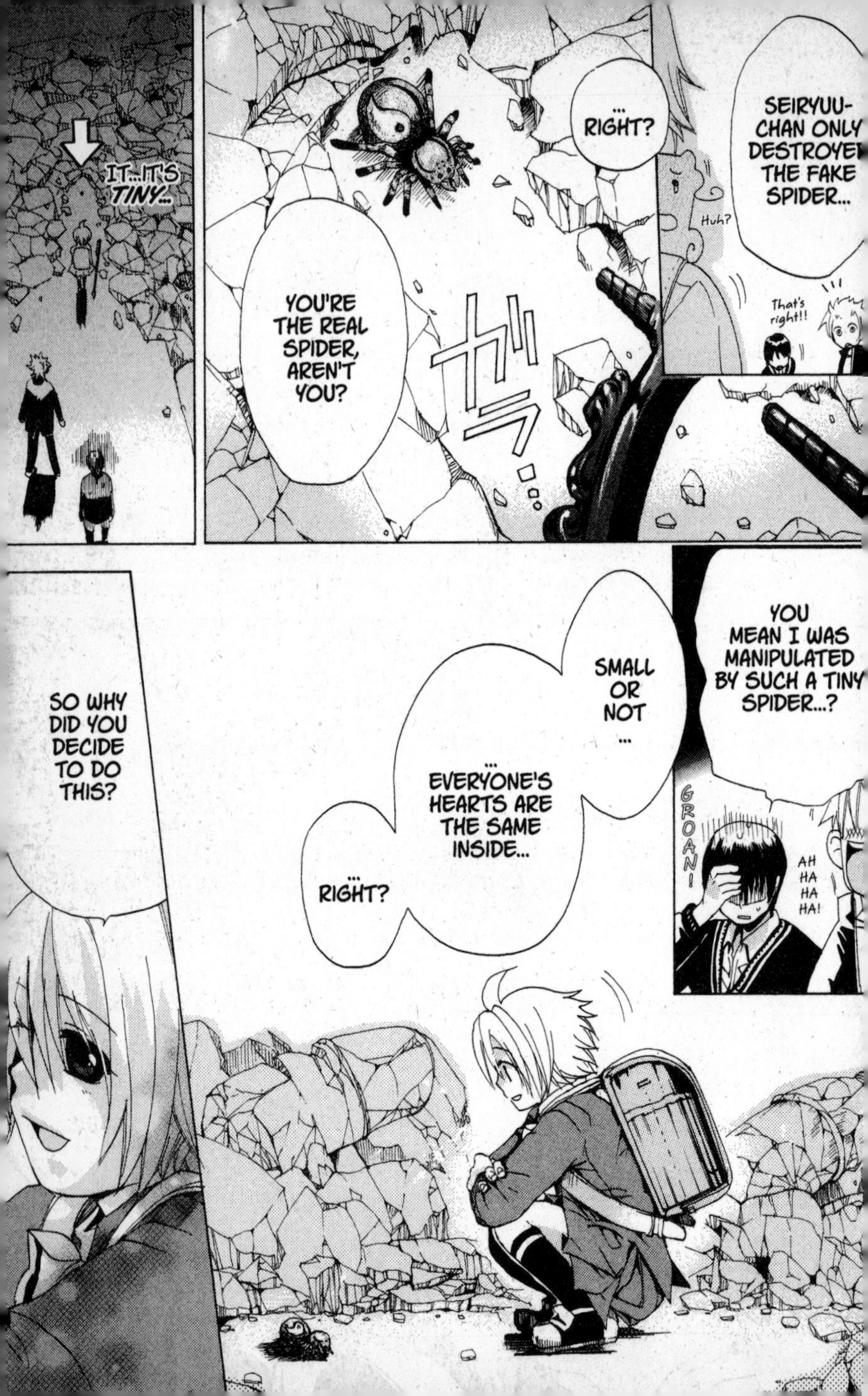
SEIRYUU-CHAN ONLY DESTROYED THE FAKE SPIDER...
Huh?
That's right!!
... RIGHT?
YOU'RE THE REAL SPIDER, AREN'T YOU?
ガラ
IT...IT'S TINY...
YOU MEAN I WAS MANIPULATED BY SUCH A TINY SPIDER...?
GROAN!
AH HA HA HA!
SMALL OR NOT ...
... EVERYONE'S HEARTS ARE THE SAME INSIDE...
... RIGHT?
SO WHY DID YOU DECIDE TO DO THIS?

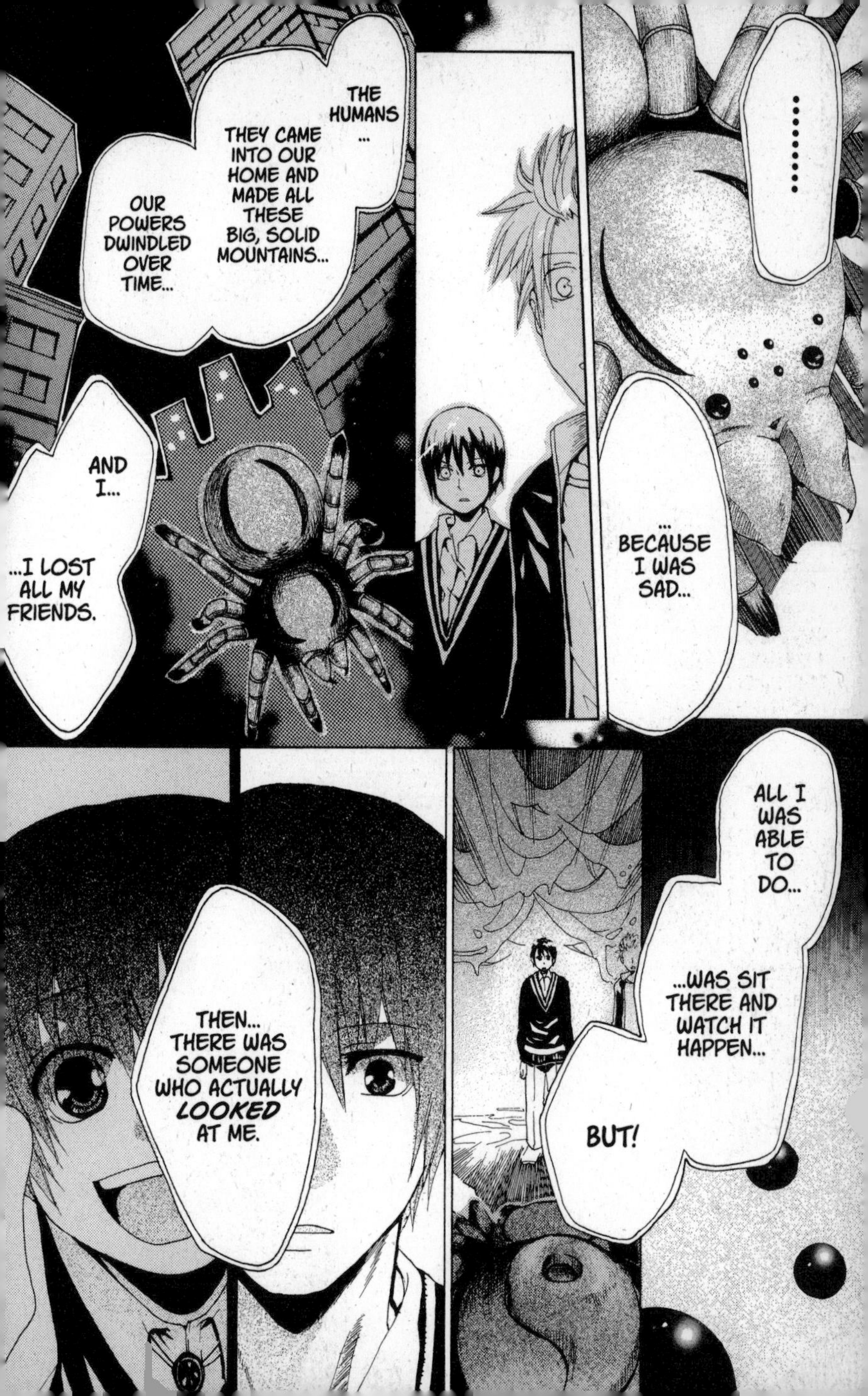
......
...BECAUSE I WAS SAD...
THE HUMANS...
THEY CAME INTO OUR HOME AND MADE ALL THESE BIG, SOLID MOUNTAINS...
OUR POWERS DWINDLED OVER TIME...
AND I...
...I LOST ALL MY FRIENDS.
ALL I WAS ABLE TO DO...
...WAS SIT THERE AND WATCH IT HAPPEN...
BUT!
THEN... THERE WAS SOMEONE WHO ACTUALLY *LOOKED* AT ME.

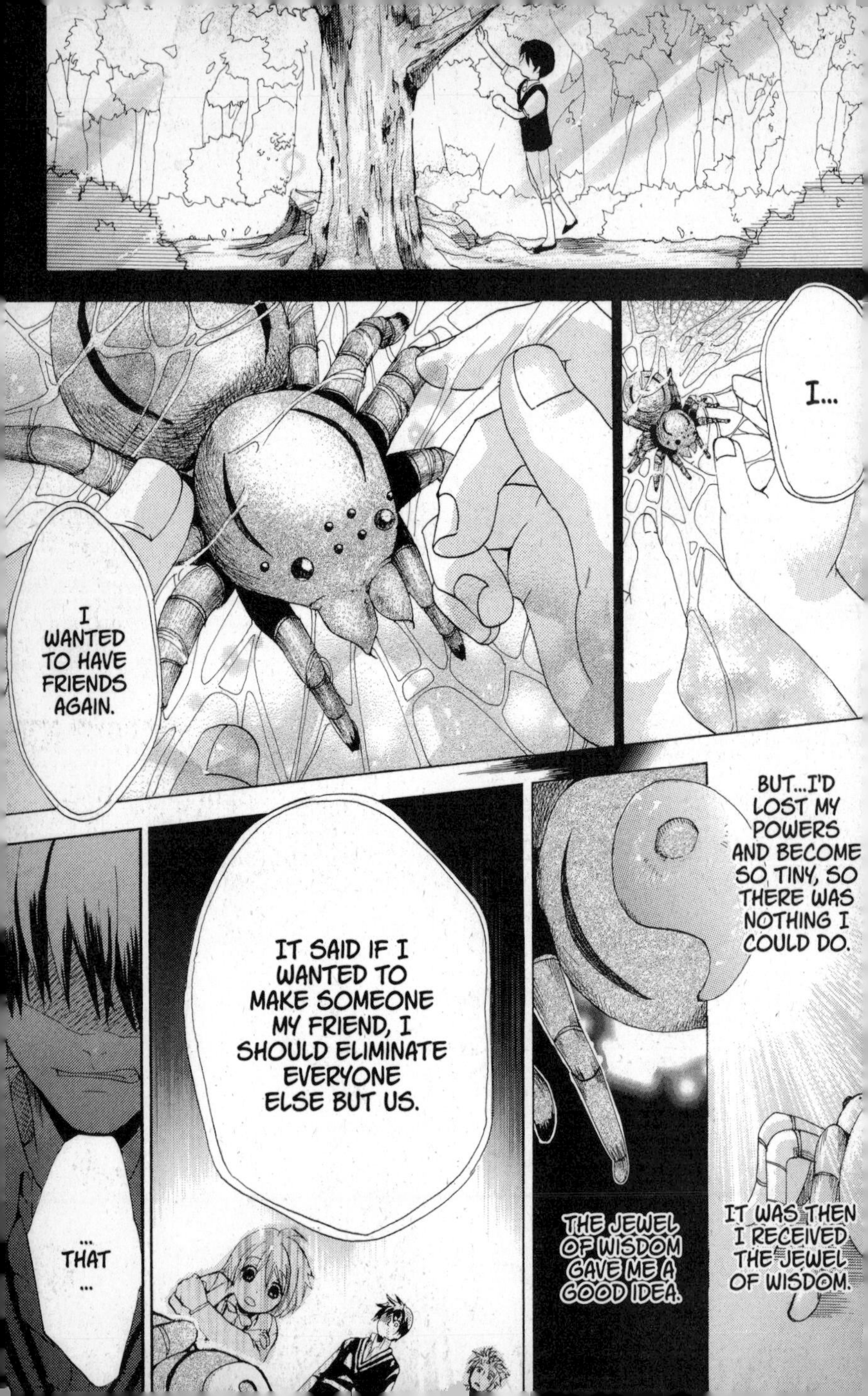
I...
I WANTED TO HAVE FRIENDS AGAIN.
BUT...I'D LOST MY POWERS AND BECOME SO TINY, SO THERE WAS NOTHING I COULD DO.
IT WAS THEN I RECEIVED THE JEWEL OF WISDOM.
THE JEWEL OF WISDOM GAVE ME A GOOD IDEA.
IT SAID IF I WANTED TO MAKE SOMEONE MY FRIEND, I SHOULD ELIMINATE EVERYONE ELSE BUT US.
...THAT...

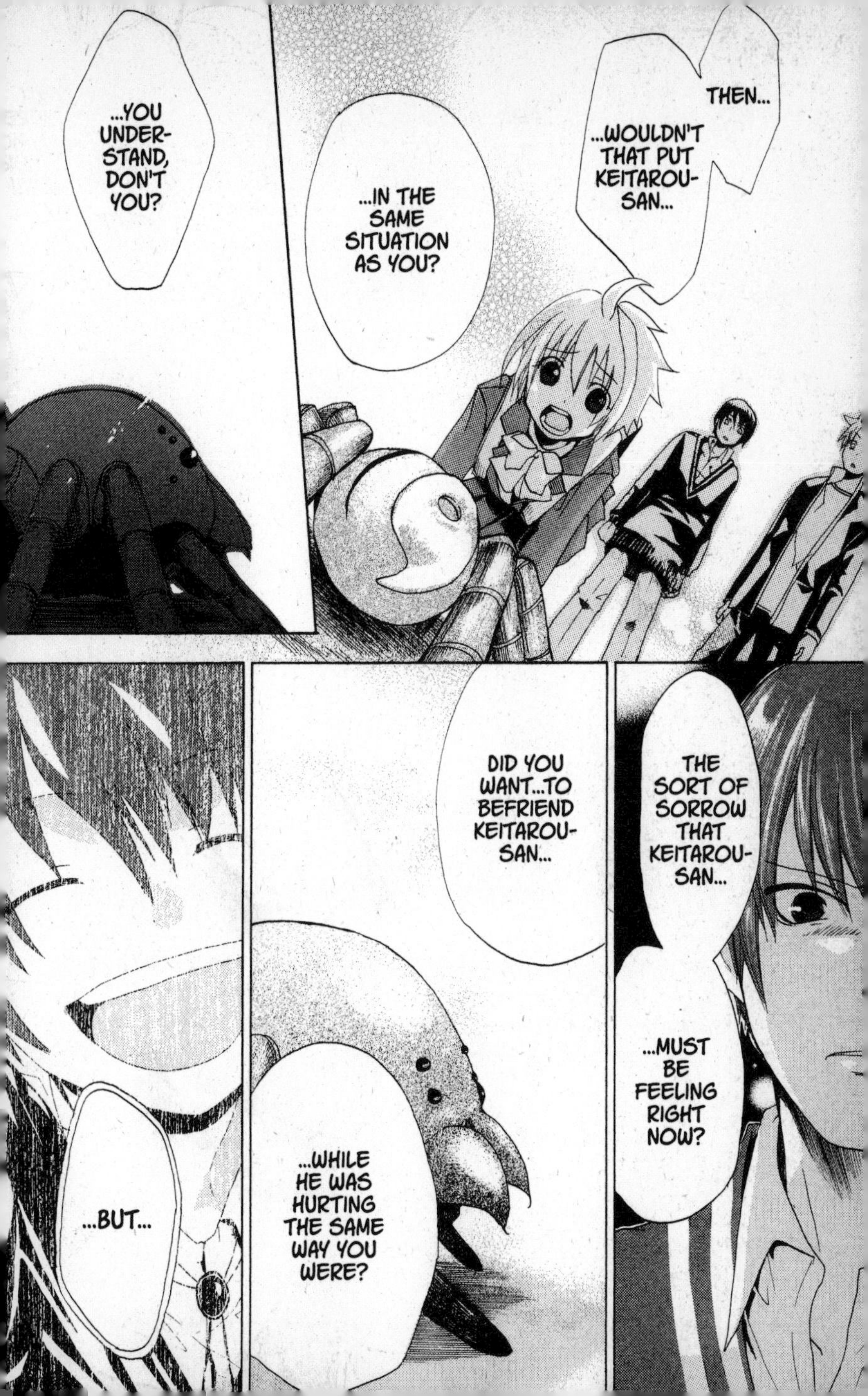
THEN...
...WOULDN'T THAT PUT KEITAROU-SAN...
...IN THE SAME SITUATION AS YOU?
...YOU UNDERSTAND, DON'T YOU?
THE SORT OF SORROW THAT KEITAROU-SAN...
...MUST BE FEELING RIGHT NOW?
DID YOU WANT...TO BEFRIEND KEITAROU-SAN...
...WHILE HE WAS HURTING THE SAME WAY YOU WERE?
...BUT...

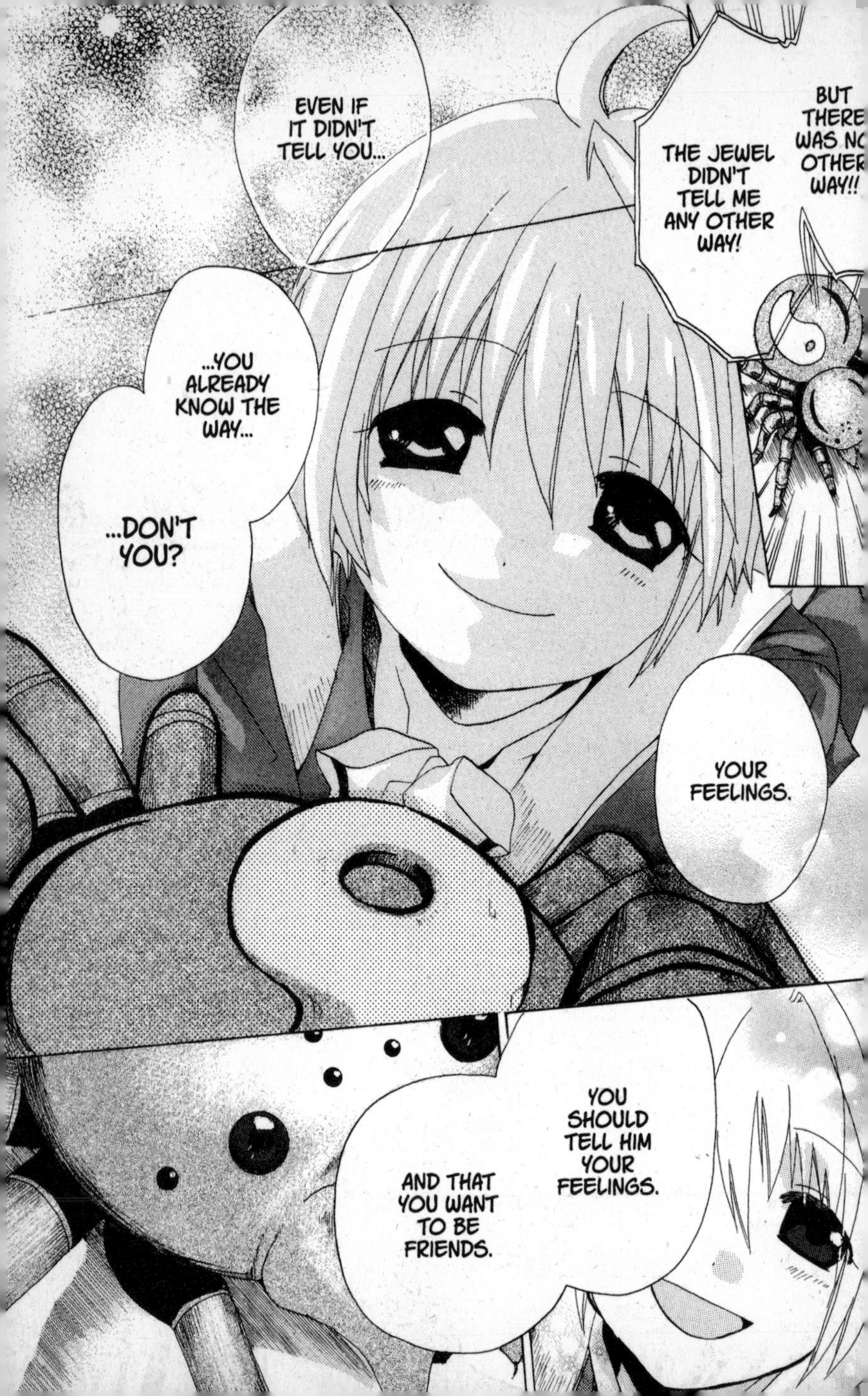
BUT THERE WAS NO OTHER WAY!!
THE JEWEL DIDN'T TELL ME ANY OTHER WAY!
EVEN IF IT DIDN'T TELL YOU...
...YOU ALREADY KNOW THE WAY...
...DON'T YOU?
YOUR FEELINGS.
YOU SHOULD TELL HIM YOUR FEELINGS.
AND THAT YOU WANT TO BE FRIENDS.

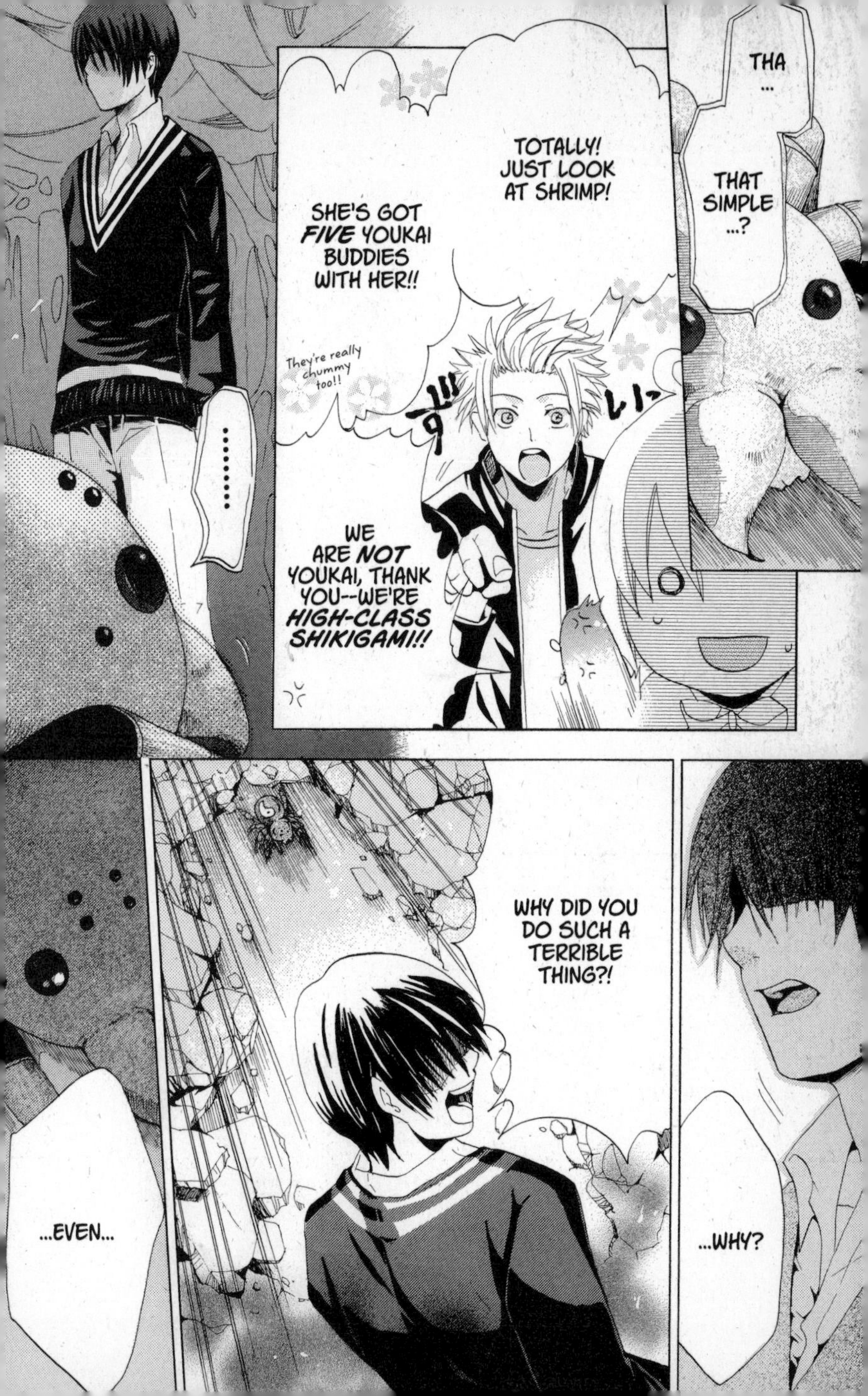

THA...
THAT SIMPLE...?
TOTALLY! JUST LOOK AT SHRIMP!
SHE'S GOT FIVE YOUKAI BUDDIES WITH HER!!
They're really chummy too!!
WE ARE NOT YOUKAI, THANK YOU--WE'RE HIGH-CLASS SHIKIGAMI!!
....
...WHY?
WHY DID YOU DO SUCH A TERRIBLE THING?!
...EVEN...

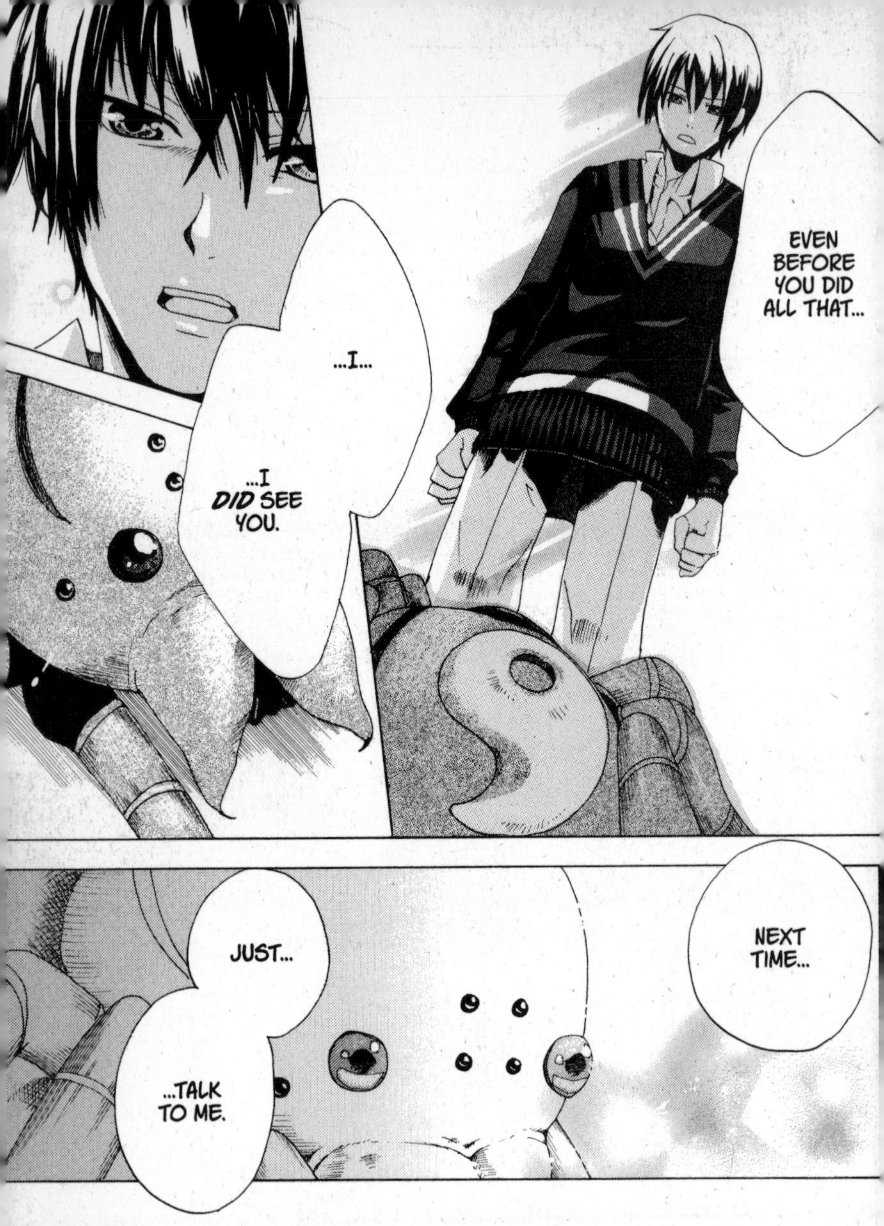
EVEN BEFORE YOU DID ALL THAT...
...I...
...I *DID* SEE YOU.
NEXT TIME...
JUST...
...TALK TO ME.

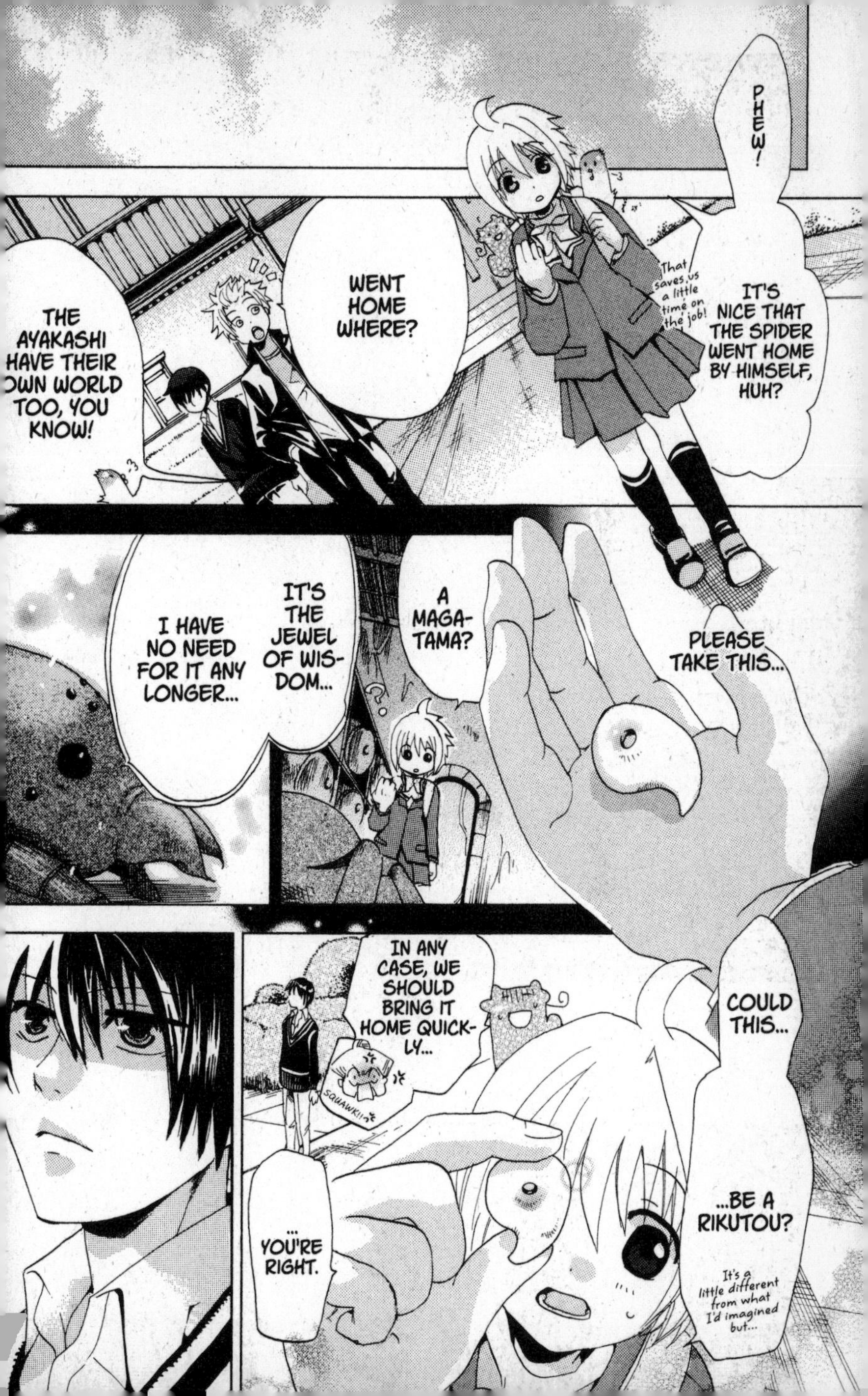
PHEW!
IT'S NICE THAT THE SPIDER WENT HOME BY HIMSELF, HUH?
That saves us a little time on the job!
WENT HOME WHERE?
THE AYAKASHI HAVE THEIR OWN WORLD TOO, YOU KNOW!
PLEASE TAKE THIS...
A MAGA-TAMA?
IT'S THE JEWEL OF WIS-DOM...
I HAVE NO NEED FOR IT ANY LONGER...
COULD THIS...
...BE A RIKUTOU?
It's a little different from what I'd imagined but...
IN ANY CASE, WE SHOULD BRING IT HOME QUICK-LY...
SQUAWK!!
... YOU'RE RIGHT.

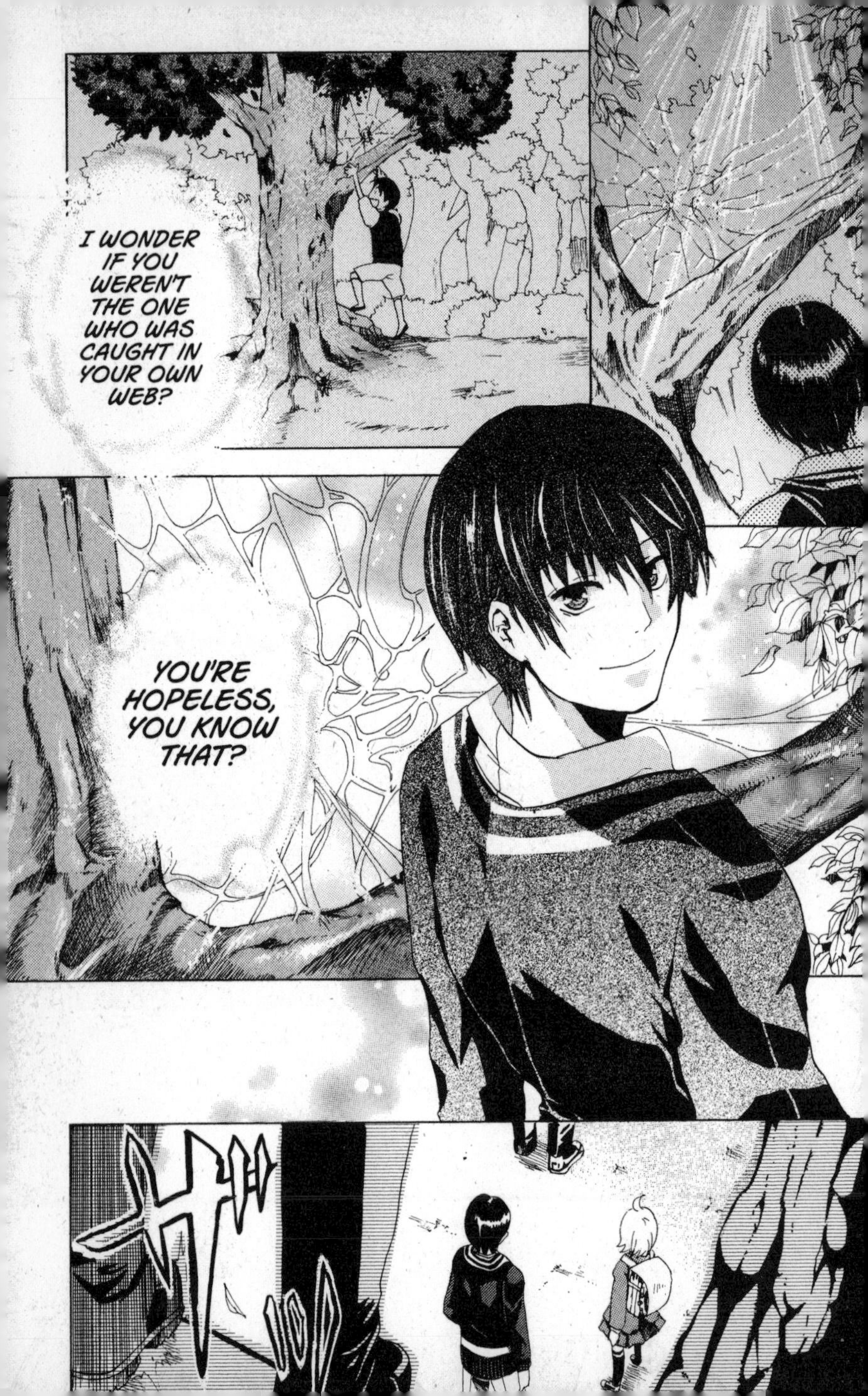
I WONDER IF YOU WEREN'T THE ONE WHO WAS CAUGHT IN YOUR OWN WEB?
YOU'RE HOPELESS, YOU KNOW THAT?

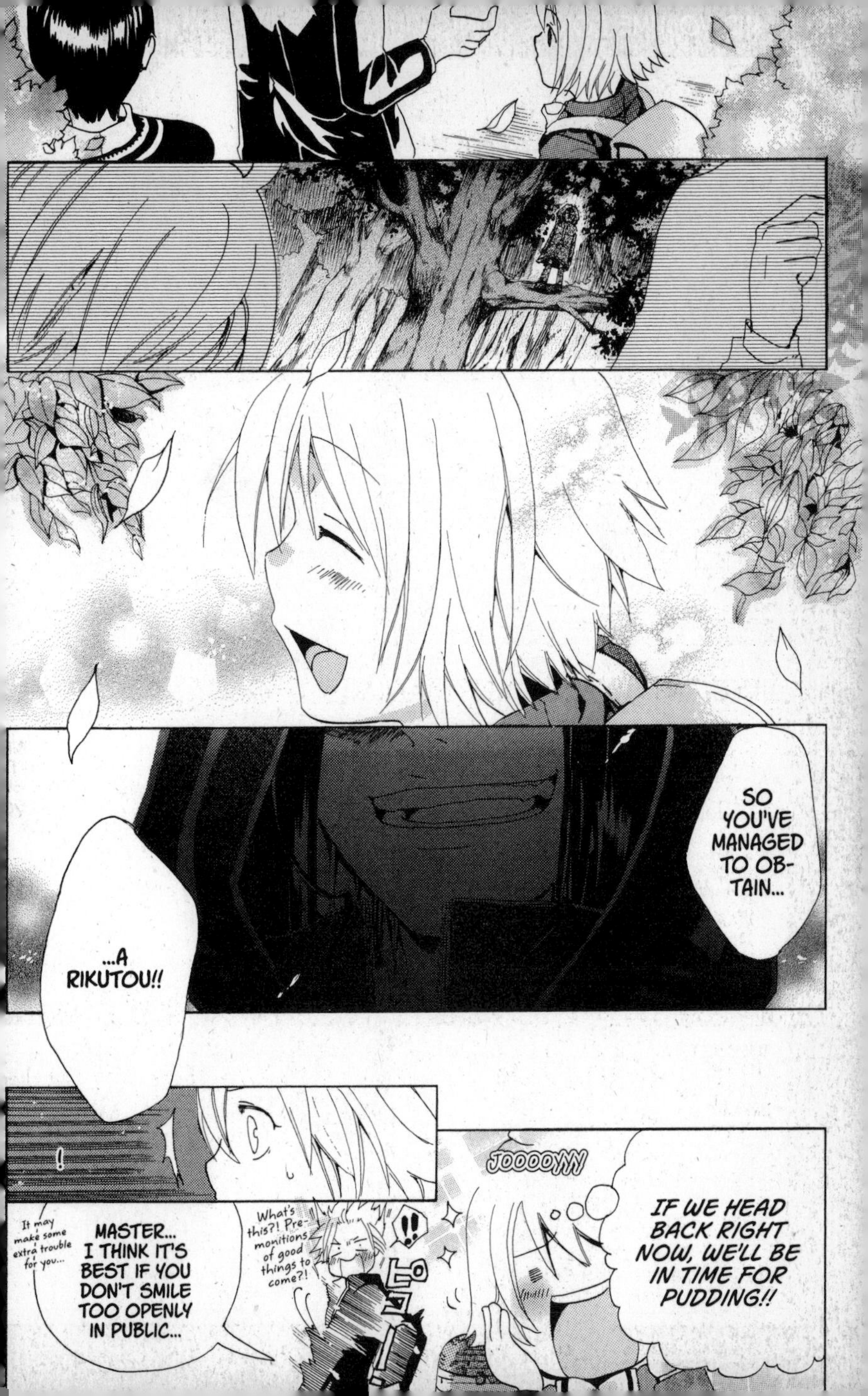
SO YOU'VE MANAGED TO OB-TAIN...
...A RIKUTOU!!
JOOOOYYY
IF WE HEAD BACK RIGHT NOW, WE'LL BE IN TIME FOR PUDDING!!
!
What's this?! Pre-monitions of good things to come?!
!!
MASTER... I THINK IT'S BEST IF YOU DON'T SMILE TOO OPENLY IN PUBLIC...
It may make some extra trouble for you...

MID-VOLUME BONUS COMIC.

A DAY IN THE LIFE OF A SHIKIGAMI (PART 2).

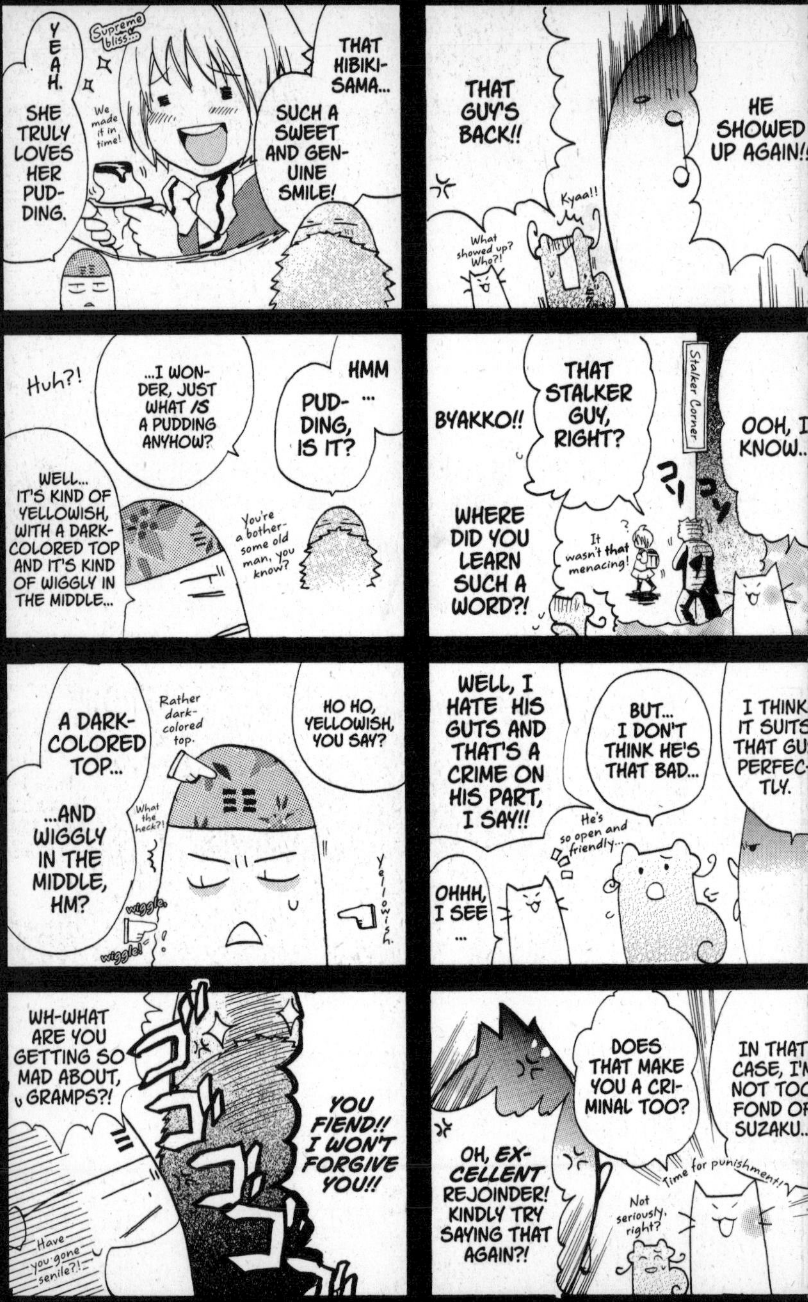
HE SHOWED UP AGAIN!!
THAT GUY'S BACK!!
Kyaa!!
What showed up? Who?!
OOH, I KNOW...
Stalker Corner
THAT STALKER GUY, RIGHT?
BYAKKO!!
It wasn't that menacing!
WHERE DID YOU LEARN SUCH A WORD?!
I THINK IT SUITS THAT GU PERFEC-TLY.
BUT... I DON'T THINK HE'S THAT BAD...
WELL, I HATE HIS GUTS AND THAT'S A CRIME ON HIS PART, I SAY!!
He's so open and friendly...
OHHH, I SEE ...
IN THAT CASE, I'M NOT TOO FOND OF SUZAKU...
DOES THAT MAKE YOU A CRI-MINAL TOO?
Time for punishment!
OH, EX-CELLENT REJOINDER! KINDLY TRY SAYING THAT AGAIN?!
Not seriously, right?
THAT HIBIKI-SAMA... SUCH A SWEET AND GEN-UINE SMILE!
Supreme bliss...
We made it in time!
YEAH. SHE TRULY LOVES HER PUD-DING.
HMM... PUD-DING, IS IT?
...I WON-DER, JUST WHAT IS A PUDDING ANYHOW?
Huh?!
You're a bother-some old man, you know?
WELL... IT'S KIND OF YELLOWISH, WITH A DARK-COLORED TOP AND IT'S KIND OF WIGGLY IN THE MIDDLE...
HO HO, YELLOWISH, YOU SAY?
Rather dark-colored top.
A DARK-COLORED TOP... ...AND WIGGLY IN THE MIDDLE, HM?
What the heck?!
Yellowish.
wiggle. wiggle!
YOU FIEND!! I WON'T FORGIVE YOU!!
WH-WHAT ARE YOU GETTING SO MAD ABOUT, GRAMPS?!
Have you gone senile?!

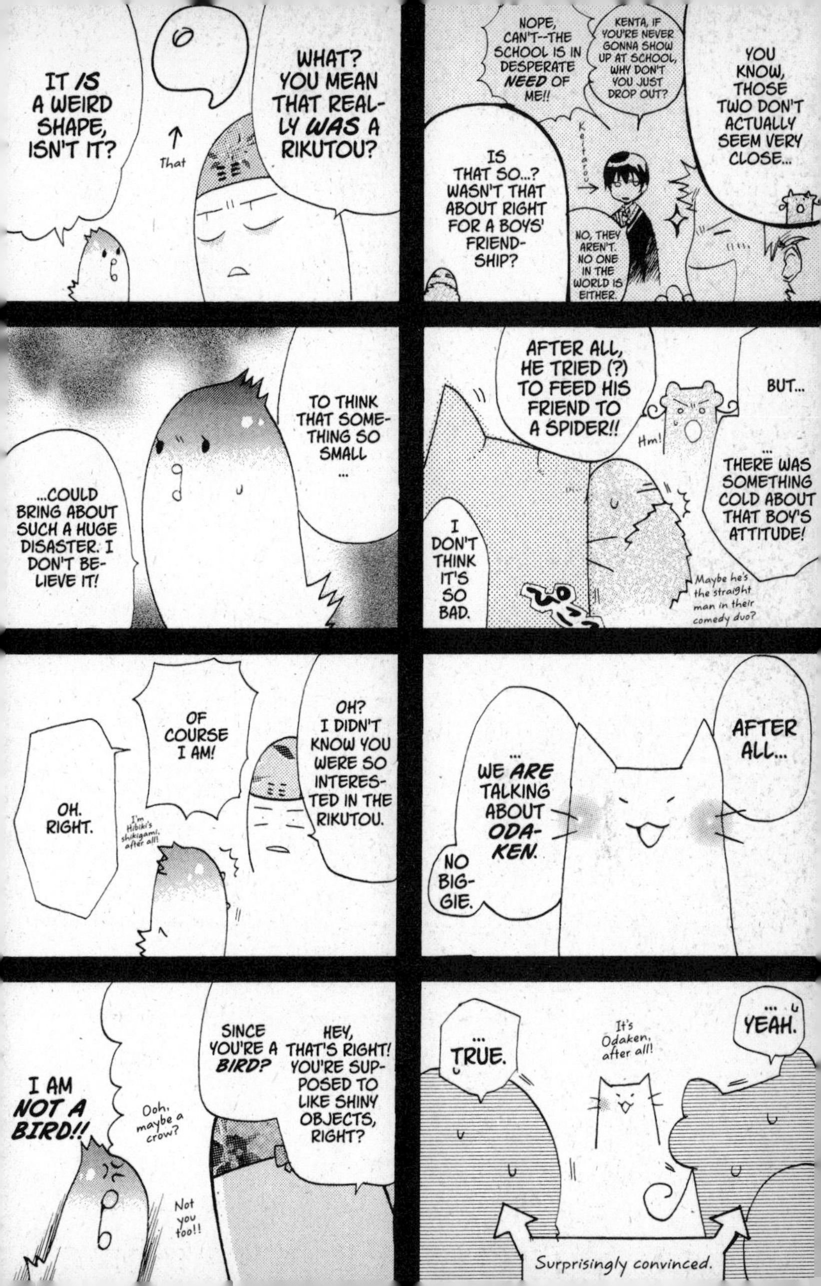
YOU KNOW, THOSE TWO DON'T ACTUALLY SEEM VERY CLOSE...
KENTA, IF YOU'RE NEVER GONNA SHOW UP AT SCHOOL, WHY DON'T YOU JUST DROP OUT?
NOPE, CAN'T--THE SCHOOL IS IN DESPERATE NEED OF ME!!
Keitarou
IS THAT SO...? WASN'T THAT ABOUT RIGHT FOR A BOYS' FRIENDSHIP?
NO, THEY AREN'T. NO ONE IN THE WORLD IS EITHER.
BUT...
AFTER ALL, HE TRIED (?) TO FEED HIS FRIEND TO A SPIDER!!
Hm!
... THERE WAS SOMETHING COLD ABOUT THAT BOY'S ATTITUDE!
Maybe he's the straight man in their comedy duo?
I DON'T THINK IT'S SO BAD.
AFTER ALL...
... WE ARE TALKING ABOUT ODAKEN.
NO BIGGIE.
... YEAH.
It's Odaken, after all!
... TRUE.
Surprisingly convinced.
WHAT? YOU MEAN THAT REALLY WAS A RIKUTOU?
That
IT IS A WEIRD SHAPE, ISN'T IT?
TO THINK THAT SOMETHING SO SMALL ...
...COULD BRING ABOUT SUCH A HUGE DISASTER. I DON'T BELIEVE IT!
OH? I DIDN'T KNOW YOU WERE SO INTERESTED IN THE RIKUTOU.
OF COURSE I AM!
I'm Hibiki's shikigami, after all!
OH. RIGHT.
HEY, THAT'S RIGHT! YOU'RE SUPPOSED TO LIKE SHINY OBJECTS, RIGHT?
SINCE YOU'RE A BIRD?
Ooh, maybe a crow?
I AM NOT A BIRD!!
Not you too!!

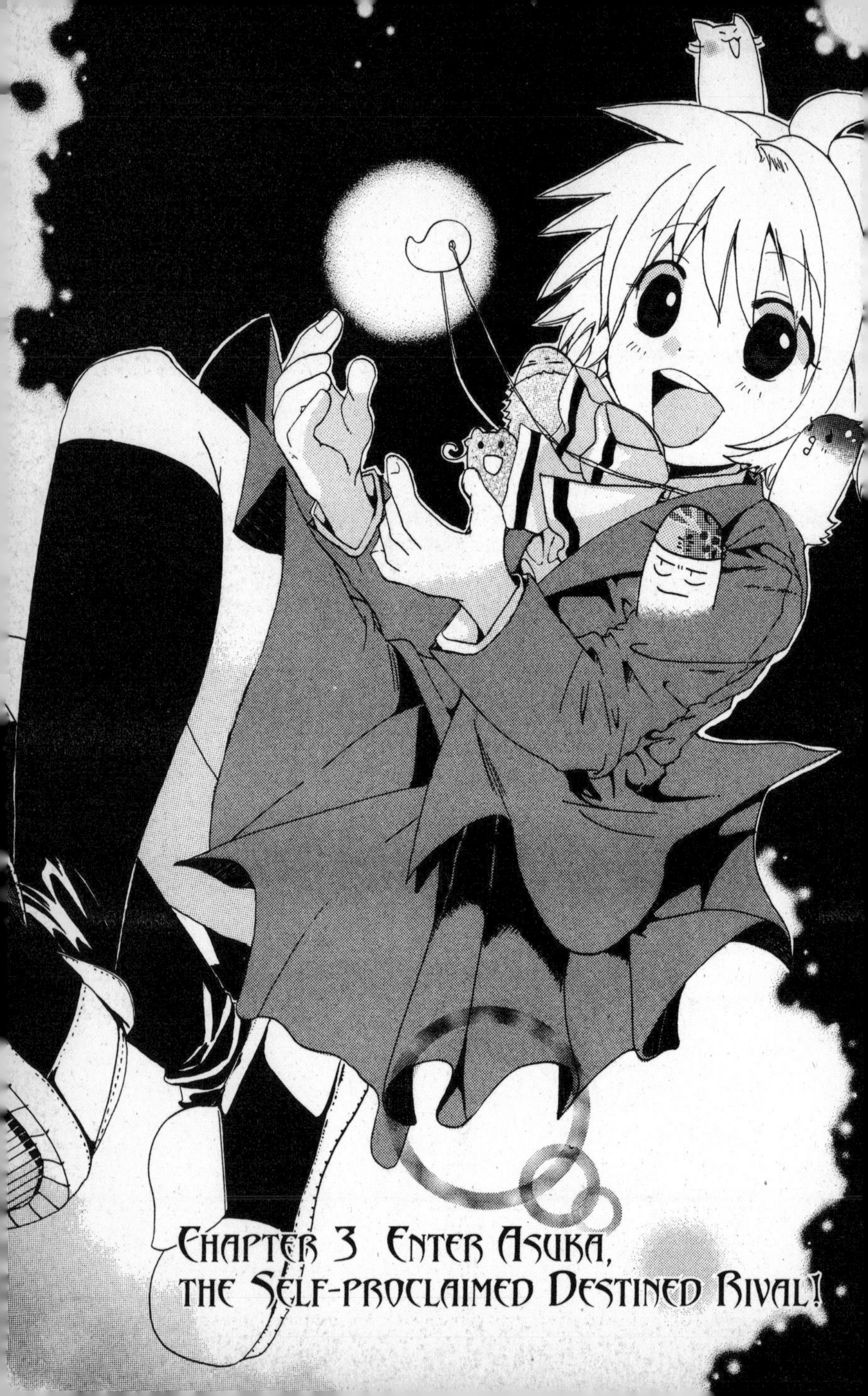

Chapter 3 Enter Asuka, the Self-proclaimed Destined Rival!

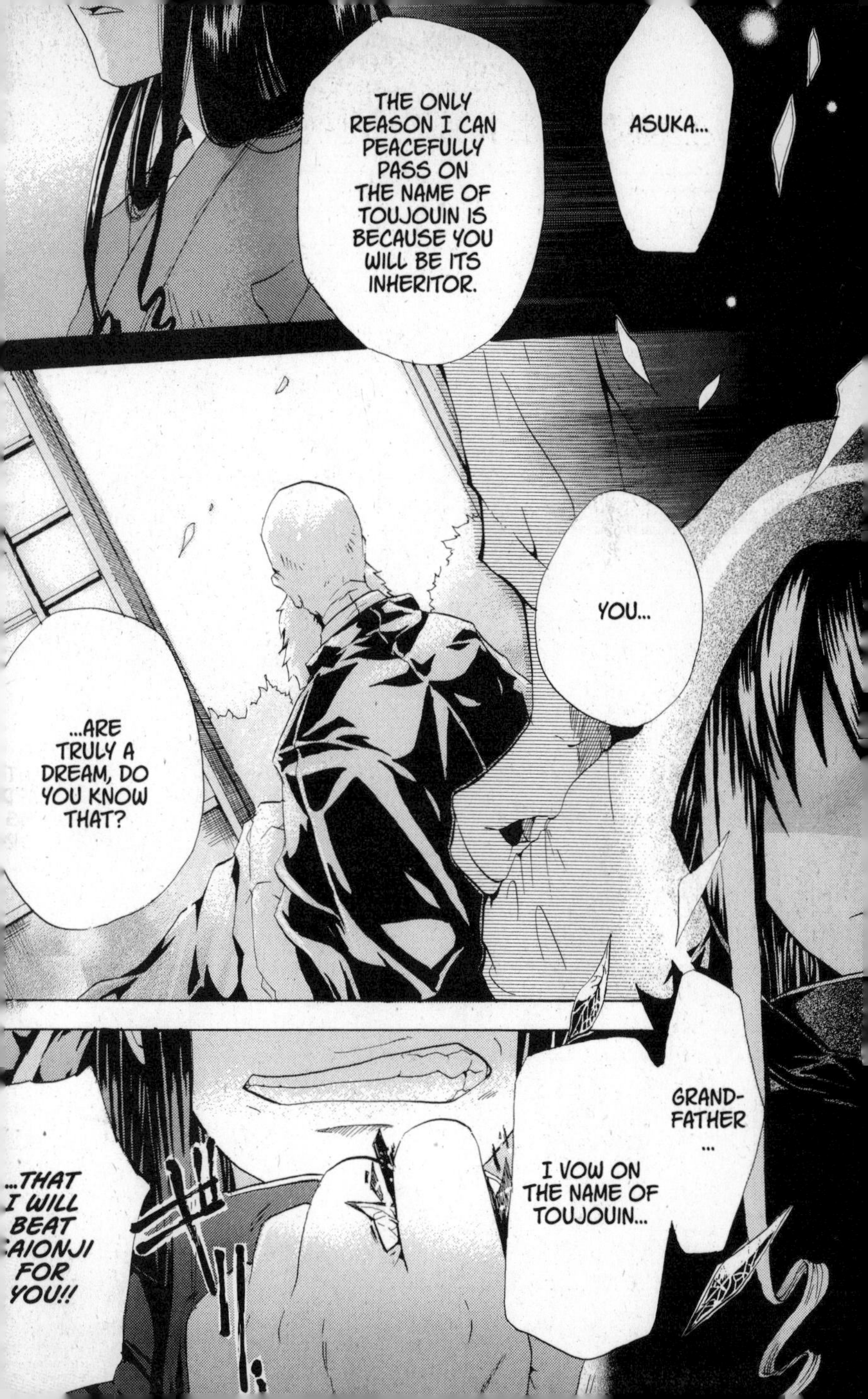
ASUKA...
THE ONLY REASON I CAN PEACEFULLY PASS ON THE NAME OF TOUJOUIN IS BECAUSE YOU WILL BE ITS INHERITOR.
YOU...
...ARE TRULY A DREAM, DO YOU KNOW THAT?
GRAND-FATHER ...
I VOW ON THE NAME OF TOUJOUIN...
...THAT I WILL BEAT AIONJI FOR YOU!!

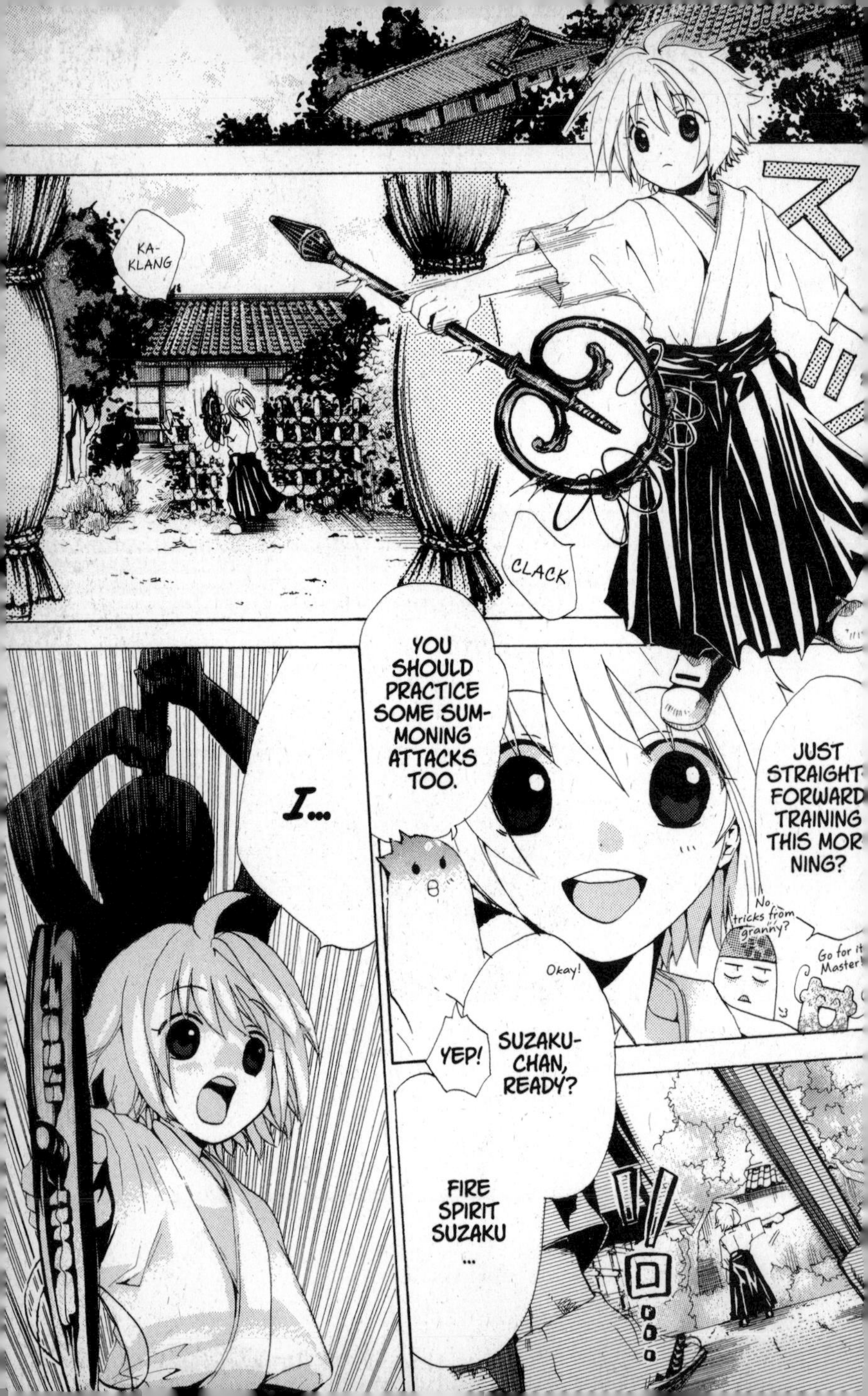
CLACK
KA-KLANG
JUST STRAIGHTFORWARD TRAINING THIS MORNING?
No tricks from granny?
Go for it Master!
YOU SHOULD PRACTICE SOME SUMMONING ATTACKS TOO.
Okay!
SUZAKU-CHAN, READY?
YEP!
FIRE SPIRIT SUZAKU ...
I...

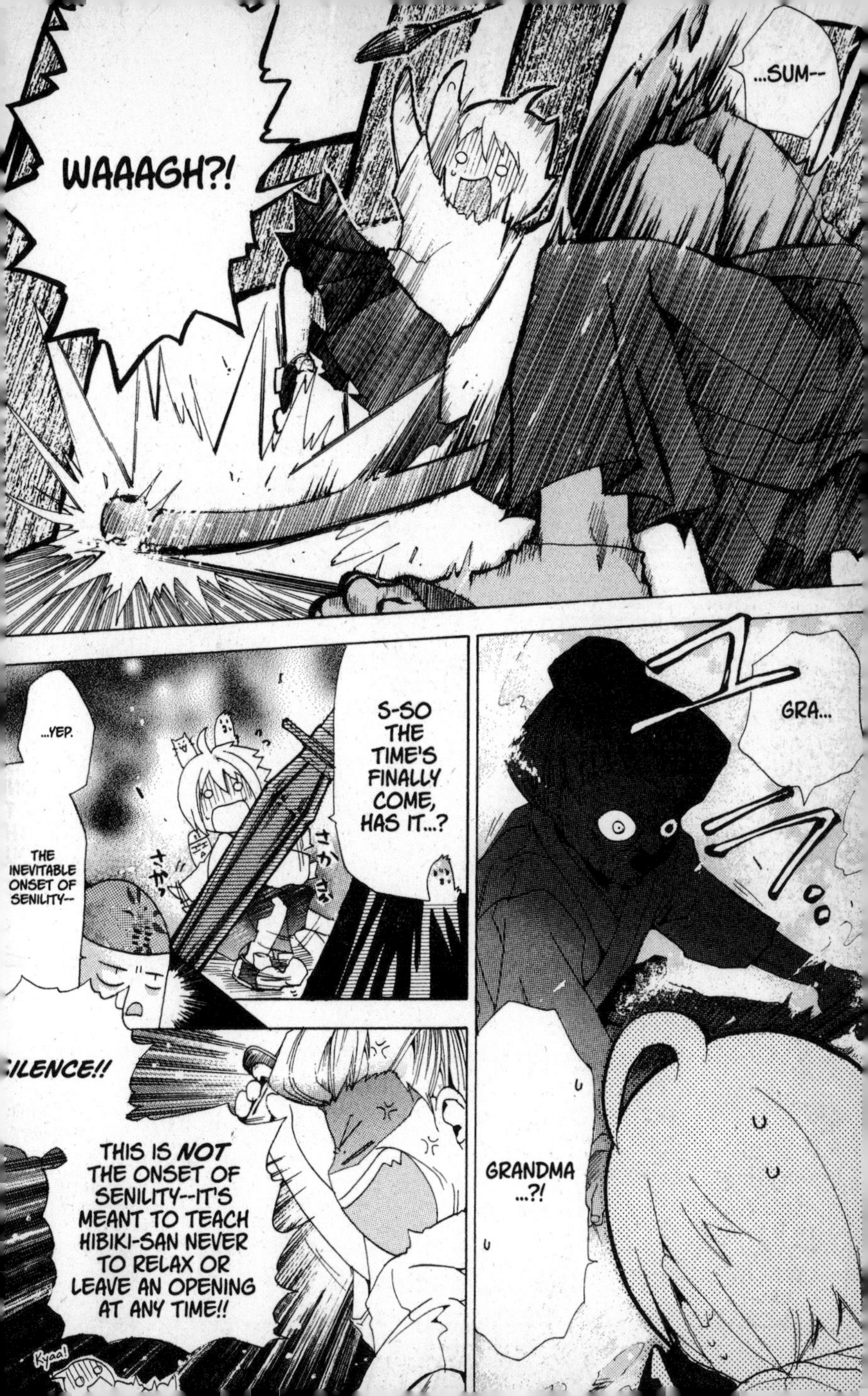
...SUM--
WAAAGH?!
GRA...
GRANDMA ...?!
S-SO THE TIME'S FINALLY COME, HAS IT...?
...YEP.
THE INEVITABLE ONSET OF SENILITY--
SILENCE!!
THIS IS *NOT* THE ONSET OF SENILITY--IT'S MEANT TO TEACH HIBIKI-SAN NEVER TO RELAX OR LEAVE AN OPENING AT ANY TIME!!
Kyaa!

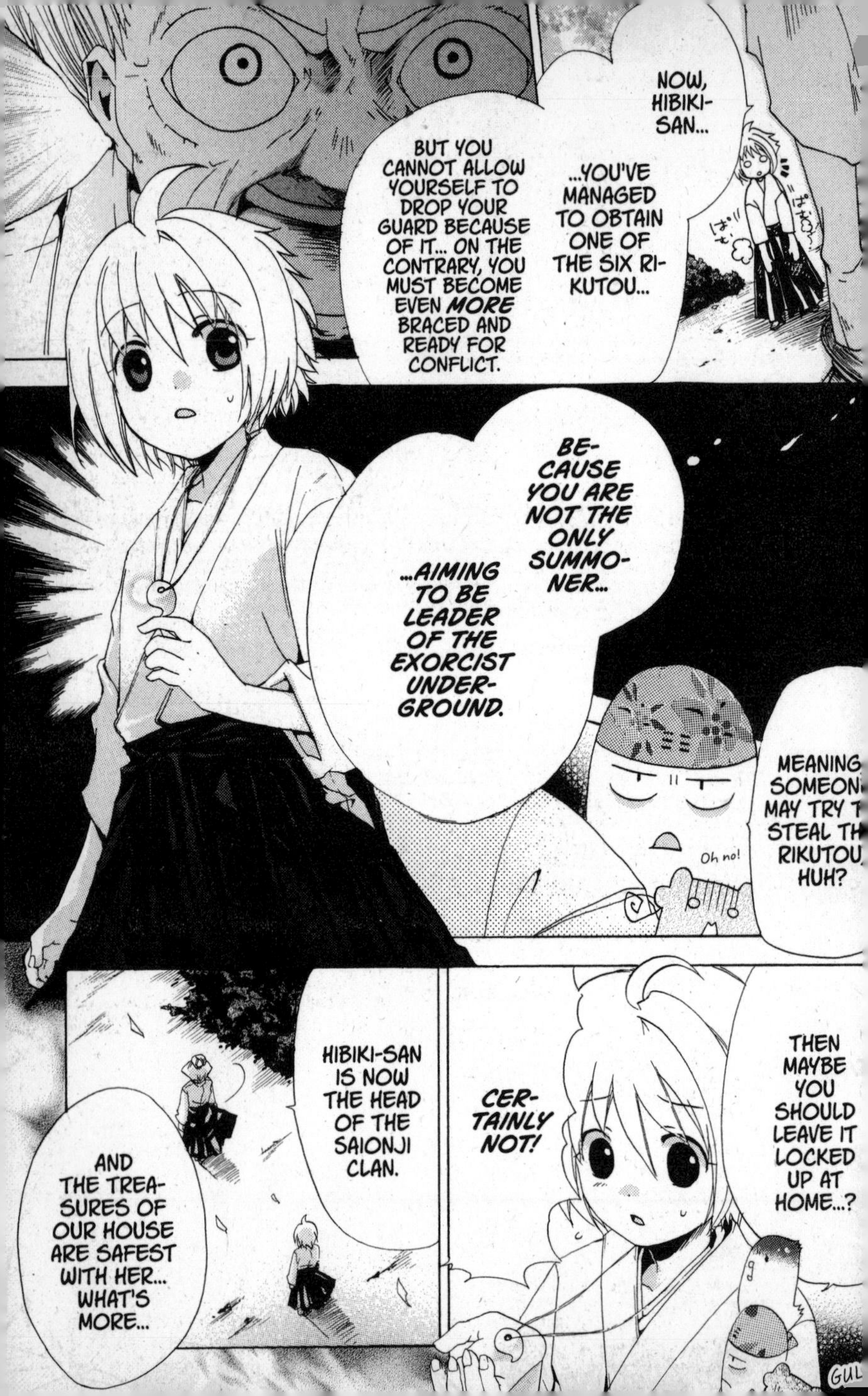
NOW, HIBIKI-SAN...
...YOU'VE MANAGED TO OBTAIN ONE OF THE SIX RI-KUTOU...
BUT YOU CANNOT ALLOW YOURSELF TO DROP YOUR GUARD BECAUSE OF IT... ON THE CONTRARY, YOU MUST BECOME EVEN *MORE* BRACED AND READY FOR CONFLICT.
BE-CAUSE YOU ARE NOT THE ONLY SUMMONO-NER...
...AIMING TO BE LEADER OF THE EXORCIST UNDER-GROUND.
MEANING SOMEON MAY TRY T STEAL TH RIKUTOU, HUH?
Oh no!
THEN MAYBE YOU SHOULD LEAVE IT LOCKED UP AT HOME...?
CER-TAINLY NOT!
HIBIKI-SAN IS NOW THE HEAD OF THE SAIONJI CLAN.
AND THE TREA-SURES OF OUR HOUSE ARE SAFEST WITH HER... WHAT'S MORE...
GUL

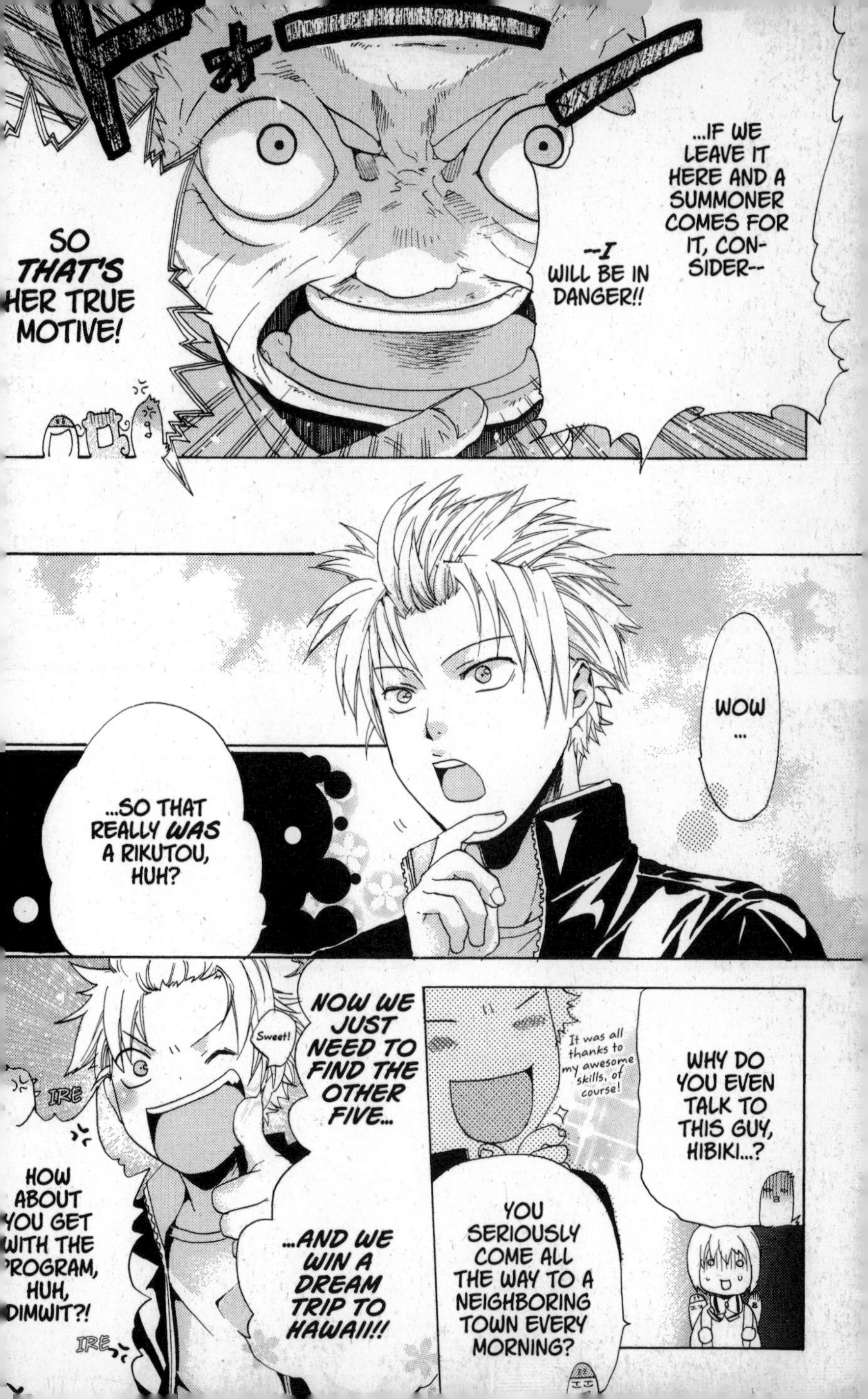
...IF WE LEAVE IT HERE AND A SUMMONER COMES FOR IT, CONSIDER--
--I WILL BE IN DANGER!!
SO THAT'S HER TRUE MOTIVE!
WOW...
...SO THAT REALLY WAS A RIKUTOU, HUH?
WHY DO YOU EVEN TALK TO THIS GUY, HIBIKI...?
It was all thanks to my awesome skills, of course!
YOU SERIOUSLY COME ALL THE WAY TO A NEIGHBORING TOWN EVERY MORNING?
NOW WE JUST NEED TO FIND THE OTHER FIVE...
Sweet!
...AND WE WIN A DREAM TRIP TO HAWAII!!
IRE
HOW ABOUT YOU GET WITH THE PROGRAM, HUH, DIMWIT?!
IRE

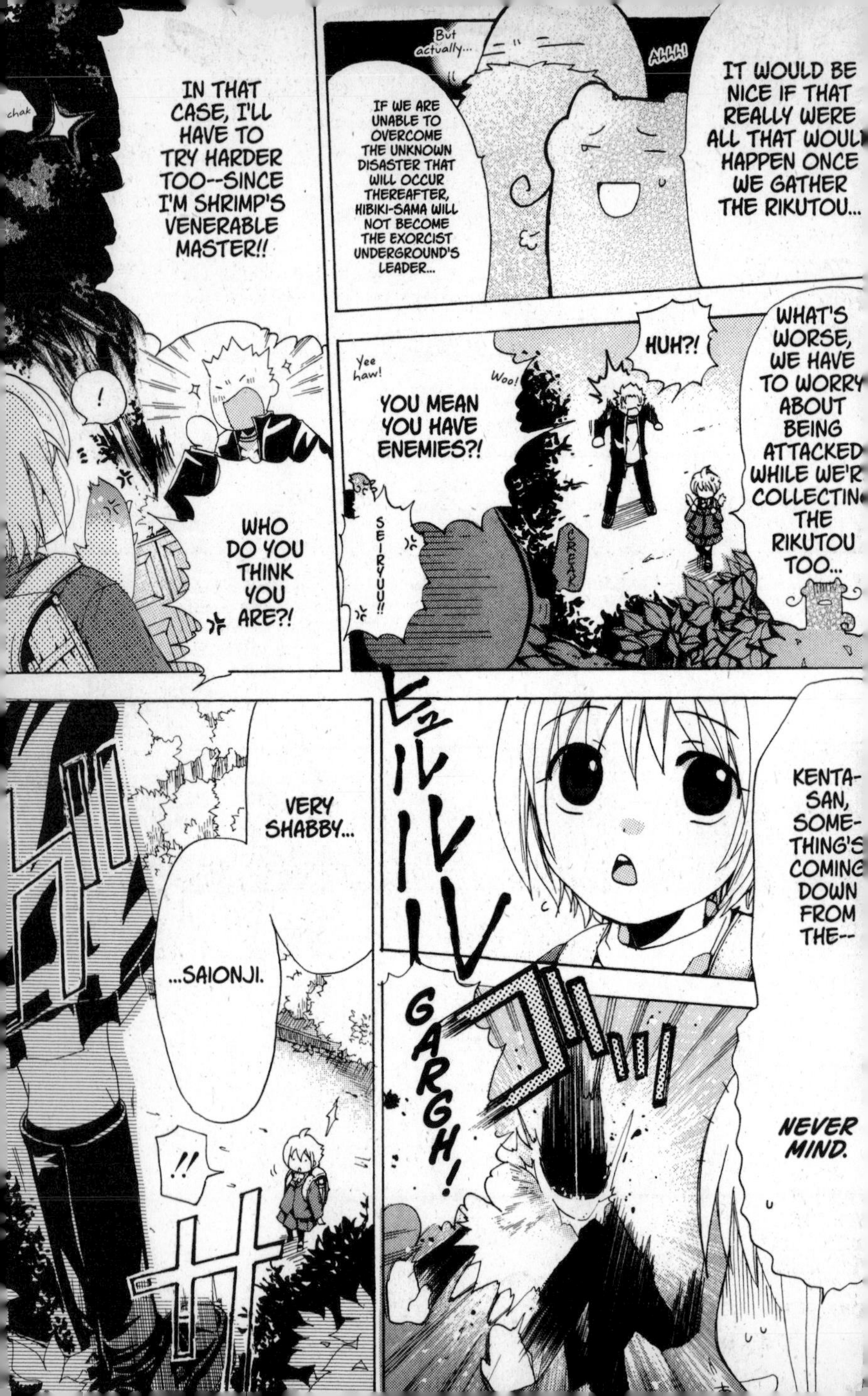
IT WOULD BE NICE IF THAT REALLY WERE ALL THAT WOULD HAPPEN ONCE WE GATHER THE RIKUTOU...
Ahhh!
But actually...
IF WE ARE UNABLE TO OVERCOME THE UNKNOWN DISASTER THAT WILL OCCUR THEREAFTER, HIBIKI-SAMA WILL NOT BECOME THE EXORCIST UNDERGROUND'S LEADER...
WHAT'S WORSE, WE HAVE TO WORRY ABOUT BEING ATTACKED WHILE WE'RE COLLECTING THE RIKUTOU TOO...
HUH?!
Woo!
Yee haw!
YOU MEAN YOU HAVE ENEMIES?!
CREAK
SEIRYUU!!
chak
IN THAT CASE, I'LL HAVE TO TRY HARDER TOO--SINCE I'M SHRIMP'S VENERABLE MASTER!!
!
WHO DO YOU THINK YOU ARE?!
KENTA-SAN, SOMETHING'S COMING DOWN FROM THE--
ヒュルルル
GARGH!
NEVER MIND.
VERY SHABBY...
...SAIONJI.
!!

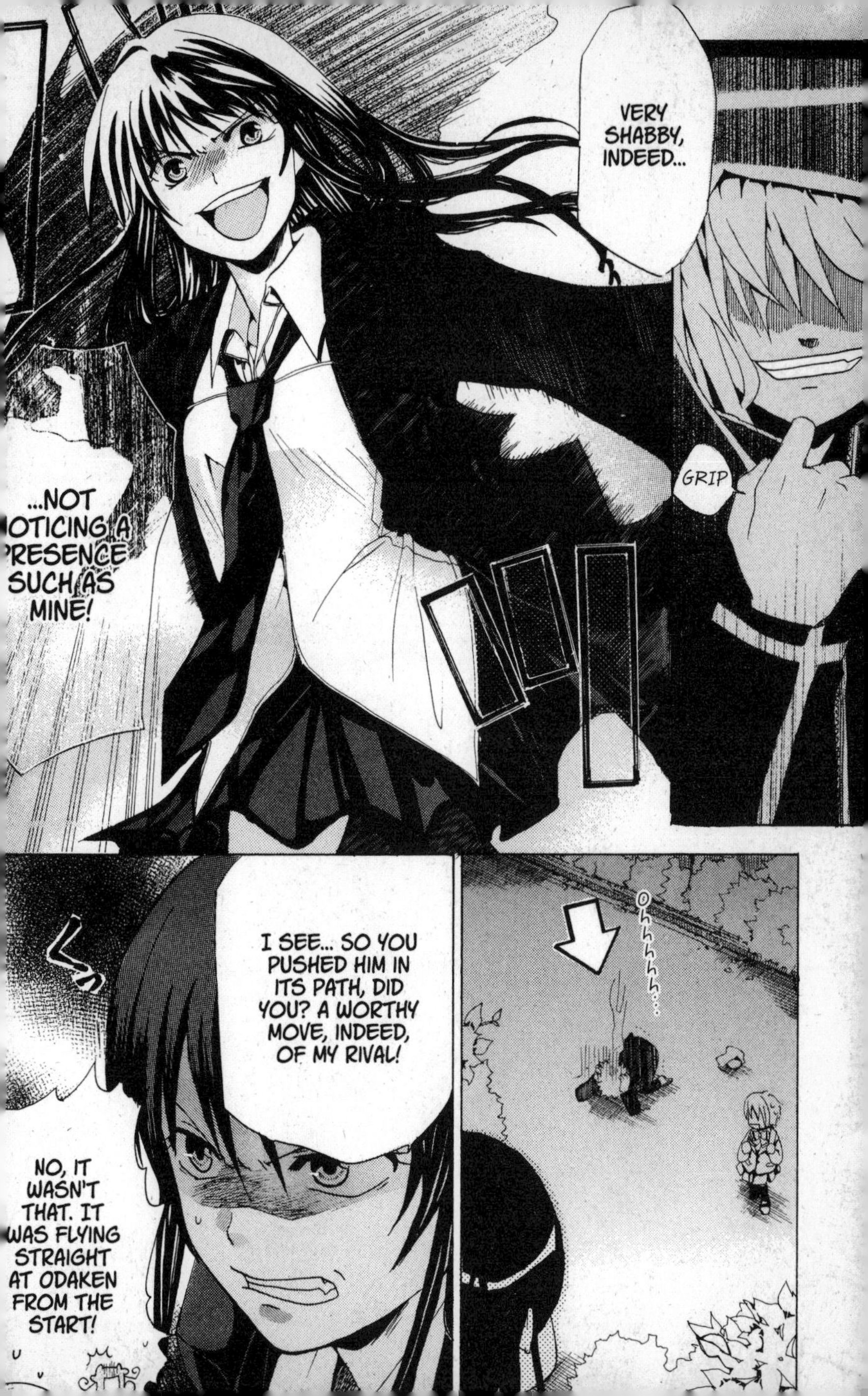
VERY SHABBY, INDEED...
GRIP
...NOT OTICING A RESENCE SUCH AS MINE!
Ohhhhh...
I SEE... SO YOU PUSHED HIM IN ITS PATH, DID YOU? A WORTHY MOVE, INDEED, OF MY RIVAL!
NO, IT WASN'T THAT. IT WAS FLYING STRAIGHT AT ODAKEN FROM THE START!

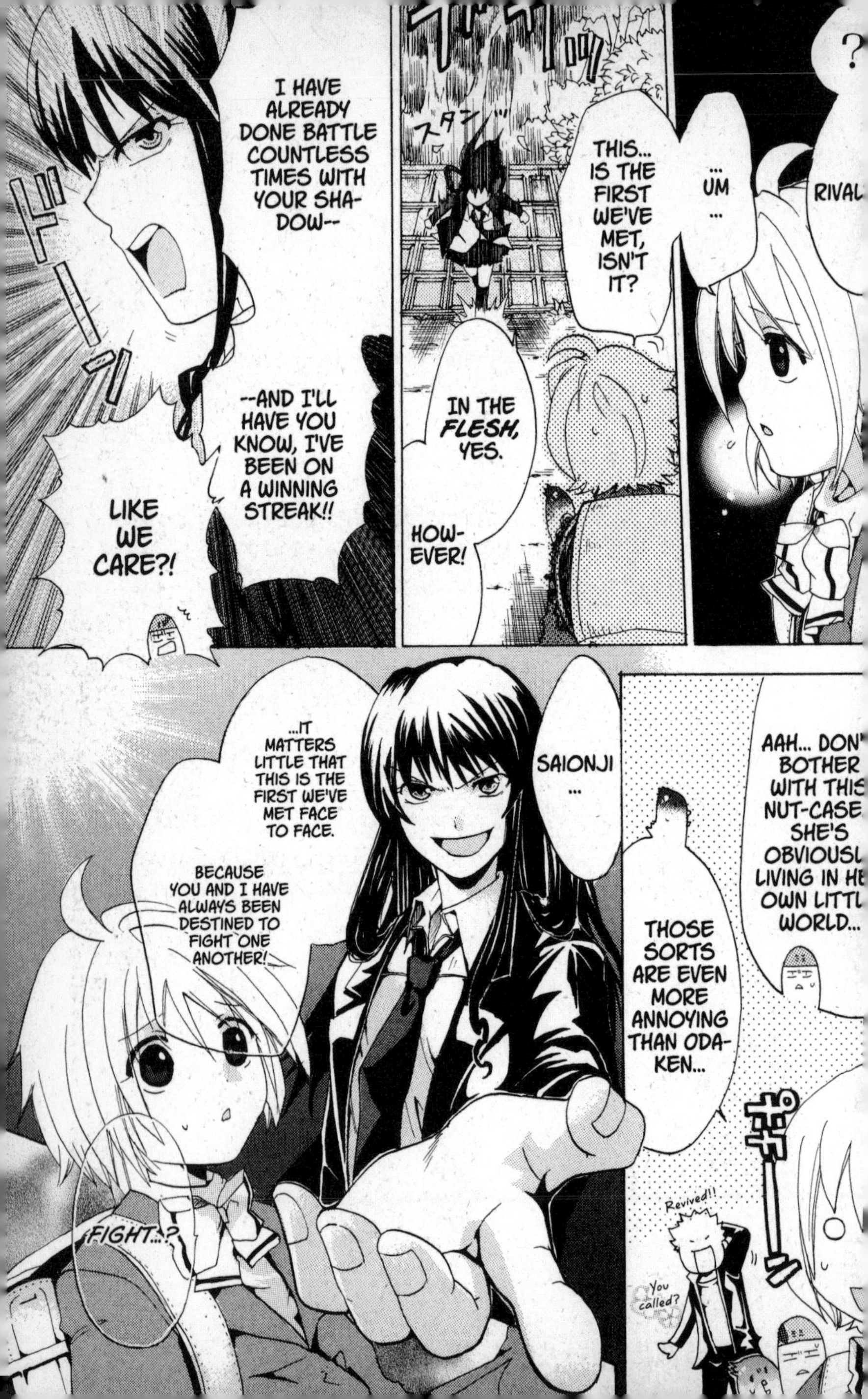
?
RIVAL
... UM ...
THIS... IS THE FIRST WE'VE MET, ISN'T IT?
IN THE *FLESH,* YES.
HOW-EVER!
I HAVE ALREADY DONE BATTLE COUNTLESS TIMES WITH YOUR SHA-DOW--
--AND I'LL HAVE YOU KNOW, I'VE BEEN ON A WINNING STREAK!!
LIKE WE CARE?!
AAH... DON'T BOTHER WITH THIS NUT-CASE SHE'S OBVIOUSL LIVING IN HE OWN LITTL WORLD...
THOSE SORTS ARE EVEN MORE ANNOYING THAN ODA-KEN...
Revived!!
You called?
SAIONJI ...
...IT MATTERS LITTLE THAT THIS IS THE FIRST WE'VE MET FACE TO FACE.
BECAUSE YOU AND I HAVE ALWAYS BEEN DESTINED TO FIGHT ONE ANOTHER!
FIGHT...?

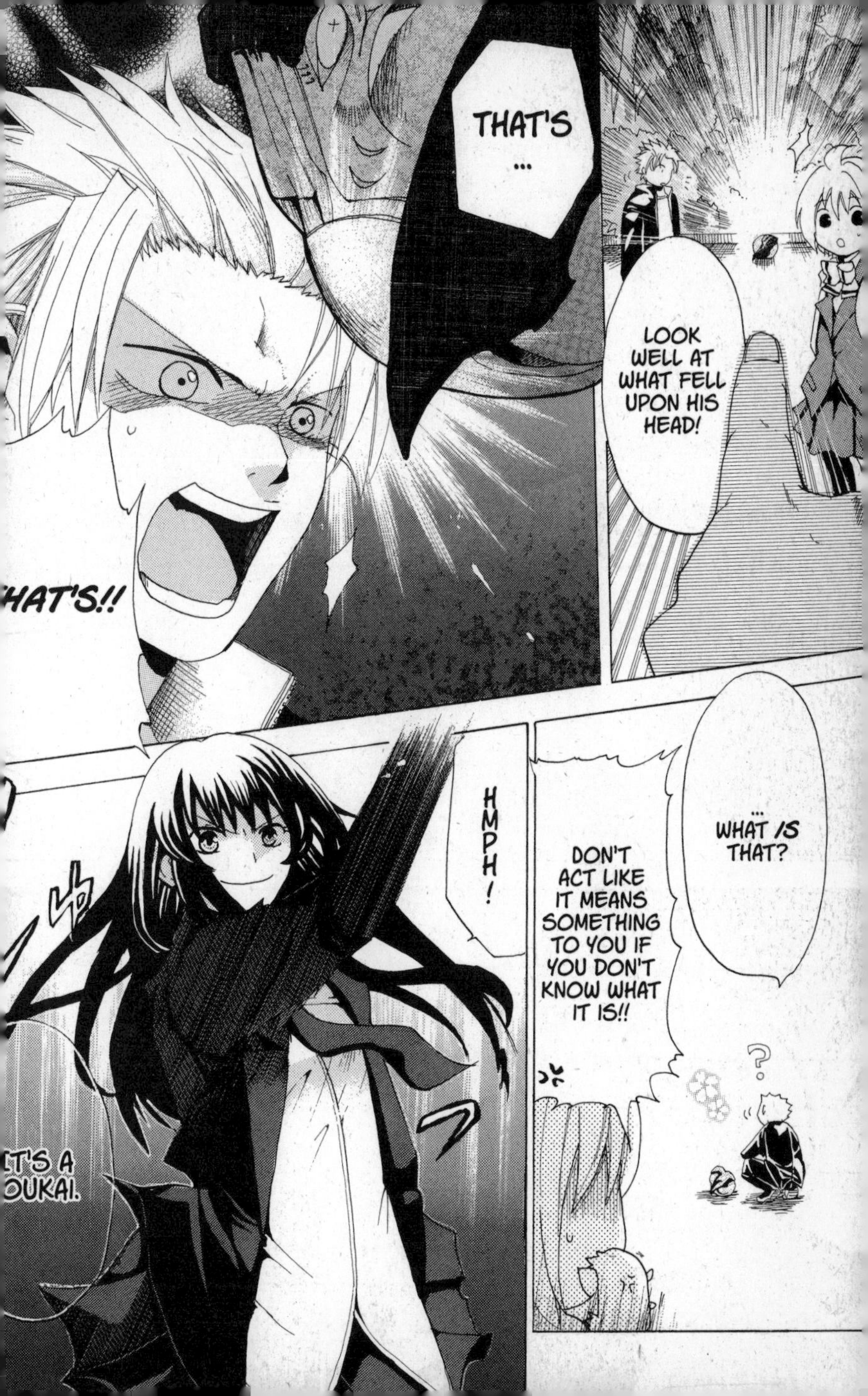

LOOK WELL AT WHAT FELL UPON HIS HEAD!
THAT'S ...
HAT'S!!
... WHAT IS THAT?
DON'T ACT LIKE IT MEANS SOMETHING TO YOU IF YOU DON'T KNOW WHAT IT IS!!
HMPH!
T'S A
OUKAI.

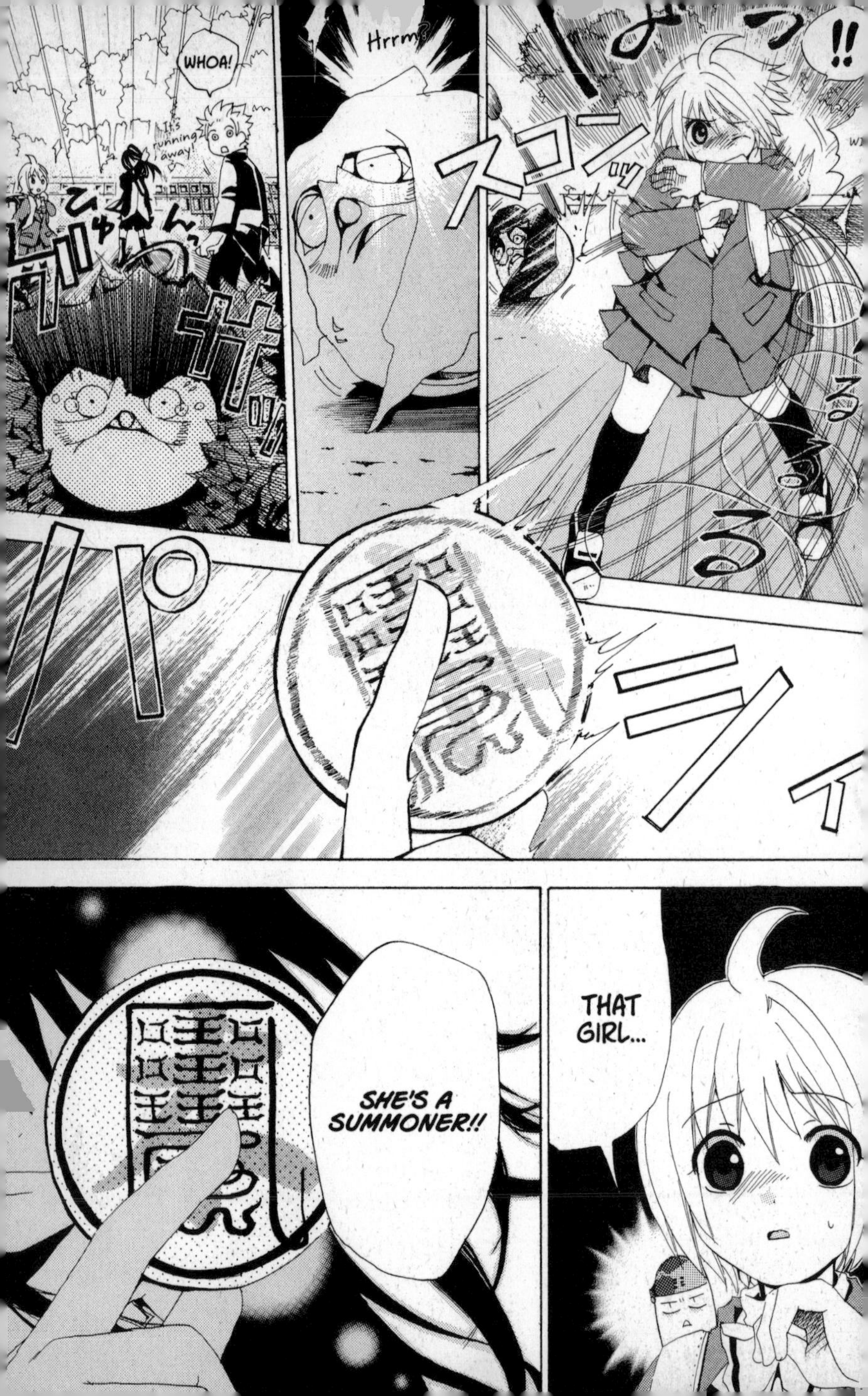
よっ!!
スコーンッ
Hrrm?
WHOA!
It's running away!
ひゅんっ
パシィ
THAT GIRL...
SHE'S A SUMMONER!!

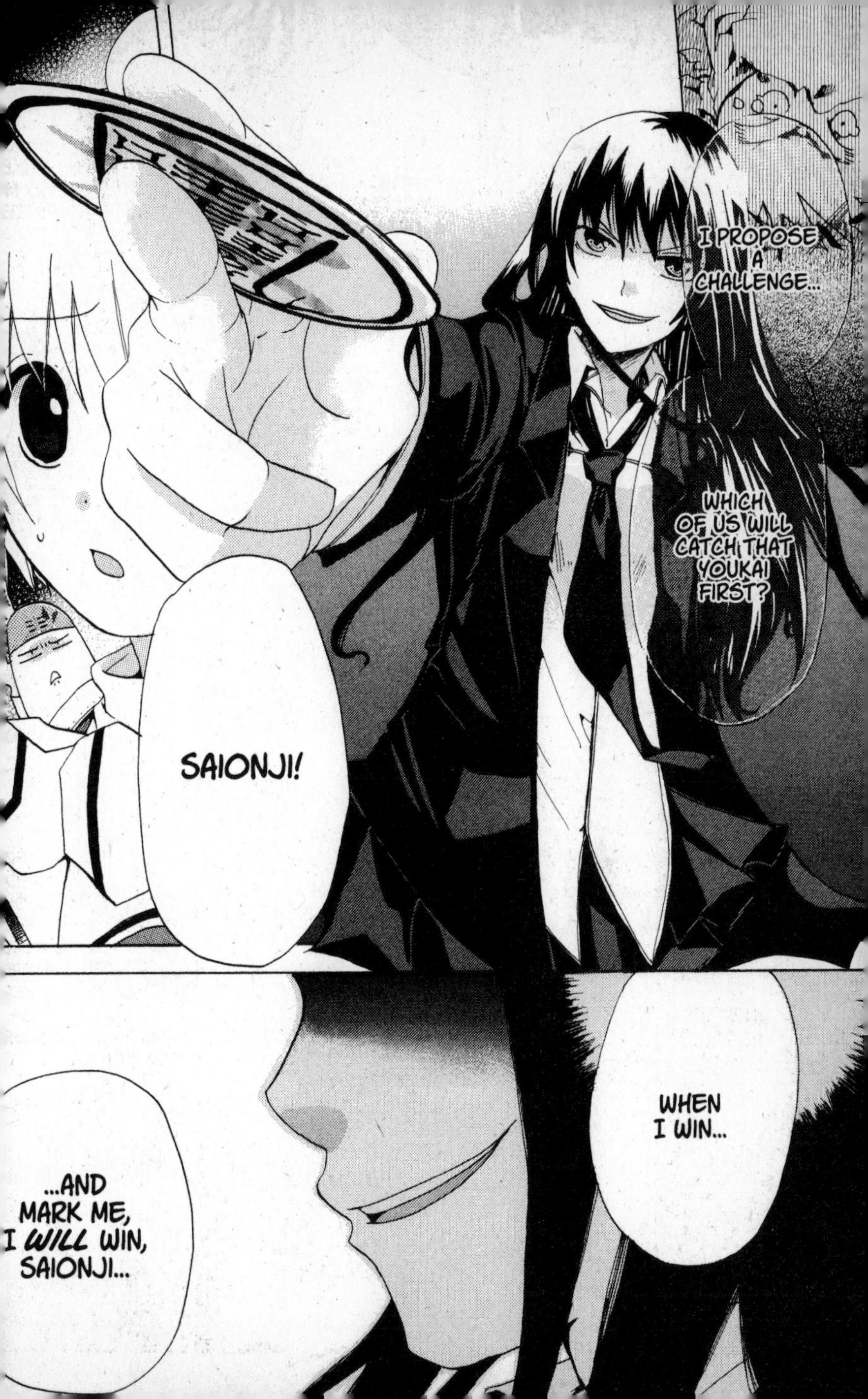
I PROPOSE A CHALLENGE...
WHICH OF US WILL CATCH THAT YOUKAI FIRST?
SAIONJI!
WHEN I WIN...
...AND MARK ME, I *WILL* WIN, SAIONJI...

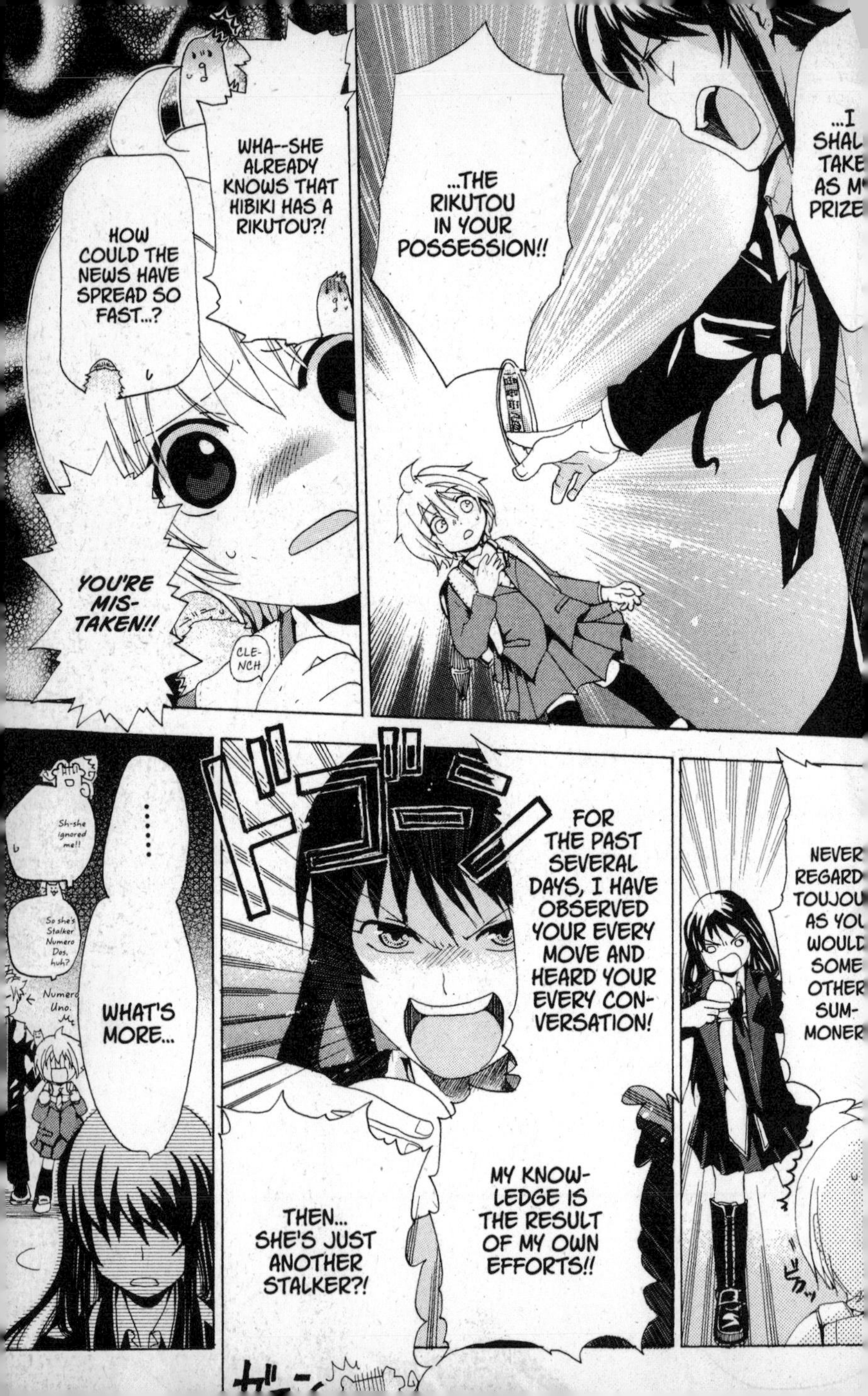
...I SHAL TAKE AS M PRIZE
...THE RIKUTOU IN YOUR POSSESSION!!
WHA--SHE ALREADY KNOWS THAT HIBIKI HAS A RIKUTOU?!
HOW COULD THE NEWS HAVE SPREAD SO FAST...?
YOU'RE MIS-TAKEN!!
CLE-NCH
NEVER REGARD TOUJOU AS YOU WOULD SOME OTHER SUM-MONER
FOR THE PAST SEVERAL DAYS, I HAVE OBSERVED YOUR EVERY MOVE AND HEARD YOUR EVERY CON-VERSATION!
MY KNOW-LEDGE IS THE RESULT OF MY OWN EFFORTS!!
THEN... SHE'S JUST ANOTHER STALKER?!
......
WHAT'S MORE...
Sh-she ignored me!!
So she's Stalker Numero Dos, huh?
Numero Uno.

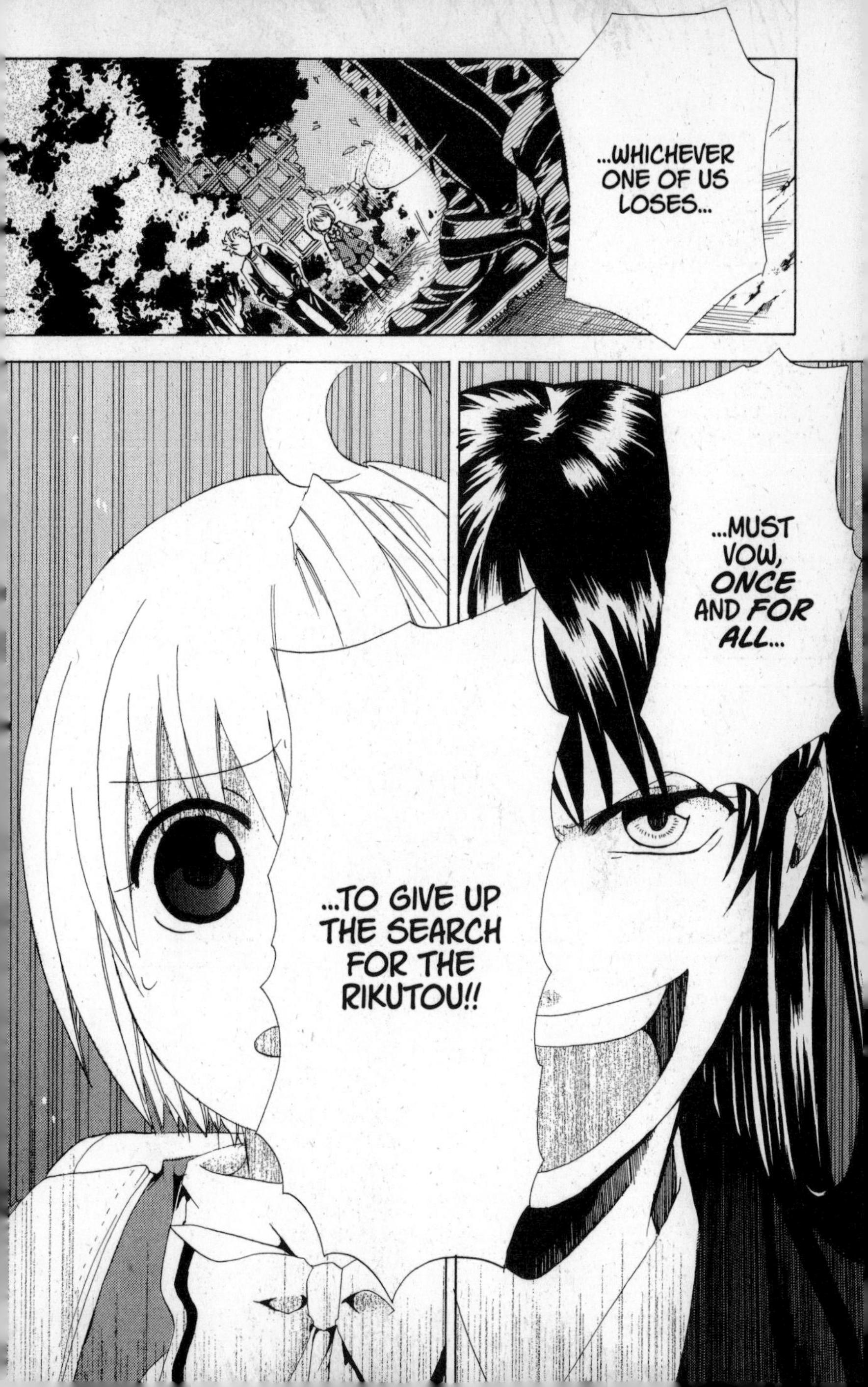
...WHICHEVER ONE OF US LOSES...
...MUST VOW, ONCE AND FOR ALL...
...TO GIVE UP THE SEARCH FOR THE RIKUTOU!!

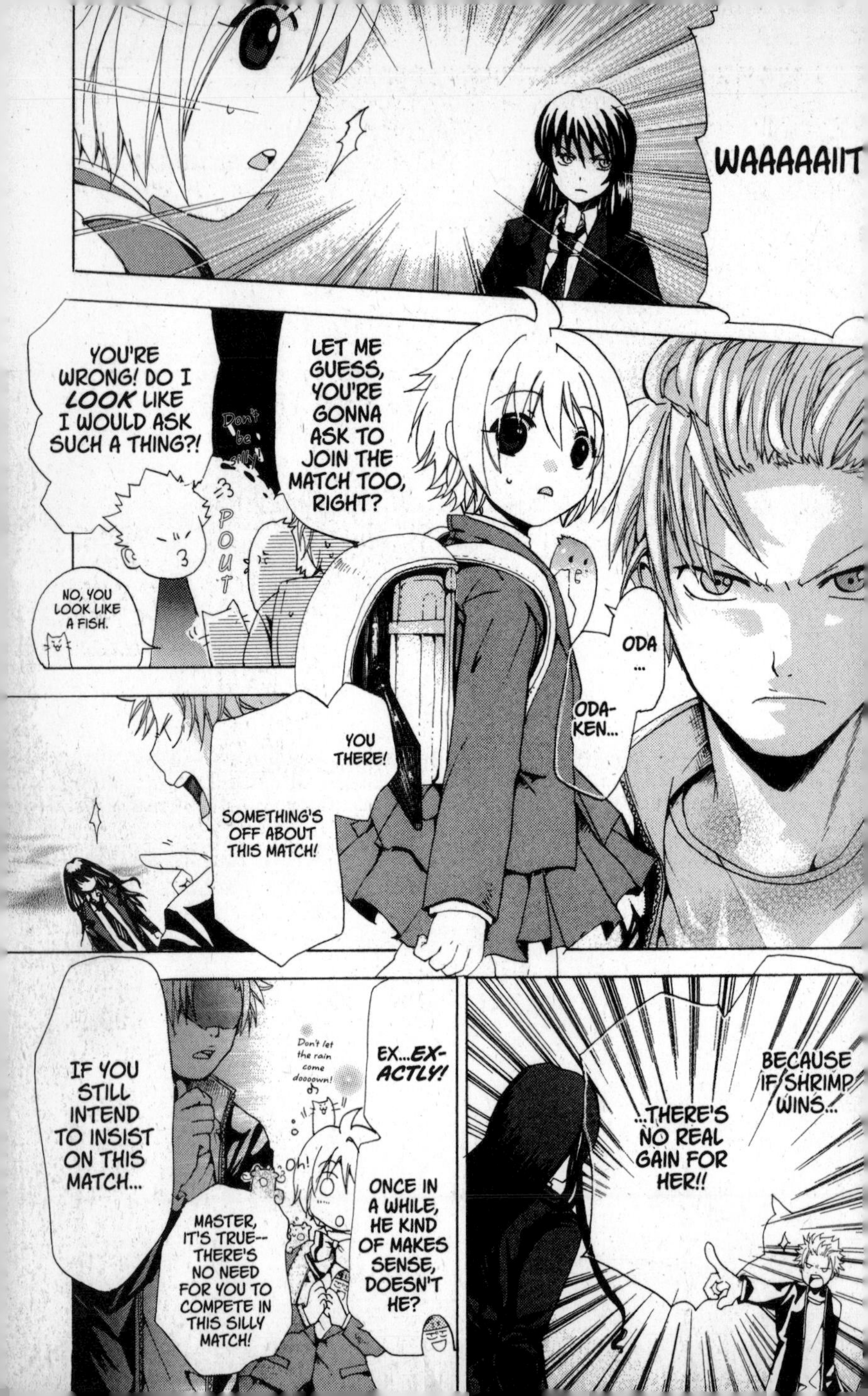
WAAAAAIIT
ODA...
ODA-KEN...
LET ME GUESS, YOU'RE GONNA ASK TO JOIN THE MATCH TOO, RIGHT?
YOU'RE WRONG! DO I *LOOK* LIKE I WOULD ASK SUCH A THING?!
Don't be silly!
POUT
NO, YOU LOOK LIKE A FISH.
YOU THERE!
SOMETHING'S OFF ABOUT THIS MATCH!
BECAUSE IF SHRIMP WINS...
...THERE'S NO REAL GAIN FOR HER!!
EX...*EX-ACTLY!*
Don't let the rain come doooown!
Oh!
ONCE IN A WHILE, HE KIND OF MAKES SENSE, DOESN'T HE?
IF YOU STILL INTEND TO INSIST ON THIS MATCH...
MASTER, IT'S TRUE-- THERE'S NO NEED FOR YOU TO COMPETE IN THIS SILLY MATCH!

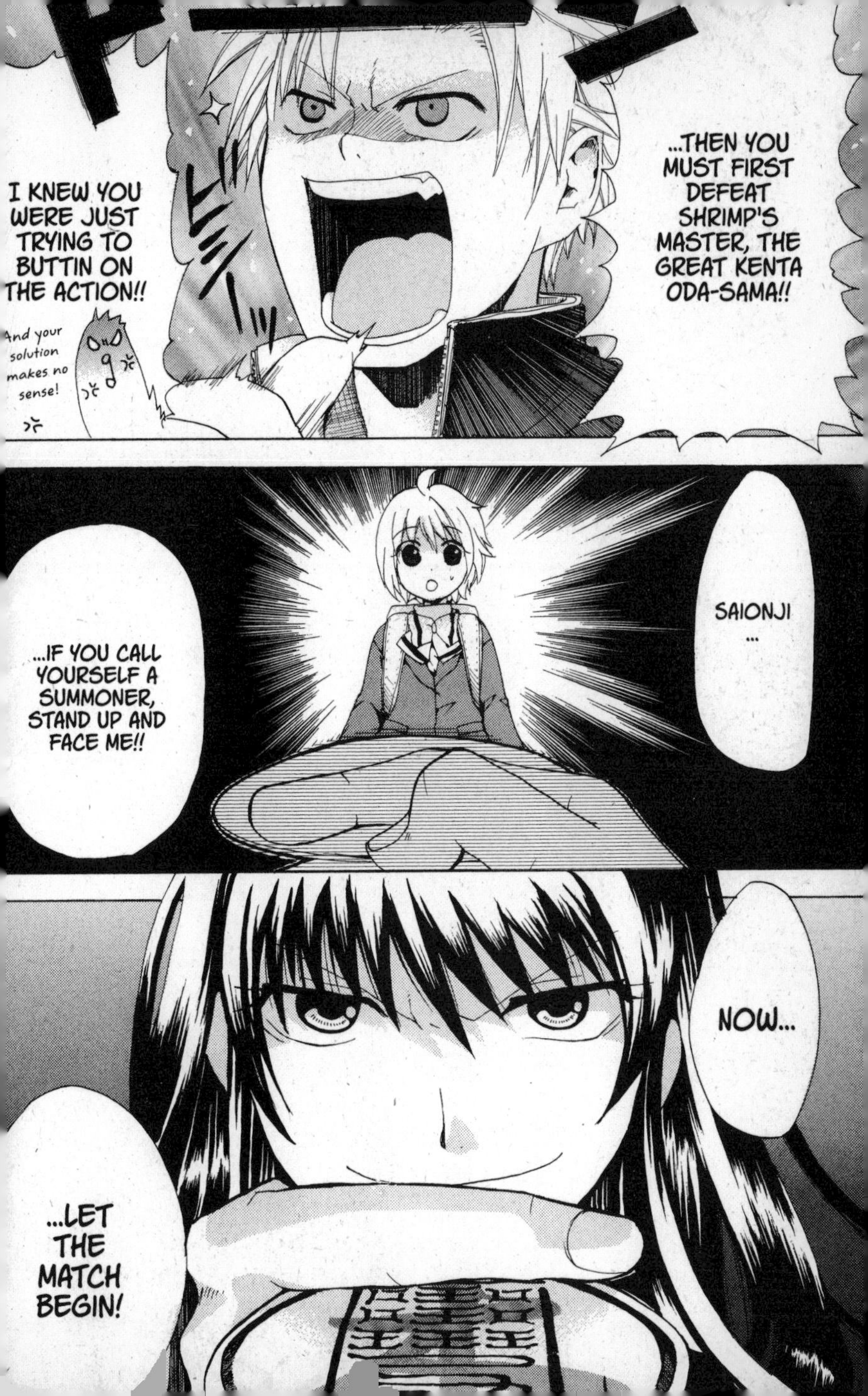
...THEN YOU MUST FIRST DEFEAT SHRIMP'S MASTER, THE GREAT KENTA ODA-SAMA!!
I KNEW YOU WERE JUST TRYING TO BUTTIN ON THE ACTION!!
And your solution makes no sense!
SAIONJI ...
...IF YOU CALL YOURSELF A SUMMONER, STAND UP AND FACE ME!!
NOW...
...LET THE MATCH BEGIN!

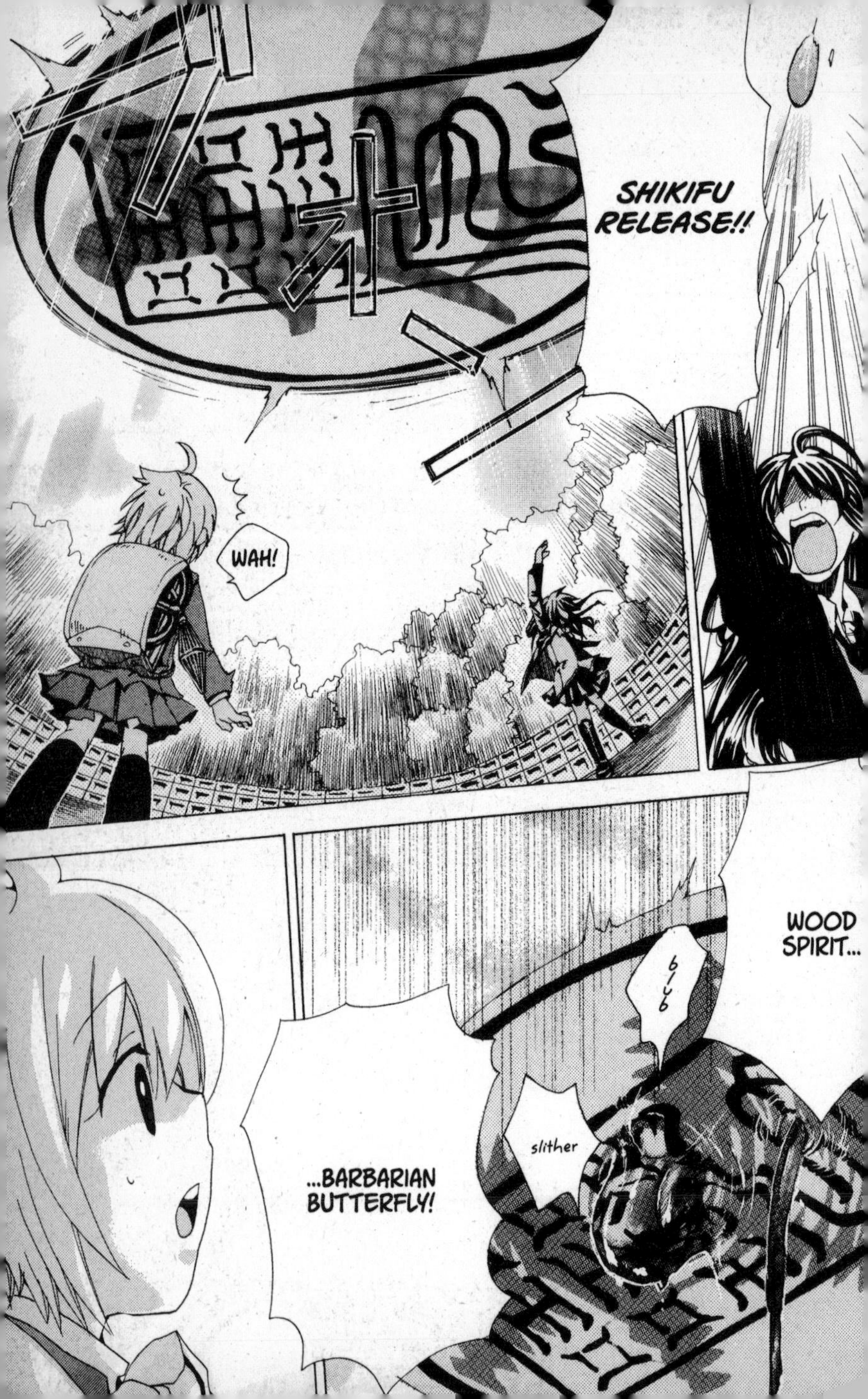
SHIKIFU RELEASE!!
WAH!
WOOD SPIRIT...
blub
slither
...BARBARIAN BUTTERFLY!

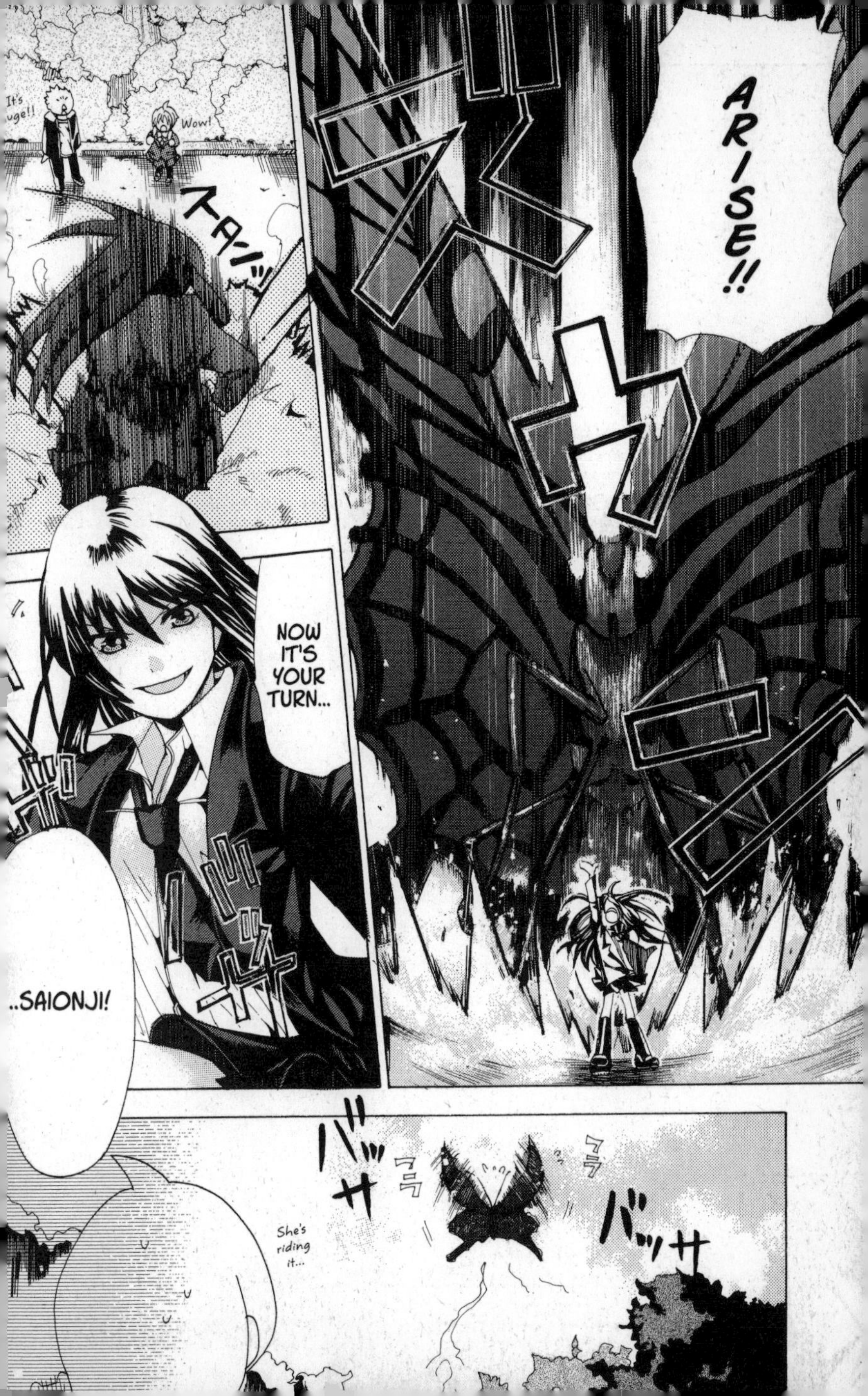
ARISE!!
It's
uge!!
Wow!
スタンッ
NOW IT'S YOUR TURN...
..SAIONJI!
バッサ
フラ
フラ
バッサ
She's riding it...

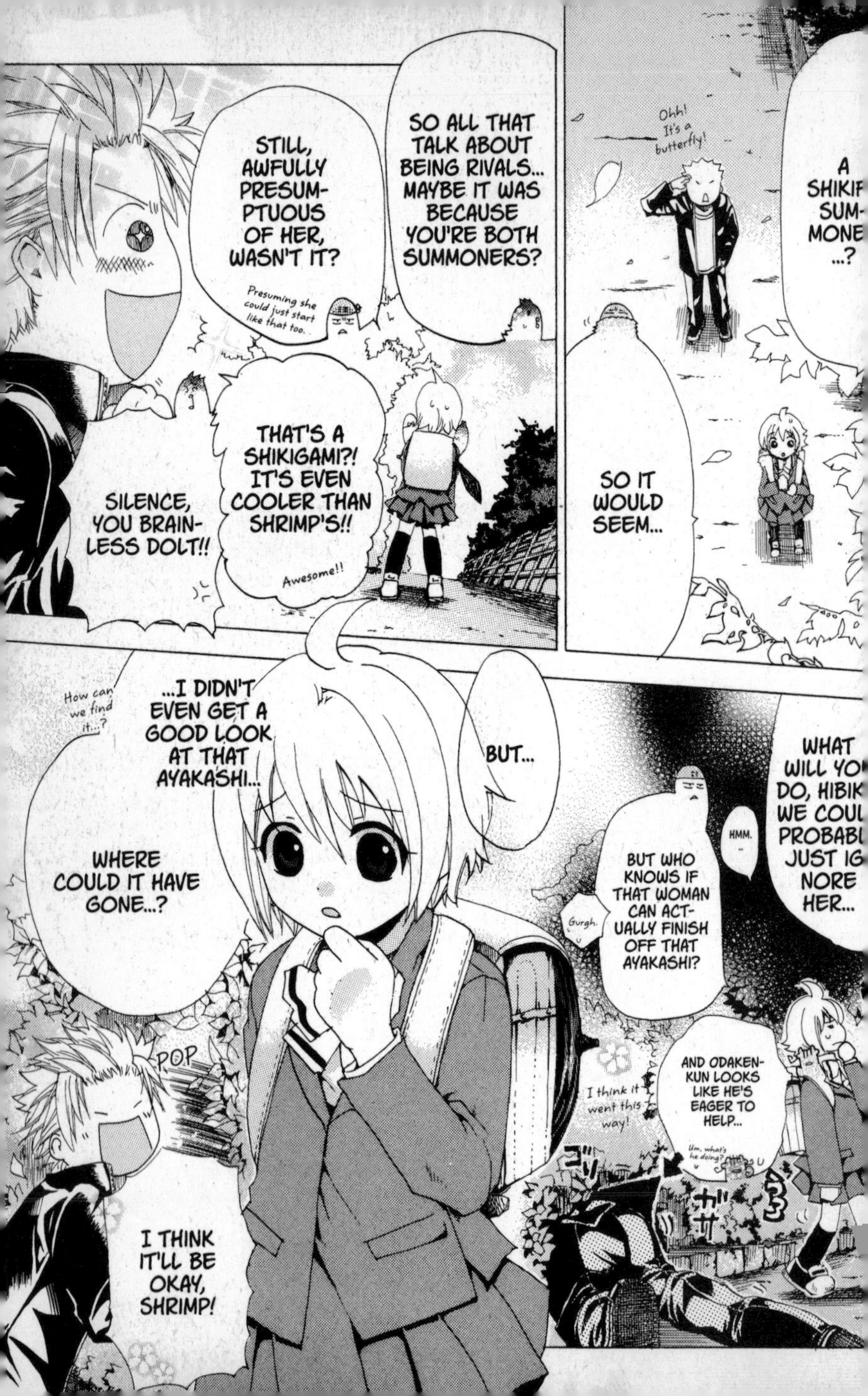
A SHIKI SUM- MONE ...?
Ohh! It's a butterfly!
SO IT WOULD SEEM...
SO ALL THAT TALK ABOUT BEING RIVALS... MAYBE IT WAS BECAUSE YOU'RE BOTH SUMMONERS?
STILL, AWFULLY PRESUMPTUOUS OF HER, WASN'T IT?
Presuming she could just start like that too..
THAT'S A SHIKIGAMI?! IT'S EVEN COOLER THAN SHRIMP'S!!
Awesome!!
SILENCE, YOU BRAINLESS DOLT!!
WHAT WILL YO DO, HIBIK WE COUL PROBABL JUST IG NORE HER...
HMM..
BUT WHO KNOWS IF THAT WOMAN CAN ACTUALLY FINISH OFF THAT AYAKASHI?
Gurgh.
AND ODAKEN-KUN LOOKS LIKE HE'S EAGER TO HELP...
Um, what's he doing?
I think it went this way!
BUT...
...I DIDN'T EVEN GET A GOOD LOOK AT THAT AYAKASHI...
How can we find it...?
WHERE COULD IT HAVE GONE...?
POP
I THINK IT'LL BE OKAY, SHRIMP!

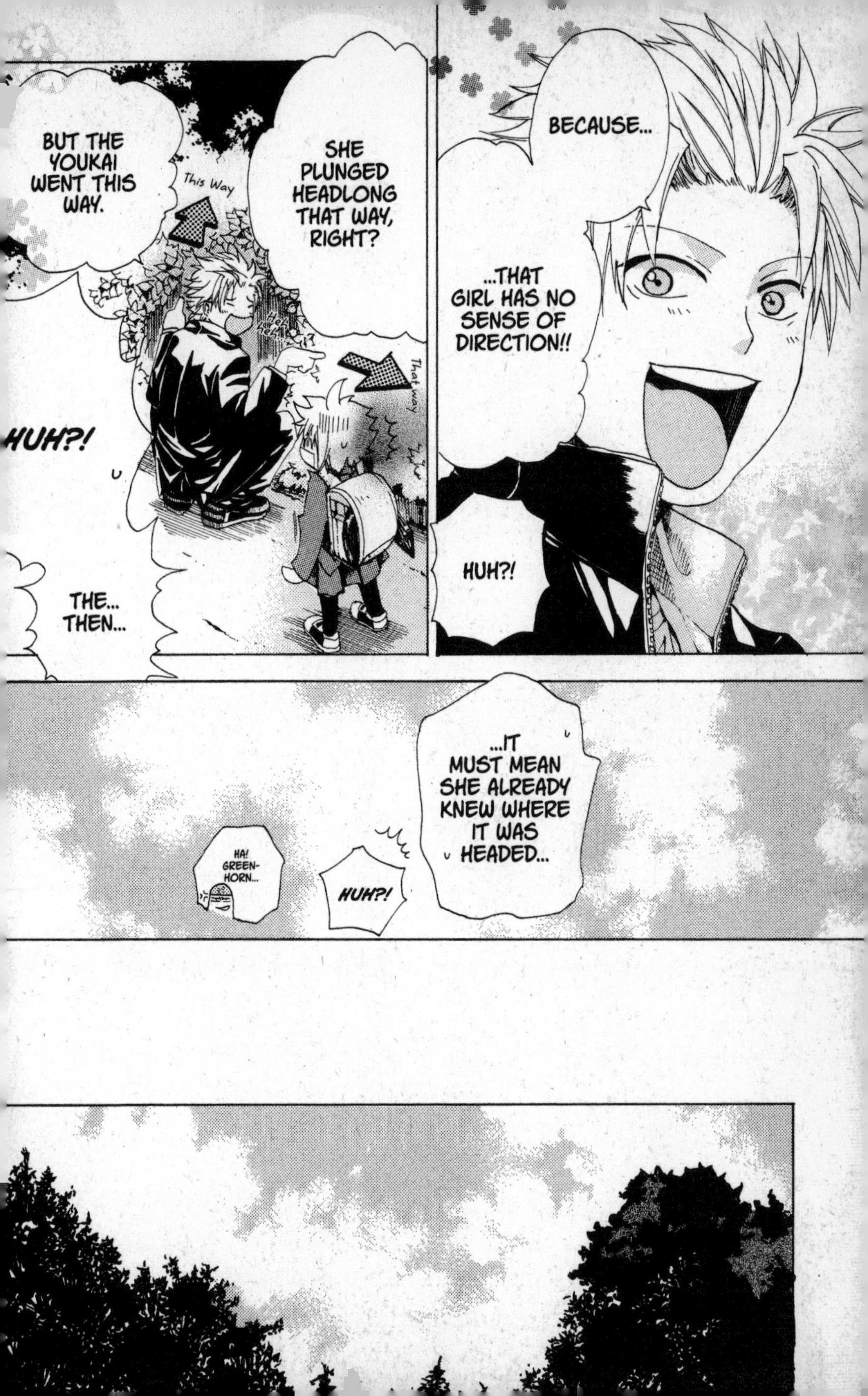
BECAUSE...
...THAT GIRL HAS NO SENSE OF DIRECTION!!
HUH?!
SHE PLUNGED HEADLONG THAT WAY, RIGHT?
That way
Heh heh
This Way
BUT THE YOUKAI WENT THIS WAY.
HUH?!
THE... THEN...
...IT MUST MEAN SHE ALREADY KNEW WHERE IT WAS HEADED...
HUH?!
HA! GREEN-HORN...

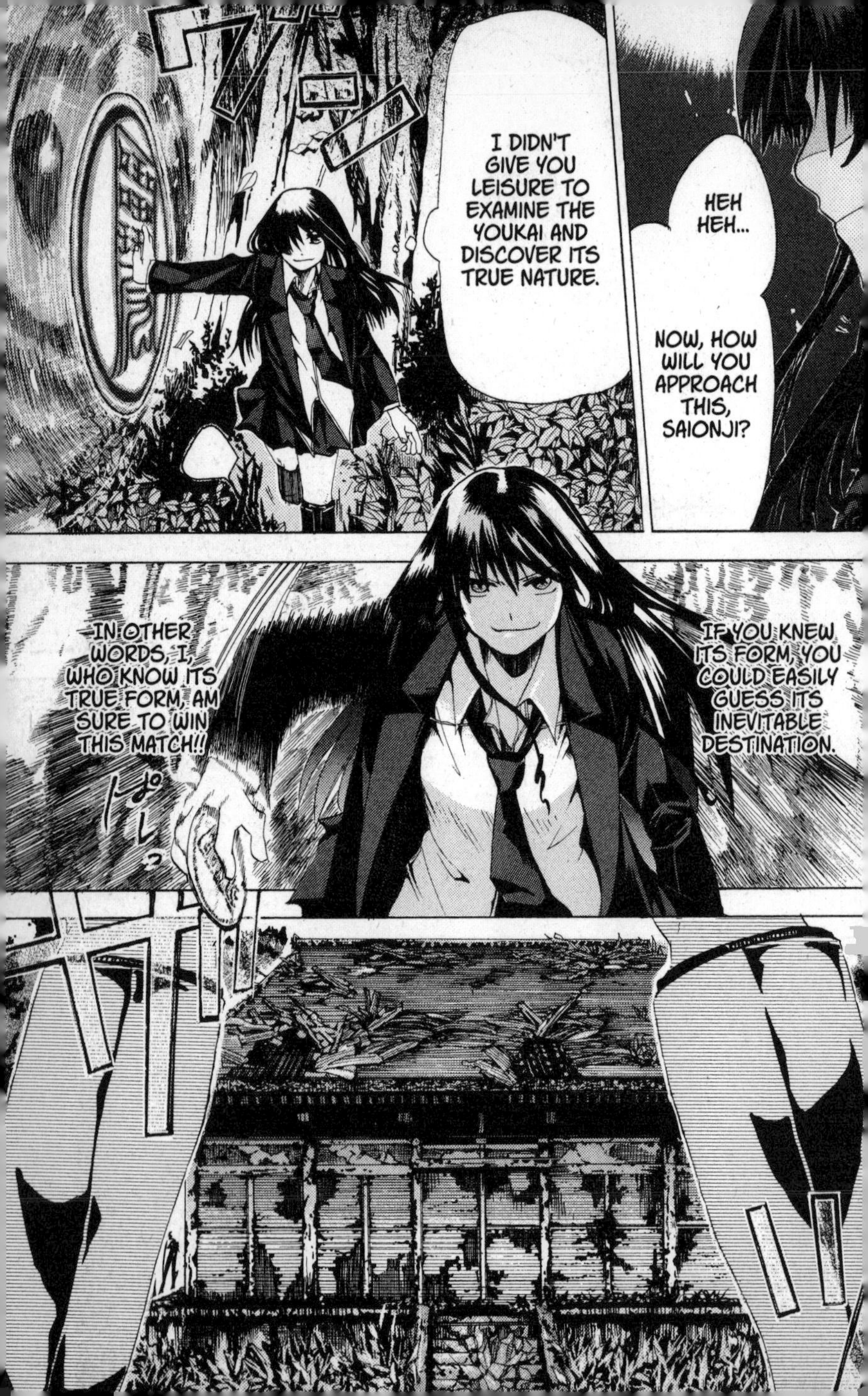
HEH HEH...
NOW, HOW WILL YOU APPROACH THIS, SAIONJI?
I DIDN'T GIVE YOU LEISURE TO EXAMINE THE YOUKAI AND DISCOVER ITS TRUE NATURE.
IF YOU KNEW ITS FORM, YOU COULD EASILY GUESS ITS INEVITABLE DESTINATION.
IN OTHER WORDS, I, WHO KNOW ITS TRUE FORM, AM SURE TO WIN THIS MATCH!!

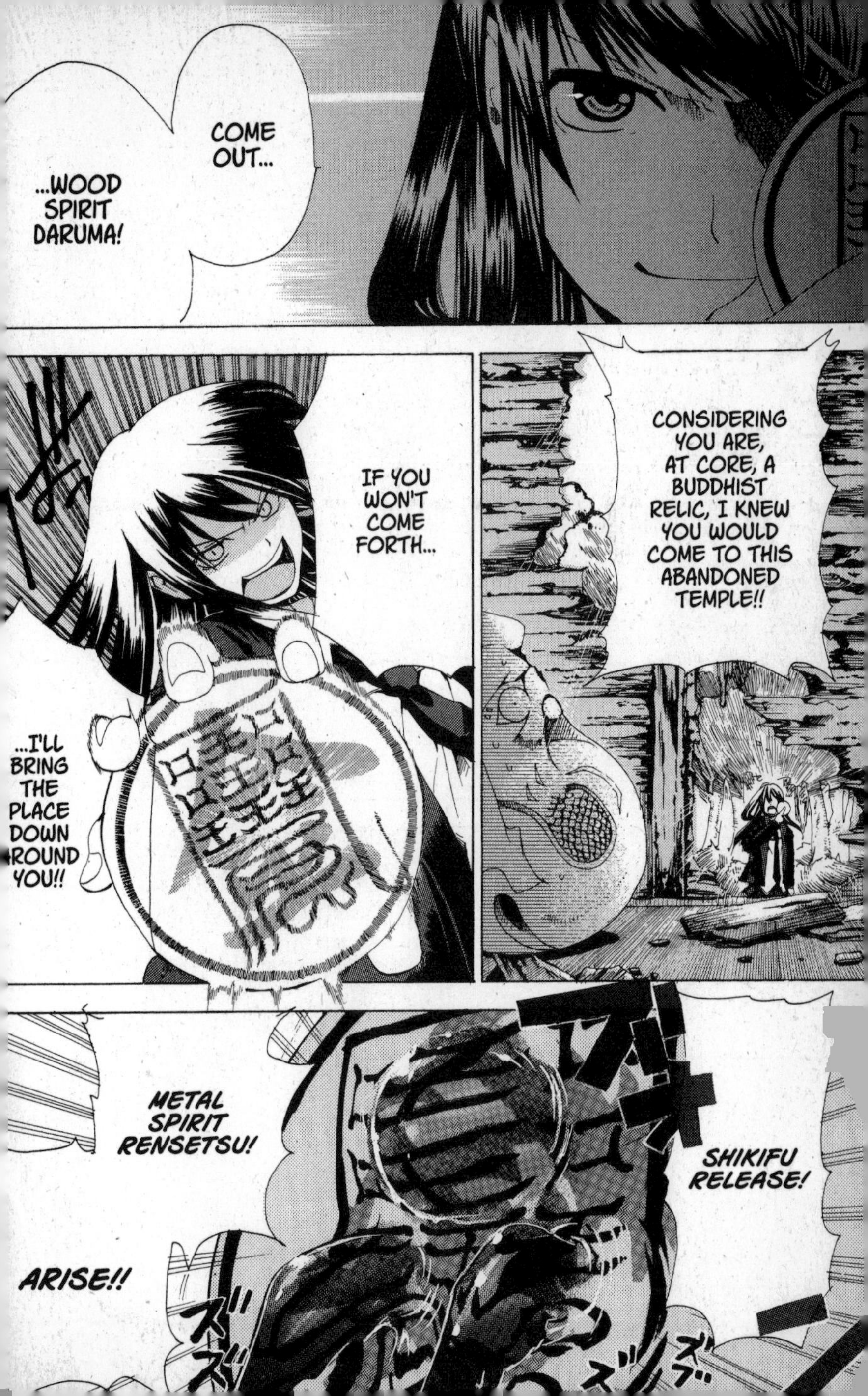
COME OUT...
...WOOD SPIRIT DARUMA!
CONSIDERING YOU ARE, AT CORE, A BUDDHIST RELIC, I KNEW YOU WOULD COME TO THIS ABANDONED TEMPLE!!
IF YOU WON'T COME FORTH...
...I'LL BRING THE PLACE DOWN AROUND YOU!!
SHIKIFU RELEASE!
METAL SPIRIT RENSETSU!
ARISE!!

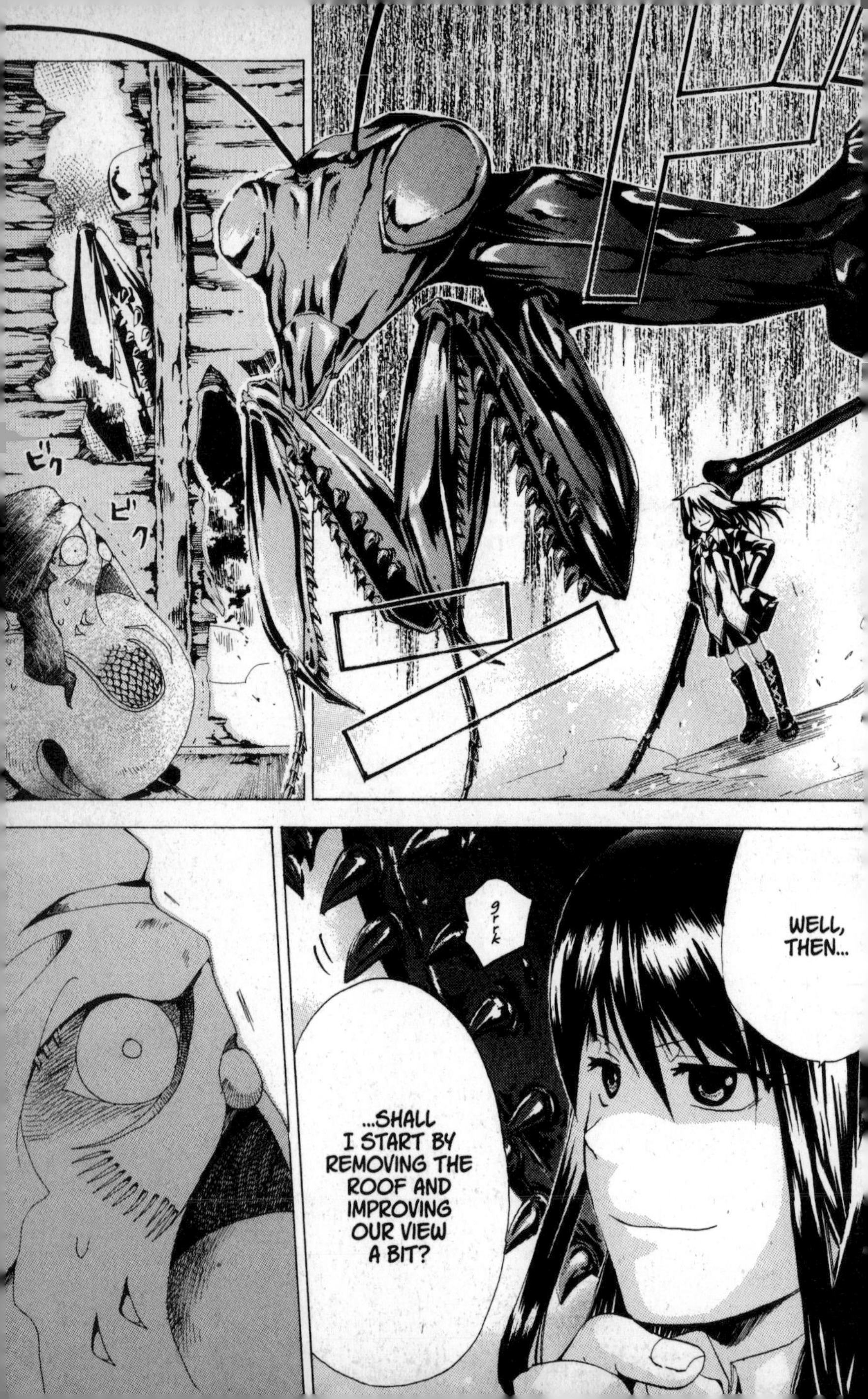
ビク
ビク
WELL, THEN...
grrk
...SHALL I START BY REMOVING THE ROOF AND IMPROVING OUR VIEW A BIT?

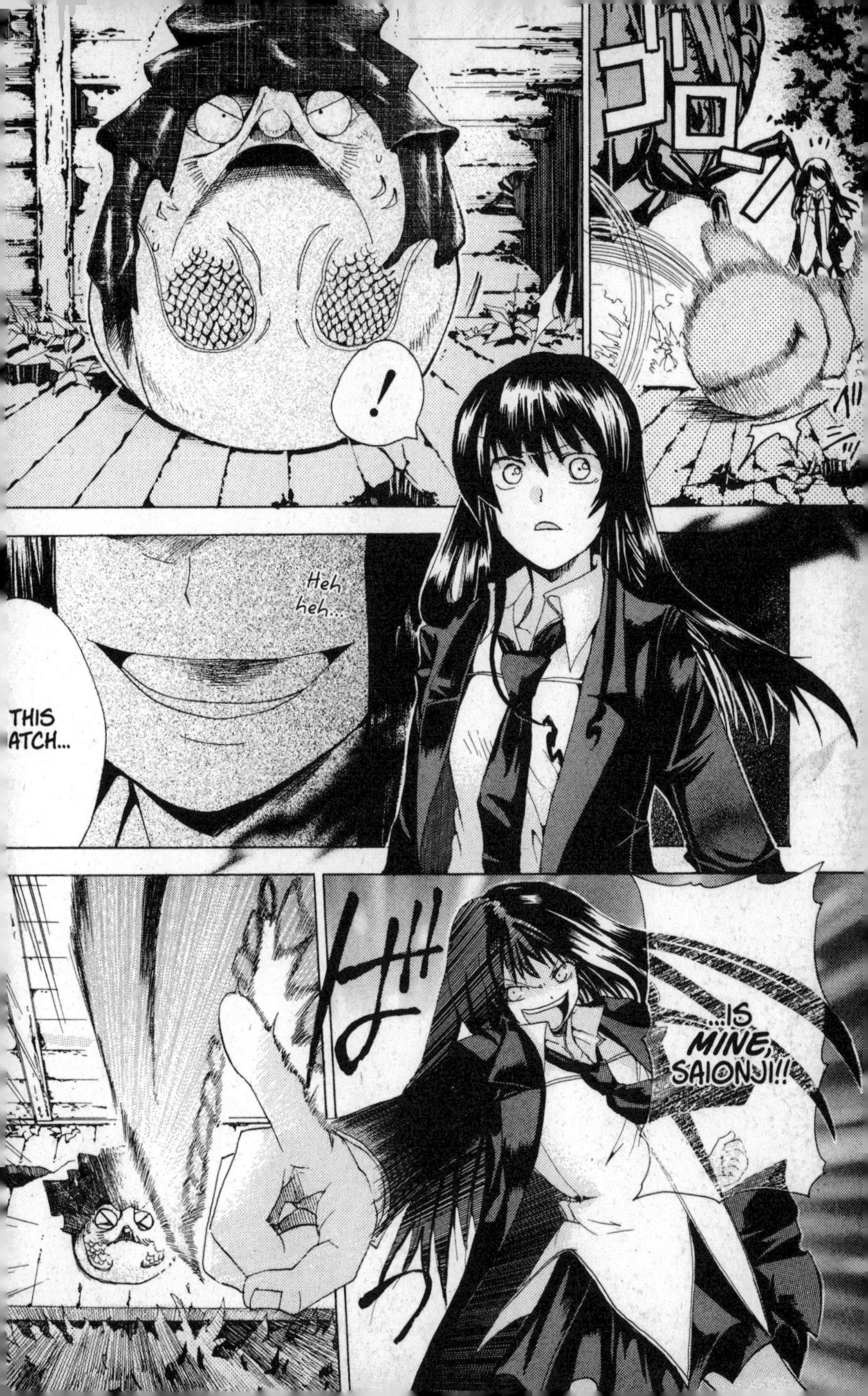
!
Heh heh...
THIS
ATCH...
...IS MINE, SAIONJI!!

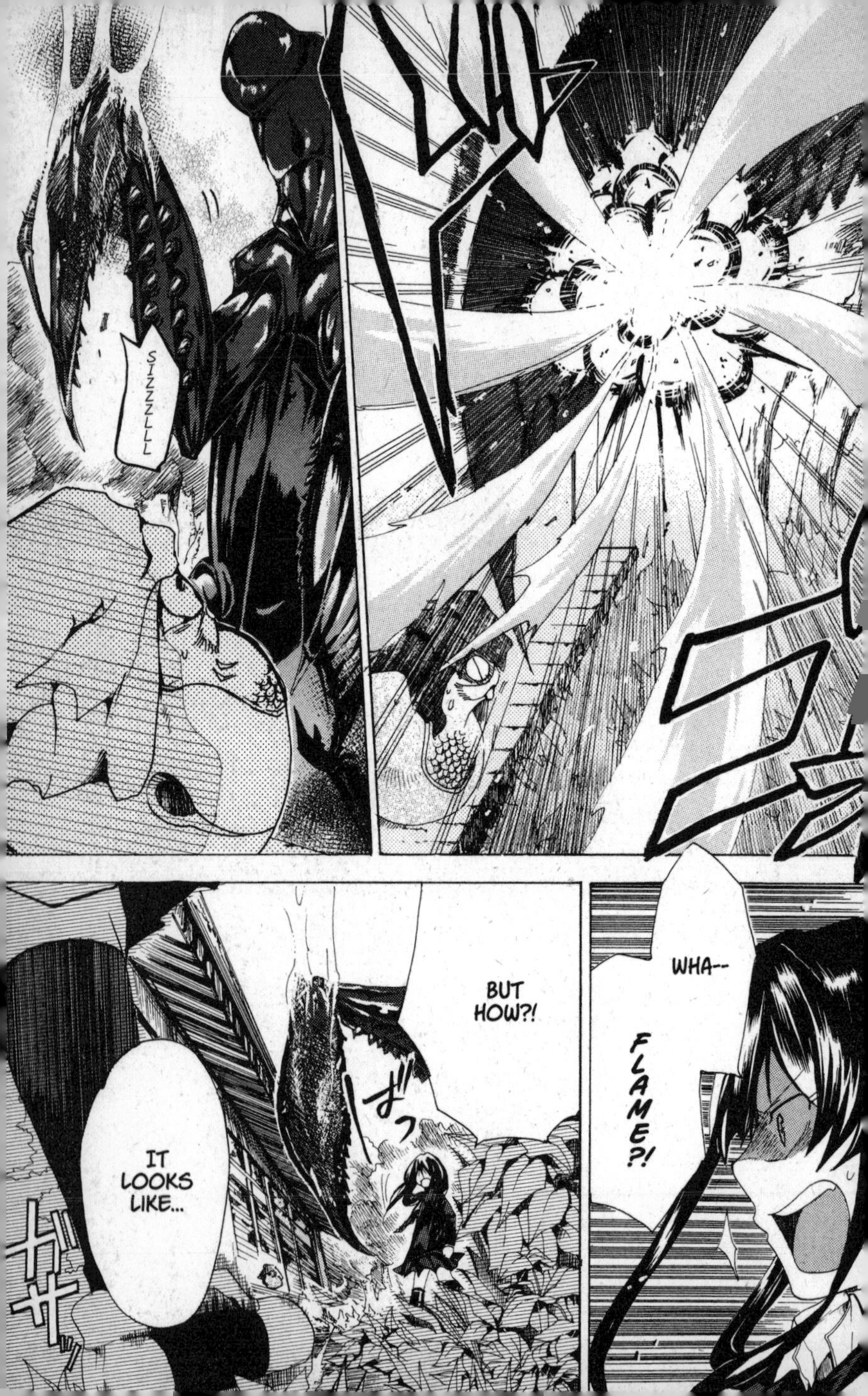
SIZZZLLL
WHA--
FLAME?!
BUT HOW?!
ずっ
IT LOOKS LIKE...

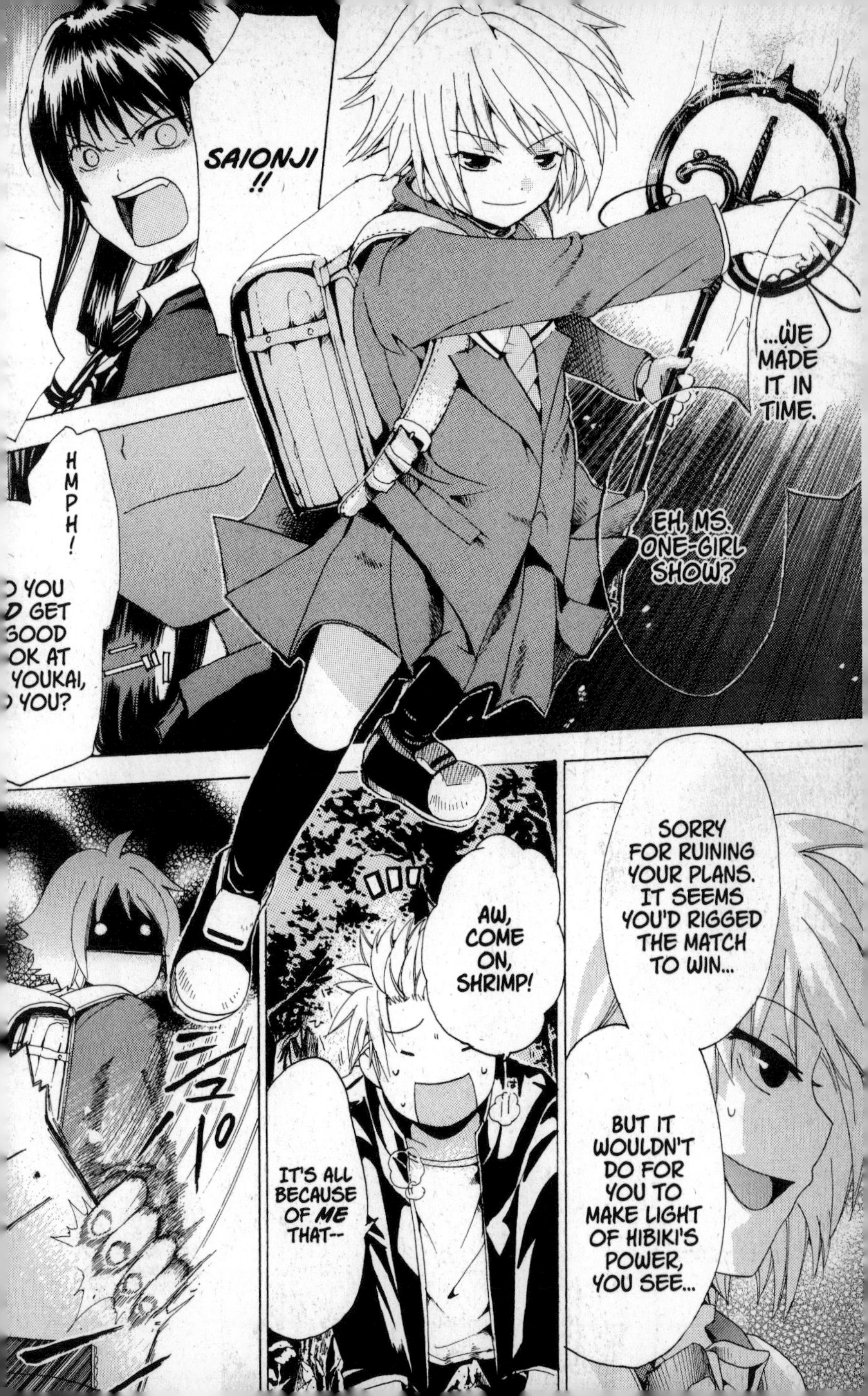

...WE MADE IT IN TIME.
EH, MS. ONE-GIRL SHOW?
SAIONJI!!
HMPH!
D YOU D GET GOOD OK AT YOUKAI, D YOU?
SORRY FOR RUINING YOUR PLANS. IT SEEMS YOU'D RIGGED THE MATCH TO WIN...
BUT IT WOULDN'T DO FOR YOU TO MAKE LIGHT OF HIBIKI'S POWER, YOU SEE...
AW, COME ON, SHRIMP!
IT'S ALL BECAUSE OF ME THAT--

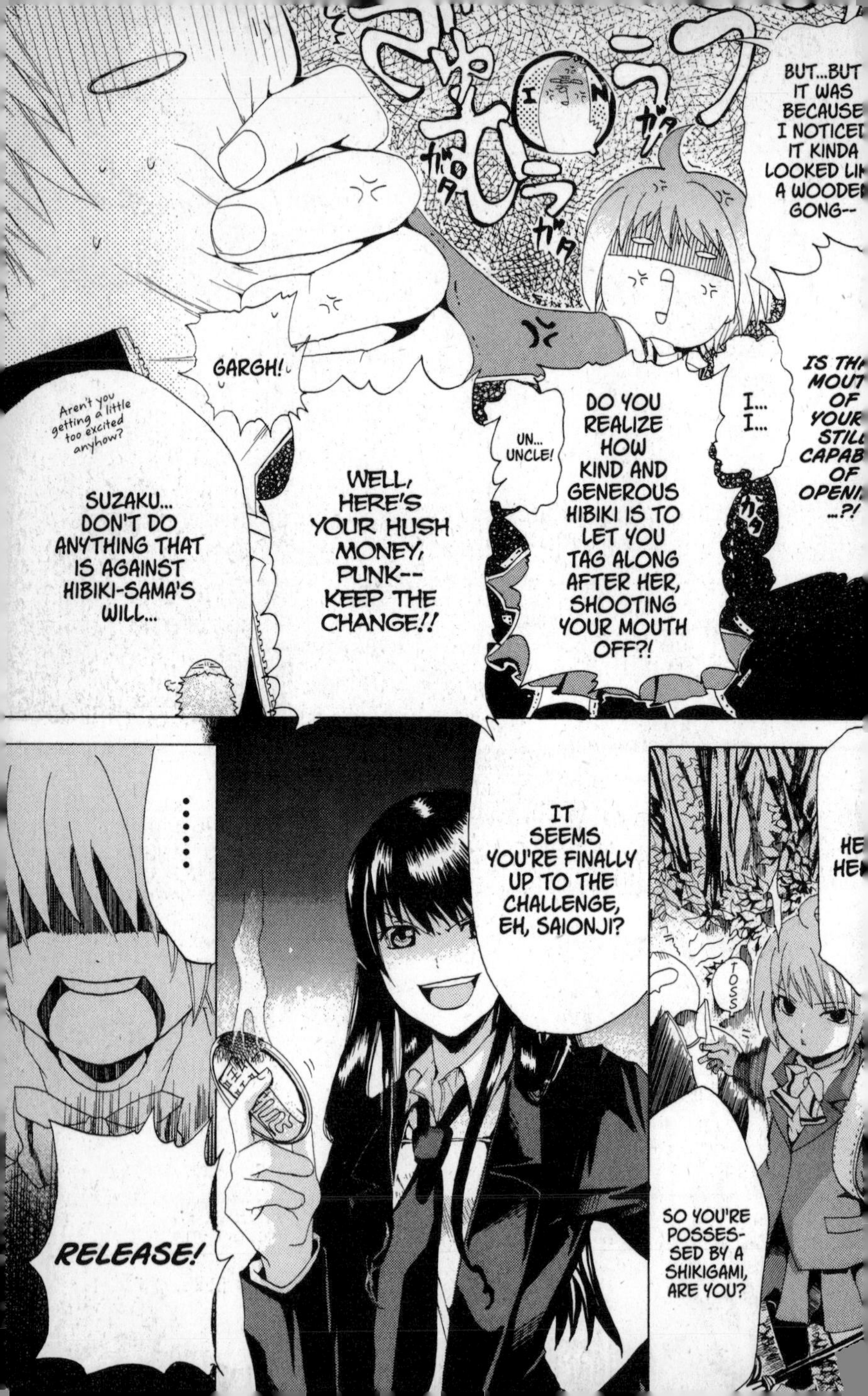
BUT...BUT IT WAS BECAUSE I NOTICE IT KINDA LOOKED LI A WOODE GONG--
IS TH MOUT OF YOUR STILL CAPAB OF OPENI ...?!
I... I...
DO YOU REALIZE HOW KIND AND GENEROUS HIBIKI IS TO LET YOU TAG ALONG AFTER HER, SHOOTING YOUR MOUTH OFF?!
UN... UNCLE!
GARGH!
WELL, HERE'S YOUR HUSH MONEY, PUNK-- KEEP THE CHANGE!!
SUZAKU... DON'T DO ANYTHING THAT IS AGAINST HIBIKI-SAMA'S WILL...
Aren't you getting a little too excited anyhow?
HE HE
TOSS
SO YOU'RE POSSES-SED BY A SHIKIGAMI, ARE YOU?
IT SEEMS YOU'RE FINALLY UP TO THE CHALLENGE, EH, SAIONJI?
......
RELEASE!

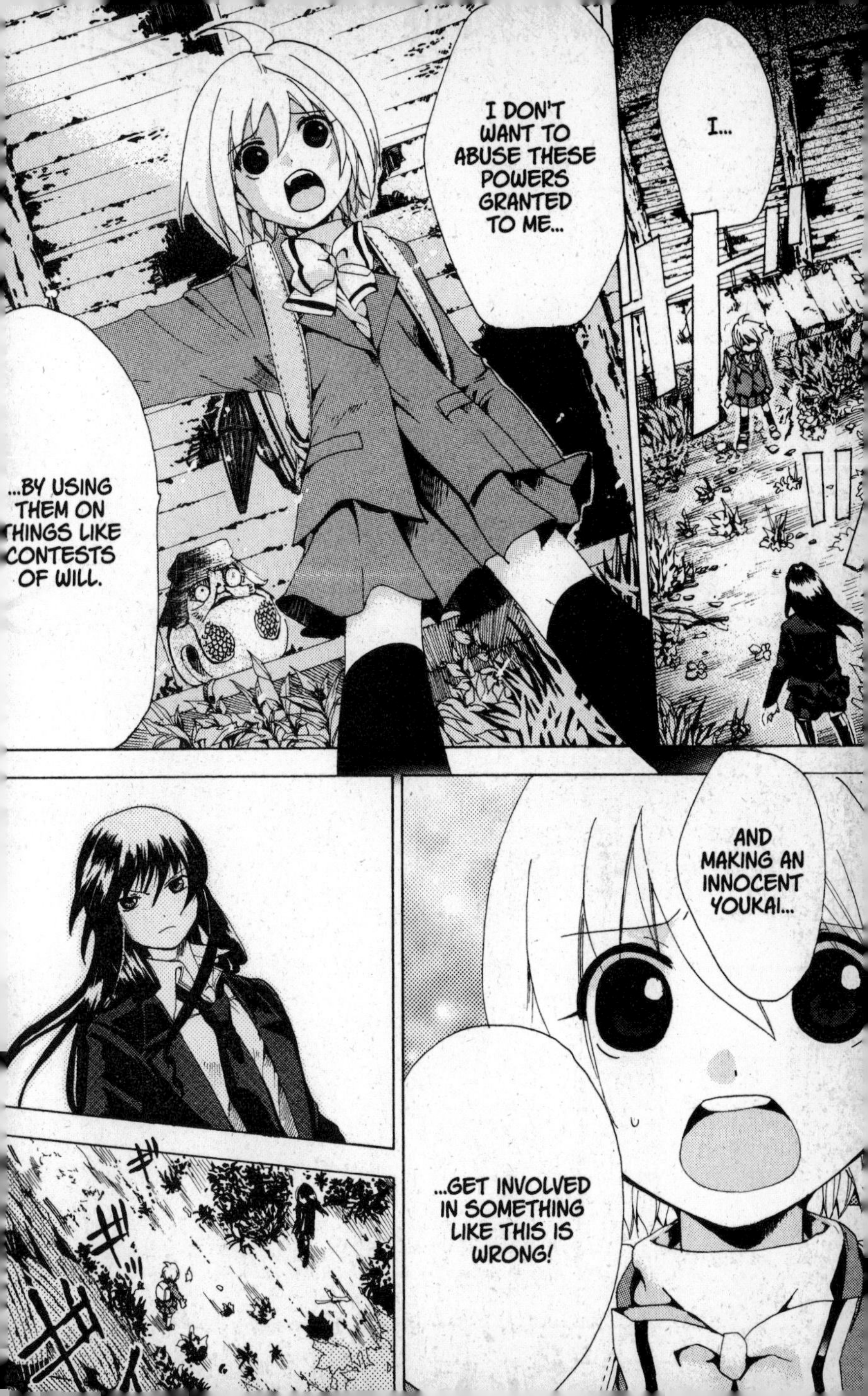
I...
I DON'T WANT TO ABUSE THESE POWERS GRANTED TO ME...
...BY USING THEM ON THINGS LIKE CONTESTS OF WILL.
AND MAKING AN INNOCENT YOUKAI...
...GET INVOLVED IN SOMETHING LIKE THIS IS WRONG!

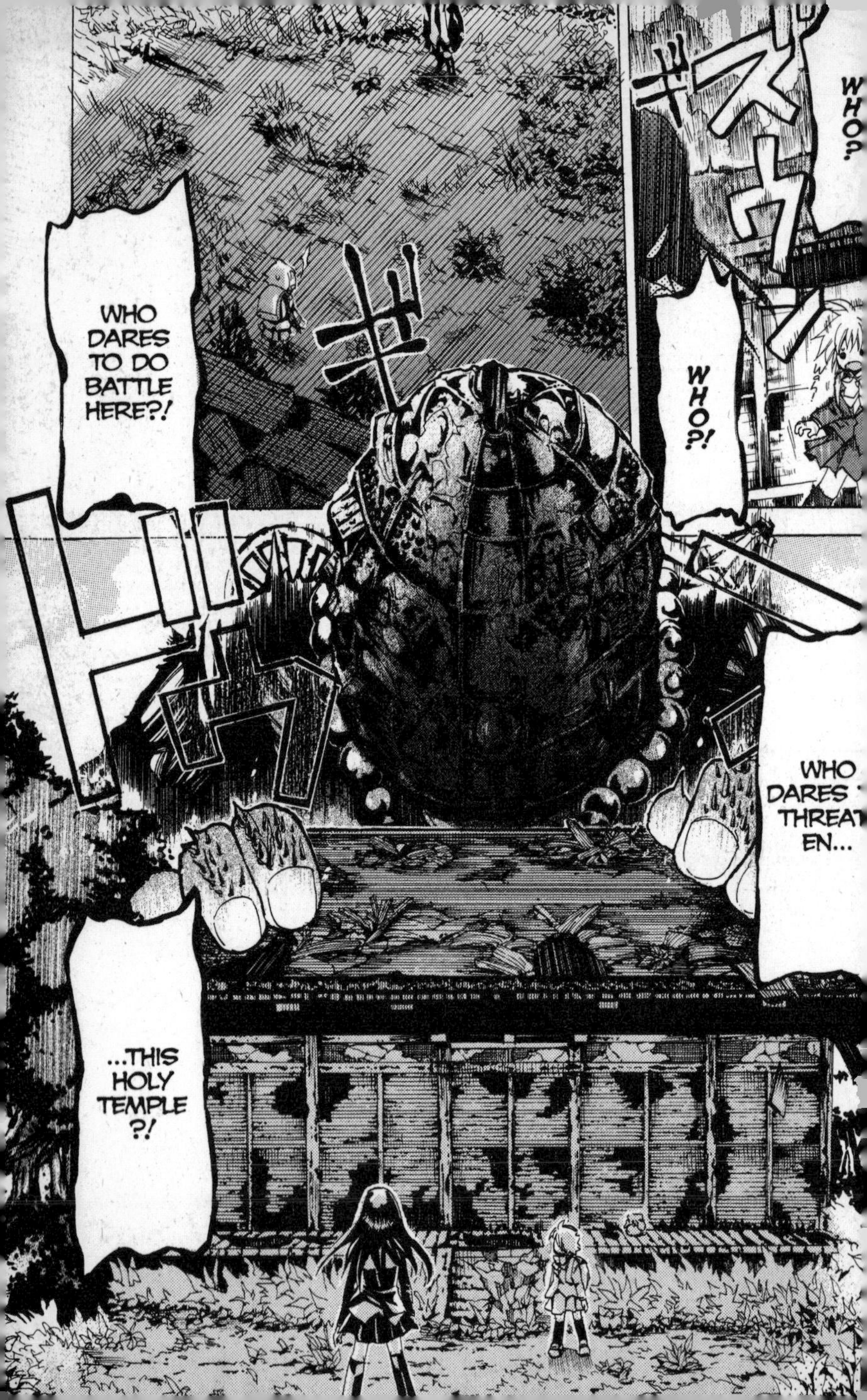
WHO?
WHO?!
WHO DARES TO DO BATTLE HERE?!
WHO DARES THREATEN...
...THIS HOLY TEMPLE?!

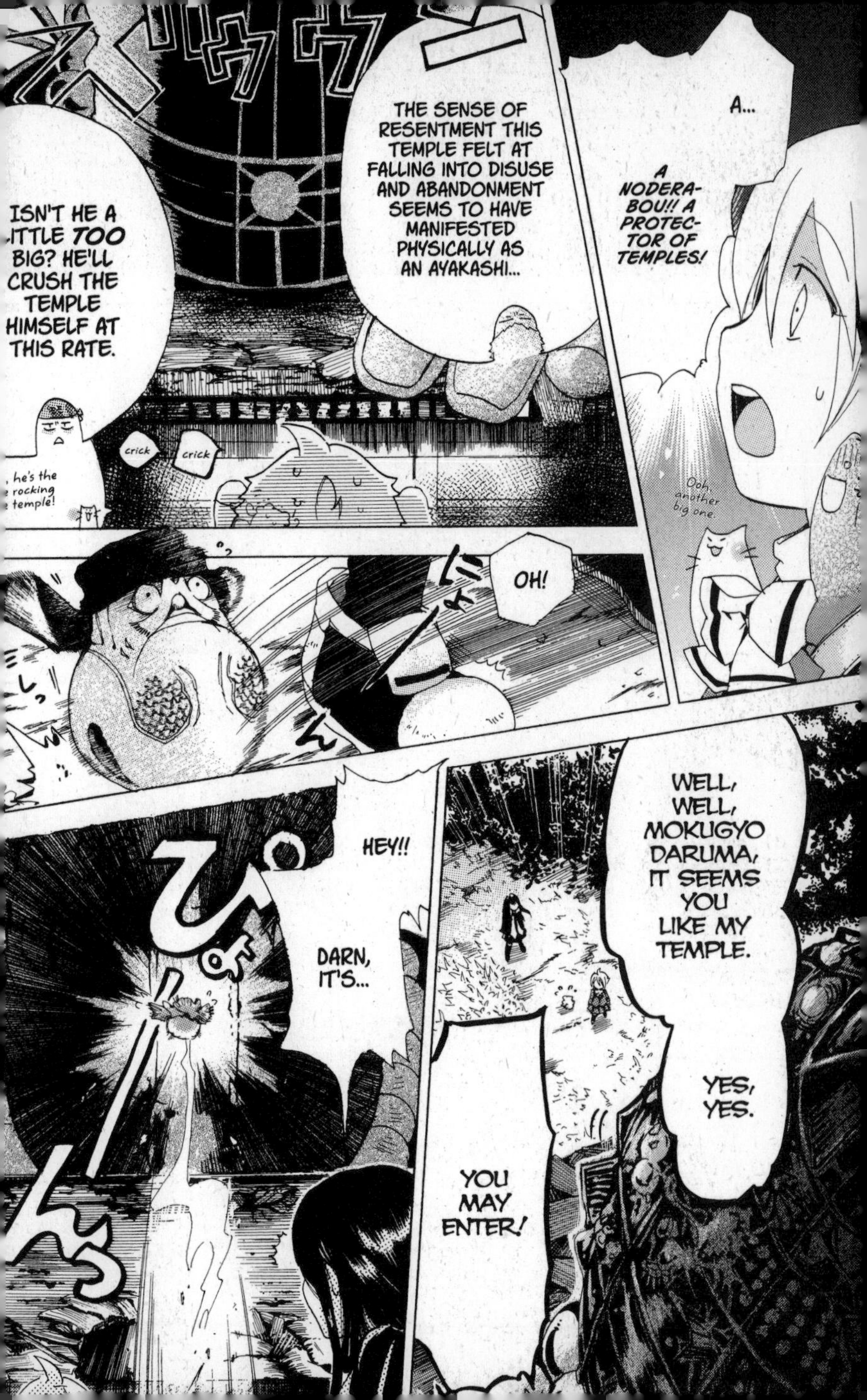

A...
A NODERA-BOU!! A PROTECTOR OF TEMPLES!
Ooh, another big one.
THE SENSE OF RESENTMENT THIS TEMPLE FELT AT FALLING INTO DISUSE AND ABANDONMENT SEEMS TO HAVE MANIFESTED PHYSICALLY AS AN AYAKASHI...
ISN'T HE A LITTLE TOO BIG? HE'LL CRUSH THE TEMPLE HIMSELF AT THIS RATE.
crick
crick
he's the rocking temple!
OH!
WELL, WELL, MOKUGYO DARUMA, IT SEEMS YOU LIKE MY TEMPLE.
YES, YES.
YOU MAY ENTER!
HEY!!
DARN, IT'S...

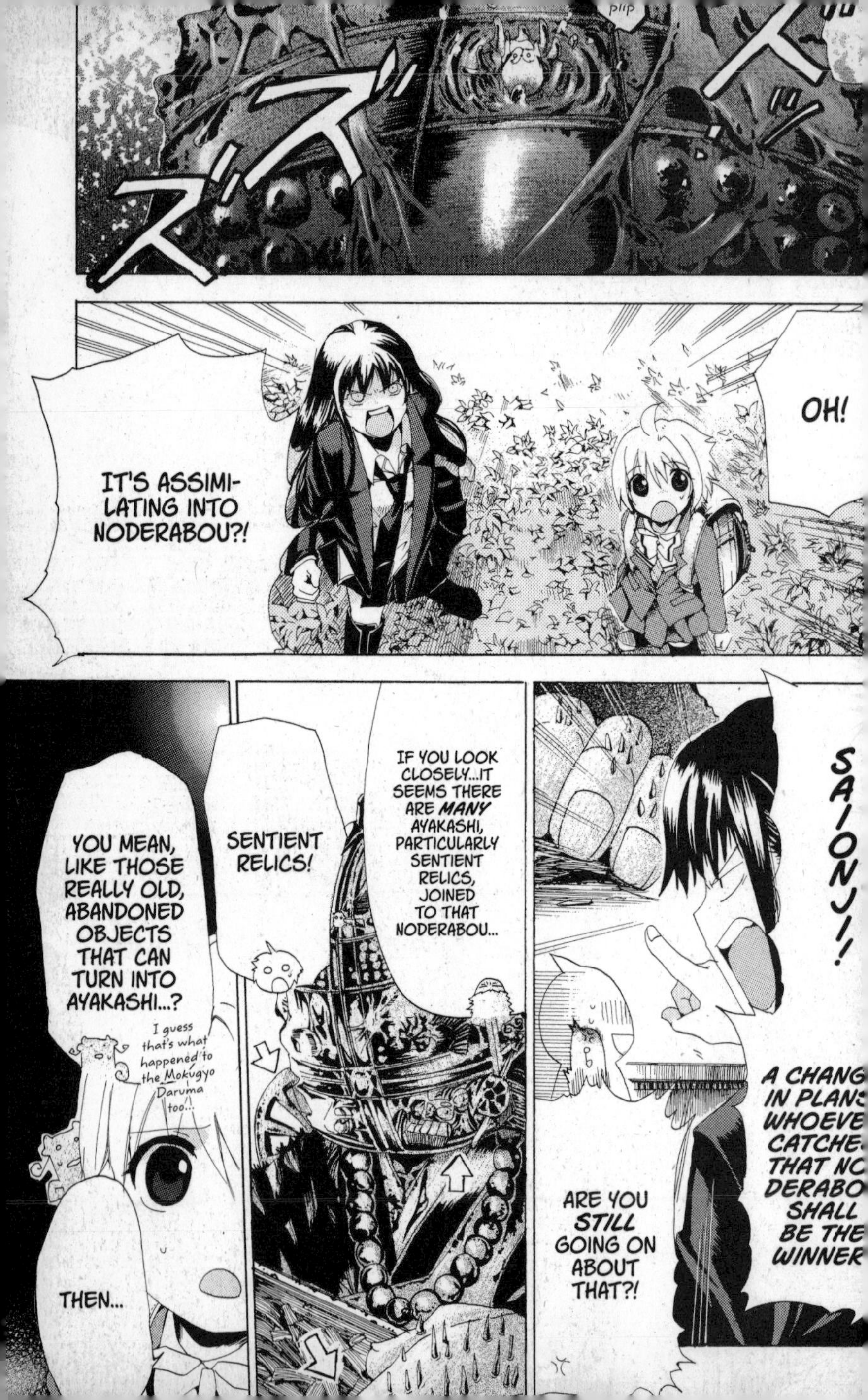
plip
OH!
IT'S ASSIMI-LATING INTO NODERABOU?!
SAIONJI!!
A CHANG IN PLAN WHOEVE CATCHE THAT NO DERABO SHALL BE THE WINNER
ARE YOU STILL GOING ON ABOUT THAT?!
IF YOU LOOK CLOSELY...IT SEEMS THERE ARE MANY AYAKASHI, PARTICULARLY SENTIENT RELICS, JOINED TO THAT NODERABOU...
SENTIENT RELICS!
YOU MEAN, LIKE THOSE REALLY OLD, ABANDONED OBJECTS THAT CAN TURN INTO AYAKASHI...?
I guess that's what happened to the Mokugyo Daruma too...
THEN...

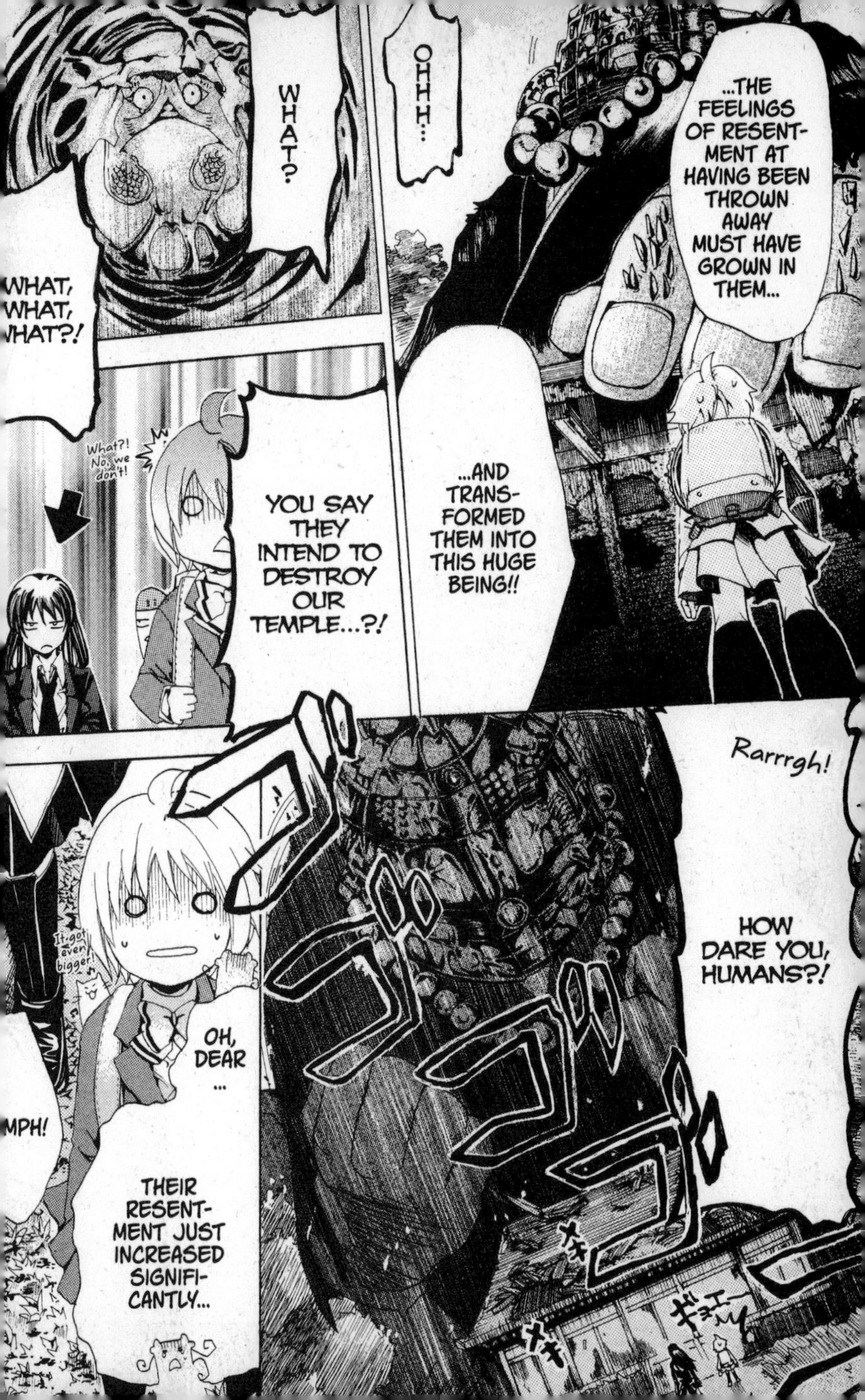
...THE FEELINGS OF RESENTMENT AT HAVING BEEN THROWN AWAY MUST HAVE GROWN IN THEM...
...AND TRANSFORMED THEM INTO THIS HUGE BEING!!
OHHH...
WHAT?
WHAT, WHAT, WHAT?!
YOU SAY THEY INTEND TO DESTROY OUR TEMPLE...?!
What?! No, we don't!
Rarrrgh!
HOW DARE YOU, HUMANS?!
OH, DEAR...
It got even bigger!
MPH!
THEIR RESENTMENT JUST INCREASED SIGNIFICANTLY...

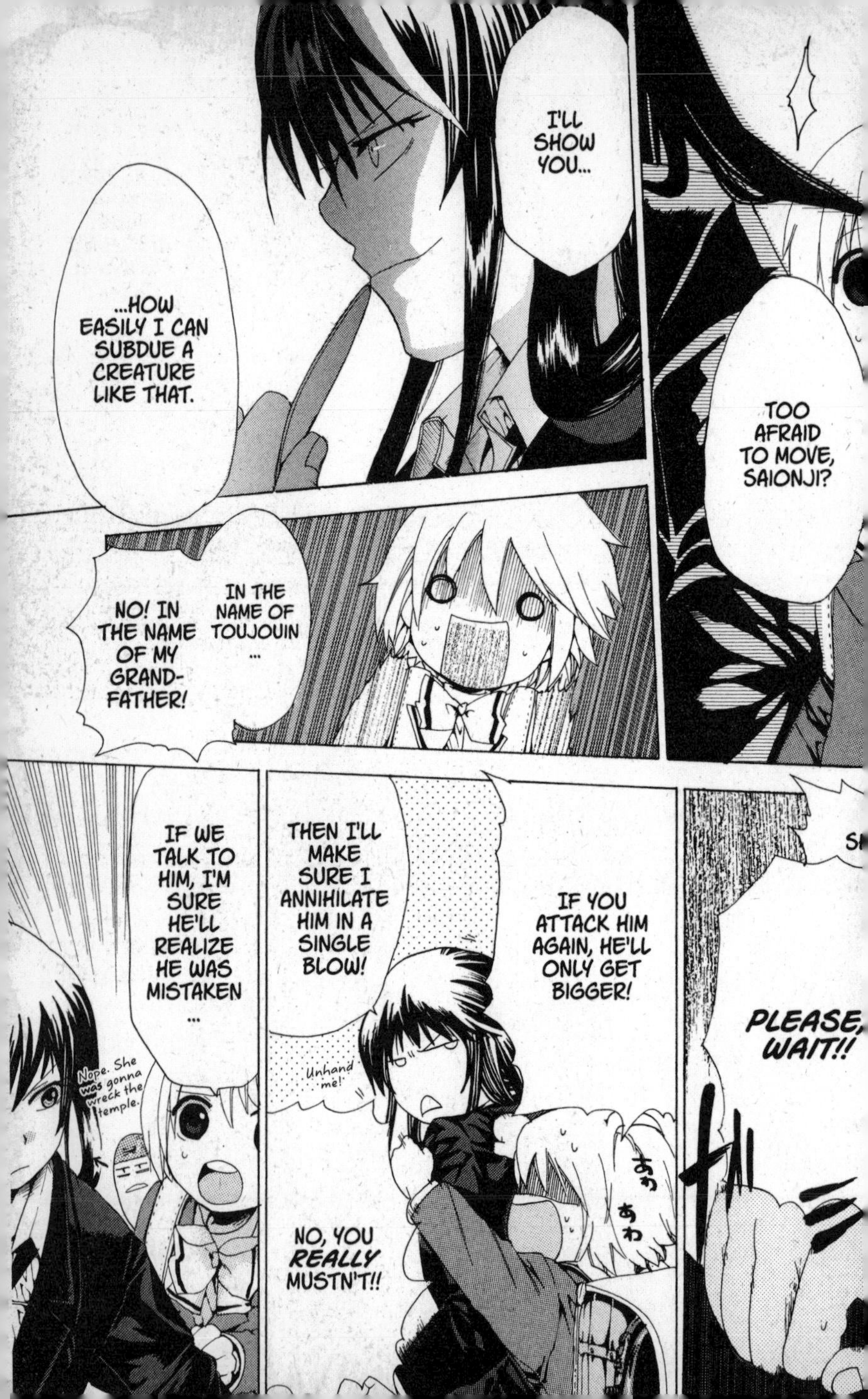
TOO AFRAID TO MOVE, SAIONJI?
I'LL SHOW YOU...
...HOW EASILY I CAN SUBDUE A CREATURE LIKE THAT.
IN THE NAME OF TOUJOUIN...
NO! IN THE NAME OF MY GRAND-FATHER!
PLEASE, WAIT!!
IF YOU ATTACK HIM AGAIN, HE'LL ONLY GET BIGGER!
THEN I'LL MAKE SURE I ANNIHILATE HIM IN A SINGLE BLOW!
Unhand me!
あわ
あわ
NO, YOU REALLY MUSTN'T!!
IF WE TALK TO HIM, I'M SURE HE'LL REALIZE HE WAS MISTAKEN...
Nope. She was gonna wreck the temple.

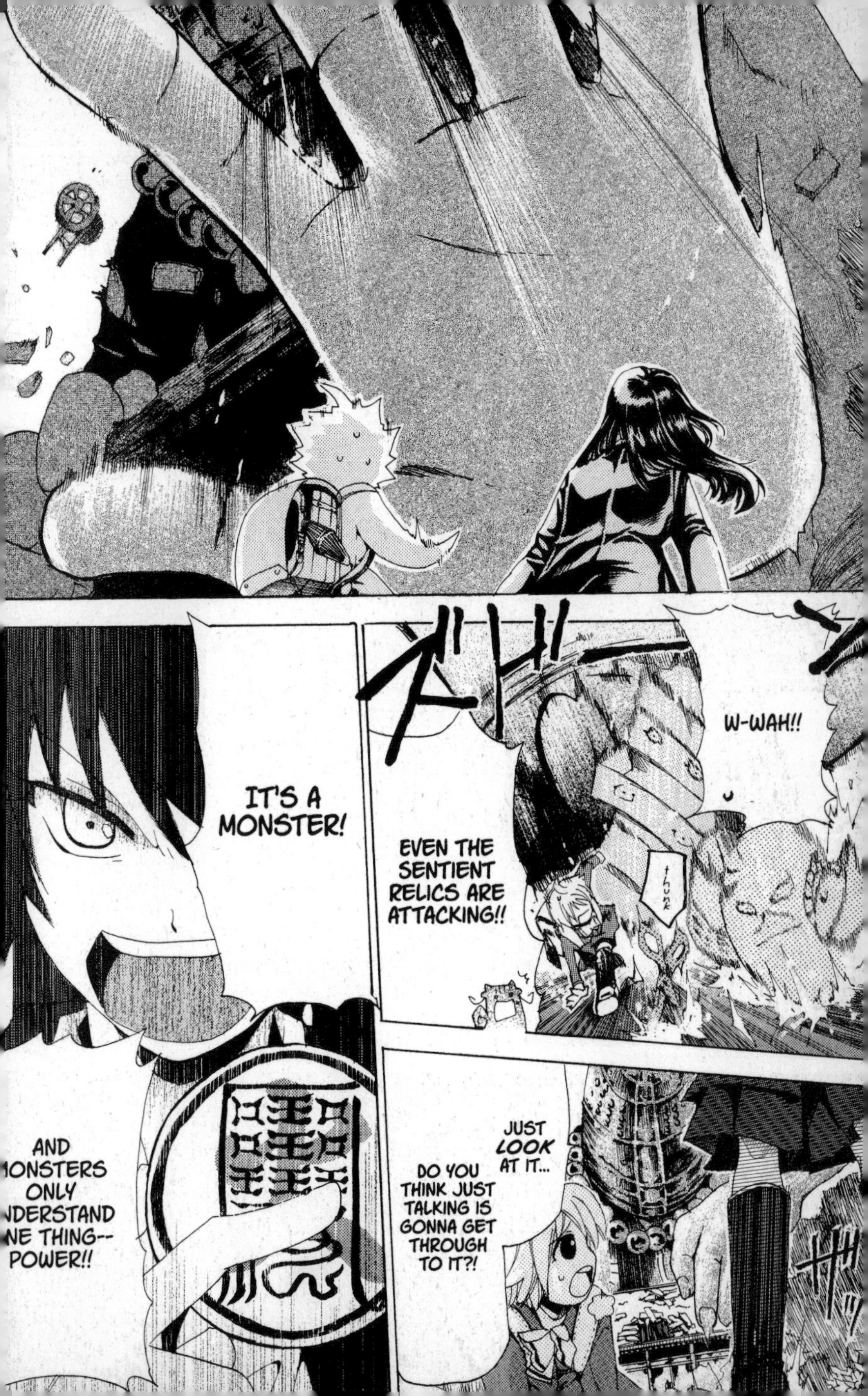
W-WAH!!
EVEN THE SENTIENT RELICS ARE ATTACKING!!
IT'S A MONSTER!
JUST *LOOK* AT IT...
DO YOU THINK JUST TALKING IS GONNA GET THROUGH TO IT?!
AND ONSTERS ONLY NDERSTAND NE THING-- POWER!!

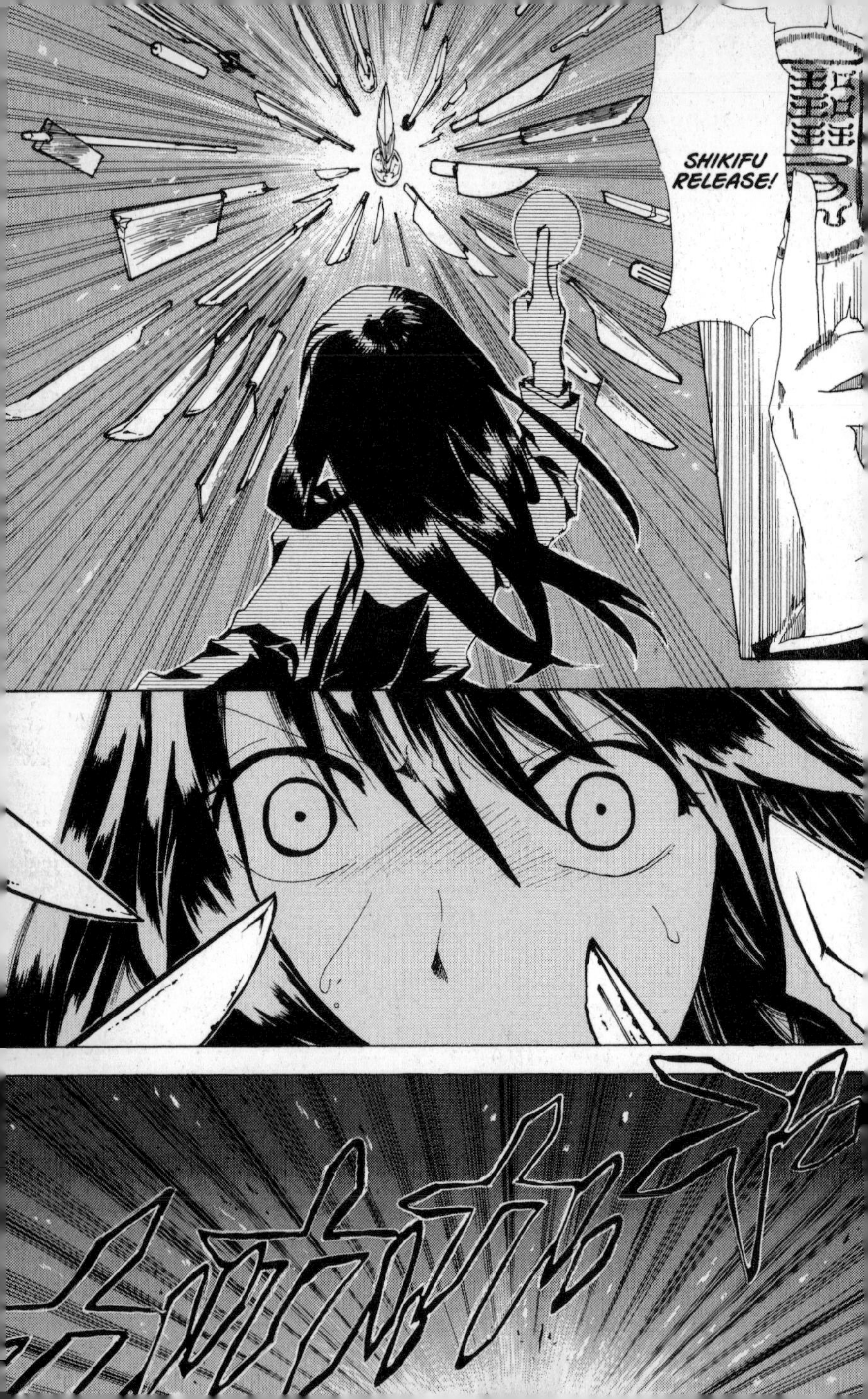
SHIKIFU RELEASE!

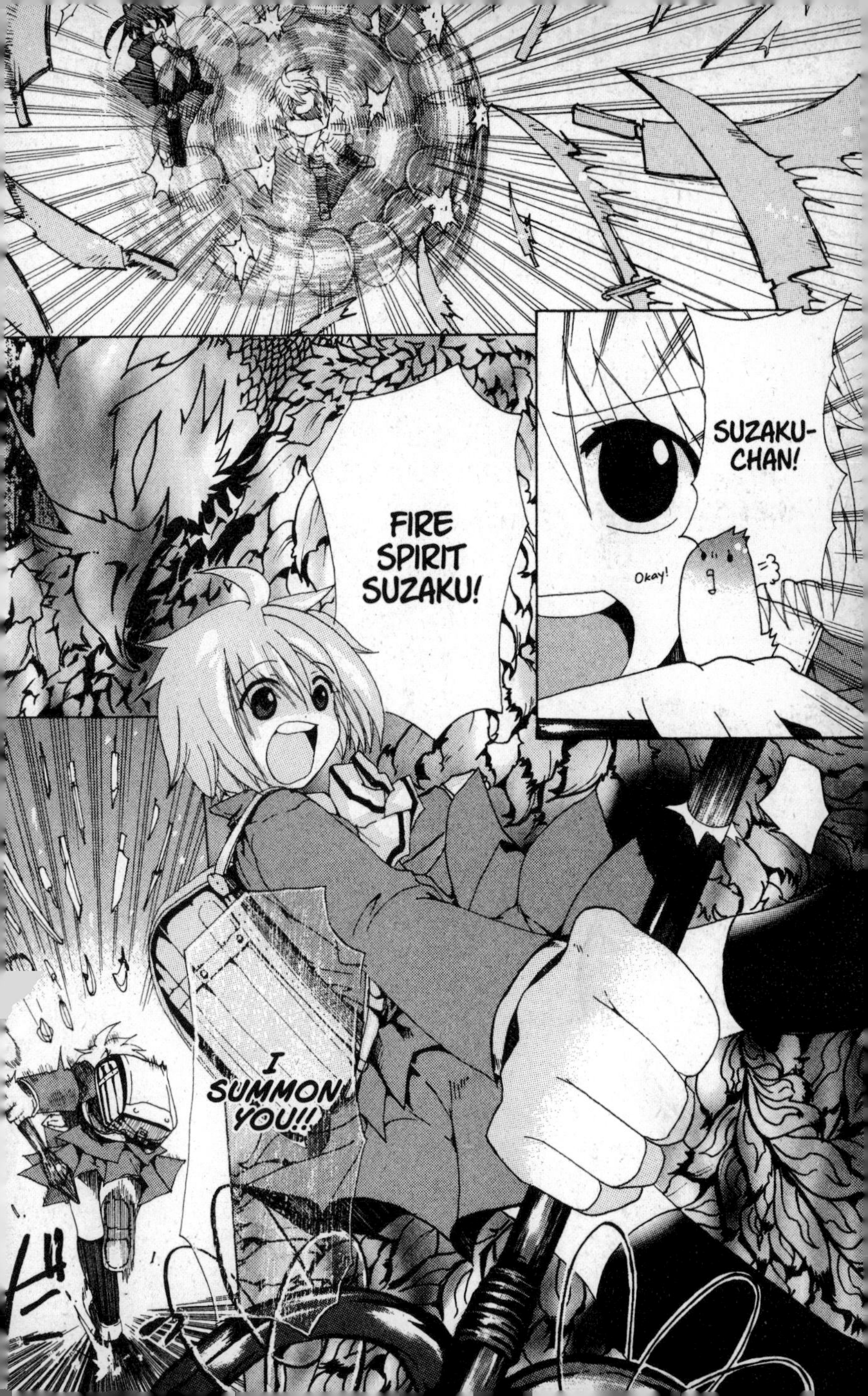
SUZAKU-CHAN!
Okay!
FIRE SPIRIT SUZAKU!
I SUMMON YOU!!

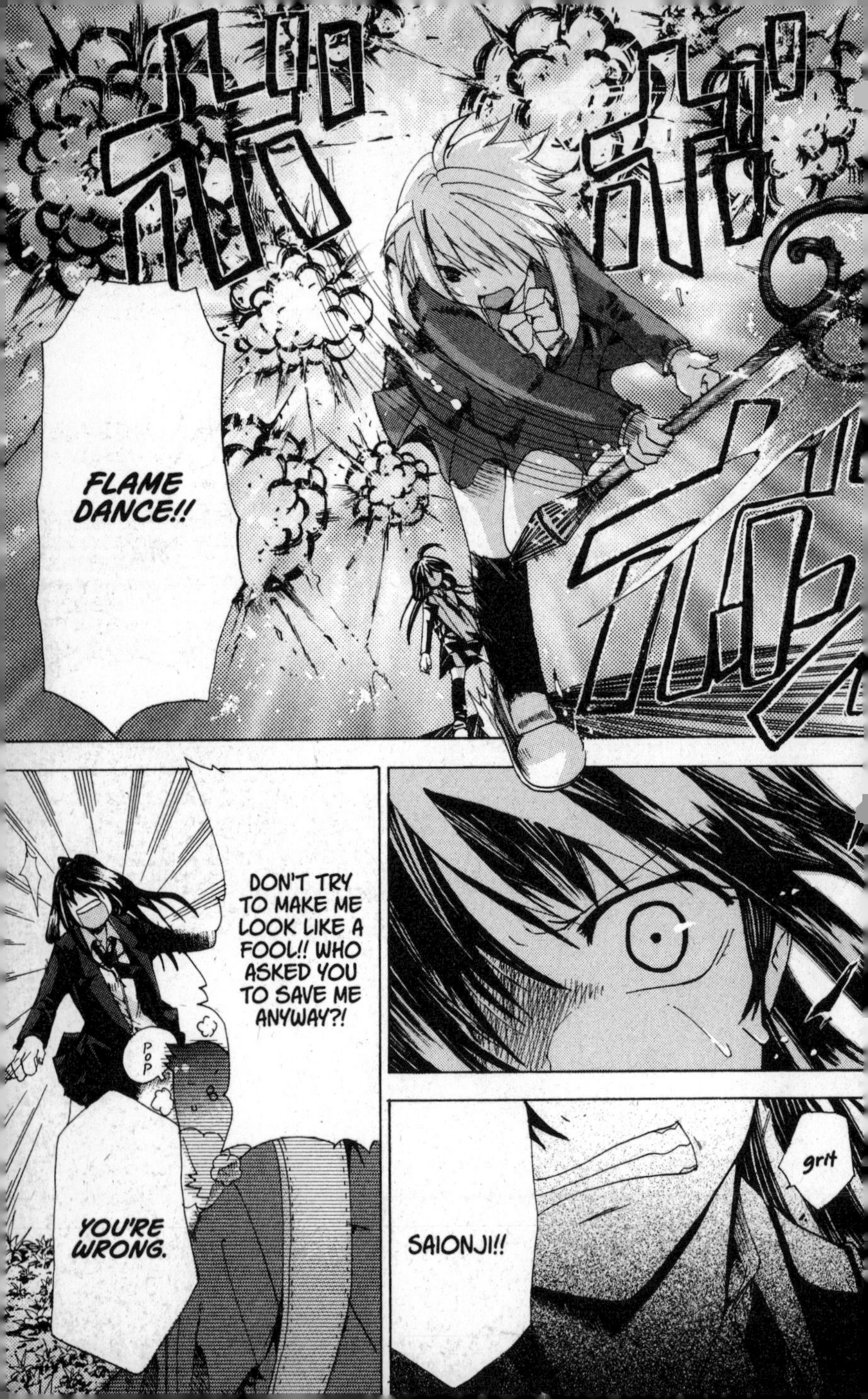
FLAME DANCE!!
grit
SAIONJI!!
DON'T TRY TO MAKE ME LOOK LIKE A FOOL!! WHO ASKED YOU TO SAVE ME ANYWAY?!
POP
YOU'RE WRONG.

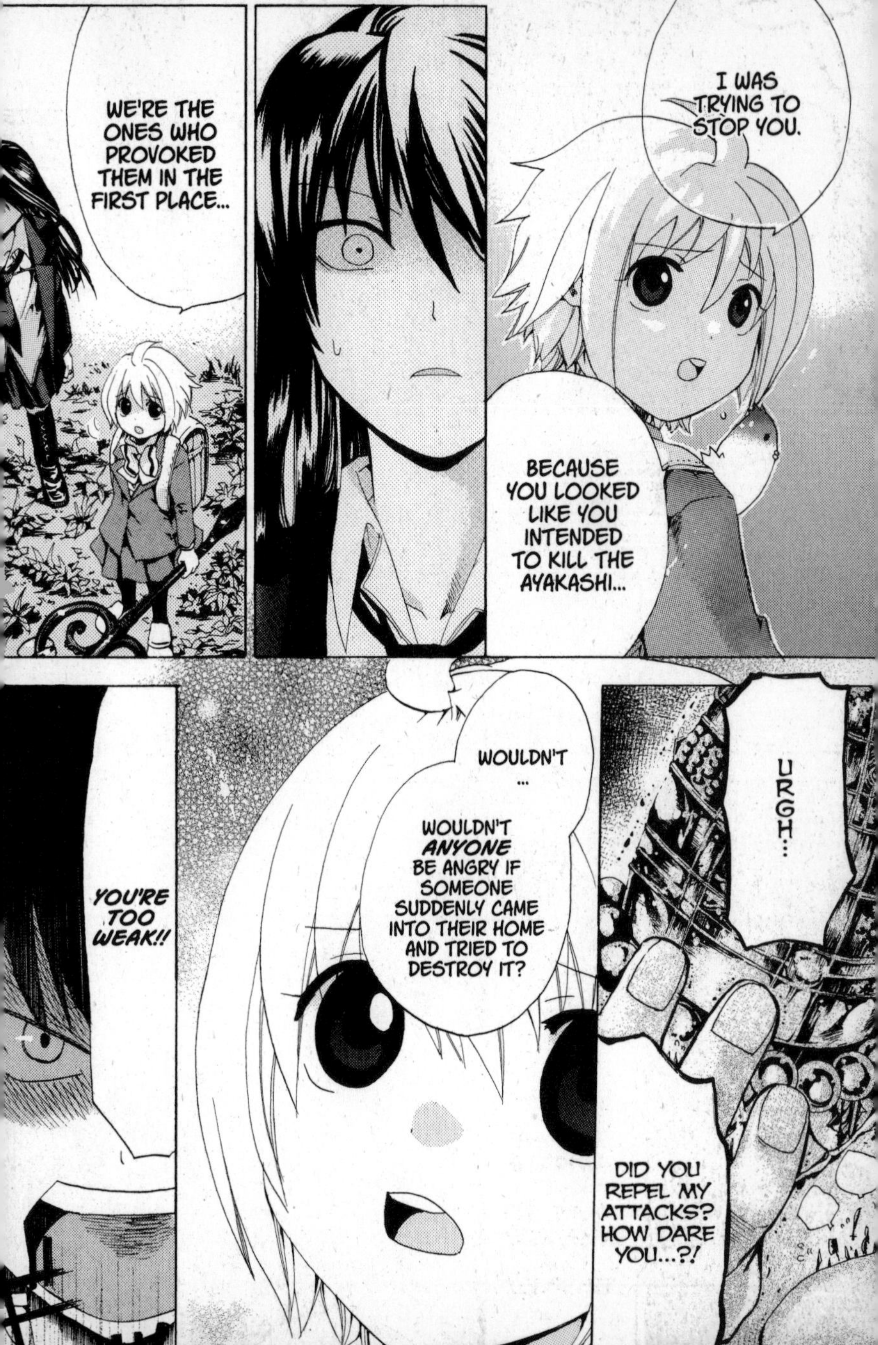
I WAS TRYING TO STOP YOU.
BECAUSE YOU LOOKED LIKE YOU INTENDED TO KILL THE AYAKASHI...
WE'RE THE ONES WHO PROVOKED THEM IN THE FIRST PLACE...
URGH...
DID YOU REPEL MY ATTACKS? HOW DARE YOU...?!
WOULDN'T ...
WOULDN'T ANYONE BE ANGRY IF SOMEONE SUDDENLY CAME INTO THEIR HOME AND TRIED TO DESTROY IT?
YOU'RE TOO WEAK!!

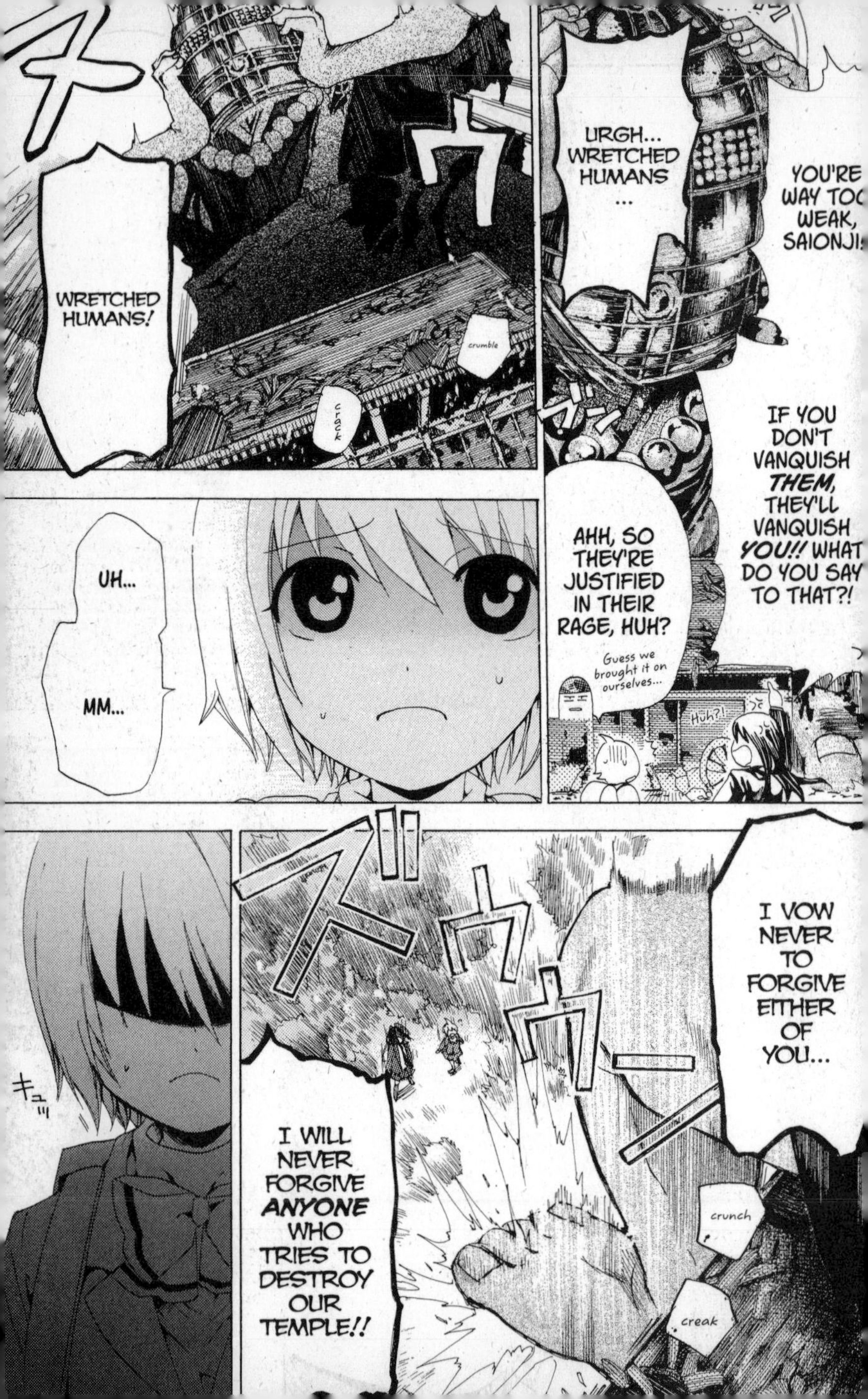
URGH... WRETCHED HUMANS ...
YOU'RE WAY TOO WEAK, SAIONJI!
IF YOU DON'T VANQUISH **THEM,** THEY'LL VANQUISH **YOU!!** WHAT DO YOU SAY TO THAT?!
WRETCHED HUMANS!
crumble
crack
AHH, SO THEY'RE JUSTIFIED IN THEIR RAGE, HUH?
Guess we brought it on ourselves...
Huh?!
UH...
MM...
I VOW NEVER TO FORGIVE EITHER OF YOU...
I WILL NEVER FORGIVE **ANYONE** WHO TRIES TO DESTROY OUR TEMPLE!!
crunch
creak
キュッ

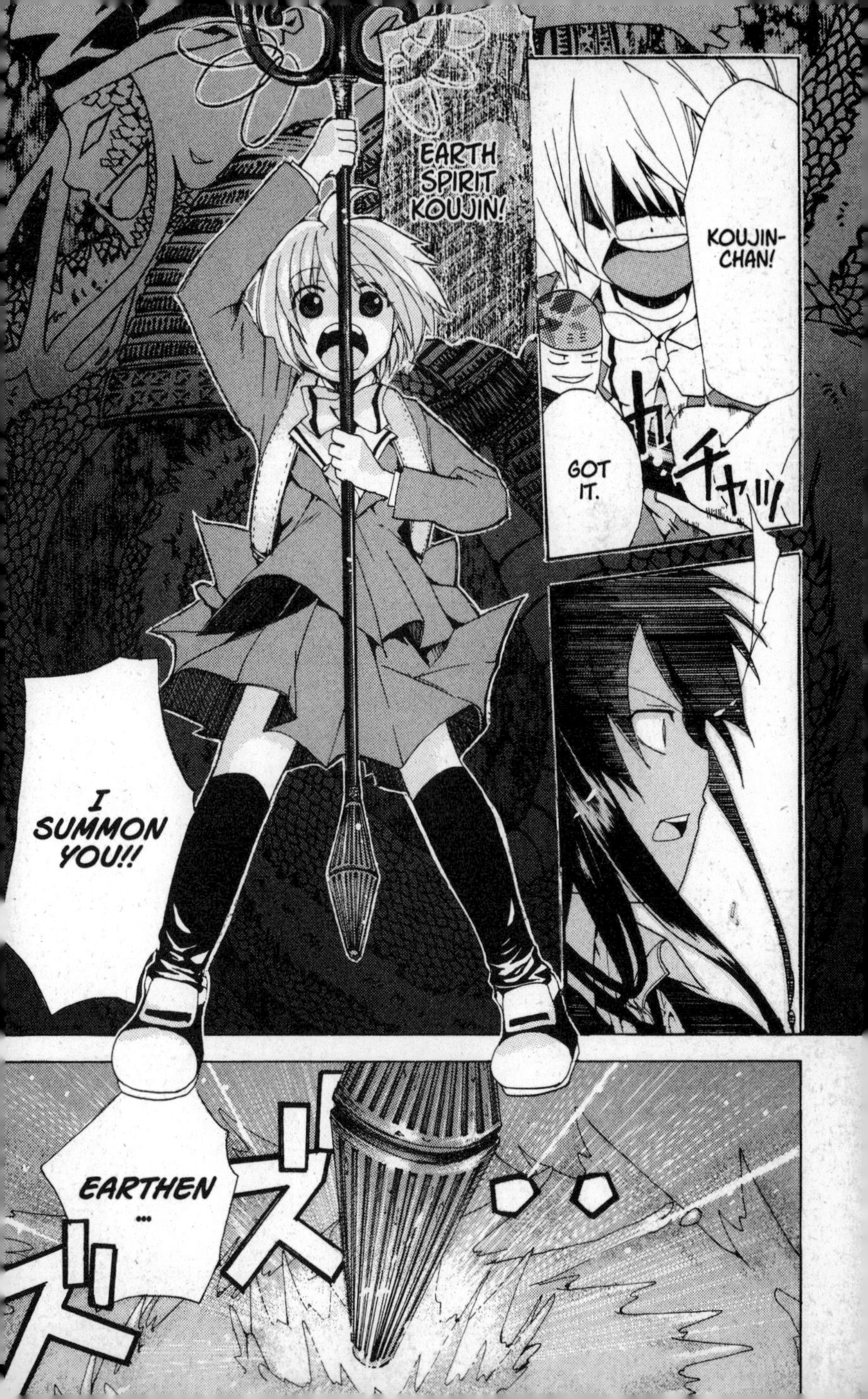
KOUJIN-CHAN!
GOT IT.
カチャッ
EARTH SPIRIT KOUJIN!
I SUMMON YOU!!
EARTHEN ...

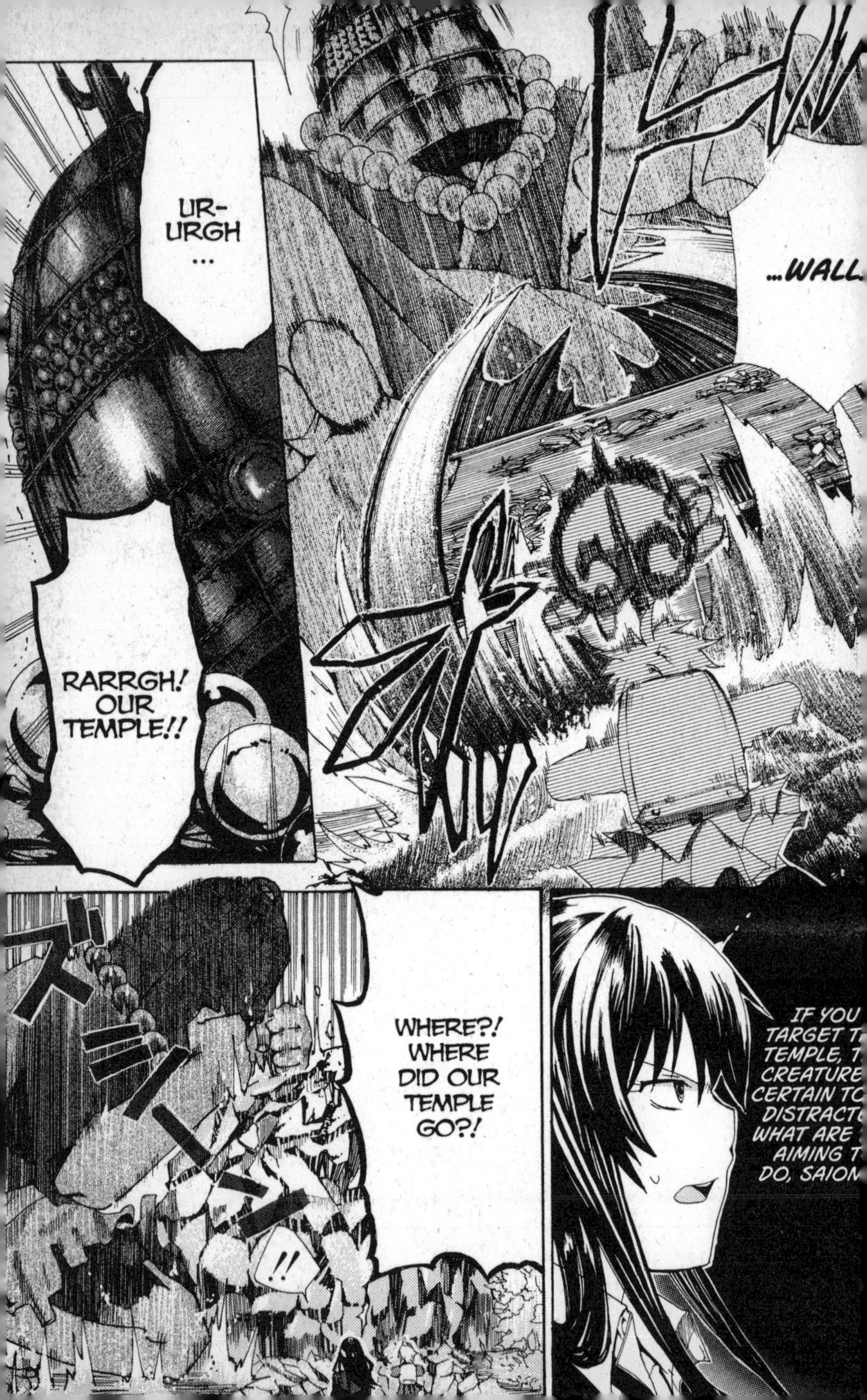
...WALL...
UR-URGH ...
RARRGH! OUR TEMPLE!!
IF YOU TARGET T TEMPLE, T CREATURE CERTAIN TO DISTRACT WHAT ARE AIMING T DO, SAIOM
WHERE?! WHERE DID OUR TEMPLE GO?!
!!

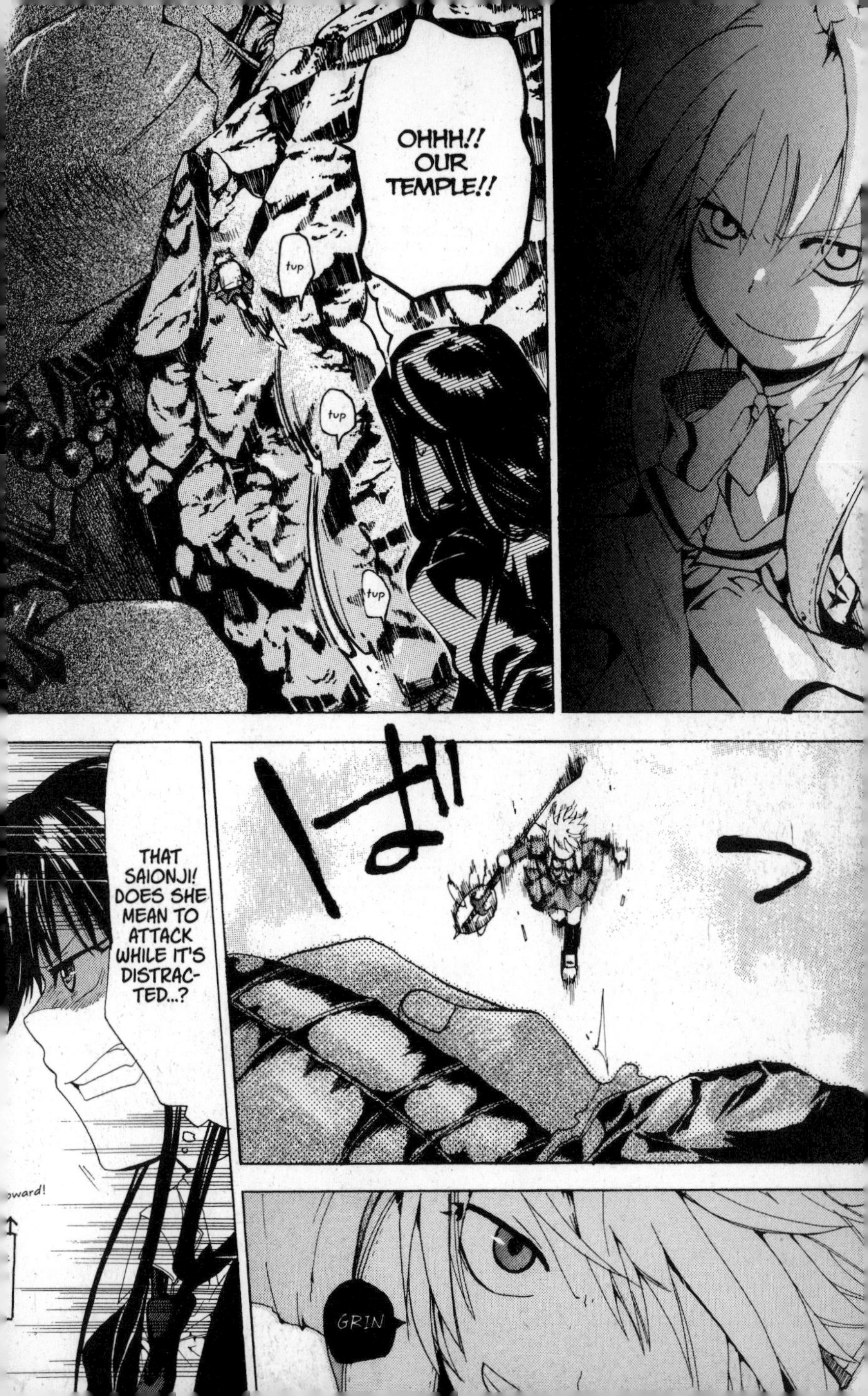
OHHH!! OUR TEMPLE!!
tup
tup
tup
GRIN
THAT SAIONJI! DOES SHE MEAN TO ATTACK WHILE IT'S DISTRAC-TED...?

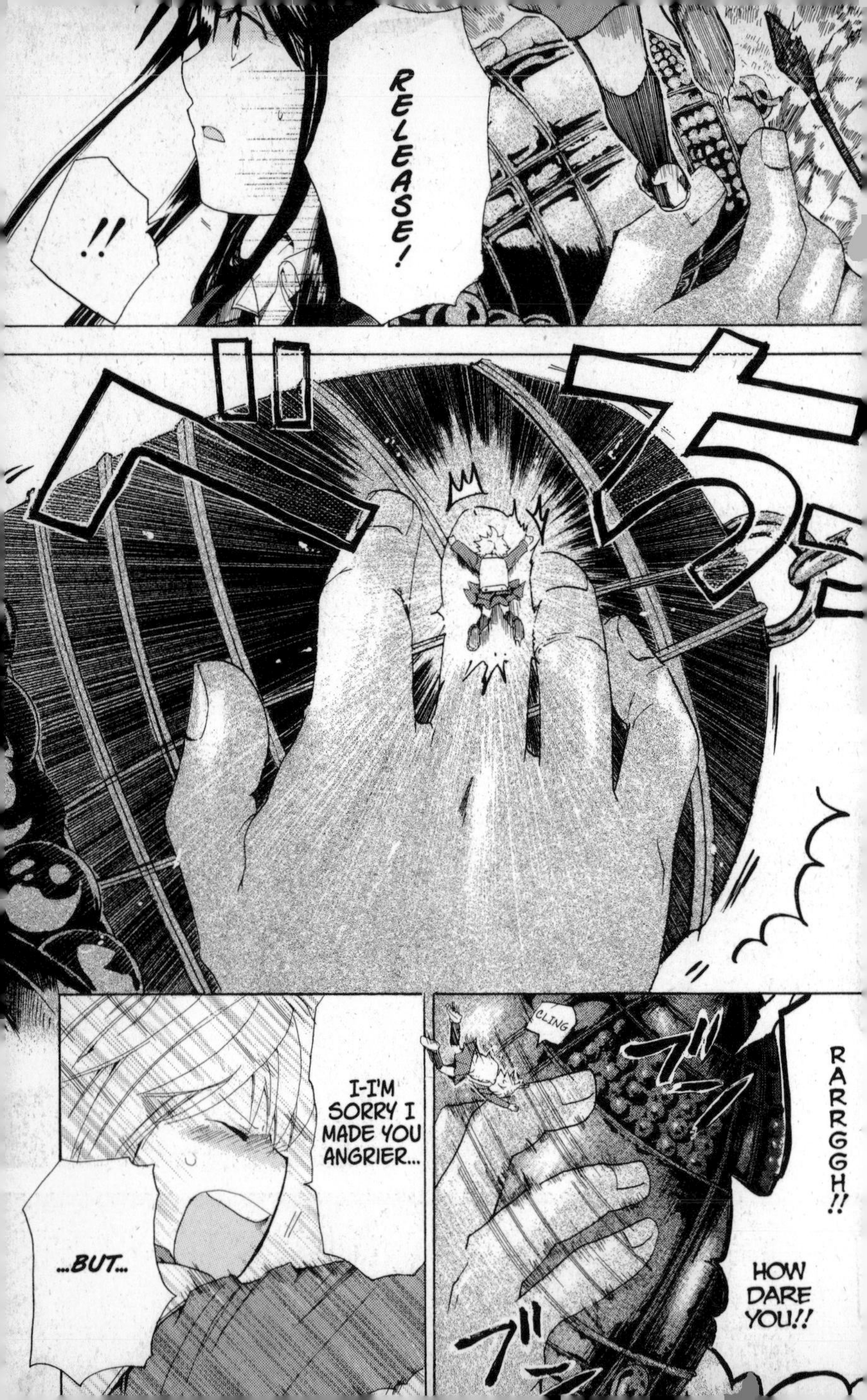
RELEASE!
!!
RARRGGH!!
CLING
HOW DARE YOU!!
I-I'M SORRY I MADE YOU ANGRIER...
...BUT...

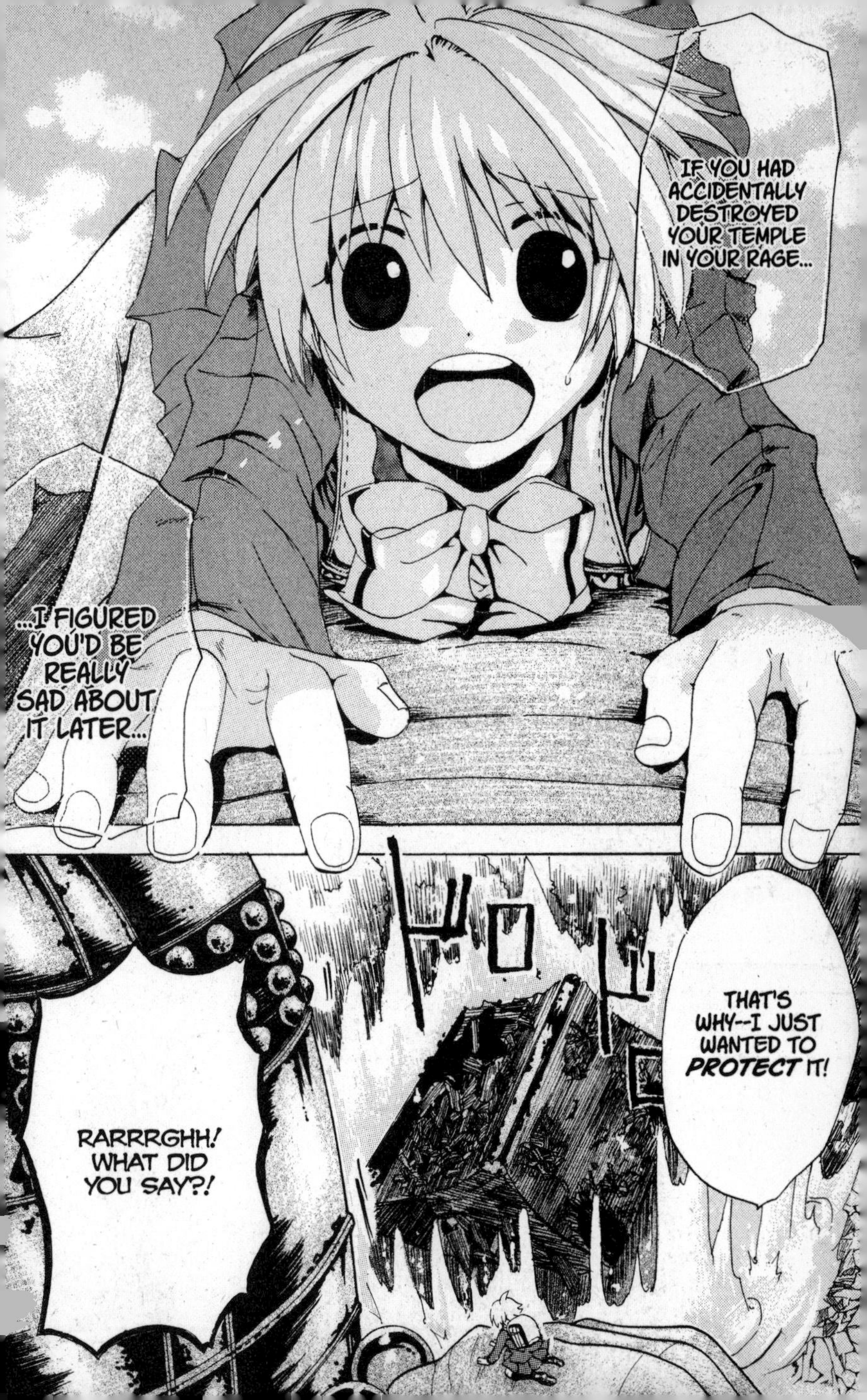
IF YOU HAD ACCIDENTALLY DESTROYED YOUR TEMPLE IN YOUR RAGE...
...I FIGURED YOU'D BE REALLY SAD ABOUT IT LATER...
THAT'S WHY--I JUST WANTED TO *PROTECT* IT!
RARRRGHH! WHAT DID YOU SAY?!

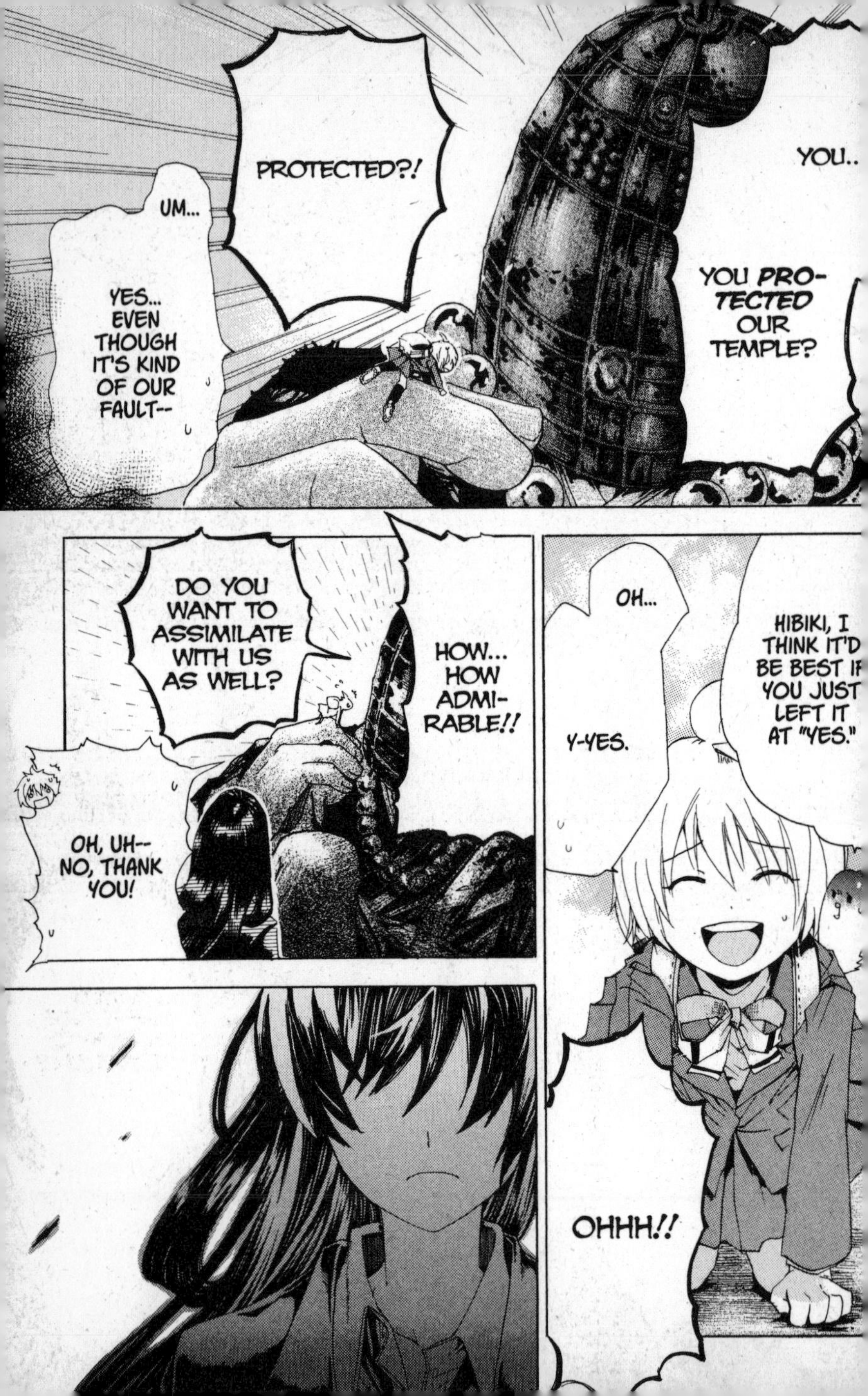
YOU..
YOU *PROTECTED* OUR TEMPLE?
PROTECTED?!
UM...
YES... EVEN THOUGH IT'S KIND OF OUR FAULT--
HIBIKI, I THINK IT'D BE BEST IF YOU JUST LEFT IT AT "YES."
OH...
Y-YES.
OHHH!!
HOW... HOW ADMIRABLE!!
DO YOU WANT TO ASSIMILATE WITH US AS WELL?
OH, UH-- NO, THANK YOU!

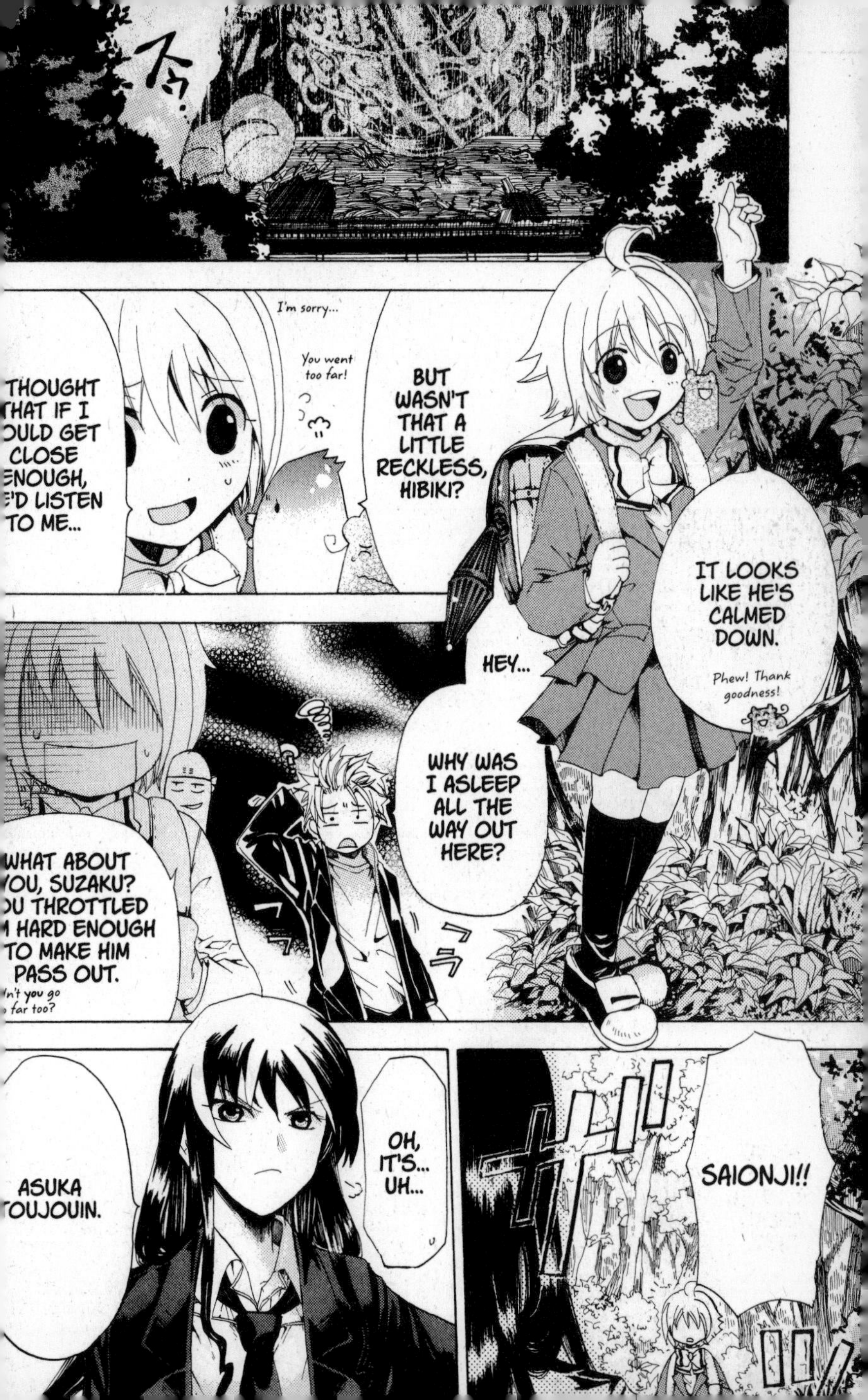
IT LOOKS LIKE HE'S CALMED DOWN.
Phew! Thank goodness!
BUT WASN'T THAT A LITTLE RECKLESS, HIBIKI?
You went too far!
I'm sorry...
THOUGHT THAT IF I OULD GET CLOSE ENOUGH, E'D LISTEN TO ME...
HEY...
WHY WAS I ASLEEP ALL THE WAY OUT HERE?
WHAT ABOUT YOU, SUZAKU? OU THROTTLED M HARD ENOUGH TO MAKE HIM PASS OUT.
n't you go far too?
SAIONJI!!
OH, IT'S... UH...
ASUKA OUJOUIN.

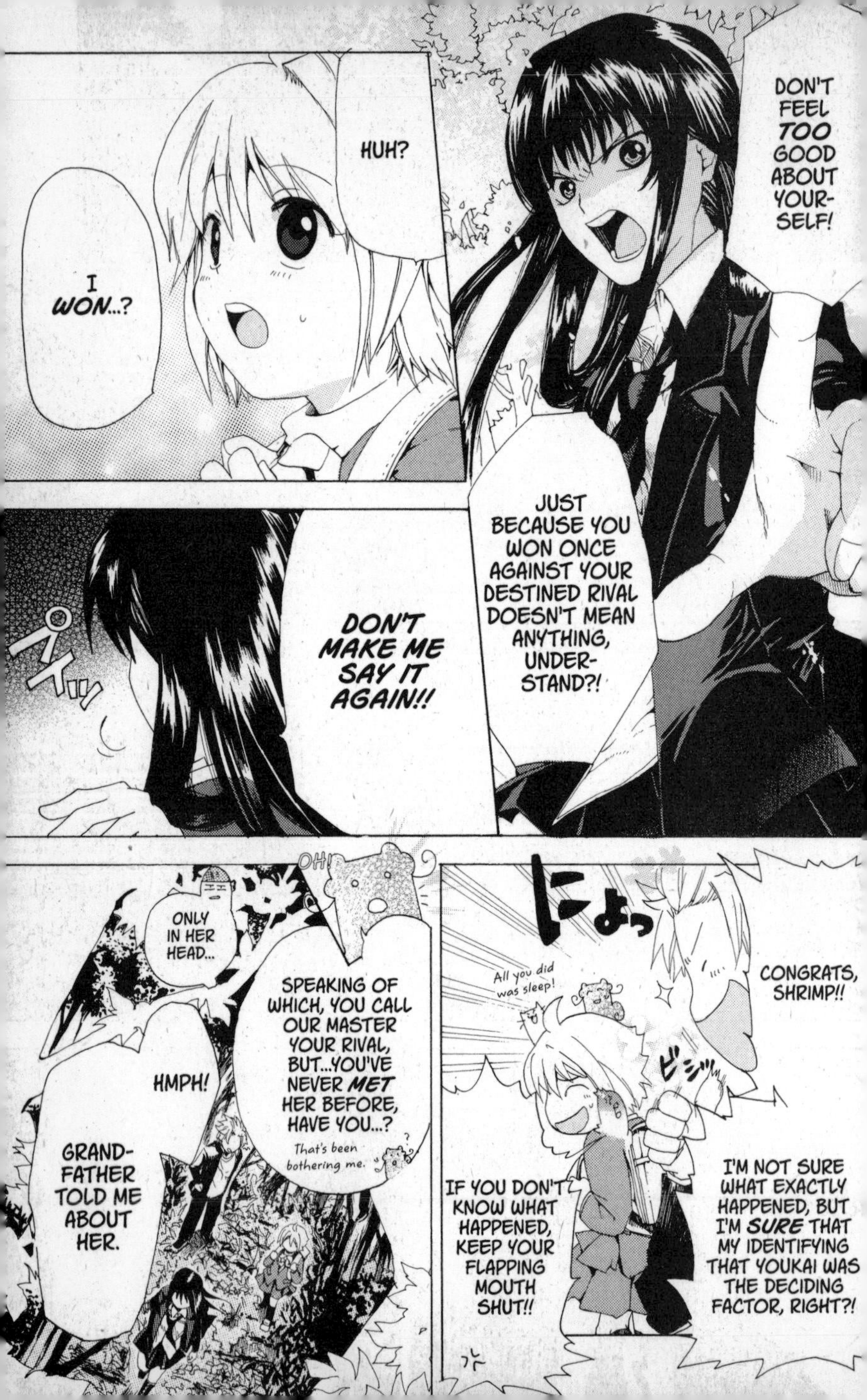
DON'T FEEL TOO GOOD ABOUT YOURSELF!
JUST BECAUSE YOU WON ONCE AGAINST YOUR DESTINED RIVAL DOESN'T MEAN ANYTHING, UNDERSTAND?!
HUH?
I WON...?
DON'T MAKE ME SAY IT AGAIN!!
にょっ
CONGRATS, SHRIMP!!
All you did was sleep!
I'M NOT SURE WHAT EXACTLY HAPPENED, BUT I'M SURE THAT MY IDENTIFYING THAT YOUKAI WAS THE DECIDING FACTOR, RIGHT?!
IF YOU DON'T KNOW WHAT HAPPENED, KEEP YOUR FLAPPING MOUTH SHUT!!
OH!
ONLY IN HER HEAD...
SPEAKING OF WHICH, YOU CALL OUR MASTER YOUR RIVAL, BUT...YOU'VE NEVER MET HER BEFORE, HAVE YOU...?
That's been bothering me.
HMPH!
GRANDFATHER TOLD ME ABOUT HER.

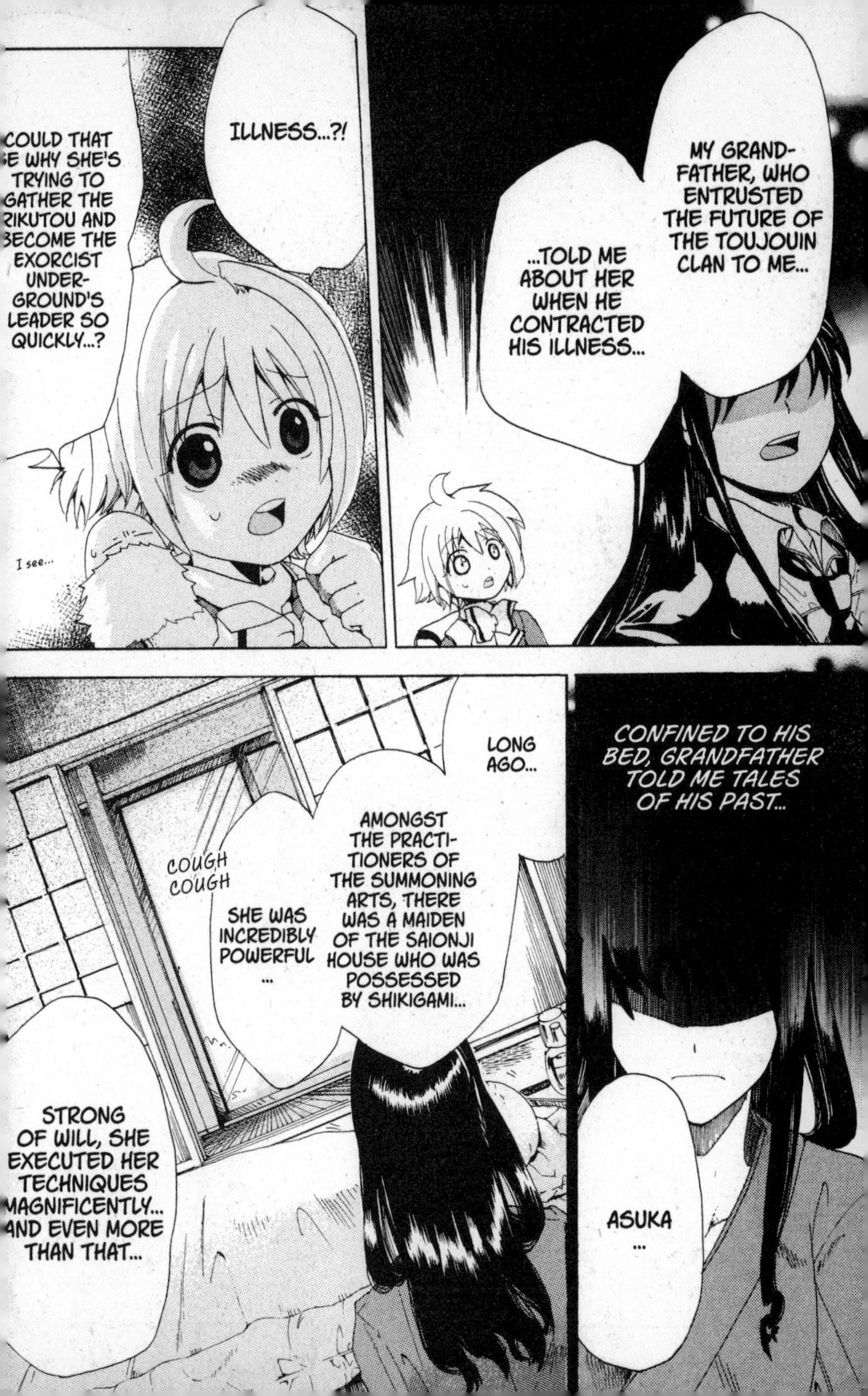
MY GRAND-FATHER, WHO ENTRUSTED THE FUTURE OF THE TOUJOUIN CLAN TO ME...
...TOLD ME ABOUT HER WHEN HE CONTRACTED HIS ILLNESS...
ILLNESS...?!
COULD THAT E WHY SHE'S TRYING TO GATHER THE IKUTOU AND ECOME THE EXORCIST UNDER-GROUND'S LEADER SO QUICKLY...?
I see...
CONFINED TO HIS BED, GRANDFATHER TOLD ME TALES OF HIS PAST...
ASUKA ...
LONG AGO...
AMONGST THE PRACTI-TIONERS OF THE SUMMONING ARTS, THERE WAS A MAIDEN OF THE SAIONJI HOUSE WHO WAS POSSESSED BY SHIKIGAMI...
COUGH COUGH
SHE WAS INCREDIBLY POWERFUL ...
STRONG OF WILL, SHE EXECUTED HER TECHNIQUES MAGNIFICENTLY... AND EVEN MORE THAN THAT...

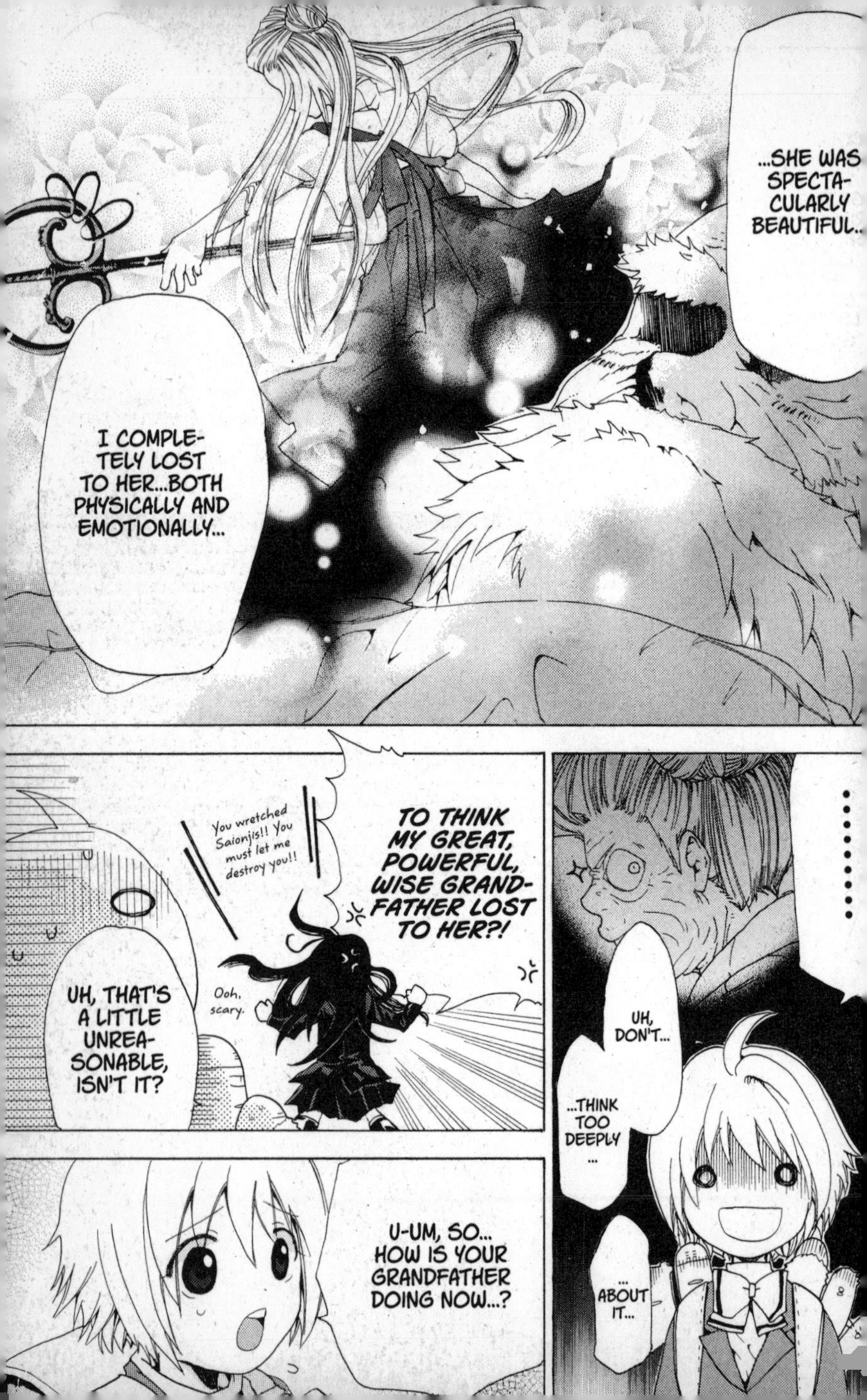
...SHE WAS SPECTA-CULARLY BEAUTIFUL...
I COMPLE-TELY LOST TO HER...BOTH PHYSICALLY AND EMOTIONALLY...
......
UH, DON'T...
...THINK TOO DEEPLY ...
... ABOUT IT...
TO THINK MY GREAT, POWERFUL, WISE GRAND-FATHER LOST TO HER?!
You wretched Saionjis!! You must let me destroy you!!
Ooh, scary.
UH, THAT'S A LITTLE UNREA-SONABLE, ISN'T IT?
U-UM, SO... HOW IS YOUR GRANDFATHER DOING NOW...?

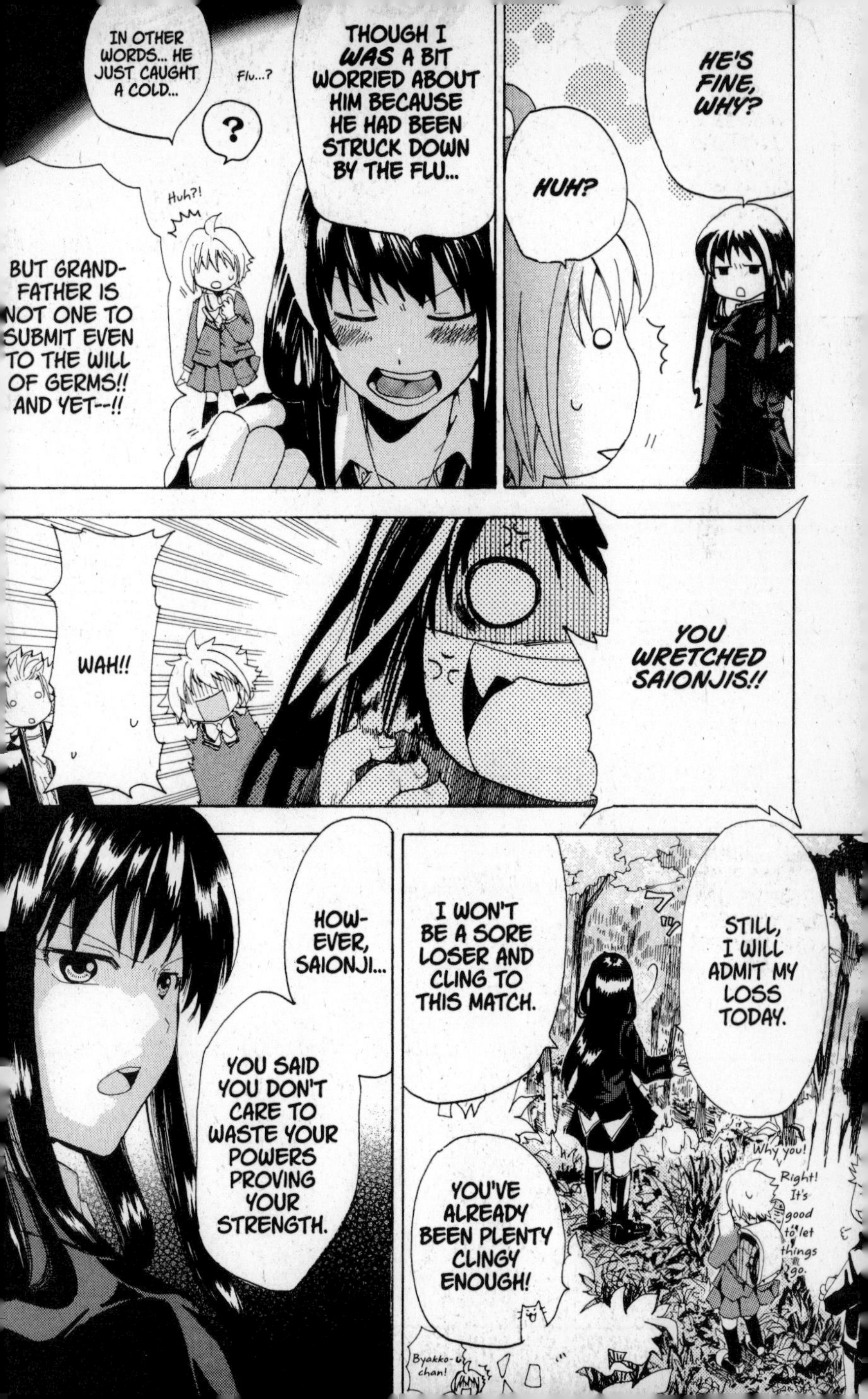
HE'S FINE, WHY?
HUH?
THOUGH I WAS A BIT WORRIED ABOUT HIM BECAUSE HE HAD BEEN STRUCK DOWN BY THE FLU...
Flu...?
?
IN OTHER WORDS... HE JUST CAUGHT A COLD...
Huh?!
BUT GRAND-FATHER IS NOT ONE TO SUBMIT EVEN TO THE WILL OF GERMS!! AND YET--!!
YOU WRETCHED SAIONJIS!!
WAH!!
STILL, I WILL ADMIT MY LOSS TODAY.
I WON'T BE A SORE LOSER AND CLING TO THIS MATCH.
Why you!
Right! It's good to let things go.
YOU'VE ALREADY BEEN PLENTY CLINGY ENOUGH!
Byakko-chan!
HOW-EVER, SAIONJI...
YOU SAID YOU DON'T CARE TO WASTE YOUR POWERS PROVING YOUR STRENGTH.

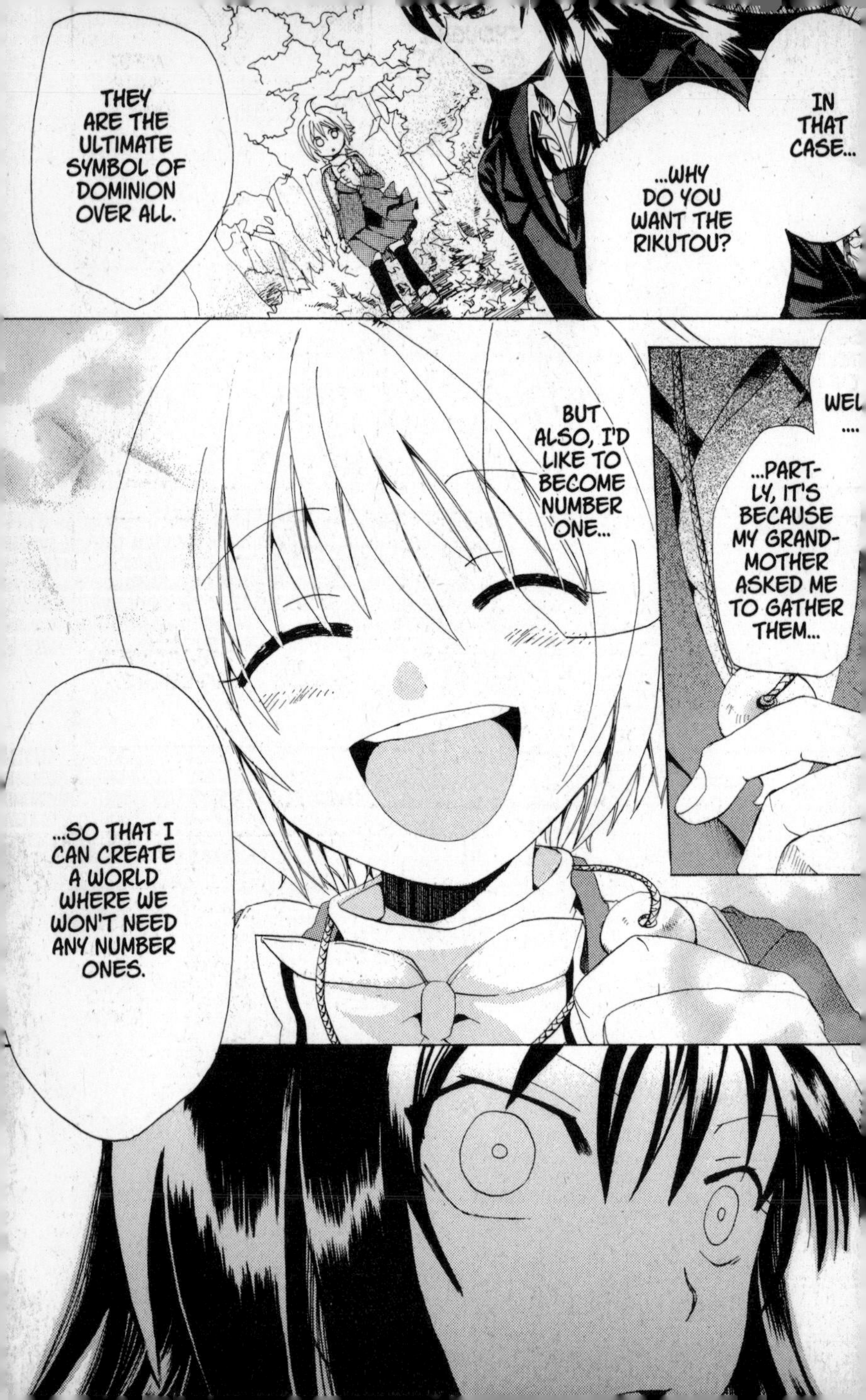
IN THAT CASE...
...WHY DO YOU WANT THE RIKUTOU?
THEY ARE THE ULTIMATE SYMBOL OF DOMINION OVER ALL.
WEL ....
...PART-LY, IT'S BECAUSE MY GRAND-MOTHER ASKED ME TO GATHER THEM...
BUT ALSO, I'D LIKE TO BECOME NUMBER ONE...
...SO THAT I CAN CREATE A WORLD WHERE WE WON'T NEED ANY NUMBER ONES.

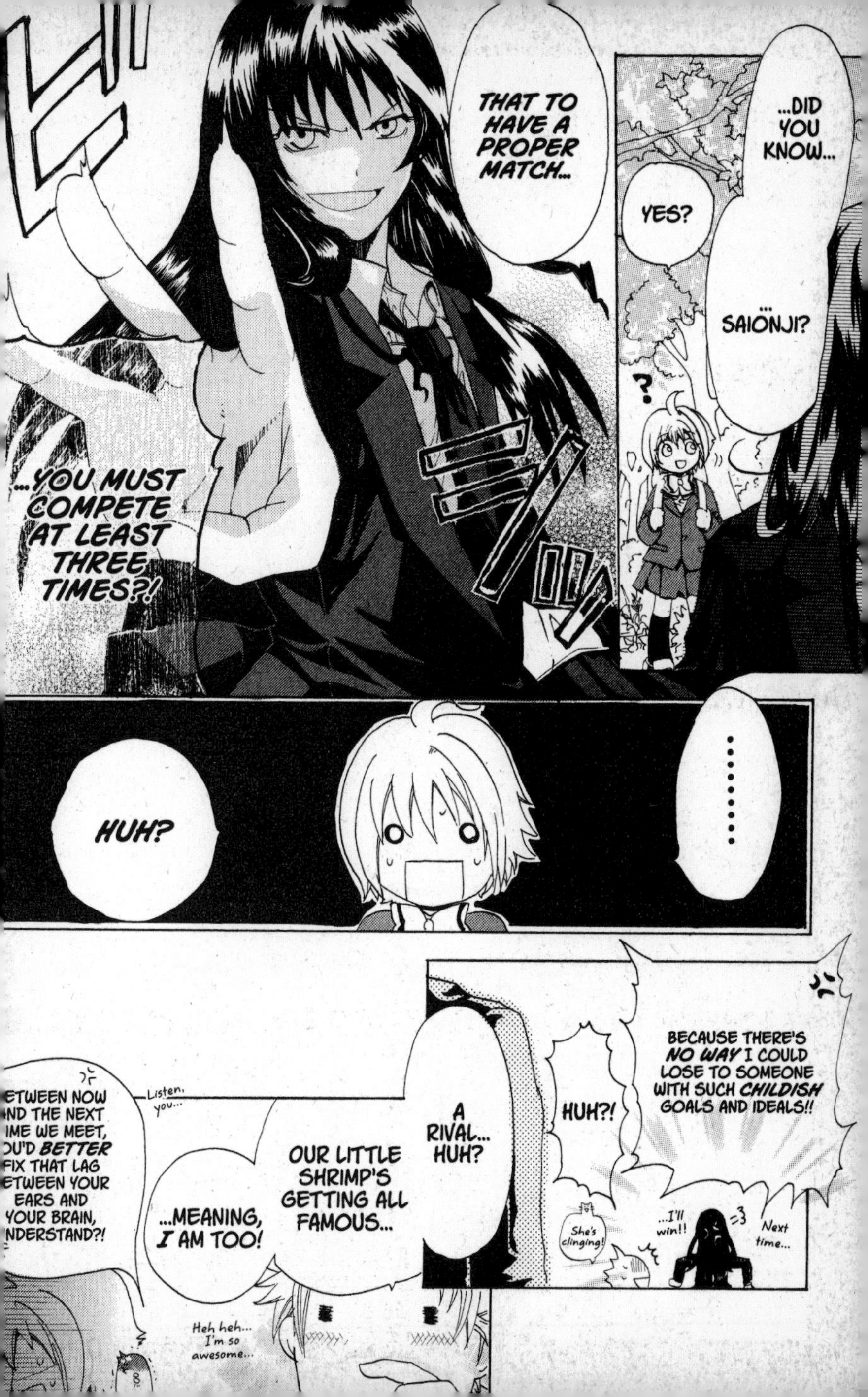
...DID YOU KNOW...
YES?
...SAIONJI?
THAT TO HAVE A PROPER MATCH...
...YOU MUST COMPETE AT LEAST THREE TIMES?!
....
HUH?
BECAUSE THERE'S *NO WAY* I COULD LOSE TO SOMEONE WITH SUCH *CHILDISH* GOALS AND IDEALS!!
HUH?!
Next time...
...I'll win!!
She's clinging!
A RIVAL... HUH?
OUR LITTLE SHRIMP'S GETTING ALL FAMOUS...
...MEANING, *I* AM TOO!
Listen, you...
ETWEEN NOW ND THE NEXT IME WE MEET, OU'D *BETTER* FIX THAT LAG ETWEEN YOUR EARS AND YOUR BRAIN, NDERSTAND?!
Heh heh... I'm so awesome...

MID-VOLUME BONUS COMIC.

A DAY IN THE LIFE OF A SHIKIGAMI (PART 3).

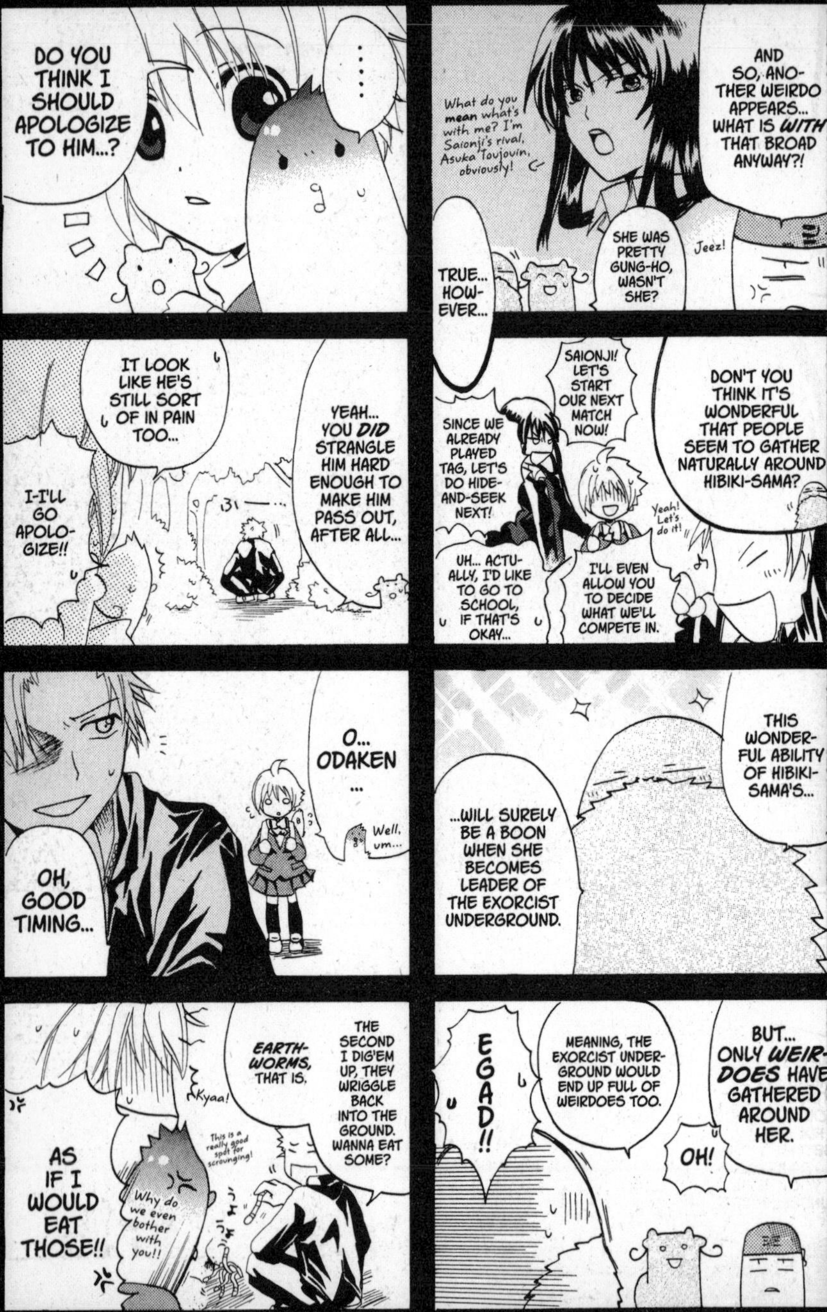
AND SO, ANOTHER WEIRDO APPEARS... WHAT IS WITH THAT BROAD ANYWAY?!
What do you mean what's with me? I'm Saionji's rival, Asuka Toujouin, obviously!
Jeez!
SHE WAS PRETTY GUNG-HO, WASN'T SHE?
TRUE... HOWEVER...
DON'T YOU THINK IT'S WONDERFUL THAT PEOPLE SEEM TO GATHER NATURALLY AROUND HIBIKI-SAMA?
SAIONJI! LET'S START OUR NEXT MATCH NOW!
Yeah! Let's do it!
SINCE WE ALREADY PLAYED TAG, LET'S DO HIDE-AND-SEEK NEXT!
I'LL EVEN ALLOW YOU TO DECIDE WHAT WE'LL COMPETE IN.
UH... ACTUALLY, I'D LIKE TO GO TO SCHOOL, IF THAT'S OKAY...
THIS WONDERFUL ABILITY OF HIBIKI-SAMA'S...
...WILL SURELY BE A BOON WHEN SHE BECOMES LEADER OF THE EXORCIST UNDERGROUND.
BUT... ONLY WEIRDOES HAVE GATHERED AROUND HER.
OH!
MEANING, THE EXORCIST UNDERGROUND WOULD END UP FULL OF WEIRDOES TOO.
EGAD!!
......
DO YOU THINK I SHOULD APOLOGIZE TO HIM...?
YEAH... YOU DID STRANGLE HIM HARD ENOUGH TO MAKE HIM PASS OUT, AFTER ALL...
IT LOOK LIKE HE'S STILL SORT OF IN PAIN TOO...
I-I'LL GO APOLOGIZE!!
O... ODAKEN ...
Well, um...
OH, GOOD TIMING...
THE SECOND I DIG'EM UP, THEY WRIGGLE BACK INTO THE GROUND. WANNA EAT SOME?
EARTHWORMS, THAT IS.
Kyaa!
This is a really good spot for scrounging!
AS IF I WOULD EAT THOSE!!
Why do we even bother with you!!

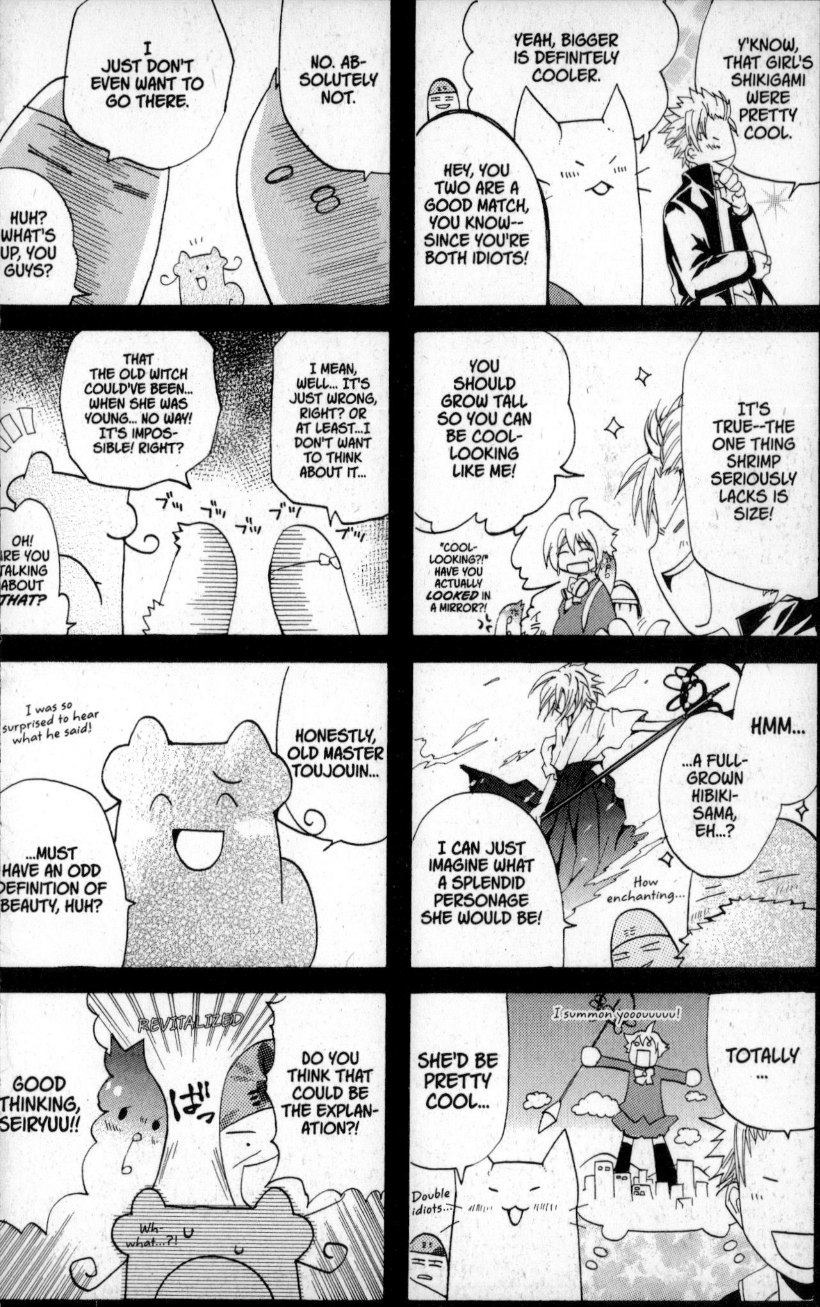
Y'KNOW, THAT GIRL'S SHIKIGAMI WERE PRETTY COOL.
YEAH, BIGGER IS DEFINITELY COOLER.
HEY, YOU TWO ARE A GOOD MATCH, YOU KNOW-- SINCE YOU'RE BOTH IDIOTS!
IT'S TRUE--THE ONE THING SHRIMP SERIOUSLY LACKS IS SIZE!
YOU SHOULD GROW TALL SO YOU CAN BE COOL-LOOKING LIKE ME!
"COOL-LOOKING?!" HAVE YOU ACTUALLY LOOKED IN A MIRROR?!
HMM...
...A FULL-GROWN HIBIKI-SAMA, EH...?
How enchanting...
I CAN JUST IMAGINE WHAT A SPLENDID PERSONAGE SHE WOULD BE!
TOTALLY...
I summon yooouuuuu!
SHE'D BE PRETTY COOL...
Double idiots...
NO. ABSOLUTELY NOT.
I JUST DON'T EVEN WANT TO GO THERE.
HUH? WHAT'S UP, YOU GUYS?
I MEAN, WELL... IT'S JUST WRONG, RIGHT? OR AT LEAST...I DON'T WANT TO THINK ABOUT IT...
THAT THE OLD WITCH COULD'VE BEEN... WHEN SHE WAS YOUNG... NO WAY! IT'S IMPOSSIBLE! RIGHT?
OH! RE YOU TALKING ABOUT THAT?
HONESTLY, OLD MASTER TOUJOUIN...
I was so surprised to hear what he said!
...MUST HAVE AN ODD DEFINITION OF BEAUTY, HUH?
DO YOU THINK THAT COULD BE THE EXPLANATION?!
REVITALIZED
ぱっ
GOOD THINKING, SEIRYUU!!
Wh-what...?!

O BE CONTINUED...?

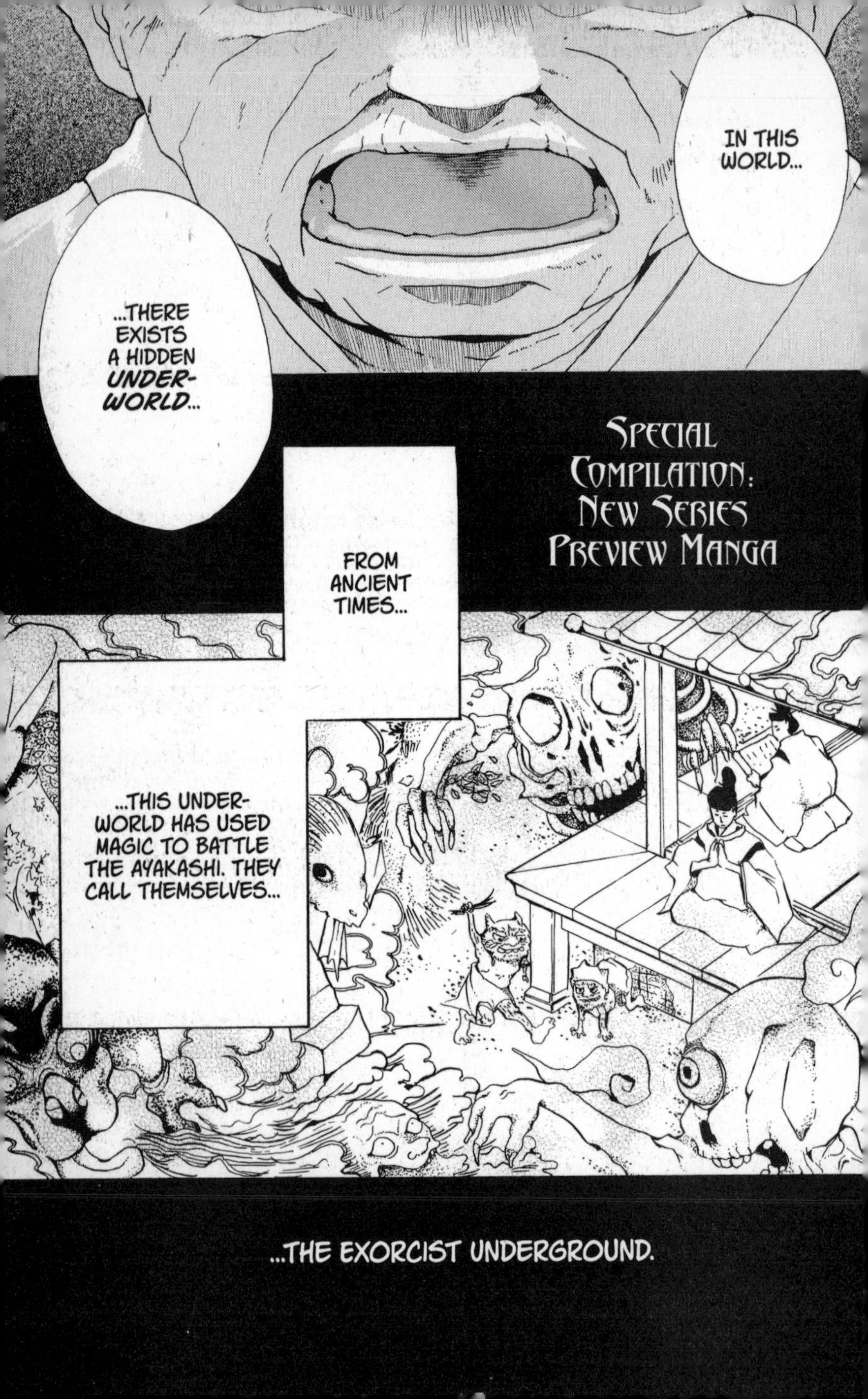
IN THIS WORLD...
...THERE EXISTS A HIDDEN UNDER-WORLD...
SPECIAL COMPILATION: NEW SERIES PREVIEW MANGA
FROM ANCIENT TIMES...
...THIS UNDER-WORLD HAS USED MAGIC TO BATTLE THE AYAKASHI. THEY CALL THEMSELVES...
...THE EXORCIST UNDERGROUND.

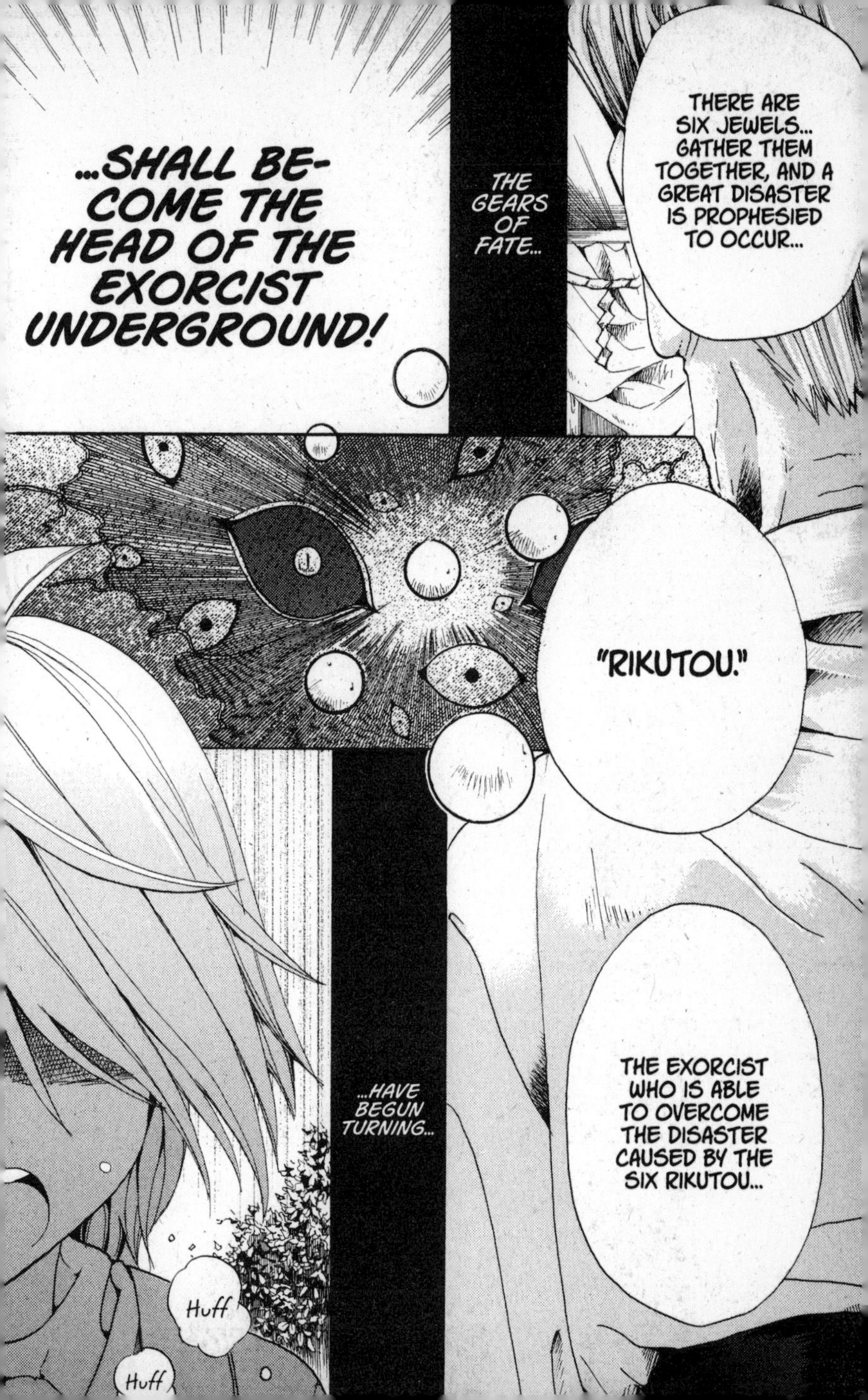
THERE ARE SIX JEWELS... GATHER THEM TOGETHER, AND A GREAT DISASTER IS PROPHESIED TO OCCUR...
"RIKUTOU."
THE EXORCIST WHO IS ABLE TO OVERCOME THE DISASTER CAUSED BY THE SIX RIKUTOU...
...SHALL BE-COME THE HEAD OF THE EXORCIST UNDERGROUND!
THE GEARS OF FATE...
...HAVE BEGUN TURNING...
Huff
Huff

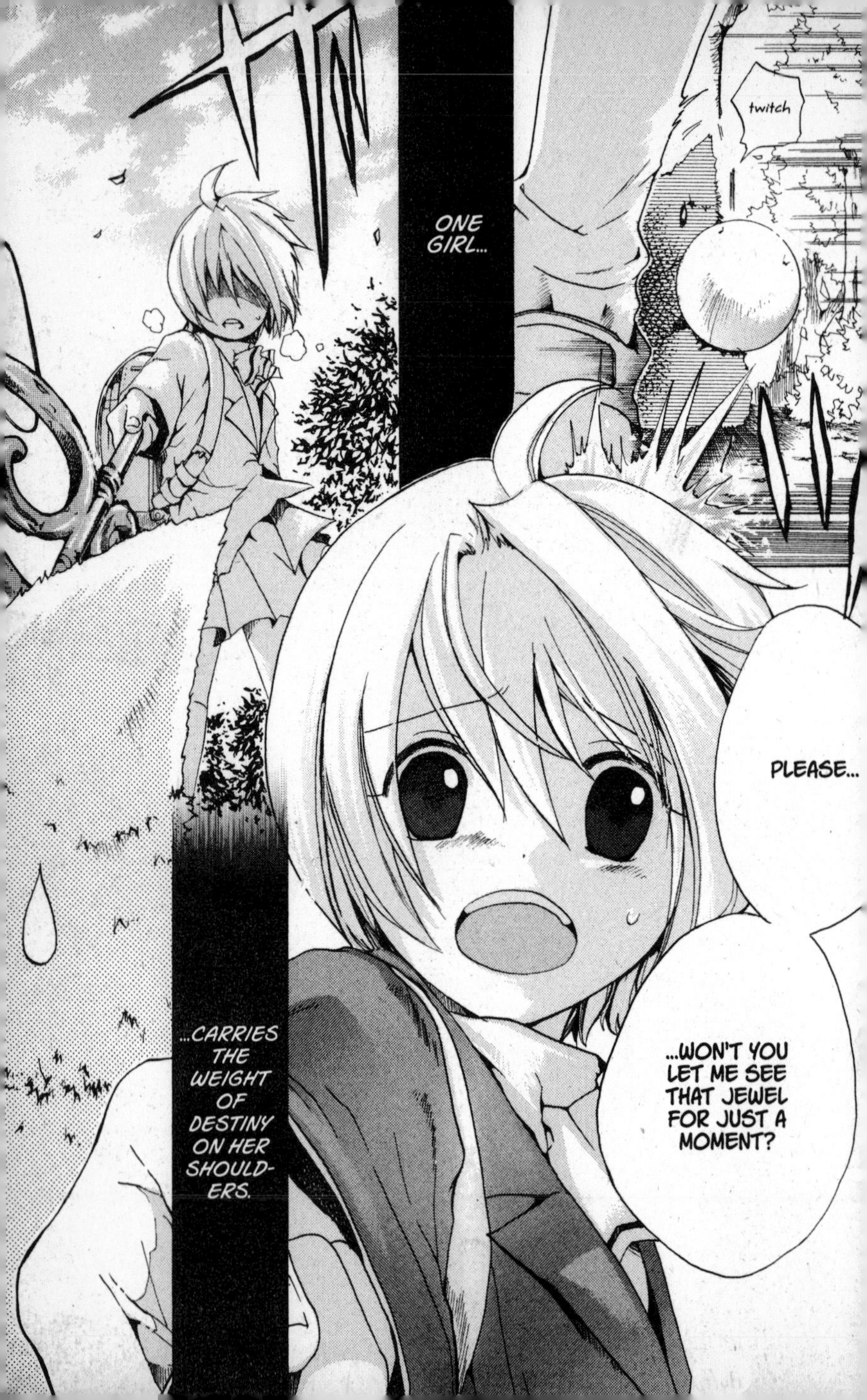
twitch
ONE GIRL...
PLEASE...
...WON'T YOU LET ME SEE THAT JEWEL FOR JUST A MOMENT?
...CARRIES THE WEIGHT OF DESTINY ON HER SHOULDERS.

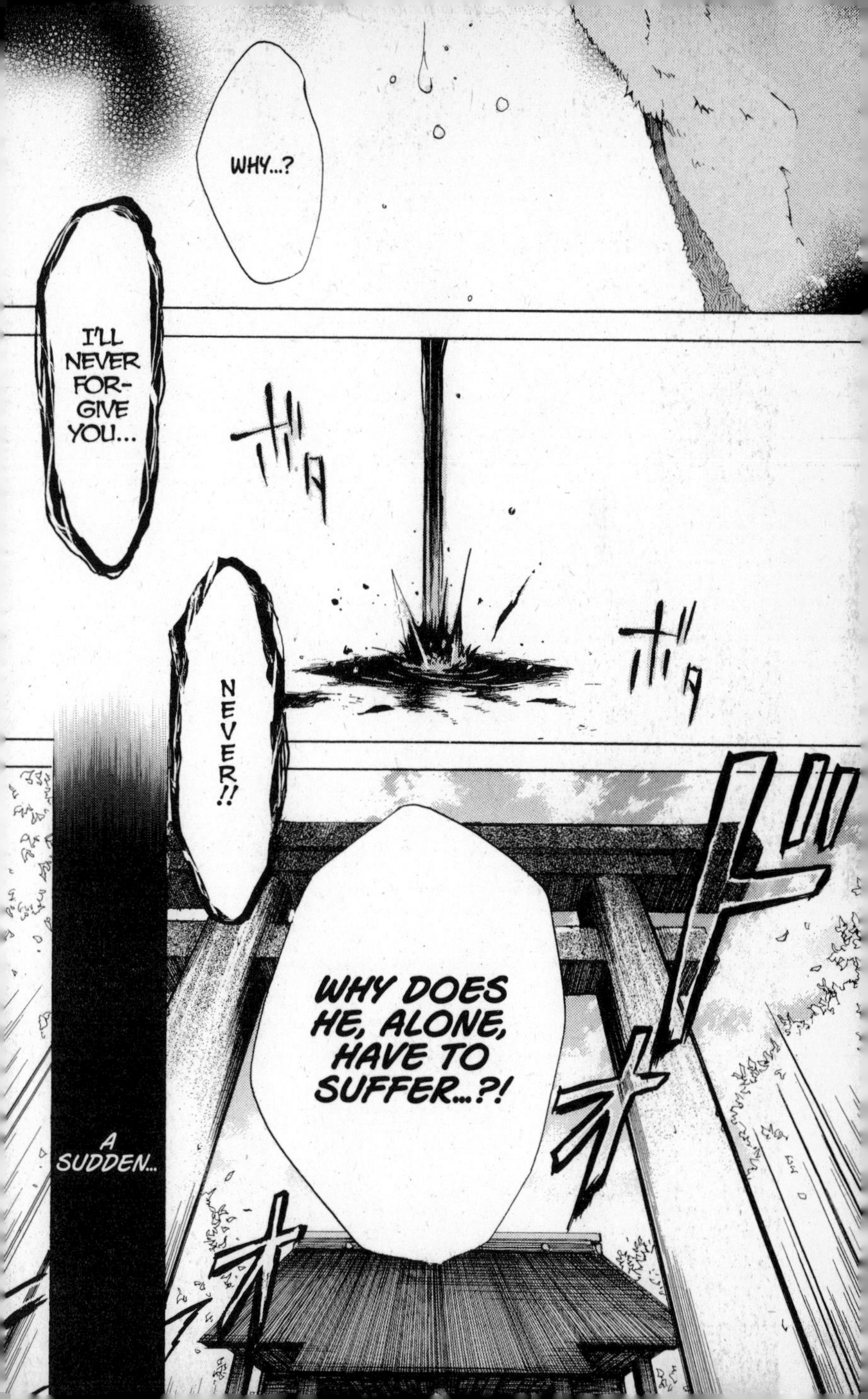
WHY...?
I'LL NEVER FOR-GIVE YOU...
ボタ
ボタ
NEVER!!
WHY DOES HE, ALONE, HAVE TO SUFFER...?!
A SUDDEN...

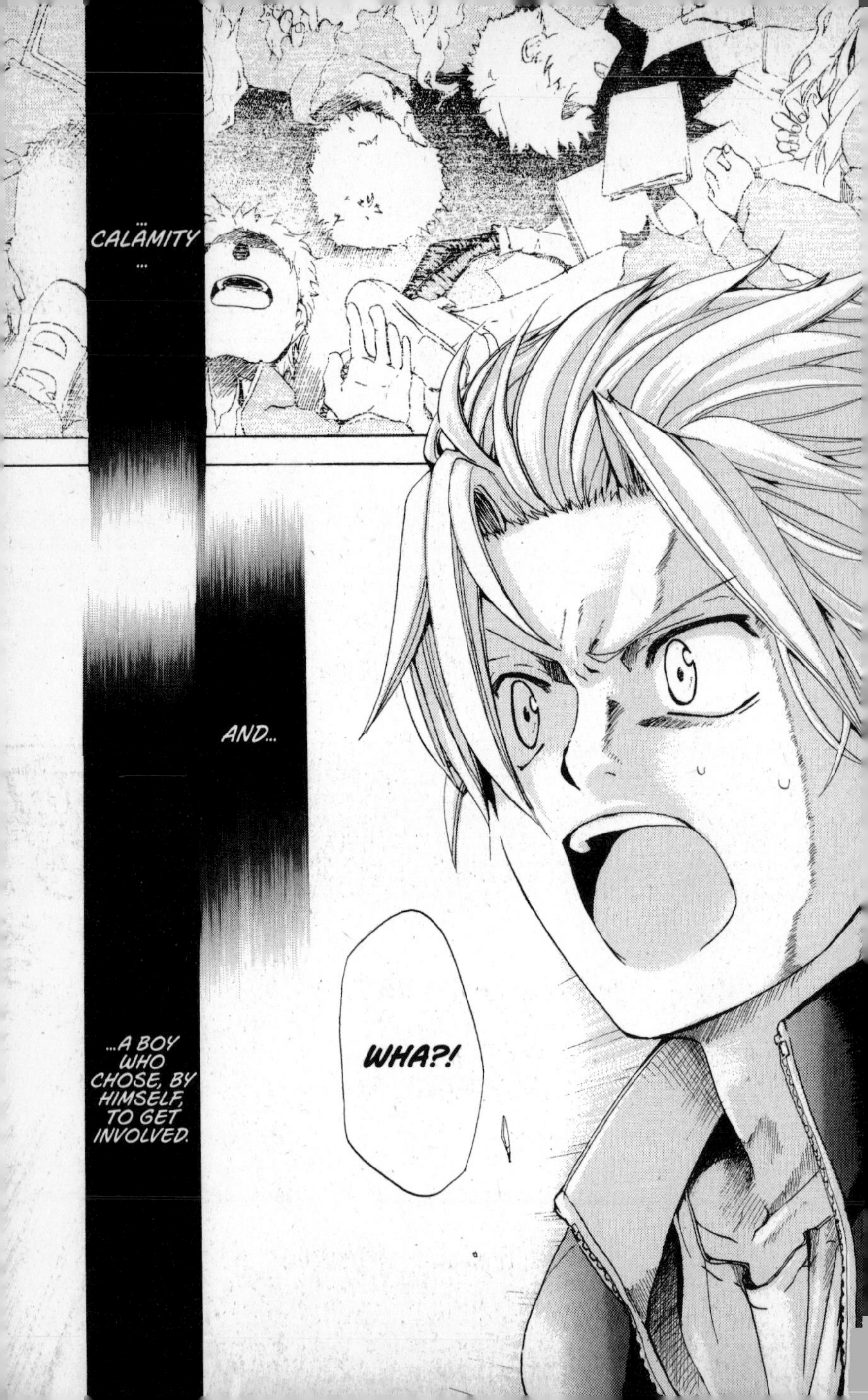
...CALAMITY...
AND...
...A BOY WHO CHOSE, BY HIMSELF, TO GET INVOLVED.
WHA?!

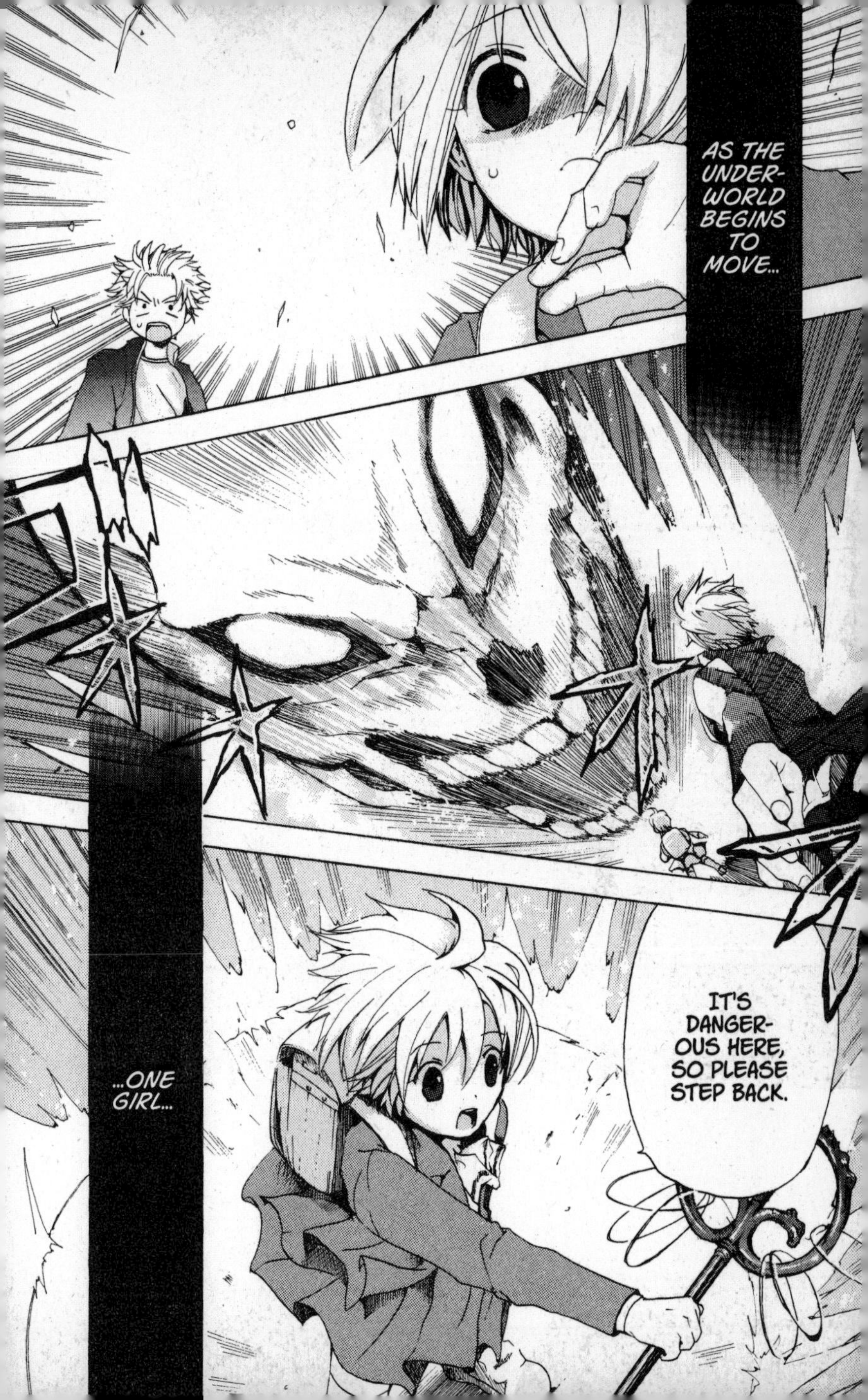
AS THE UNDER-WORLD BEGINS TO MOVE...
IT'S DANGER-OUS HERE, SO PLEASE STEP BACK.
...ONE GIRL...

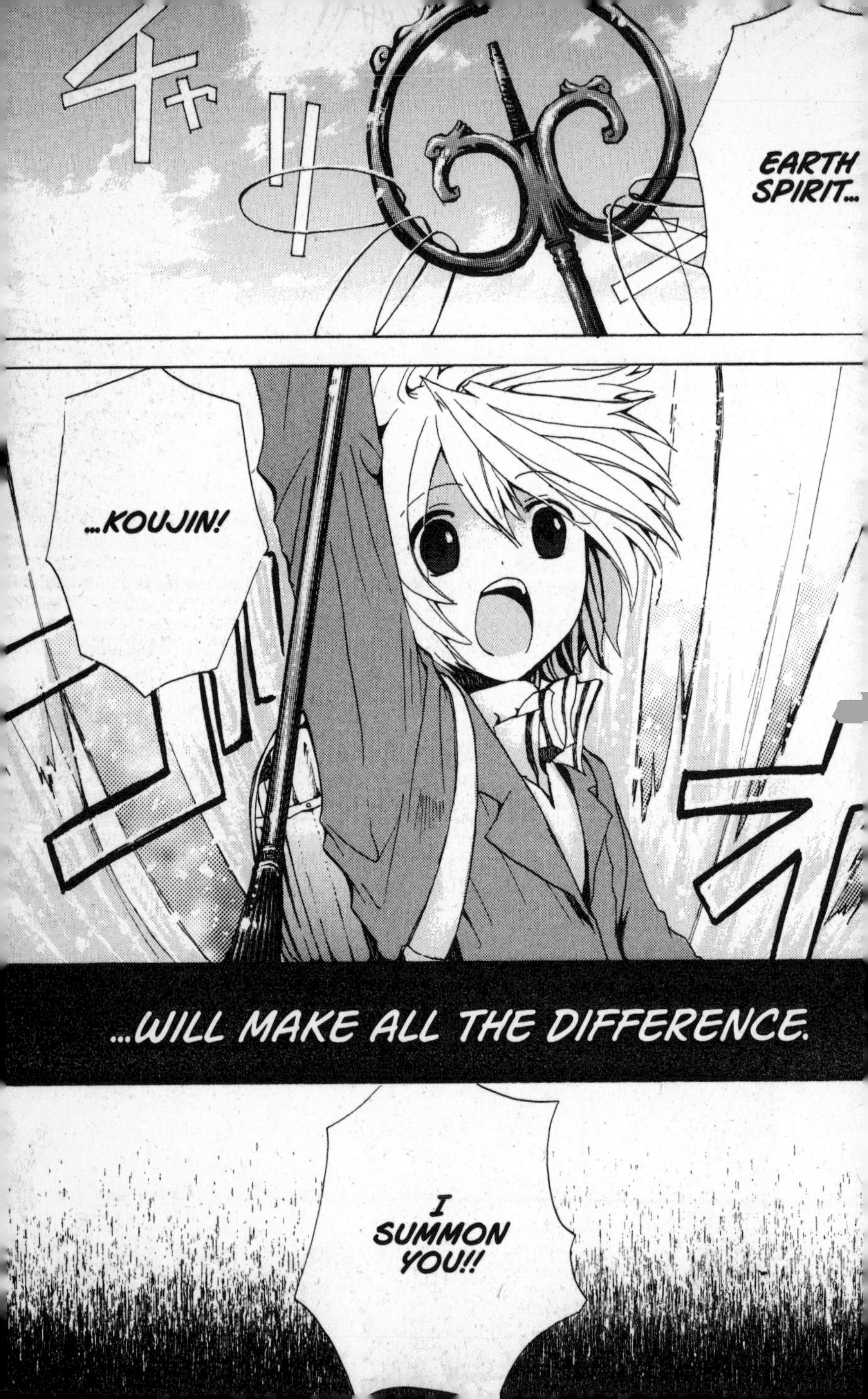
EARTH SPIRIT...
...KOUJIN!
...WILL MAKE ALL THE DIFFERENCE.
I SUMMON YOU!!

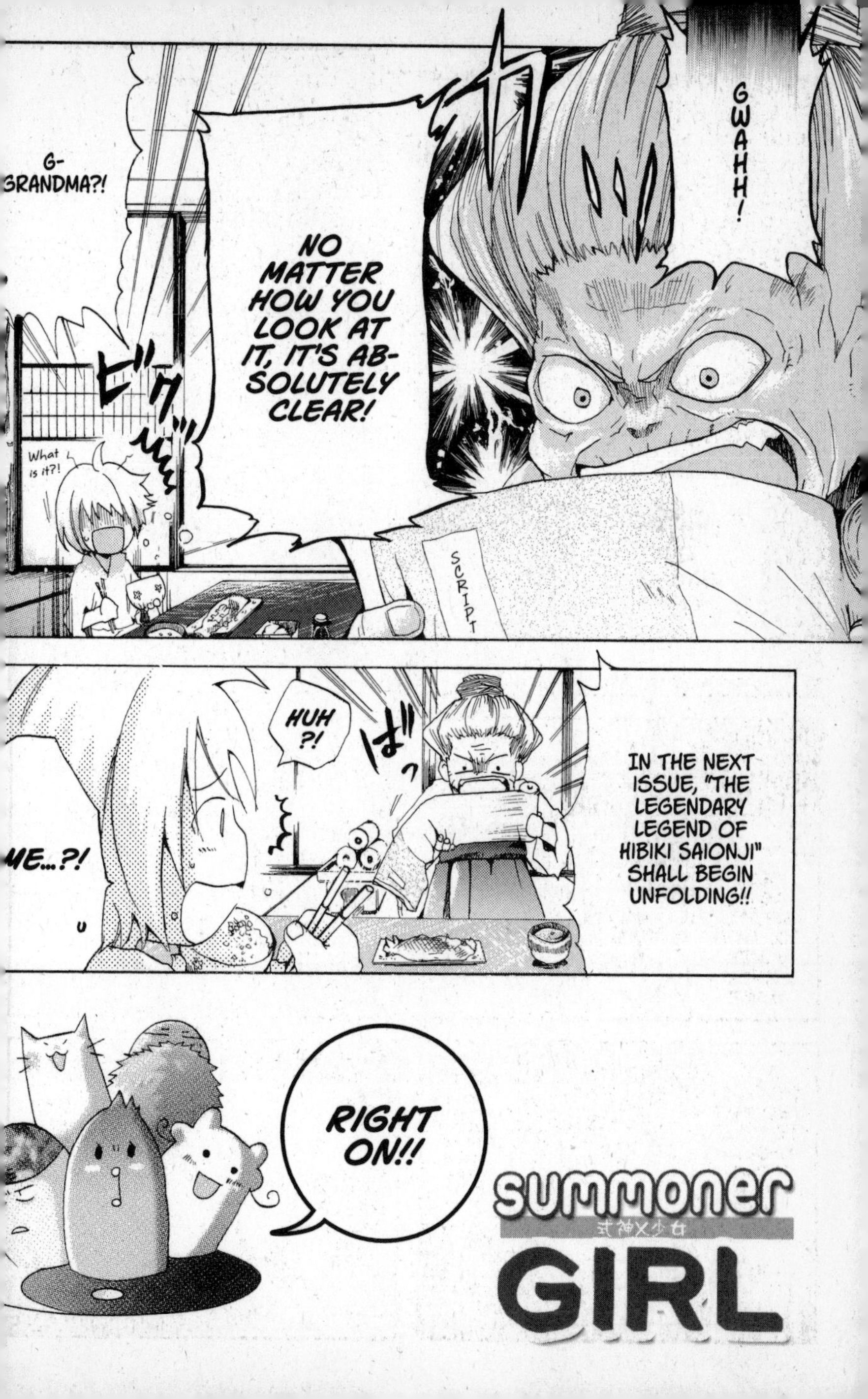
GWAHH!
NO MATTER HOW YOU LOOK AT IT, IT'S ABSOLUTELY CLEAR!
G-GRANDMA?!
What is it?!
SCRIPT
IN THE NEXT ISSUE, "THE LEGENDARY LEGEND OF HIBIKI SAIONJI" SHALL BEGIN UNFOLDING!!
HUH?!
ME...?!
RIGHT ON!!
summoner
式神×少女
GIRL

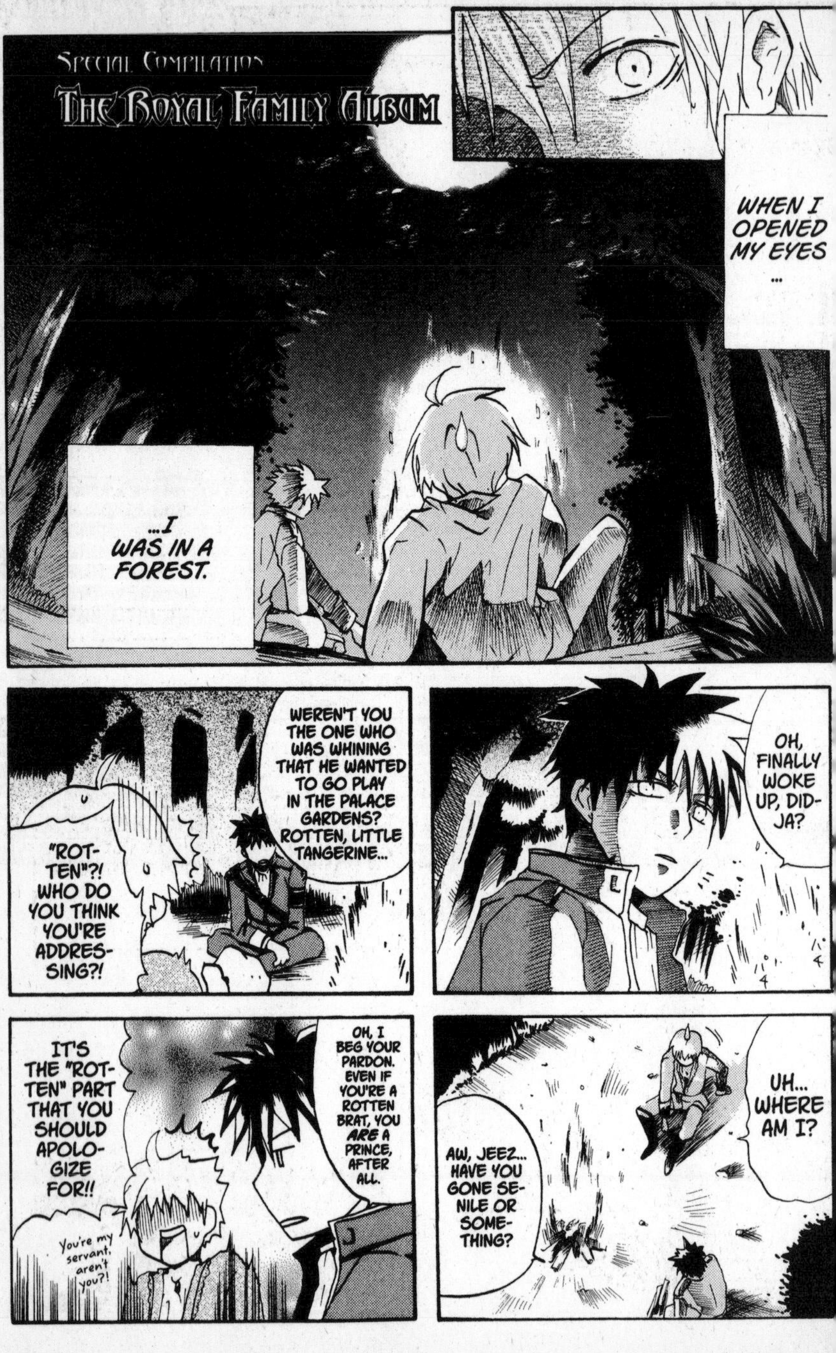
SPECIAL COMPILATION
THE ROYAL FAMILY ALBUM
WHEN I OPENED MY EYES ...
...I WAS IN A FOREST.
OH, FINALLY WOKE UP, DIDJA?
WEREN'T YOU THE ONE WHO WAS WHINING THAT HE WANTED TO GO PLAY IN THE PALACE GARDENS? ROTTEN, LITTLE TANGERINE...
"ROT-TEN"?! WHO DO YOU THINK YOU'RE ADDRES-SING?!
UH... WHERE AM I?
AW, JEEZ... HAVE YOU GONE SE-NILE OR SOME-THING?
OH, I BEG YOUR PARDON. EVEN IF YOU'RE A ROTTEN BRAT, YOU ARE A PRINCE, AFTER ALL.
IT'S THE "ROT-TEN" PART THAT YOU SHOULD APOLO-GIZE FOR!!
You're my servant, aren't you?!

MONSTER HUSTLE

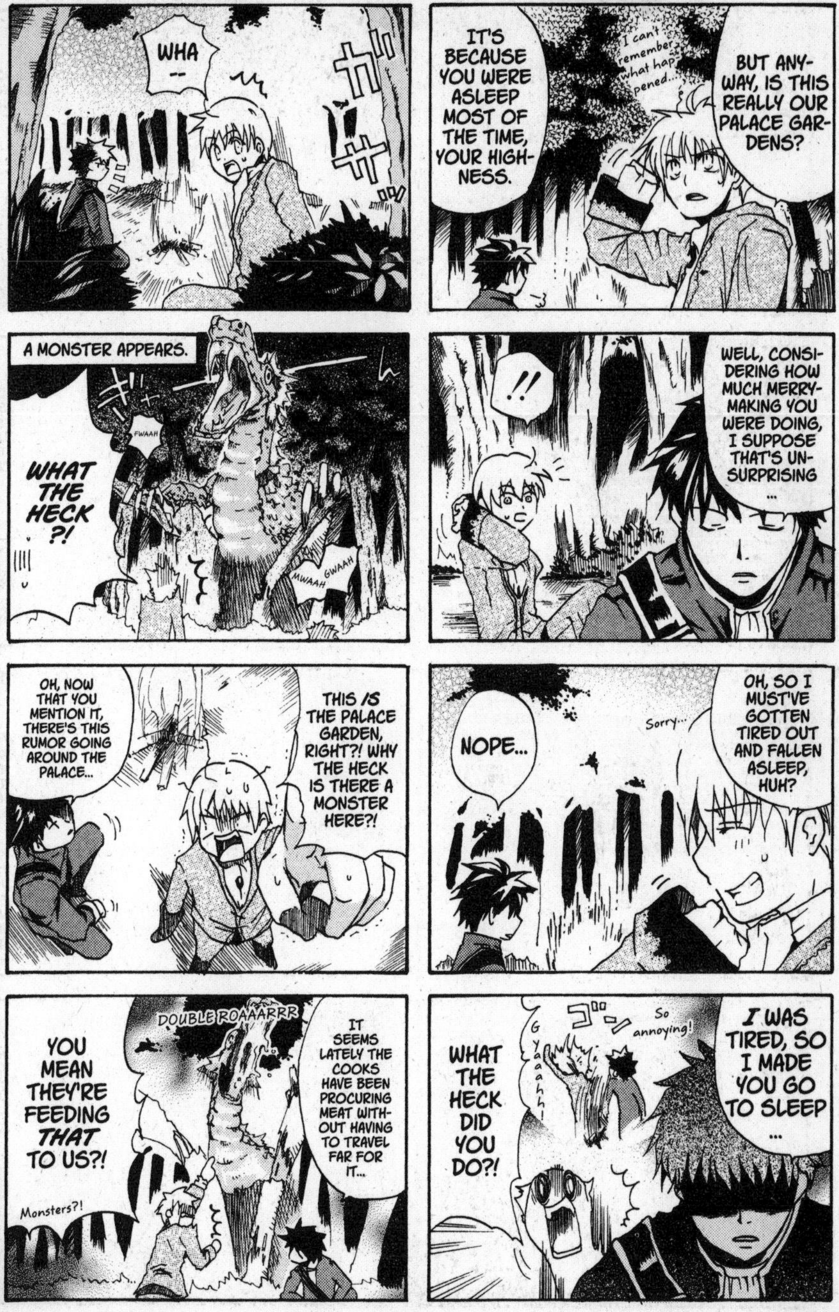

BUT ANY-WAY, IS THIS REALLY OUR PALACE GAR-DENS?
I can't remember what hap-pened...
IT'S BECAUSE YOU WERE ASLEEP MOST OF THE TIME, YOUR HIGH-NESS.
WELL, CONSI-DERING HOW MUCH MERRY-MAKING YOU WERE DOING, I SUPPOSE THAT'S UN-SURPRISING ...
!!
OH, SO I MUST'VE GOTTEN TIRED OUT AND FALLEN ASLEEP, HUH?
Sorry...
NOPE...
I WAS TIRED, SO I MADE YOU GO TO SLEEP ...
So annoying!
Gyaaahh!
WHAT THE HECK DID YOU DO?!
WHA --
A MONSTER APPEARS.
FWAAH
GWAAH
MWAAH
WHAT THE HECK ?!
THIS IS THE PALACE GARDEN, RIGHT?! WHY THE HECK IS THERE A MONSTER HERE?!
OH, NOW THAT YOU MENTION IT, THERE'S THIS RUMOR GOING AROUND THE PALACE...
IT SEEMS LATELY THE COOKS HAVE BEEN PROCURING MEAT WITH-OUT HAVING TO TRAVEL FAR FOR IT...
DOUBLE ROAAARRR
YOU MEAN THEY'RE FEEDING THAT TO US?!
Monsters?!

The King's Troubles

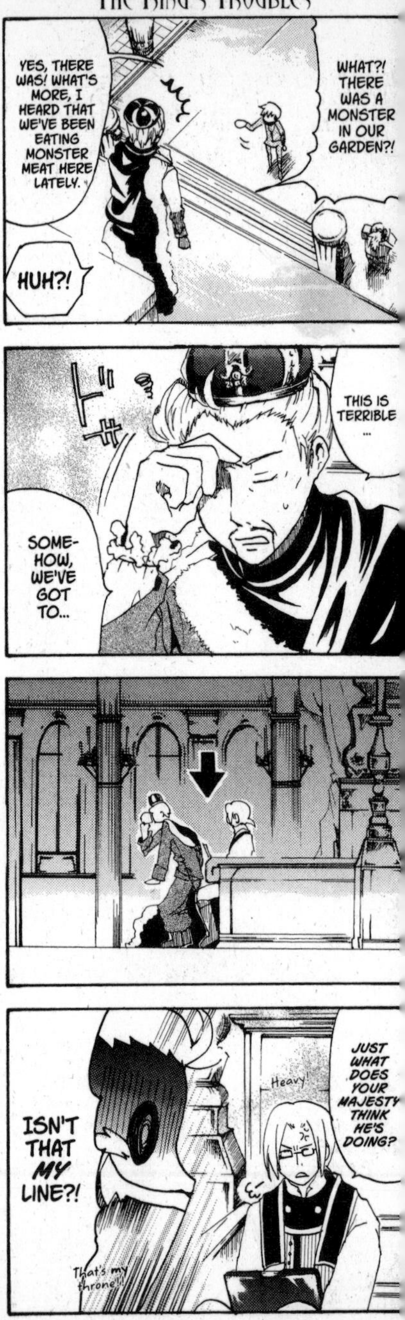
WHAT?! THERE WAS A MONSTER IN OUR GARDEN?!
YES, THERE WAS! WHAT'S MORE, I HEARD THAT WE'VE BEEN EATING MONSTER MEAT HERE LATELY.
HUH?!
THIS IS TERRIBLE ...
SOMEHOW, WE'VE GOT TO...
JUST WHAT DOES YOUR MAJESTY THINK HE'S DOING?
Heavy!
ISN'T THAT MY LINE?!
That's my throne!!

A Hero Appears

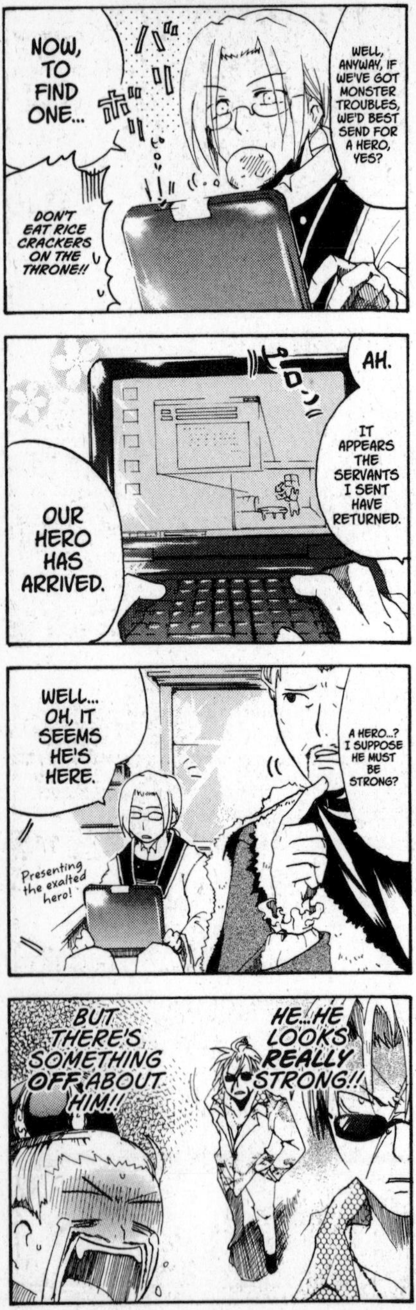
WELL, ANYWAY, IF WE'VE GOT MONSTER TROUBLES, WE'D BEST SEND FOR A HERO, YES?
NOW, TO FIND ONE...
DON'T EAT RICE CRACKERS ON THE THRONE!!
AH.
IT APPEARS THE SERVANTS I SENT HAVE RETURNED.
OUR HERO HAS ARRIVED.
A HERO...? I SUPPOSE HE MUST BE STRONG?
WELL... OH, IT SEEMS HE'S HERE.
Presenting the exalted hero!
HE...HE LOOKS REALLY STRONG!!
BUT THERE'S SOMETHING OFF ABOUT HIM!!

THE HERO'S TRUE CHARACTER

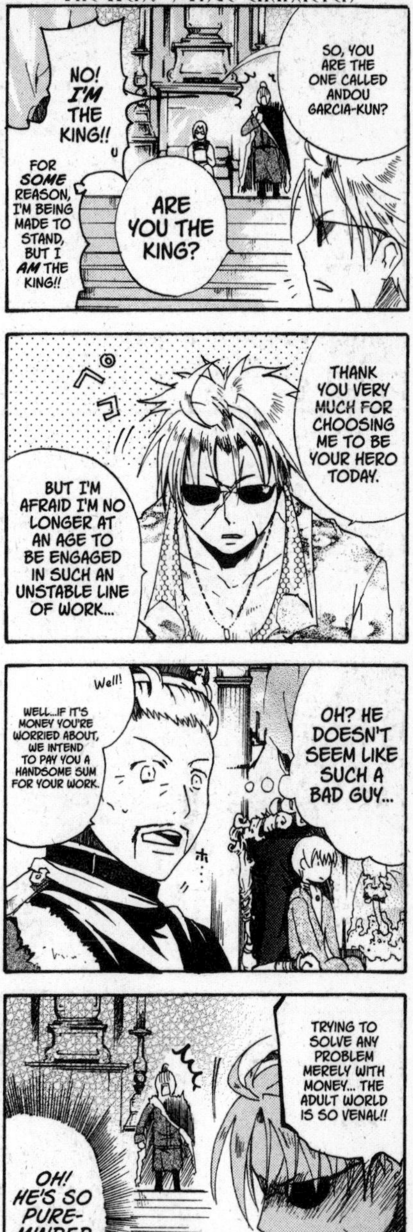
SO, YOU ARE THE ONE CALLED ANDOU GARCIA-KUN?
ARE YOU THE KING?
NO! I'M THE KING!!
FOR SOME REASON, I'M BEING MADE TO STAND, BUT I AM THE KING!!
THANK YOU VERY MUCH FOR CHOOSING ME TO BE YOUR HERO TODAY.
BUT I'M AFRAID I'M NO LONGER AT AN AGE TO BE ENGAGED IN SUCH AN UNSTABLE LINE OF WORK...
OH? HE DOESN'T SEEM LIKE SUCH A BAD GUY...
Well!
WELL...IF IT'S MONEY YOU'RE WORRIED ABOUT, WE INTEND TO PAY YOU A HANDSOME SUM FOR YOUR WORK.
TRYING TO SOLVE ANY PROBLEM MERELY WITH MONEY... THE ADULT WORLD IS SO VENAL!!
OH! HE'S SO PURE-MINDED TOO!!
Urgh!

THE KING ENDANGERED

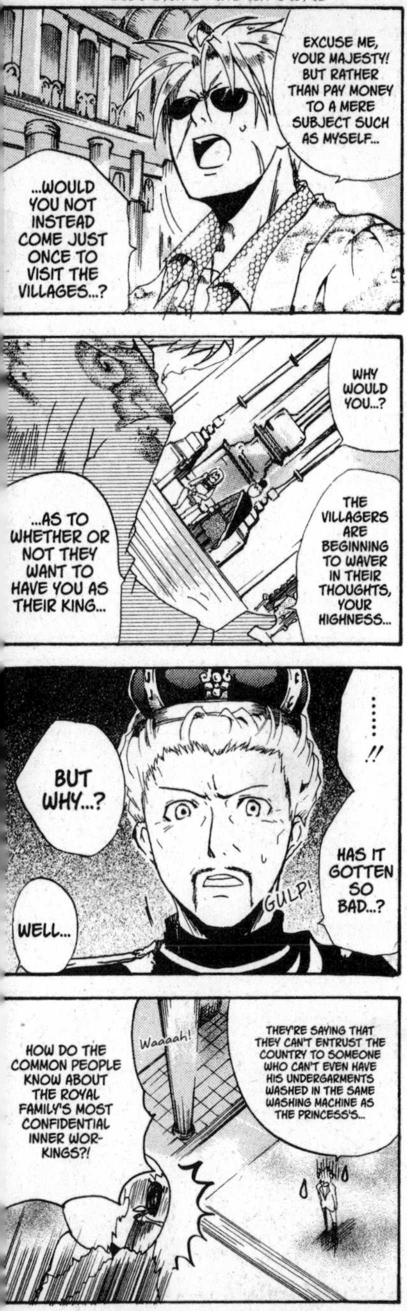
EXCUSE ME, YOUR MAJESTY! BUT RATHER THAN PAY MONEY TO A MERE SUBJECT SUCH AS MYSELF...
...WOULD YOU NOT INSTEAD COME JUST ONCE TO VISIT THE VILLAGES...?
WHY WOULD YOU...?
THE VILLAGERS ARE BEGINNING TO WAVER IN THEIR THOUGHTS, YOUR HIGHNESS...
...AS TO WHETHER OR NOT THEY WANT TO HAVE YOU AS THEIR KING...
......!!
HAS IT GOTTEN SO BAD...?
GULP!
BUT WHY...?
WELL...
THEY'RE SAYING THAT THEY CAN'T ENTRUST THE COUNTRY TO SOMEONE WHO CAN'T EVEN HAVE HIS UNDERGARMENTS WASHED IN THE SAME WASHING MACHINE AS THE PRINCESS'S...
Waaaah!
HOW DO THE COMMON PEOPLE KNOW ABOUT THE ROYAL FAMILY'S MOST CONFIDENTIAL INNER WOR-KINGS?!

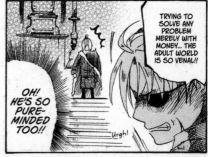

DEGREE OF SUSPICION

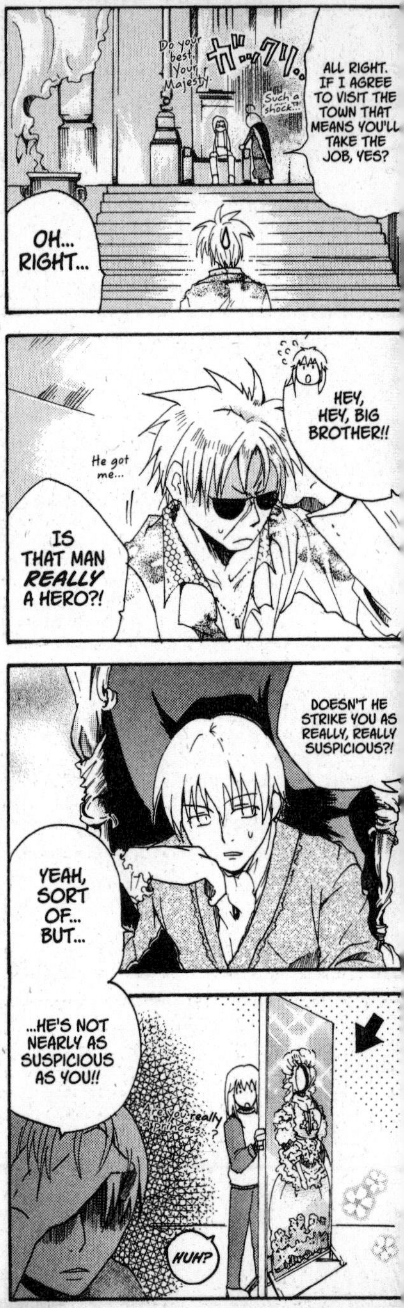
ALL RIGHT. IF I AGREE TO VISIT THE TOWN THAT MEANS YOU'LL TAKE THE JOB, YES?
Do your best, Your Majesty
ガッ…クリ。。
Such a shock...
OH... RIGHT...
HEY, HEY, BIG BROTHER!!
He got me...
IS THAT MAN *REALLY* A HERO?!
DOESN'T HE STRIKE YOU AS REALLY, REALLY SUSPICIOUS?!
YEAH, SORT OF... BUT...
...HE'S NOT NEARLY AS SUSPICIOUS AS YOU!!
Are you really a Princess?
HUH?

THE KING'S STAND-IN

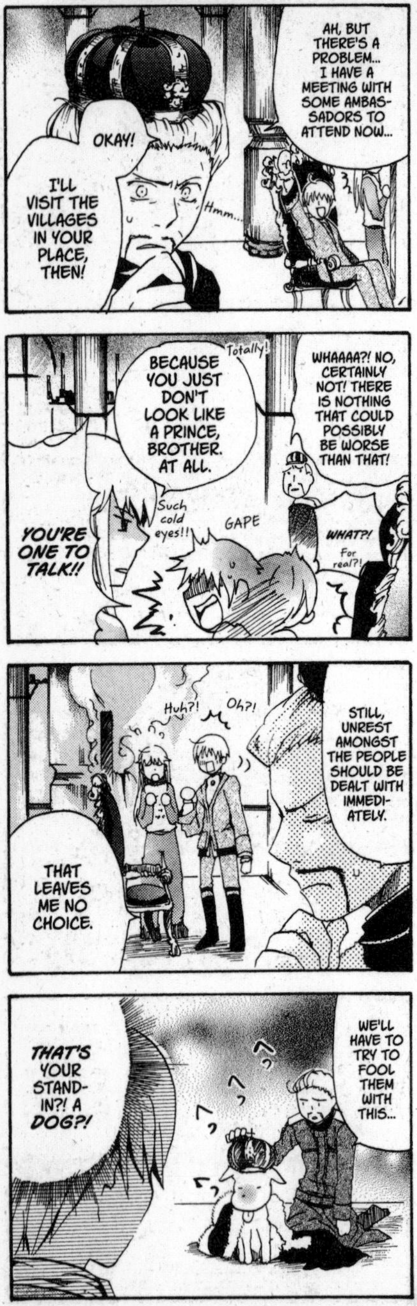
AH, BUT THERE'S A PROBLEM... I HAVE A MEETING WITH SOME AMBASSADORS TO ATTEND NOW...
Hmm...
OKAY!
I'LL VISIT THE VILLAGES IN YOUR PLACE, THEN!
WHAAAA?! NO, CERTAINLY NOT! THERE IS NOTHING THAT COULD POSSIBLY BE WORSE THAN THAT!
Totally!
BECAUSE YOU JUST DON'T LOOK LIKE A PRINCE, BROTHER. AT ALL.
WHAT?!
For real?!
GAPE
Such cold eyes!!
YOU'RE ONE TO TALK!!
STILL, UNREST AMONGST THE PEOPLE SHOULD BE DEALT WITH IMMEDIATELY.
Oh?!
Huh?!
THAT LEAVES ME NO CHOICE.
WE'LL HAVE TO TRY TO FOOL THEM WITH THIS...
THAT'S YOUR STAND-IN?! A *DOG?!*

In the End, the Prince Goes...

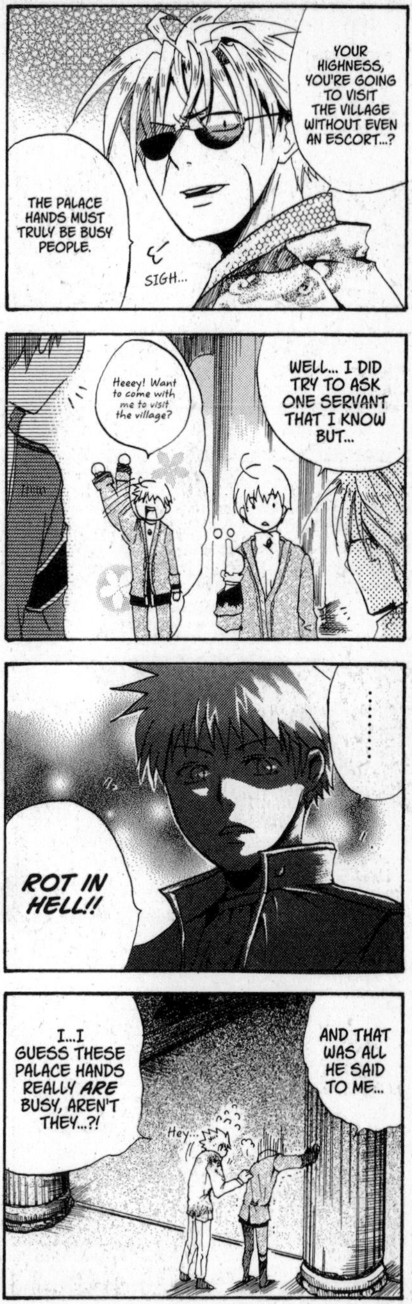
YOUR HIGHNESS, YOU'RE GOING TO VISIT THE VILLAGE WITHOUT EVEN AN ESCORT...?
THE PALACE HANDS MUST TRULY BE BUSY PEOPLE.
SIGH...
WELL... I DID TRY TO ASK ONE SERVANT THAT I KNOW BUT...
Heeey! Want to come with me to visit the village?
......
ROT IN HELL!!
AND THAT WAS ALL HE SAID TO ME...
I...I GUESS THESE PALACE HANDS REALLY *ARE* BUSY, AREN'T THEY...?!
Hey...

The Servant Who Wouldn't Go

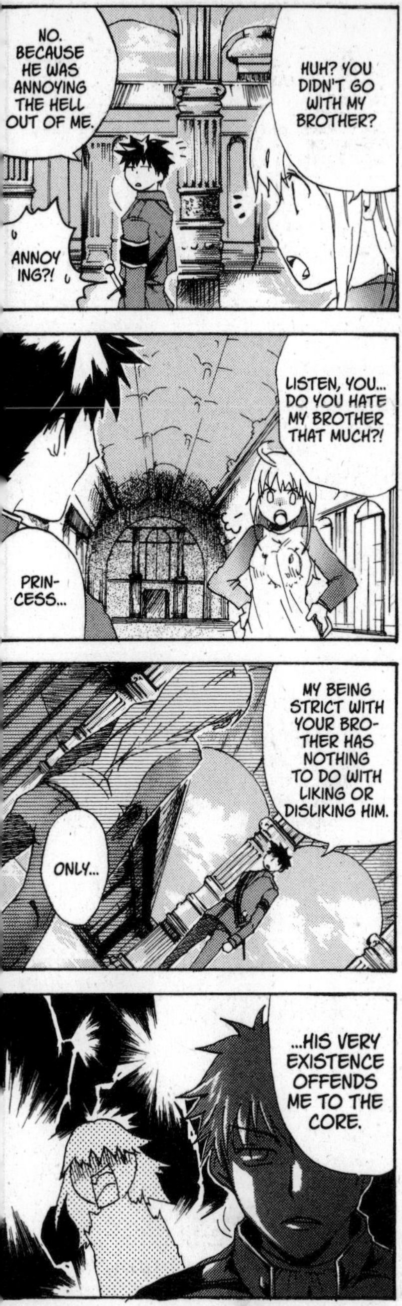
HUH? YOU DIDN'T GO WITH MY BROTHER?
NO. BECAUSE HE WAS ANNOYING THE HELL OUT OF ME.
ANNOYING?!
LISTEN, YOU... DO YOU HATE MY BROTHER THAT MUCH?!
PRINCESS...
MY BEING STRICT WITH YOUR BROTHER HAS NOTHING TO DO WITH LIKING OR DISLIKING HIM.
ONLY...
...HIS VERY EXISTENCE OFFENDS ME TO THE CORE.

FAITH IN THE KING

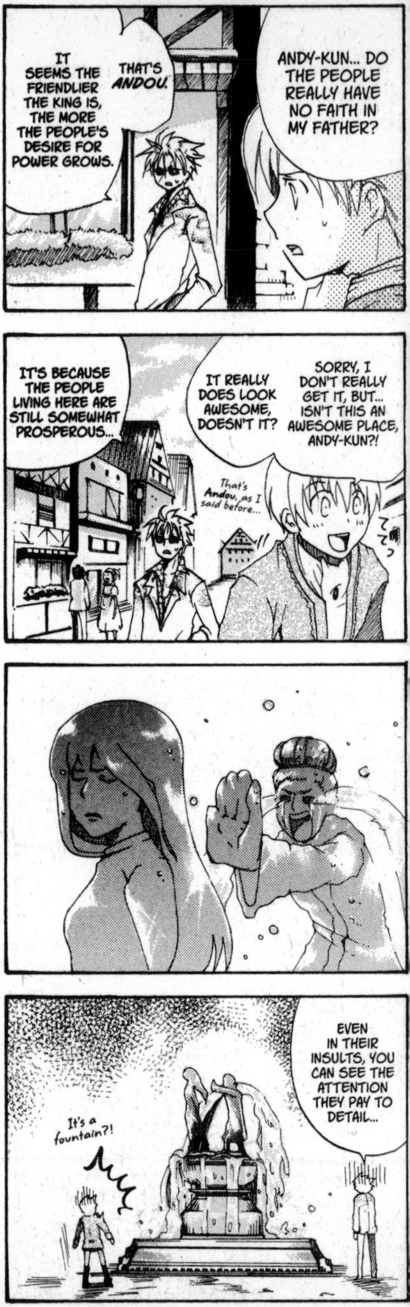
ANDY-KUN... DO THE PEOPLE REALLY HAVE NO FAITH IN MY FATHER?
THAT'S ANDOU.
IT SEEMS THE FRIENDLIER THE KING IS, THE MORE THE PEOPLE'S DESIRE FOR POWER GROWS.
SORRY, I DON'T REALLY GET IT, BUT... ISN'T THIS AN AWESOME PLACE, ANDY-KUN?!
IT REALLY DOES LOOK AWESOME, DOESN'T IT?
That's Andou, as I said before...
IT'S BECAUSE THE PEOPLE LIVING HERE ARE STILL SOMEWHAT PROSPEROUS...
EVEN IN THEIR INSULTS, YOU CAN SEE THE ATTENTION THEY PAY TO DETAIL...
It's a fountain?!

THE STRONG

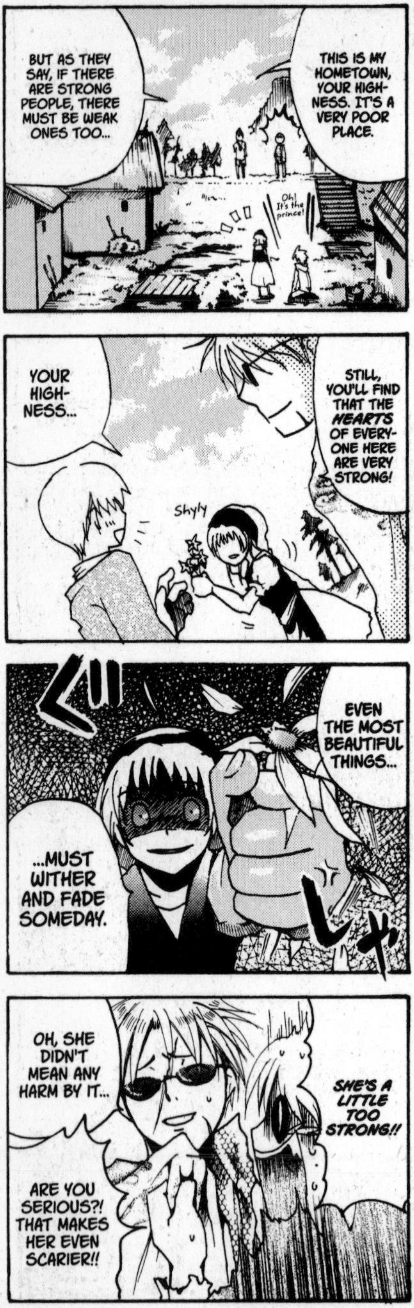
THIS IS MY HOMETOWN, YOUR HIGHNESS. IT'S A VERY POOR PLACE.
Oh! It's the prince!
BUT AS THEY SAY, IF THERE ARE STRONG PEOPLE, THERE MUST BE WEAK ONES TOO...
STILL, YOU'LL FIND THAT THE HEARTS OF EVERYONE HERE ARE VERY STRONG!
YOUR HIGHNESS...
Shyly
EVEN THE MOST BEAUTIFUL THINGS...
...MUST WITHER AND FADE SOMEDAY.
SHE'S A LITTLE TOO STRONG!!
OH, SHE DIDN'T MEAN ANY HARM BY IT...
ARE YOU SERIOUS?! THAT MAKES HER EVEN SCARIER!!

That's Not What I Meant...

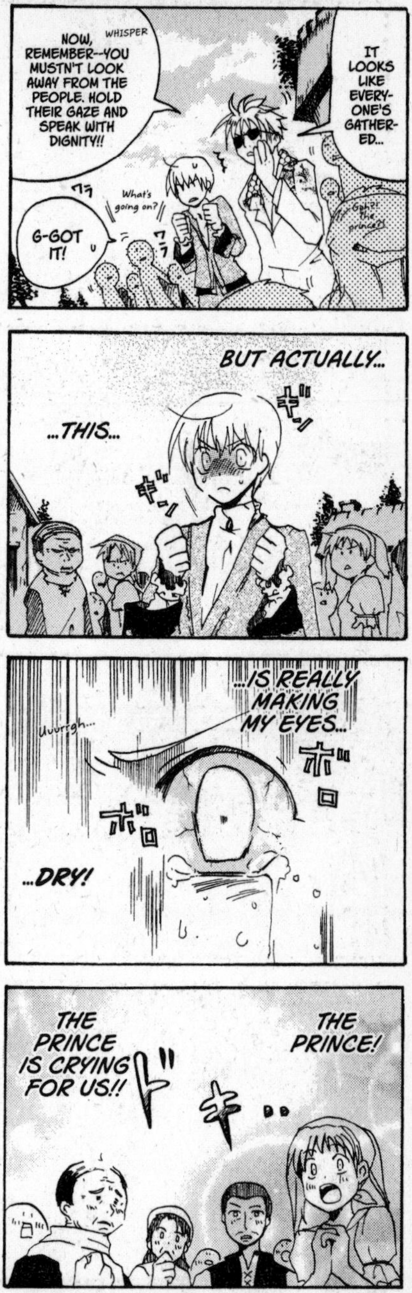
IT LOOKS LIKE EVERYONE'S GATHERED...
WHISPER
NOW, REMEMBER--YOU MUSTN'T LOOK AWAY FROM THE PEOPLE. HOLD THEIR GAZE AND SPEAK WITH DIGNITY!!
What's going on?
G-GOT IT!
BUT ACTUALLY...
...THIS...
...IS REALLY MAKING MY EYES...
Uuurgh...
...DRY!
THE PRINCE!
THE PRINCE IS CRYING FOR US!!

Hard Contacts

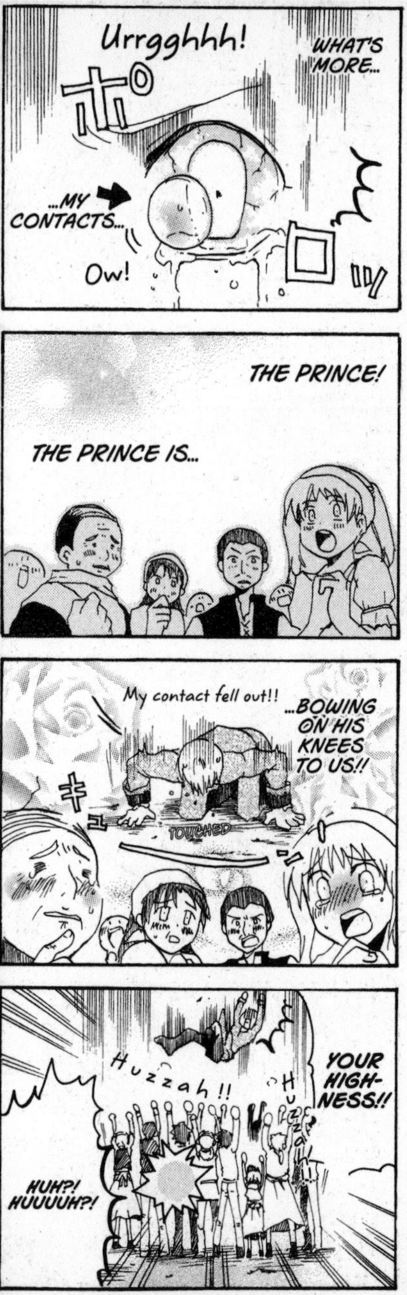
WHAT'S MORE...
Urrgghhh!
...MY CONTACTS...
Ow!
THE PRINCE!
THE PRINCE IS...
...BOWING ON HIS KNEES TO US!!
My contact fell out!!
TOUCHED
YOUR HIGHNESS!!
Huzzah!!
Huzzah!!
HUH?! HUUUUH?!

The Dissident

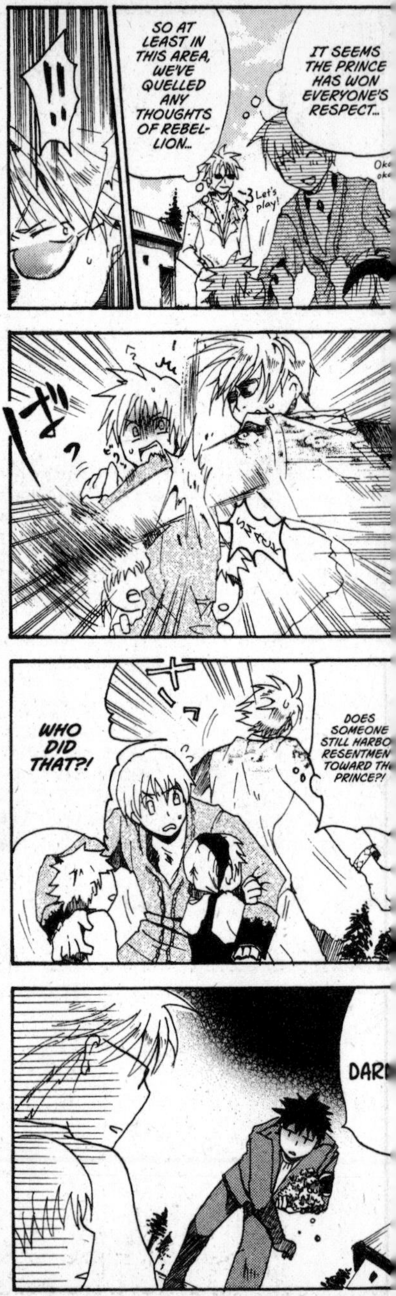
IT SEEMS THE PRINCE HAS WON EVERYONE'S RESPECT...
SO AT LEAST IN THIS AREA, WE'VE QUELLED ANY THOUGHTS OF REBEL-LION...
Let's play!
!!
DOES SOMEONE STILL HARBO RESENTMEN TOWARD TH PRINCE?!
WHO DID THAT?!
DAR

Mission Accomplished

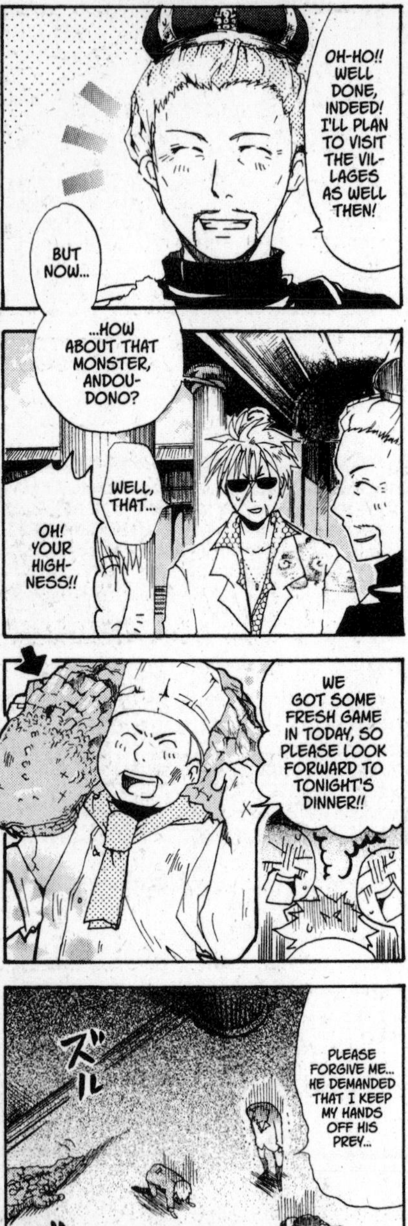
OH-HO!! WELL DONE, INDEED! I'LL PLAN TO VISIT THE VIL-LAGES AS WELL THEN!
BUT NOW...
...HOW ABOUT THAT MONSTER, ANDOU-DONO?
WELL, THAT...
OH! YOUR HIGH-NESS!!
WE GOT SOME FRESH GAME IN TODAY, SO PLEASE LOOK FORWARD TO TONIGHT'S DINNER!!
PLEASE FORGIVE ME... HE DEMANDED THAT I KEEP MY HANDS OFF HIS PREY...
ズル
ズル

The Royal Family Album / End

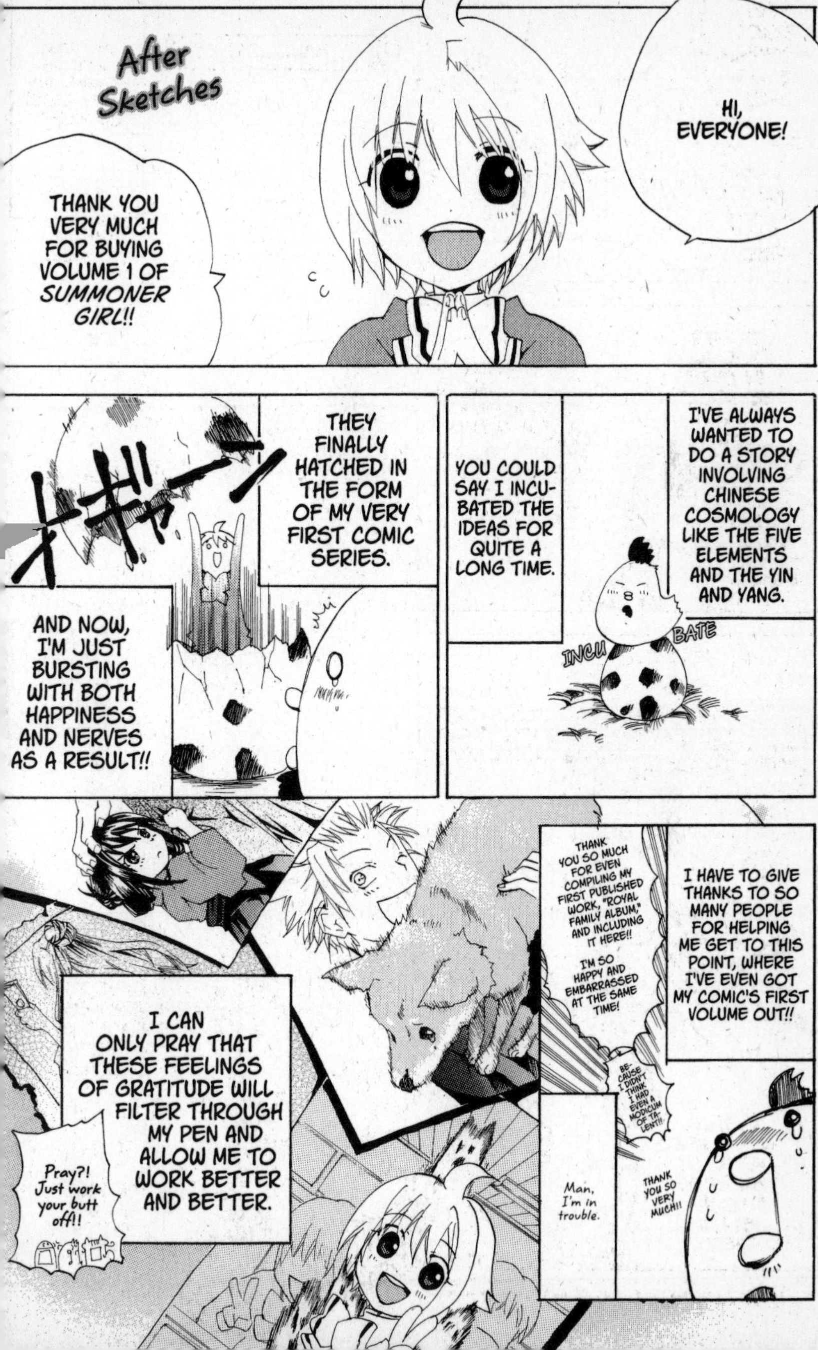
HI, EVERYONE!
After Sketches
THANK YOU VERY MUCH FOR BUYING VOLUME 1 OF *SUMMONER GIRL!!*
I'VE ALWAYS WANTED TO DO A STORY INVOLVING CHINESE COSMOLOGY LIKE THE FIVE ELEMENTS AND THE YIN AND YANG.
YOU COULD SAY I INCUBATED THE IDEAS FOR QUITE A LONG TIME.
INCU BATE
THEY FINALLY HATCHED IN THE FORM OF MY VERY FIRST COMIC SERIES.
AND NOW, I'M JUST BURSTING WITH BOTH HAPPINESS AND NERVES AS A RESULT!!
I HAVE TO GIVE THANKS TO SO MANY PEOPLE FOR HELPING ME GET TO THIS POINT, WHERE I'VE EVEN GOT MY COMIC'S FIRST VOLUME OUT!!
THANK YOU SO MUCH FOR EVEN COMPILING MY FIRST PUBLISHED WORK, "ROYAL FAMILY ALBUM," AND INCLUDING IT HERE!!
I'M SO HAPPY AND EMBARRASSED AT THE SAME TIME!
BECAUSE I DIDN'T THINK I HAD EVEN A MODICUM OF TALENT!!
THANK YOU SO VERY MUCH!!
Man, I'm in trouble.
I CAN ONLY PRAY THAT THESE FEELINGS OF GRATITUDE WILL FILTER THROUGH MY PEN AND ALLOW ME TO WORK BETTER AND BETTER.
Pray?! Just work your butt off!!

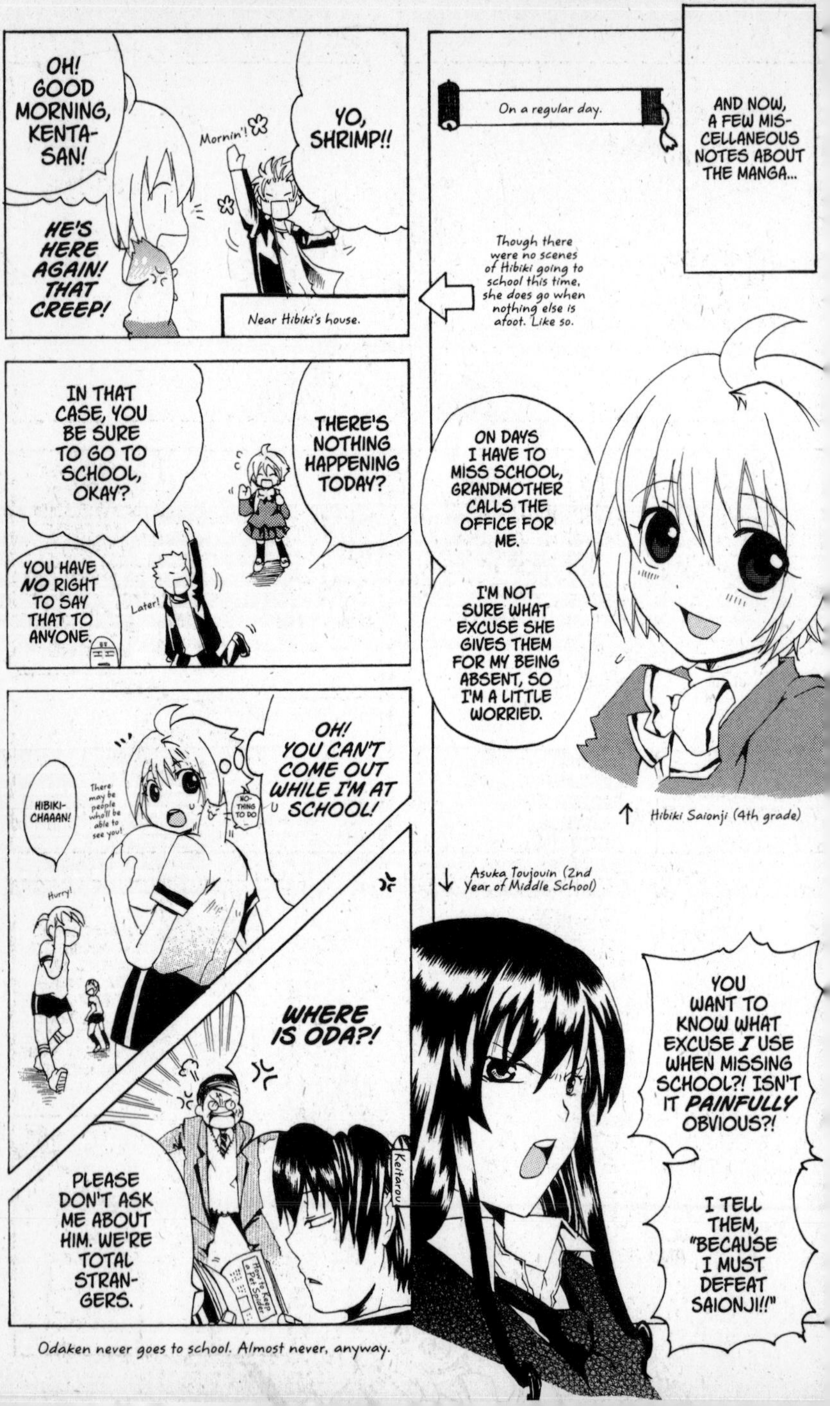
AND NOW, A FEW MISCELLANEOUS NOTES ABOUT THE MANGA...
On a regular day.
Though there were no scenes of Hibiki going to school this time, she does go when nothing else is afoot. Like so.
ON DAYS I HAVE TO MISS SCHOOL, GRANDMOTHER CALLS THE OFFICE FOR ME.
I'M NOT SURE WHAT EXCUSE SHE GIVES THEM FOR MY BEING ABSENT, SO I'M A LITTLE WORRIED.
↑ Hibiki Saionji (4th grade)
↓ Asuka Toujouin (2nd Year of Middle School)
YOU WANT TO KNOW WHAT EXCUSE *I* USE WHEN MISSING SCHOOL?! ISN'T IT *PAINFULLY* OBVIOUS?!
I TELL THEM, "BECAUSE I MUST DEFEAT SAIONJI!!"
Near Hibiki's house.
YO, SHRIMP!!
Mornin'!
OH! GOOD MORNING, KENTA-SAN!
HE'S HERE AGAIN! THAT CREEP!
THERE'S NOTHING HAPPENING TODAY?
IN THAT CASE, YOU BE SURE TO GO TO SCHOOL, OKAY?
Later!
YOU HAVE *NO* RIGHT TO SAY THAT TO ANYONE.
OH! YOU CAN'T COME OUT WHILE I'M AT SCHOOL!
NOTHING TO DO
There may be people who'll be able to see you!
HIBIKI-CHAAAN!
Hurry!
WHERE IS ODA?!
Keitarou
PLEASE DON'T ASK ME ABOUT HIM. WE'RE TOTAL STRANGERS.
How to Keep a Pet Spider

Odaken never goes to school. Almost never, anyway.

The Saionji Dining Table.

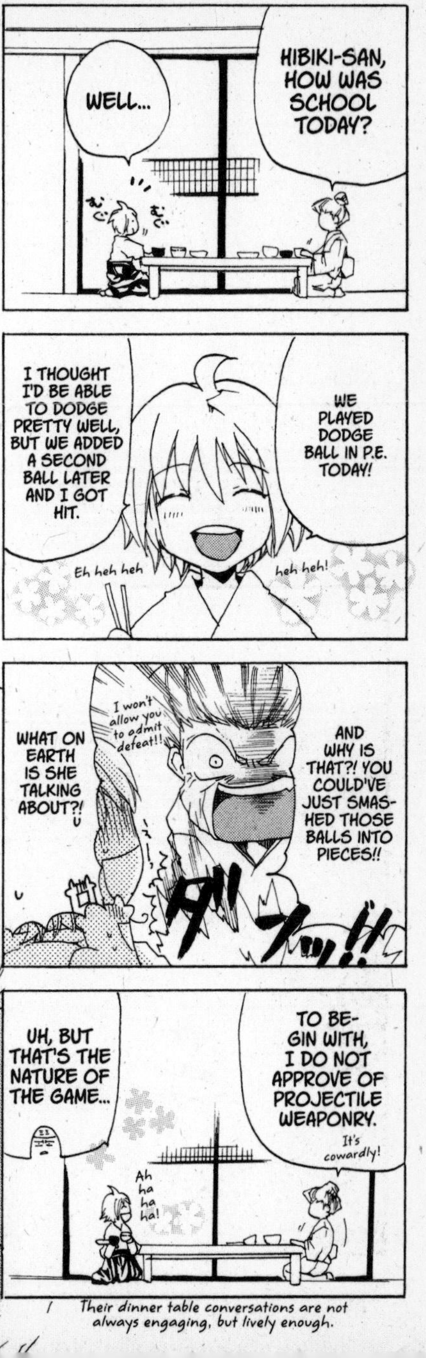
HIBIKI-SAN, HOW WAS SCHOOL TODAY?
WELL...
むぐ むぐ
WE PLAYED DODGE BALL IN P.E. TODAY!
I THOUGHT I'D BE ABLE TO DODGE PRETTY WELL, BUT WE ADDED A SECOND BALL LATER AND I GOT HIT.
heh heh!
Eh heh heh
AND WHY IS THAT?! YOU COULD'VE JUST SMASHED THOSE BALLS INTO PIECES!!
I won't allow you to admit defeat!!
WHAT ON EARTH IS SHE TALKING ABOUT?!
TO BEGIN WITH, I DO NOT APPROVE OF PROJECTILE WEAPONRY.
It's cowardly!
UH, BUT THAT'S THE NATURE OF THE GAME...
Ah ha ha ha!

Their dinner table conversations are not always engaging, but lively enough.

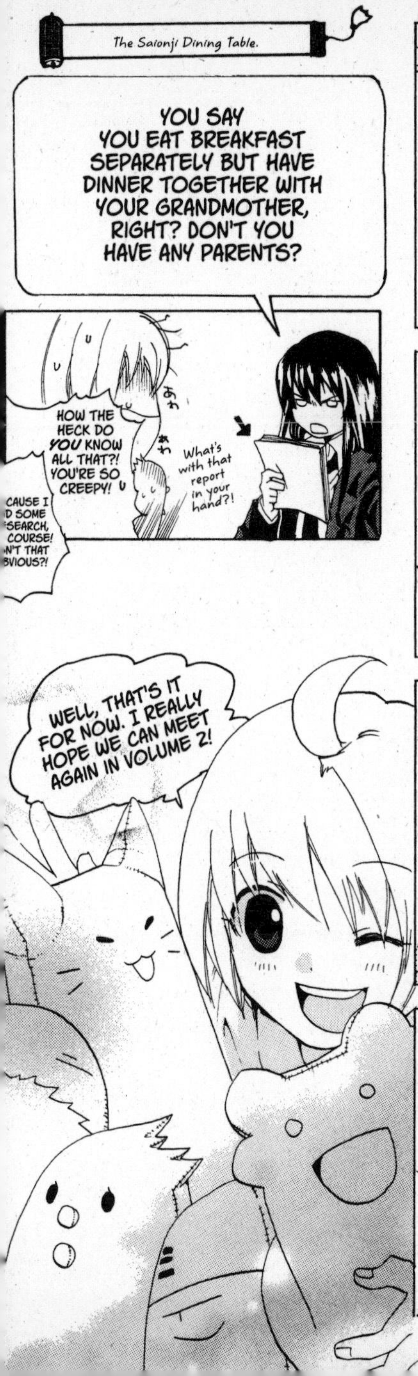
YOU SAY YOU EAT BREAKFAST SEPARATELY BUT HAVE DINNER TOGETHER WITH YOUR GRANDMOTHER, RIGHT? DON'T YOU HAVE ANY PARENTS?
What's with that report in your hand?!
HOW THE HECK DO YOU KNOW ALL THAT?! YOU'RE SO CREEPY!
あれ あれ
CAUSE I D SOME SEARCH, COURSE! N'T THAT BVIOUS?!
WELL, THAT'S IT FOR NOW. I REALLY HOPE WE CAN MEET AGAIN IN VOLUME 2!

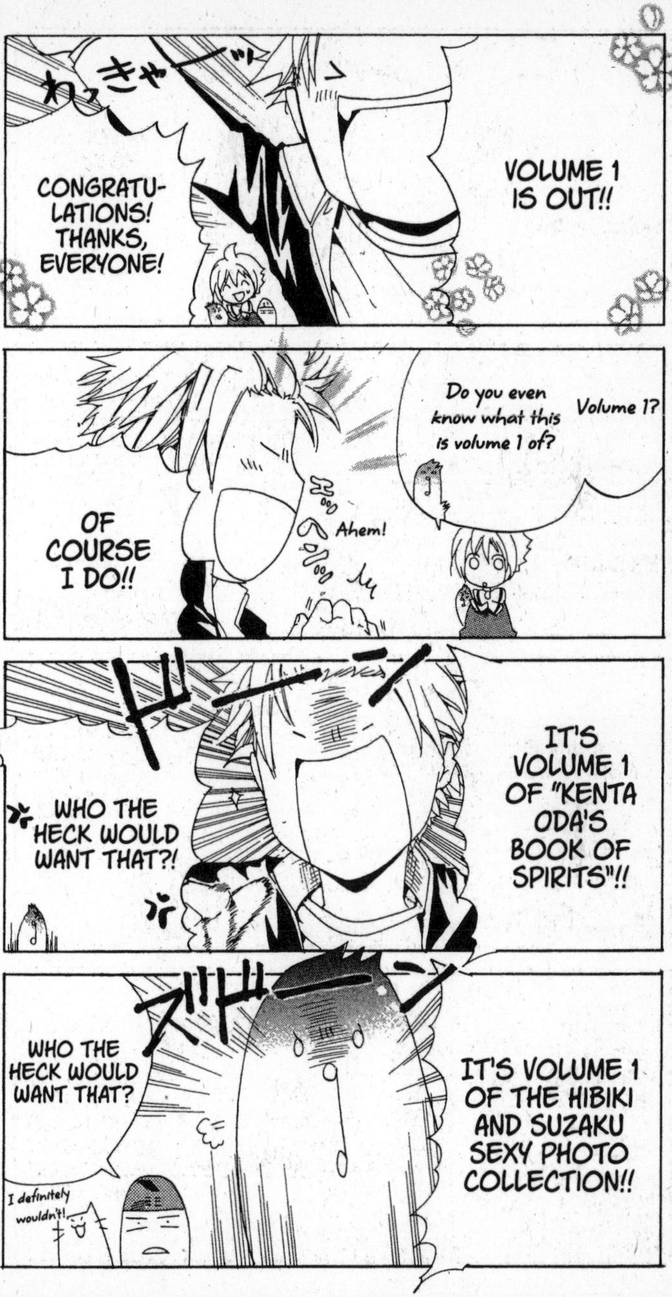
VOLUME 1 IS OUT!!
わっきゃーッ
CONGRATULATIONS! THANKS, EVERYONE!
Volume 1?
Do you even know what this is volume 1 of?
Ahem!
OF COURSE I DO!!
IT'S VOLUME 1 OF "KENTA ODA'S BOOK OF SPIRITS"!!
WHO THE HECK WOULD WANT THAT?!
IT'S VOLUME 1 OF THE HIBIKI AND SUZAKU SEXY PHOTO COLLECTION!!
WHO THE HECK WOULD WANT THAT?
I definitely wouldn't!

DID YOU SAY, "PHOTO COLLECTION"?
And she appears!
ASUKA-SAN!!
TO BE BUSYING YOURSELF WITH SOMETHING OTHER THAN THE RIKUTOU, YOU MUST FEEL PRETTY CONFIDENT YOU'LL FIND THEM ALL.
Hmph!
N-NO ...
NO, THAT'S NOT IT AT ALL!!
HOWEVER ...
...SINCE THIS IS A CHALLENGE ISSUED FROM YOU, MY SWORN RIVAL...
...I CANNOT BACK DOWN!!
Now what's she up to?
Huh?!
SO LET'S COMPETE AND SEE WHICH OF US SELLS MORE PHOTO COLLECTIONS, SAIONJI!!
Asuka Toujouin Photo Collection On Sale Now!
Wah!
H-HOW DID SHE GET THEM PUBLISHED ALREADY?!
She has a photo collection?!
Where'd she get that stand?!

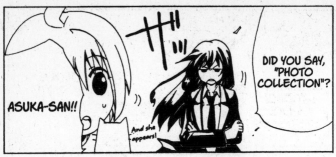

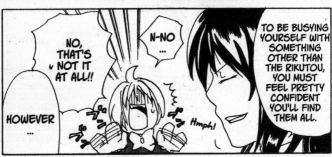

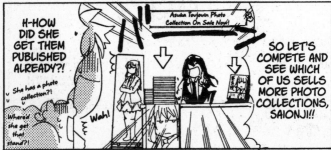

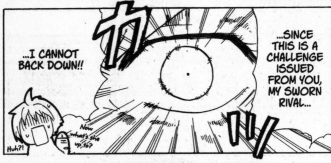

IN THE NEXT VOLUME OF...

summoner GIRL

THE HUNT FOR THE RIKUTOU CONTINUES! HIBIKI'S GOT HER SHIKIGAMI ON HER SIDE, BUT SHE'S ALSO GOT THE EVERY-ANNOYING KENTA WHO OFTEN HURTS MORE THAN HE HELPS, IN SPITE OF HIS BEST INTENTIONS. NOT TO MENTION THAT ASUKA'S GRUDGE SHOWS NO SIGNS OF ABATING! CAN'T THEY ALL JUST GET ALONG? WHAT'S A SUMMONER TO DO?!

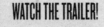

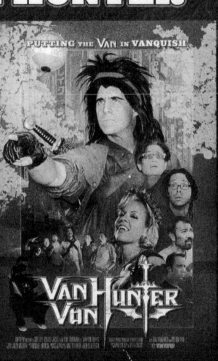

STOP!

This is the back of the book.
You wouldn't want to spoil a great ending!

This book is printed "manga-~~URBANA FREE LIBRARY~~
format. Since none of the art
get to experience the story ju
asking for it, so TOKYOPOP®
and far more fun!

| 3 | 1 |

DIRECTIONS

If this is your first time